Springer Series on
LIFE STYLES AND ISSUES IN AGING

Series Editor: Bernard D. Starr, PhD
Marymount Manhattan College
New York, NY

Advisory Board: Robert C. Atchley, PhD; M. Powell Lawton, PhD;
Marjorie Cantor, PhD (Hon); Harvey L. Sterns, PhD

Max B. Rothman, JD, LLM, is the Executive Director of the Southeast Florida Center on Aging and former Acting Director of the School of Social Work in the College of Urban and Public Affairs of Florida International University. He holds an AB from Lafayette College, a JD from the University of Michigan, and an LLM from the George Washington University Graduate School of Public Law. He has served as an attorney for the Department of Health, Education and Welfare; a Peace Corps Volunteer in Venezuela; director of three legal services programs for the indigent in New Jersey, Florida, and Colorado; director of Florida's health and human services programs in Dade and Monroe counties, Florida; and founder of the Center on Aging in 1984. His extensive publications are primarily in the areas of aging, long-term care, and public policy.

Burton D. Dunlop, PhD, is the Director of Research at the Southeast Florida Center on Aging of Florida International University, where he is responsible for directing the Center's research agenda, involving faculty throughout the University in research on aging, and managing ongoing research and evaluation projects. He holds a BA from Eastern Nazarene College and a MA and PhD from the University of Illinois at Urbana-Champaign. He has 25 years experience in directing research and evaluating issues and programs in aging, health, disability, social services and long-term care, including residencies at the Urban Institute, and Project HOPE Center for Health Affairs, both in Washington, DC. He is the author of numerous scholarly articles, reports, book chapters, and books, and is a frequent speaker at state, national, and international conferences.

Pamela Entzel, JD, studied international relations at the University of Minnesota and then law at the University of Miami. She is a member of the Florida Bar Association and has experience in the areas of civil rights, international human rights, immigration, and refugee and asylum law. She was a research assistant at the Southeast Florida Center on Aging from 1998 to 1999. She is currently pursuing a master's degree in epidemiology and public health at the University of Miami School of Medicine and is engaged in research on refugee health.

Elders, Crime, and the Criminal Justice System

Myth, Perceptions, and Reality in the 21st Century

Max B. Rothman, JD, LLM
Burton D. Dunlop, PhD
Pamela Entzel, JD
Editors

 Springer Series on
Life Styles and Issues in Aging

Springer Publishing Company, Inc.
536 Broadway
New York, NY 10012-3955

Acquisitions Editor: Bill Tucker
Production Editor: Pamela Lankas
Cover design by James Scotto-Lavino

Library of Congress Cataloging-in-Publication Data

Elders, crime, and the criminal justice system : myth, perception, and reality in the 21st century / Max B. Rothman, Burton D. Dunlop, and Pamela Entzel, editors.
    p. cm. — (Springer series on life styles and issues in aging)
    Includes bibliographical references and index.
    ISBN 0-8261-1145-9
    1. Crime and age—United States. 2. Aged offenders—United States. 3. Aged—Crimes against—United States. 4. Victims of crimes—United States. 5. Criminal justice, Administration of—United States. I. Rothman, Max B. II. Dunlop, Burton David. III. Entzel, Pamela. IV. Series.
HV6789.E43 2000
364.3'0846'0983—dc21
                                             99-088403
                                               CIP

This book is dedicated to my late parents, Eve B. and Herbert Rothman, who understood that education and the discovery of new ideas were the keys to our progress as individuals and as a nation.

M.B.R.

To my late parents, Burton David and Marion Ida Dickinson Dunlop, already elders during my childhood, whose high ideals and high regard for knowledge and truth were passed on to their very grateful children.

B.D.D.

Contents

Contributors

W. Andrew Achenbaum, PhD
College of Humanities, Fine
   Arts & Communications
University of Houston
Houston, TX

William E. Adams, Jr., JD
Shepard Broad Law Center
Southeastern Nova University
Ft. Lauderdale, FL

Malca Alek, PhD
Department of Criminology
Bar Ilan University
Ramat-Gan, Israel

Sarah Ben-David, PhD
Department of Criminology
Bar Ilan University
Ramat-Gan, Israel

Brian H. Bornstein, PhD
Department of Psychology
Louisiana State University
Baton Rouge, LA

Alison Brammer, PhD
Department of Law
Keele University
Keele, Staffordshire, United
   Kingdom

Katie E. Cherry, PhD
Department of Psychology
Louisiana State University
Baton Rouge, LA

Sanford I. Finkel, MD
Department of Psychiatry and
   Behavioral Sciences
Northwestern University
   Medical School
Chicago, IL

Edith Elisabeth Flynn, PhD
College of Criminal Justice
Northeastern University
Boston, MA

Ulrike Grasberger, PhD
Universität Giessen
Giessen, Germany

Edith Greene, PhD
Department of Psychology
University of Colorado
Colorado Springs, CO

Elmer H. Johnson, PhD
Center for the Study of Crime,
    Delinquency, and
    Corrections
Southern Illinois University at
    Carbondale
Carbondale, IL

John J. Kerbs, MSN
306 South Main Street
Ann Arbor, MI

Arthur Kreuzer, PhD
Universität Giessen
Giessen, Germany

Inez J. Macko, PhD
Leonard Schanfield Research
    Institute & Geriatric Institute
Council for Jewish Elderly
Chicago, IL

Mark Motivans, PhD
Deparment of Psychology
Pennsylvania State University
University Park, PA

Judith Phillips, PhD
Department of Applied Social
    Studies
Keele University
Keele, Staffordshire, United
    Kingdom

Mary A. Schieve, JD
Private Attorney
301 E. Liberty
Ann Arbor, MI

Darrell Steffensmeier, PhD
Department of Sociology
Pennsylvania State University
University Park, PA

W. Clinton Terry III, PhD
College of Urban and Public
    Affairs
Florida International University
North Miami, FL

Christy J. Witt, PhD
Department of Psychology
Louisiana State University
Baton Rouge, LA

Rosalie S. Wolf, PhD
Institute on Aging
U Mass Memorial Health Care
Worcester, MA

Anne Worrall, PhD
Department of Criminology
Keele University
Keele, Staffordshire, United
    Kingdom

A. Daniel Yarmey, PhD
Department of Psychology
University of Guelph
Guelph, Ontario, Canada

Acknowledgments

The editors wish to express their appreciation to Dr. Irene Prager, who helped identify and gain the early interest of many of the contributors to this book, and to Rosanne Greaves, who helped with word processing and tracking of chapters during the last phase of this project.

Foreword: Putting Elders, Crime, and the Criminal Justice System into Historical Perspective

Scriptural Precedents

In recounting the history of Israel from the exodus from Egypt to the establishment of the House of David, a psalmist long ago in a single verse captured several aspects of how older men and women were situated in human legal systems—a relationship that affected the workings of the ancient Hebrews' version of criminal justice:

> He established a decree in Jacob.
>   and appointed a law in Israel.
> which he commanded our ancestors
>   to teach to their children (Psalm 78:5).[1]

"He" refers to YHWH, who ordained a special destiny for His chosen people (the children of Jacob) in the world. The Israelites, after receiving the Ten Commandments, then were commissioned to create a code of behavior that was consistent with the Divine Order. Members of the older generation also were commanded to instruct rising generations in the way of the Law, just as parents taught children.

Why start a volume on *Elders, Crime, and the Criminal Justice System* with a biblical verse? We do so in order to orient readers to the fact that

---

[1]All biblical references and quotations come from the *New Revised Standard Version* (New York: Oxford University Press, 1991).

they should make the effort to digest the contents of this collection of essays utilizing several levels of analysis. This volume helps to fill a major gap in the gerontological literature. Not only do subject matters vary but so do authors' foci. The facts and issues presented herein do not lend themselves to neat categorization. In some essays, older people are viewed as victims of crime. Elsewhere, they are witnesses or jurors. Sometimes researchers describe how older ones render verdicts. Max Rothman and his collaborators rarely cross-reference one another's studies. The editors have (wisely) resisted the temptation to craft a template that might, in the absence of compelling evidence, preclude subsequent efforts to organize crosscutting themes.

We thus had two aims in preparing this Foreword. First, we wanted to contextualize some of the key findings presented here. We have paid attention to points of convergence in ideas about older people's varied roles in the U.S. criminal justice system. We highlight differences in images of old age and legal institutions in various countries. To facilitate further work in this area, we underscore holes in the literature that various authors indicate; we also identify a few areas where we think that more spadework usefully could be done. This Foreword ideally provides a road map for what follows.

In an admittedly more sketchy manner, we have a second purpose in writing. Most of the chapters in *Elders, Crime, and the Criminal Justice System* focus on developments in American society since World War II. This is an appropriate temporal framework for Professor Rothman and his colleagues to select. After all, gerontologists demand the latest data; that means emphasizing recent history. Too much present-mindedness, however, can blind readers to continuities in older people's roles. Researchers on aging have sometimes been too hasty in describing as "distinctive" relationships (such as what constitutes a marriage or a family under the law) that actually transcend any particular era or specific locale. Thus, in a preliminary way we have tried to historicize the contents of these chapters that follow by making a few "then" and "now" comparisons in the prologue.

We acknowledge that an historical presentation that focuses on continuities runs counter to conventional gerontological knowledge. Much research on aging, it is worth recalling, deals primarily with "change." It is commonplace for gerontologists to begin with evidence (or at least an assertion) demonstrating that there are larger proportions of senior citizens in our midst than ever before. Increasing numbers of older people, we are instructed, prompt public-policy initiatives that stipulate age-specific eligiblity criteria for entitlements. Advertisements with gray-haired and fuller-figured models cater to Baby-Boomer consumers whose disposable income lately has attracted the notice of Madison Avenue executives. The noticeable presence of unretired/part-time workers in places such as McDonald's (just to mention one more example) similarly reflects the impact of demographic aging on 21st-century cultural values, social norms, and economic arrangements. But we should not exaggerate the novelty of present circumstances. There have been old people since the beginning of civilization. Just because their relative proportional share of the population was smaller than now does not mean that the aged's lives were simple, or that their ascribed roles in society were monolithic. Older people have always had special relationships to the law— ranging from miserable offenders to august magistrates.

So we begin with this verse from the Psalms because it is an ancient text. Its inclusion over the centuries in various editions of the Bible "proves" its authenticity. Furthermore, the verse's references to how older people fit into a particular set of human relationships (in this case those governed by laws and criminal codes) sounds familiar to us. Comparing the Psalmist's message with other verses in Hebrew Scripture and the New Testament, in fact, demonstrates its unexceptional quality. Consistency with other themes in Hebrew Scripture, especially in the Bible's opening chapters, makes it an appropriate baseline for measuring continuities and changes over a broad sweep of historical time.

The Pentateuch (the first five biblical books) provides an extraordinary range of rules and regulations concerning how the children of Israel were required to behave themselves if they wished to remain holy in the eyes of the Lord. Laws governing dietary codes, worship practices, and relations between family members and other human beings were elaborately prescribed. Amidst the distinctions and details therein, it is sometimes easy to forget that the ancient Hebrews considered these codes to be universal. According to Leviticus 11:46, the laws of God applied to "every living creature." A bit later in that book (Lev. 24:22), YHWH reminded His people that "you shall have one law for the alien and for the citizen," a theme reiterated in Numbers 15:16. Failure to adhere to the Law of the Lord brought a devastating punishment: "Whoever acts high-handedly, whether a native or alien, affronts the Lord, and shall be cut off from among the people" (Num. 15:30). No sacrifice seemed sufficient to repay the community for the damage done by a person who had broken the Law by committing a deliberate sin. Actions that harmed other people were not only deemed sinful but also were considered to be crimes. Thus people must be instructed by responsible teachers so that they would know how to conduct their affairs as God desired (Sturdy, 1976).

Moses traditionally is recognized by Jews, Christians, and Moslems as the one who received the Ten Commandments from God on Mount Sinai sometime during the 15th to 13th centuries B.C.E. Those of us who saw the movie imagine that Moses was a young person when he encountered the Lord. Moses looked like Charlton Heston, a trim man, fit and strong. Yet biblical evidence indicates that Moses actually must have been past his prime. According to Deuteronomy 34:7, Moses was 120 years old when he died. Working backwards, bearing in mind that the Hebrews wandered for 40 years through the wilderness and desert, Moses probably received the tablets when he was 80. Even if we allow for some literary license and historical fallacy, Moses was a bona fide elder.

Once given the Covenant, Moses tried to arrange things so that the Israelites would abide by God's stipulations. He was worried about his people's rebelliousness, especially after his death. Thus Moses assembled "all the elders of your tribes and your officials" (Deut. 31:28) so that they could assume responsibility for enforcing order and for ensuring that their families, relatives, and neighbors would bear witness to YHWH. Biblical scholars claim that it was at Sinai that Moses established the Hebrews' judicial system. Judges were appointed to preside over hearings in which civil aspects of community life were resolved. Ways of atoning for violations of the Law were promulgated. If this is what happened, then Moses the Lawgiver also served his people as a legal administrator during his later years.

Elders played a central role in the Hebrew legal system after Moses died. "All Israel, alien as well as citizen, with their elders and officers and their judges, stood on opposite sides of the ark in front of the levitical priests, who carried the ark of the covenant of the Lord" (Josh. 8:33). Criminal procedures were established. The elders, priests, and civil authorities proclaimed fasts as public occasions wherein the children of Israel could collectively atone for their sins. The rulers set punishments: for instance, they ordered that scoundrels be stoned. They prescribed methods for expiating the murders of unknown persons in their territories (1 Kings 21: 8-11; Deut. 21: 2-3). Elder Israelites played one other central role. They were, above all, expected to teach their children how to observe the laws. Hence, young people's behavior reflected, for good and ill, on the old:

> Those who keep the law are wise
>   children.
> but companions of gluttons
>   shame their parents (Prov. 28:7)

Note how writers underscored the generational reciprocity encoded in Israel's efforts to adhere to God's laws. Under the Law as well as most other aspects of life, deference was paid to age. Children should seek to emulate their parents' wisdom. Those who failed to abide by cultic laws and honor tribal injunctions brought shame to themselves, their families, and their community.

The legal gerontocracy instituted by the ancient Israelites held sway for centuries. According to the Book of Acts (5: 33–9), a Pharisee named Gamaliel, "a teacher of the law, respected by the people" persuaded the Jews to flog rather than murder Stephen and other apostles who gave witness to the divinity of Christ. Gamaliel probably did not share Stephen's views, but he nonetheless thought that killing him would be more dangerous than silencing him. (Apparently Gamaliel's colleagues disagreed. Without benefit of a trial, Stephen was stoned for his blasphemy. He thus became the first Christian martyr.) Despite such theological differences, Christian congregations, like the Jewish community, recognized the value of experiences that accrued with advancing years. Members of the Jesus movement ascribed to older people important legal responsibilities. Elders were urged by Peter, who characterized himself as an old man, "to tend the flock that is in your charge, exercising the oversight, not under compulsion but willingly, as God would have you do it—not for sordid gain but eagerly" (1 Peter 5:2). Leaders were expected to be disinterested and to act in a mature manner. (Gerontologists who engage in biblical criticism reported that these two traits in Scripture were associated with a lifetime of experience wrestling with sin and trying to be good (Cole et al., 2000). Similarly, because of their presumed stature, even ordinary men and women were accorded special privileges by their fellow citizens. Christians were exhorted not to accept accusations of wrongdoing by those ordained to govern, unless there were at least two witnesses accusing an older person (1 Tim 5: 17–20).

Since the authors and compilers of both Hebrew Scripture and the New Testament readily acknowledged the ubiquity of sin, minor and criminal, it is not surprising that they tried to assess its impact on communal life. Prophets excoriated the failure of the children of Israel to uphold the Covenant. The warnings fell on deaf ears. Generation after generation, ignoring the tribulations of their wayward forebears, chose not to walk in the way of the Lord. Such disobedience, as the prophets predicted, caused misery for the body politic: the people of Israel were forced into exile. Yet far from alleviating personal guilt for collective anguish, many verses in Scripture underscore a legally pertinent theme that persists in our system of criminal justice: Individuals had to take responsibility for their wrong-doing. As a commentator in I Chronicles (25:4) put it, radically reworking earlier texts, "The parents shall not be put to death for the children, or the children be put to death for the parents, but all shall be put to death for their own sins." This passage does not contradict several biblical verses that refer to the sins of the fathers, which carries with it the implication that the dead hand of the past causes people to misbehave. Nonetheless, the legal system that unfolds in the Bible puts the onus on those who actually violate the Law (Kimble, 1995; Thomas & Eisenhandler, 1994).

Of particular interest to us is the frequency with which elders are portrayed as either victims or perpetrators of crimes. As it happens, there are relatively few instances in the Bible in which children are said to hurt their elders. When it occurs, however, the characterization is graphic. Proverbs 28:24 calls children who rob their parents "thugs." Micah (7:6) shows a variety of instances of elder abuse ranging from psychological to physical:

> The son treats the father
>   with contempt,
> The daughter rises up against
>   her mother,
> The daughter-in-law against her
>   mother-in-law;
> Your enemies are members of
>   your own household.

More frequent (than we expected at least) are the number of instances in which the elders violate the Laws of God. Ordinary people forsake YHWH (Jer. 16:11). So do kings, officials, and priests (Neh. 9: 34). When confronted with their crime, high-ranking officials tear their clothes in disgrace (2 Kings 22:11; 2 Chron. 34:19).

Key words in the Bible give a sense of the language used to describe how the legal system operated in ancient Israel. Many of the words are familiar in our vocabulary. They are used widely in *Elders, Crime, and the Criminal Justice System.* There are five instances of the word "criminal" and seventeen of "crime" between the first chapter of Genesis and the last verse of Revelations. The word "punishment" appears 93 times, usually in conjunction with a description of some judgment. "Guilt" appears 124 times, and "guilty" an additional 44, but most of these refer to people's remorse, not to their performing an act of expiation. Jeremiah 44:10 offers the Book's only allusion to "contrition." In contrast, "repentance" shows up 29 times, but it is a term mainly used in the New Testament.

Antecedents in U.S. History

Having established that older people have had variegated roles in the criminal justice system since the beginning of recorded Western history, we now leap across centuries to highlight some relevant themes and trends in the American experience that enfold in *Elders, Crime, and the Criminal Justice System.* Once again, our historical survey must be sketchy. To the best of our knowledge, no one has yet published an article or a monograph in which older Americans' place in the criminal justice system is *the* primary focus of analysis or even a major concern. In the absence of exhaustive investigations, we offer four tantalizing case studies that we hope will put the materials that follow into richer context.

Case Study One: The Salem Witchcraft Trials

We begin with a famous episode from the colonial experience. In February 1692, a group of teenagers in Salem Village, Massachusetts, began to have fits. They shrieked and thrashed about. Alarmed by this aberrant behavior, the townspeople and village elders concluded that the strange behavior was the work of the devil. Slowly, under repeated questioning, the afflicted youth identified possible witches and wizards. By the end of the summer hundreds of villagers and nearby residents had been accused. Twenty-seven were put on trial. Nineteen were executed (Foner & Garraty, 1991).

The Salem witchcraft trials disturbed several Boston clergy, notably the venerable Increase Mather, and the new provincial governor, William Phips. In October 1692, Governor Phips forbade any further trials. At the beginning of the year, a new court system was established, which imposed stricter rules for determining criminal action.[2] The new evidentiary guidelines resulted in the acquittal of 49 of the 52 remaining prisoners; the rest were released in the spring of 1693. Accusations of witchcraft in New England declined sharply thereafter.

Historians typically explain the origins of the Salem witchcraft trials in terms of divisions within a community undergoing economic and social transformations. Women and men of standing were more likely than their poorer neighbors to be accused. Their wealth apparently aroused envy and enmity. Geography also affected the choice of villains. Many of those suspected to be witches did not live in the village proper at the time of the trials. Some had recently moved to outlying areas; others were newcomers or relative strangers. Finally, the tone and style of Salem's new minister polarized the congregation. Some did not like the company that the Reverend Samuel Parris kept.

Without discounting the importance of these factors, the gerontologic element in the story is perhaps the most intriguing and salient. Historians of medicine report that the age of menarche has declined steadily over the past three centuries. In the 1690s, few 14-year-olds living in rural New England would have yet menstruated. It is striking that these young girls, possibly terrified by the changes their bodies were undergoing, should have disproportionately named postmenopausal suspects. The first three women accused were "outcasts." Tituba was a West Indian slave, who spent a lot of time—some claimed

---

[2]It is worth noting that as a consequence of the Glorious Revolution of 1688, legal codes, especially those affecting crimes, in the North American colonies were revised. For instance, a 1692 Massachusetts Bay Colony act that prohibited counterfeiting coins was disallowed because the crime did not exist in England (Papke, 1995, p. 2073).

too much time—with the Reverend Mr. Parris. Sarah Good was a pauper, who begged around Salem for food and lodging. "Gammer" Osborne was a bedridden old woman (Boyer & Nissenbaum, 1974). The men brought to trial also included several senior citizens. John Proctor, a rich barkeeper several miles from Salem, was 60. Job Tookey, who lived in nearby Beverly, on the other hand, had no wealth, but he was notorious. A sea hand and a laborer, he had been jailed several times in his life for petty theft. These men, like the women, were perceived as strangers. As David Gutmann (1987, 1997) has shown us in his brilliant ethnographic studies, unfamiliar older people who are considered "alien" are both revered for the wisdom that they are presumed to possess and feared for the evil power they may use against ordinary people. Old age clearly was a demographic factor in the criminal profile of Salem's witches and wizards.

Yet, elders played other roles in the Salem drama. Older people gave painful testimony, sometimes against kin. Consider the performance of Bray Wilkins, whose granddaughter was married to a certain John Willard. When Willard was accused of witchcraft, he sought help from his in-law. Wilkins refused assistance. Angry, Willard shot the old man an evil look. Bray Wilkins claimed that "his water was suddenly stopped, and I had no benefit of nature, but was like a man on a rack" (quoted in Boyer & Nissenbaum, 1974, p. 14). The aged were also key in adjudicating the end of the Salem witchcraft trials. For instance, the Reverend Increase Mather was 54 when he became alarmed at the incidence of accusations. In sermons and essays, Reverend Mather would recount his experiences for the rest of his life.

Case Study Two: Elder Judges

As we saw in the Salem witchcraft trials, older magistrates played an important role in determining judicial codes of evidence and meting out punishments. The extent to which we can generalize from such an "example" has generated considerable controversy among historians of aging. To wit: David Hackett Fischer in *Growing Old in America* (1977) made much of the fact that New York state in its 1777 constitution required the Chancellor, judges of the supreme court, and the ranking judge in each county court to quit the bench at the age of 60. The rule was prompted by the unpleasantness that resulted when its last colonial chief justice became demented while still on the bench. Over the next 7 decades, seven other states set an upper age-limit for judges. Fischer judges these seven cases to constitute a pattern, and he attributes the trend to a growing animus against age.

In *Old Age in the New Land* (1978), Achenbaum interpreted the facts differently. The primary author of this essay did not think that several instances represented a sufficient number of cases. Instead, he was struck by the paucity of incidences of judicial discrimination, especially given the absence of mandatory retirement ages for any other professions, such as clergy, teachers, or doctors. Achenbaum went on to note that several of the states that had imposed an age ceiling on judicial tenure, lifted them before the Civil War. Perhaps the most interesting case was New York, which revised its constitution in 1846. Lawmakers must have been chagrined by the grief the Empire State received when Chancellor James Kent was forced to resign from the bench in 1823 at the age of 60. At a banquet in his honor, a Harvard professor saluted "The James Kent—with better machinery, greater force, and greater safety than any other boat, yet constitutionally forbidden to take another trip." Three years after his removal from the bench, Kent began to publish his famous *Commentaries on American Law* (1826–30). America's Blackstone did not become infirm until a few months before his death, in 1847, at the ripe age of 84.

Some of our most memorable Supreme Court Justices were old men when they reached the height of their jurisprudential power. Two examples will suffice. Although he had no formal education and had studied the law for only 6 weeks before being admitted to the Virginia bar, John Marshall (1755–1835) was appointed chief justice by John Adams in 1801. During his 34 years on the bench Marshall dominated the court. Similarly, Oliver Wendell Holmes, Jr. (1841–1935) served 4 decades as an associate justice. Some of Holmes's dissents (such as in *Lochner v. New York*) are as notable as his Social Darwinian interpretation of the Constitution.

The lengthy tenures of many justices has been a mixed blessing, however. Some judges simply did not change with the times. Franklin Delano Roosevelt particularly chafed at obstructionist Court decisions that caused key programs in his New Deal to be dismantled. In 1937, FDR asked Congress for permission to overhaul the Court, which he claimed was "overworked." What the president really wanted was patently obvious: he wished to add younger justices who were liberals to ensure the survival of his political program. In a series of decisions that spring, however, the Supreme Court's voting pattern changed. FDR began to win 5–4 decisions. "A switch in time saves nine," pundits noted at the time. But the example does illustrate how ageism creeps in when commentators wish to criticize people's positions that are no longer fashionable.

Case Study Three: Old Criminals

A similar range of positive and negative perceptions and behaviors are associated with elder crimes. As is the case today, shoplifting was the crime most associated with old age a century ago. In their defense, elders tried to justify their misdeeds: they claimed that they had to steal to eat, to stay warm. Such excuses sometimes aroused pity when the older criminal was native-born or female. Welfare programs, like the justice system, accorded special considerations to poor elders who were deemed deserving. When immigrants committed petty larceny, however, it tended to fan resentment against the foreign-born (Haber & Gratton, 1996).

The exploits of some aged criminals, on the other hand, made them notorious. Take, for instance, the saga of Billy Miner (1846–1919). As a youth he stole horses in Michigan. He then robbed stage coaches in his prime. Miner's Robin Hood style gained him admirers, but his criminal record put him behind bars in San Quentin for 30 years. Once set free, Miner went back to what he knew best. Only this time, he went after trains. The legend of Grey Fox became a movie.

Of course not all old crooks are endearing. Clark Clifford, a major fixture in Washington policy and legal circles for decades, aroused pity among those who admired the man's contributions to the nation over the last half-century. Others, less generous, thought Clifford had disgraced himself decades earlier. Nor did many object when Leona Helmsley went to jail for tax evasion. But age does stir compassion. The fate of older husbands and wives sent to jail for engaging in what they claimed was "mercy killing" of their disabled spouses troubles many people. We sympathize with their desire to spare their loved ones suffering in a slow and painful death. We also recognize that the deliberate taking of another person's life is murder, and that taking a life cannot be condoned despite mitigating circumstances or even the purported consent of the victim.

Case Study Four: Crime Statistics

Several chapters in this volume give us a current baseline for studying the criminal patterns of older Americans. Here, it is important to note the paucity of reliable historical data. It is hard to find national statistics on the ages of older people arrested prior to the New Deal. Then and now, the data show that young adults (those between the ages of 15 and 30) commit the majority of crimes. Even among that age subset, the data are rarely broken down by the nature or magnitude of the offense (U.S. Department of Commerce, 1975: 415). It would appear, using national census data tracking crimes since 1930, that percentage of crimes committed by men and women over the age of 55 fluctuates between 6% and 16%. Confirming data in this volume, gerontologists have already reported a drop in the level of crimes committed by senior citizens since the 1970s (Cutler, 1995, p. 244). The decline has not been steady over the 20th century, however.

Conclusions

Even this spare historical overview provides enough of a bulwark for the tripartite contextual framework set forth by Edith Elisabeth Flynn (in chapter 3), which might well serve all those who build on insights contained in this book. First, because scholars heretofore have not paid sufficient attention to understanding the nature of elder crimes, we have not fully grasped all of the darker aspects of growing older. The incidence of shoplifting among senior citizens, for instance, reveals an important insight that is not revealed in the percentages of older Americans who fall below the poverty line. And by linking old-age criminology with analyses of elder welfare, we might enrich the conceptual richness of both fields of inquiry. Nor does this limit the possibilities: we suspect that there is a link to be made between elder abuse and crimes committed by elders. And it is troubling that there is no commonly accepted age at which a person is considered an "older" or "geriatric" prisoner.

Second, if we assume (as we must, in the absence of sufficient empirical data) that older people do not always commit crimes for the reasons that younger people do, then we must ask whether definitions of various crimes and sentencing should take account of a suspect's years or should remain as age-irrelevant as possible. Here the discussions of recidivism are particularly interesting. *Are* there certain crimes that older people commit that do not warrant imprisonment? If we look the other way, will we encourage aberrant behavior among our elders? Here, too, the wide differences in cross-national patterns are fascinating. Should the United States emulate the Japanese in exercising more leniency in dealing with older suspects? Or, should we continue to adhere to patterns that we share with the British, whose criminal justice system, after all, provided so many precedents for our own? Kerbs' chapters raise the unexamined issue of geriatric prisoners' medical care, barrier-free facilities, and alternatives to imprisonment for prisoners who need nursing home or hospice care.

Third, Flynn, in chapter 3, urges students of elder crimes to pay far greater attention to the theories and evidence that represents gerontological wisdom. Much is scientifically derived. But there are certain biases in the current literature that may prejudice interactions in the ways we perceive elders in the criminal justice system. For instance, several chapters in this volume note that various actors in the courtroom presume that with advancing years comes a discernible decline in cognitive capacity or visual acuity. This opinion once was accepted as a truism. We now know that the extent of intellectual decrements varies widely within older age groups and that not all older people suffer any diminished powers. Nonetheless, the image of the befuddled geezer clouds judgments in choosing older jurors, in relying on the testimony of witnesses who may be influenced by an attorney's suggestions, in selecting older attorneys, and in facing veterans on the bench.

This line of reasoning leads to the study of stereotypes in talking about elders in the criminal justice system. The gerontological literature abounds with historical and contemporary examples of instances in which gray hair is an advantage. At other times, however, advanced age seems to be a real liability. To what extent do we allow visible signs of age to influence our estimates of a person's capacity to perform a function? Thus, while we agree with Terry and Entzel (in chapter 1) that police should have some training in gerontology, so that they can be sensitive to motivations and patterns of behavior, we wish that there had been more discussion of the place of officers who age on the force before mandatory retirement. Does modern technology prolong their careers? Do the experiences of their years as rookies count for little in the contemporary era?

Elders, Crime, and the Criminal Justice System has much to offer researchers on aging. It introduces us to a field of inquiry that has been little explored. By invoking issues surrounding critical economic, psychological, and sociological aspects of the lives of older men and women—portrayed in various roles in the legal process and courts—it reopens long-standing questions about the meanings and experiences of growing older. We owe Max Rothman and his colleagues thanks for the imaginative ways they conceptualize this subfield and its links to other domains of gerontology.

—W. ANDREW ACKENBAUM AND MARY A. SCHIEVE

References

Achenbaum, W. A. (1978). *Old age in the new land: The American experience since 1790*. Baltimore, MD: Johns Hopkins University Press.

Bible (1991). *New revised standard version*. New York: Oxford University Press.

Boyer, P., & Nissenbaum, S. (1974). *Salem possessed: The social origins of witchcraft*. Cambridge, MA: Harvard University Press.

Cole, T. R., Kastenbaum, R., & Ray, R. E. (Eds.). (2000). *Handbook of the humanities and aging* (2d ed.). New York: Springer Publishing Co.

Cutler, S. (1995). Crime. In G. L. Maddox (Ed.), *Encyclopedia of aging* (2d ed.). New York: Spring Publishing Co.

Fischer, D. H. (1977). *Growing old in America*. New York: Oxford University Press.

Foner, E., & Garraty, J. A. (Eds.). (1991). *The reader's companion to American history*. Boston: Houghton Mifflin.

Gutmann, D. (1987). *Reclaimed powers: Toward a new psychology of men and women in later life*. New York: Basic Books.

Gutmann, D. (1997). *The human elder in nature, culture, and society.* San Francisco: Westview Press.

Haber, C., & Gratton, B. (1996). *Old age and the search for security.* Bloomington: Indiana University Press.

Kimble, M. (Ed.). (1995). *Aging, spirituality, and religion.* Minneapolis, MN: Fortress Press.

Lochner v. New York, 198 U.S. 45 (1905).

Sturdy, J. T. (1976). *Numbers: A commentary.* New York: Cambridge University Press.

Thomas, E., & Eisenhandler, S. (Eds.). (1994). *Aging and the religious dimension.* Westport, CT: Auburn House.

U.S. Department of Commerce. (1975). *Historical statistics of the United States to 1970.* Washington, DC: U.S. Government Printing Office.

Suggested Reading

Papke, D. R. (1995). Crime and justice. In M. K. Cayton, E. J. Gorn, & P. W. Williams (Eds.), *Encyclopedia of American social history.* New York: Scribner's.

Introduction

Max B. Rothman, Burton D. Dunlop, and Pamela Entzel

> Whether or not we can label them as stereotypes, with all that that implies, we can find in Greco-Roman literary representations traditional images of old age. These vary according to genre, gender, and author's age, which are nowhere near as predictable as they appear at first glance, and include such varying characteristics as wisdom, great dignity in the face of irreparable loss, utter defeat, fear, desperate courage, physical weakness, rigidity, foolishness, sexual frustration. It remains to be seen whether these images informed actual policies that systemically discriminated against elders.
>
> —Judith de Luce

Overview

The theme of older people and crime typically evokes images of older crime victims—the 80-year-old woman robbed of her purse or the retiree swindled in a fraudulent investment scheme! Increased vulnerability to criminal attacks is commonly thought to be an understandable, even predictable, consequence of growing older. On the other hand, older people are rarely perceived as perpetrators of crime. The older offender is viewed as an anomaly and the older prisoner seems incongruous, an oxymoron.

But are older people any more likely than younger people to be victims of criminal attacks? And what is the true nature and magnitude of elder criminality? How many older people are currently incarcerated, and what policy and ethical issues do older prisoners present? Furthermore, what other important roles, apart from victim or offender, do older people play in the criminal justice system, and how are they perceived in these roles?

For more than a quarter century, gerontologists have examined the implications of an aging America on health and long-term care, housing, employment, and economic security, leisure and recreation, and virtually every other important aspect of life in this country (see, for example, Butler, Grossman, & Oberlink, 1999 for one of the latest treatments of this topic). Indeed, there has been extensive analysis of the impact of growing numbers of older people on institutions of all kinds and, to a lesser extent, on changing perceptions of older people throughout society. To date, however, there has been virtually no research from the perspective of gerontology on elders within the context of crime and the criminal justice system. Similarly, criminologists frequently explore various aspects of crime and the criminal justice system with emphasis on race, ethnicity, and other demographic variables, while largely overlooking the factor of older age.

This book represents an effort to bridge the knowledge gap. For gerontologists and professionals in the field of aging, it provides an introduction to issues in the criminal justice system, with potential implications for understanding older people and aging in the larger society. For academics and professionals in criminal justice, it introduces a gerontological perspective and a more empirical basis for informed planning and decision making. Each chapter documents current empirical facts about elders, crime, and the criminal justice system, identifying social, policy, and ethical implications where applicable. By increasing our knowledge and understanding in this largely unexplored area, this book should serve to debunk common misperceptions about older people and crime, identify emerging policy and planning issues, and underscore important areas for future dialogue and research.

Importance of Examining Elders, Crime, and the Criminal Justice System

The elder population, usually defined as persons aged 65 and over, is undergoing rapid changes in size and composition. In 1997, there were approximately 34.1 million adults age 65 and over in the United States, representing 12.7% of the total population (American Association of Retired Persons [AARP], 1998). These numbers are expected to increase rapidly between the years 2010 and 2030 due in part to the aging of the "baby boomer" generation and increasing longevity among the old-old (age 85 and over). Current projections indicate that the number of older people will more than double by 2030, reaching about 70 million, or 20% of the American population (AARP, 1998).

Moreover, not only is the number of older Americans increasing, but the older adult population is becoming more demographically and socioeconomically diverse. The number of White non-Hispanic elders is projected to increase by 79% between 1997 and 2030, but during that same time span, increases of 368% for Hispanics, 134% for non-Hispanic Blacks, and 354% among Asians and Pacific Islanders are expected (AARP, 1998). Overall, the older minority population is projected to increase by 238% (AARP, 1998). During the last two decades, elders' levels of education and income have improved, on average, although rates vary considerably according to race and ethnic origin (see U.S. Bureau of the Census, 1996). Finally, because of such factors as improved education, economic status, and access to health care, overall, older Americans are staying healthy and active longer than ever before. In a survey of noninstitutionalized persons conducted in 1992, three out of four respondents age 65 to 74 reported being in good, very good, or excellent health as did about two in three of those age 75 and over (U.S. Bureau of the Census, 1996).

These changes have significant implications for crime and the criminal justice system. Because of the dramatic projected growth of the elder population, the number of older people involved in the criminal justice system can be expected to increase, even if crime rates remain the same. Increasingly, older people will constitute a greater proportion of all crime victims, offenders, judges, attorneys, witnesses, jurors, and prisoners. For example, recent statistics indicate that older people represent the fastest growing age group in state and federal prisons. The number of older prisoners nationally more than doubled between 1991 and 1998, from 34,845 to 83,667.

This rapid growth in the older-prisoner population is giving rise to predictions that, unless alternatives to incarceration are explored, costly correctional nursing homes for ill or frail older prisoners may soon become commonplace (see Kerbs, chapters 10 and 11).

Likewise, changes in the composition of the elder population can be expected to ripple through the criminal justice system, producing a variety of unique results. Improvements in health and socioeconomic status, for example, are redefining the roles that older people may play in the context of crime and criminal justice. Today, older people are involved with police not just as victims of crime or abuse, but as collaborators with police departments in crime prevention and public safety programs (see Terry & Entzel, chapter 1). Improvements in the health of older people, on average, also may call for a reevaluation of rationales underlying age-based exemptions from jury duty and even mandatory retirement ages for judges (see Adams, chapter 4; and Entzel, Dunlop, & Rothman, chapter 8).

In this context, there is a new demand for accurate data and informed dialogue concerning victimization of older people, elder criminality, and older participants in the criminal justice system. It is likely that changes in the size and composition of the elder population will impact the system not only in obvious and immediate ways, but in subtle ways not yet perceived. Fortunately for policymakers and planners, however, increases in the size and diversity of the elder population are foreseeable. Thus, they have an opportunity to plan and prepare for the many challenges that lie ahead. This book, then, is a first step toward producing accurate and up-to-date information and analysis of the relationships between older people and the criminal justice system.

Many chapters in this book reveal elder stereotypes and social norms at work in the criminal justice process. Thus, it is particularly meaningful to examine these issues because of what they might tell us about older people and aging generally. By observing through the lens of the criminal justice system what roles older people play, how they behave in those roles, and how others react to them, perhaps we can gain a better understanding of myths, stereotypes, and behaviors more broadly associated with aging in contemporary society.

A Gerontological Framework

What does it mean to examine crime and criminal justice from a gerontological perspective? What is current gerontological thinking, and how can this help us to conceptualize elder victimization, crime, and participation in the criminal justice system? Ferraro (1997, pp. 4–5) has attempted to articulate a "gerontological imagination"—an "analytic framework"—that fuses "the links between biological, behavioral, and social structure factors that influence human aging." Applied to the diverse chapters of this book, the "gerontological imagination" provides one useful way of examining the various data and conclusions presented herein.

According to Ferraro (1997, p. 5), the "gerontological imagination" is "a multidisciplinary sensitivity to aging that incorporates the common stock of knowledge from the core disciplines engaged in research on aging." It is a summary of the best of "scientific thinking on aging" at the present time (Ferraro, 1997, p. 5). The seven elements of this analytic framework are summarized as follows:

- Aging is not a cause of all age-related phenomena.... Age is a very important marker of life events, life transformations, social context, and resources, but age in and of itself is an impotent causal variable. (p. 6)
- Aging is a life process, not a death process.... Death often gives aging a bad name. (p. 8)
- Aging involves a series of transitions from birth to death, with both advantages and disadvantages (advantages for society include increasingly "more law-abiding behavior" as citizens age and for the individual, "less criminal victimization"). (p. 9)
- Aging involves biological, psychological, social, and spiritual changes in individuals at varying rates. The transitions associated with the life course are not linearly related to chronological age, and the process of aging itself is also multidimensional in nature. As such, the approach to the study of aging must recognize the dynamics of aging and the multidimensionality of this dynamism.... Gender, race, social class, and religious preference all shape the way in which aging occurs for individuals or groups. (pp. 10–11)
- Age is positively associated with heterogeneity in a population ... many scholars agree that people become less alike as they grow older. (p. 11)
- Although there is a tendency toward certain functional declines with aging, there are substantial individual differences in the rate of such declines. In addition, many functional abilities can be strengthened or maintained with intervention. (p. 11)

• There is a propensity toward ageism in modern societies; ageism may also exist among elder people or those who work with or for elderly people. (p. 13)

These seven elements of gerontological thought provide a key to help us unlock the meaning of age-related phenomena and how they influence behaviors and experiences of older people involved, in one way or another, in crime and the criminal justice system. The fact that aging is not a cause of age-related phenomena means, for example, that it is insufficient to explain patterns in elder victimization, elder crime, or the behaviors of older people in the courtroom.

In short, Ferraro's analytic framework helps to explain how and why, in this context, elders' behaviors differ from popular stereotypes and perceptions of older people and aging. In particular, the observation that people become less alike as they grow older suggests that many stereotypes surrounding older people and their involvement with crime and the criminal justice system reflect at best only part of the truth.

One hopes that applying Ferraro's "gerontological imagination" to the criminal justice arena will advance the study of aging in other areas. This application may even provide a model with which to disentangle age, aging, and age-related phenomena in other societal contexts, even extending to the areas of health and long-term care.

Intended Audience

This book was designed to meet the needs of readers at all levels of knowledge of gerontology and criminal justice. It is intended to be useful for both academic and professional audiences and to appeal to a wide variety of disciplinary areas within each of these groups.

Within academia, gerontologists are expected to be a primary audience. Many will have their first introduction to a variety of issues that emerge when the lives of older people intersect with the criminal justice system. From this introduction, they may be able to draw new insight and conclusions about older people and current attitudes toward aging. Ideally, faculty will use this book as a launching point for further study and discourse.

Also, because this book combines the interdisciplinary concepts of gerontology with concepts from other varied fields such as criminology and psychology, it is expected to be of interest to academics in a wide variety of other disciplines. Criminologists, sociologists, demographers, anthropologists, and legal psychologists are just a few of the social scientists who should find the book useful for its theoretical and practical implications.

Students in criminal law and criminal justice constitute another important audience. These readers will improve their awareness of and sensitivity to issues of aging within their disciplinary frameworks.

Within the professional arena, this book is intended to promote gerontologically informed decision making and action. Criminal justice professionals who work directly with elders, including police officers, lawyers, judges, jury managers, and corrections officials, as well as health and social service professionals who work with older victims and perpetrators of crime or abuse, should find the book useful for its current facts about the elder population and their impact on the criminal justice system. By gaining a larger understanding of their client populations, these readers may be better equipped to improve the quality and fairness of their policies and practices.

Additionally, administrators at both institutional and systems levels should find this introduction to a gerontological perspective useful for planning and program development. As a collection of current empirical knowledge about the roles of older people vis-à-vis crime and the criminal justice process, this book could serve well as a reference tool for researchers, consultants, planners, and policymakers charged with identifying potential problem areas within the criminal justice system and formulating appropriate responses.

Organization

In the Foreword, Achenbaum and Schieve provide a brief historical overview of the roles that older people traditionally have played in crime and criminal justice, tracing continuities in these roles from biblical times to the present. The chapters that follow pick up where this overview leaves off, focusing on current developments and trends in elder victimization, crime, participation in criminal trials, and imprisonment.

For the most part, this book is organized according to stages in the criminal justice process, beginning with crime prevention. In chapter 1 Terry and Entzel provide an overview of elder-related policing and crime prevention issues, examining specialized elder police units, joint police-and-elder crime prevention initiatives, and implications of various types of police organization for the delivery of police services to older people.

Wolf, in chapter 2, then addresses the issue of elder victimization and the question of whether older people are indeed more vulnerable to and fearful of crime than younger people. Wolf provides current empirical data on older victims of violent crime; property crime; fraud; abuse, neglect and exploitation, examining abuse and neglect in both home and residential settings.

Flynn shifts attention in chapter 3 from elders as victims to elders as offenders. In her overview and analysis of recent elder crime data and trends, Flynn highlights unexpected increases in certain types of elder crime and less-than-expected growth in others. She introduces various theoretical perspectives on elder crime, examining the roles of mental disorders, substance abuse and alcohol abuse in elder criminality.

Next, the book's focus turns from criminal acts to criminal trials and the experiences of older people in the roles of judge, attorney, defendant, witness, and juror. In chapter 4 Adams addresses perceptions and behaviors of older judges, lawyers, and criminal defendants as well as issues relating to courtroom access for older people with disabilities. In addition to physical barriers to access, older participants in the judicial process confront a number of psychological barriers and stressors, which can lead to confusion, frustration, and other psychological symptoms, which Finkel and Macko explore in chapter 5. In chapter 6 Yarmey addresses the recall and testimony of older eyewitnesses, examining whether older witnesses are judged to be less credible than their younger counterparts and whether any such disparate treatment is warranted. Bornstein, Witt, Cherry, and Greene approach a similar problem in chapter 7, providing an empirical analysis of older eyewitnesses' vulnerability to misleading information. In chapter 8, Entzel, Dunlop, and Rothman consider issues surrounding older people and jury service, including elders' perceptions of jury duty, jury duty exemptions and excuses for older people, and legal and ethical implications of age-based distinctions in the jury selection process.

Discussion of elders and the judicial process is followed by several chapters relating to the sentencing, incarceration, early release, and parole of older criminal offenders. Through detailed analysis of state and federal sentencing data, Steffensmeier and Motivans in chapter 9 test the widely held assumption that older offenders receive more lenient sentences than do younger criminals. In chapters 10 and 11 Kerbs underscores some of the many complex and pressing issues arising out of rapid growth in the number of older prisoners. Chapter 10 provides a statistical and demographic profile of the older prisoner population as well as insight into the experiences of older inmates during and after incarceration. Further exploring potential implications of and responses to increasing numbers of older prisoners in chapter 11, Kerbs presents arguments for selective decarceration.

Finally, chapters 12 through 15 address these issues as they relate to four other industrialized countries: England, Germany, Israel, and Japan. Each of these chapters presents current empirical data and analysis, making way for comparison of demographic and social trends among a number of different societies. Johnson's chapter on Japan focuses exclusively on older offenders and prisoners, whereas the other three encompass a broader scope of issues in an overview format.

The authors of each chapter were selected for their expertise in their diverse fields of study. Together, they represent the disciplines of criminology, gerontology, law, sociology, psychology, psychiatry, and social work. In bringing together these authors, the editors sought to provide a cogent and comprehensive overview of the intersection of elders, crime and the criminal justice system from both academic and applied perspectives. Because chapters have been drawn from authors in a wide variety of disciplines, they vary considerably in tone, viewpoint, and methodology. Furthermore, chapters do not necessarily reflect the views or opinions of the editors, nor were they selected for this purpose. Instead, each chapter has been included, primarily, for its potential to increase awareness and provoke thought and research in this long overlooked field of study.

Conclusions

Achenbaum and Schieve, in the Foreword, conclude that "we have not fully grasped all the darker aspects of growing older." In this book, we explore some of these darker aspects and how society, through its system of criminal justice, responds to them. The "legal gerontocracy" of the Old Testament no longer exists, but no one is certain what has replaced it. By examining what happens to older people enmeshed in one way or another with the criminal justice system today, we attempt to place these issues in the forefront of discussion among gerontologists, criminologists, and public policymakers. In doing so, we use the microcosm of the criminal justice system to raise important questions about the meaning and experience of growing older in America—and throughout the world—in the 21st century.

References

American Association of Retired Persons (AARP). (1998). *A profile of older Americans: 1998*. Washington, DC: Author.

Butler, R. N., Grossman, L. K., & Oberlink, M. R. (1999). *Life in an older America*. New York: Century Foundation Press.

de Luce, J. (1993). Ancient images of aging: Did ageism exist in Greco-Roman antiquity? *Generations, 17*, 41–45.

Ferraro, K. F. (1997). *Gerontology: Perspectives and issues* (2d ed.). New York: Springer Publishing Co.

U.S. Bureau of the Census. (1996). *65+ in the United States* (Current Population Reports, Special Studies, P23-190). Washington, DC: U.S. Government Printing Office.

PART I

Elders and Crime

Chapter 1

Police and Elders

W. Clinton Terry III and Pamela Entzel

The available literature on police and elders is basically descriptive and prescriptive in nature. Much of it describes different "crime and the elderly" programs. Since there are apparently few local programs apart from Triad and Seniors and Lawmen Together (SALT), the descriptive articles are few in number. Other articles dealing with police response to crime and elders prescribe how police should handle them. To their credit, most of these articles argue that the aging process, the changing demographics of aging within the United States, and the special problems of elders, such as abuse, should be part of the police officer's knowledge base. Most of these articles have a positive bias toward older persons. Although in our culture it might be argued that elders are ignored and relegated to a place of obscurity in our irrational embrace of things youthful, our culture also tips its hat, on occasion at least, to more kindly and caring attitudes toward older persons.

It is difficult to reconcile what is known about police work and what is known about elders and the process of aging itself. The problem, as outlined below, has less to do with understanding elders than with understanding the police. Obviously, both topics are very broad, neither is perfectly understood, and there is considerable room for different interpretations within both areas. Nevertheless, there are a number of features surrounding policing in the United States that might well be taken into consideration when thinking about police and elders.

Police Response

In responding to calls involving seniors, police officers determine the extent of elder victimization, including the presence of abuse and neglect. If the call involves elder offenders, the officer determines the seriousness of the crime, the circumstances leading up to the offense, and the degree to which the elder offenders might be criminally liable. A senile individual who wanders away from home and upon returning enters the wrong home, raids the refrigerator, and falls asleep in the bed of the master bedroom, is more likely to be returned to the proper home than to be arrested. If the case involves a referral, police are sometimes the first people on the scene. As such, they would be the first people able to provide psychological, first aid, and crisis intervention.

It is important that officers be familiar with the processes of aging and the special problems of elders when they respond to calls involving older offenders or elder abuse and neglect. Unfortunately, many officers are unfamiliar with what to look for in such cases (Weith, 1994). At police academies, where such knowledge could be imparted, there is little, if any, training in elder crime or abuse, the aging process, sensory loss characteristics, and communication with older persons (Weith, 1994). This lack of familiarity is doubly unfortunate because, according to American Association of Retired Persons (AARP), almost half of the people responding to an AARP survey indicated they would go to the police first if they were physically abused (Dolon & Hendricks, 1989). Despite these difficulties, some local police departments have developed specialized elder units and, at the national level, efforts have been underway to develop strategies conducive to the proliferation of these units at the local level.

Specialized Elder Units

In 1980, the Milwaukee Police Department created a Senior Citizen Assault Prevention Unit, which was dubbed the "Gray Squad" (Weith, 1994). This unit had a staff of five detectives, eight uniformed officers, a uniformed sergeant, and a detective lieutenant (Zevitz & Rettammel, 1990). It investigated serious crimes against seniors and worked with senior citizens in order to increase crime prevention awareness. In addition, older persons were instructed on how to identify and detect potential assailants, and the unit's members engaged in prevention and preventive patrol activities. Officers working for this unit received specialized gerontological training, including how to speak and interact with older persons (Gurnack & Zevitz, 1993; Zevitz & Gurnack, 1991; Zevitz & Rettammel, 1990).

In evaluating the effect of Milwaukee's "Gray Unit," Zevitz and his colleagues found that older victims responded favorably to the services received from this specially trained group of officers. Seventy-eight percent rated the level of police effort expended in providing services as high. An additional 18% rated these officers as making a "great effort." Seventy-four percent felt that the police were very sympathetic to the situation of elders and more than 90% felt the officers were sensitive to their needs (Zevitz & Rettammel, 1990). Compared to a group of seniors who had similar problems but who interacted with police officers not specifically trained to deal with seniors, the members of the Gray Squad were consistently rated higher (Zevitz & Gurnack, 1991; Zevitz & Rettammel, 1990). In addition, recipients of Gray Squad services felt safer in their neighborhoods, felt that their neighborhoods were receiving adequate police services, and perceived that they were less likely to be victims of a crime during the next 12 months (Gurnack & Zevitz, 1993).

In 1986, the City of Miami Police Department instituted a "Senior Citizens Specialized Policing Program" to address the issues of crime and crime prevention at designated older adult housing projects. As part of this program, the police department hired 13 part-time officers to patrol various housing and activity sites for older people during daytime hours. Other objectives of the program included providing crime prevention presentations for residents of the target housing projects and developing a crime watch network through which older citizen volunteers could alert the specially assigned police officers in the event of criminal activity (Terry, Gibbons, & Rothman, 1988).

Although not all goals of the Miami program were achieved (the crime watch network ultimately proved unworkable as first designed), the program had a number of successes. Eighteen months after the specially assigned officers were deployed, victimization of elders at the target housing projects had declined significantly, and residents reported reduced fear of crime during daytime hours. Increased police visibility, together with daily interaction between elders and the Miami police officers assigned to the HUD housing projects had given elders in the program a perception of having a "neighborhood cop" and a concomitant sense of security (Terry et al., 1988).

Triad and SALT

Perhaps the best-known police responses to the needs of elders are Triad and Seniors and Lawmen Together (SALT). In the summer of 1986, the International Association of Chiefs of Police (IACP) joined together with AARP to address the issue of elder victimization. In the spring of 1987, the IACP extended an invitation to the National Sheriff's Association (NSA) to join in these efforts (Harpold, 1994). In 1988, the AARP, IACP, and NSA passed resolutions agreeing to work toward improving the quality of life of seniors. In this way, the Triad concept was formed. By 1998, police chiefs, sheriffs, and older citizen representatives had developed 585 Triads in 46 states as well as six in the United Kingdom and one in Canada (Alliance for Aging, 1998).

The formation of a Triad generally begins with a police chief, sheriff, or representative of the elder community contacting the other two essential members to discuss a three-way cooperative effort to enhance the delivery of law enforcement services to elders. These initial participants then invite older citizens and representatives from agencies serving older citizens (e.g., Area Agencies on Aging, the public health department, adult protective services) to serve on an advisory council, often called Seniors and Lawmen Together. As one of their initial tasks, members of the SALT council conduct a preliminary survey to determine the needs and concerns of elders in the area. Once established, SALT councils generally meet monthly, often with law enforcement officials in attendance. Through these meetings, law enforcement officials learn about specific problems that impact elders as well as services and agencies that can minimize these problems, while elders serving on the council learn about the workings of law enforcement agencies and the criminal justice system (Cantrell, 1994).

Because they are designed to meet the particular needs of the local community, Triad programs vary from one jurisdiction to another. However, a critical component of all Triads is education. Many Triads train officers and deputies on the aging process, effective communication with older people, and elder victimization. They also provide various crime prevention presentations to older people in an effort to reduce elder victimization as well as elders' fear of crime. These presentations educate older people about which local crimes are most likely to affect them and what they can do to protect themselves. For example, Triads may provide elders with tips on avoiding consumer crime, emphasizing that although many older people fear violent crime, they are much more likely to be victims of frauds or scams (Cantrell, 1994).

Other Triad initiatives have involved working with local businesses and financial institutions to curtail fraud or scams targeting elders, establishing programs to prevent elder abuse, sponsoring safe outdoor exercise programs, and helping persons in high-crime-risk areas manage their grocery shopping (Cantrell, 1994). Additionally, some SALTS have begun "Adopt A Senior" and visitation programs in which law enforcement officials regularly check on the welfare of elders who are homebound or isolated ("Sheriffs," 1996). In other Triad jurisdictions, retired volunteers receive daily check-in calls from elders or place outgoing calls to those who request this service (Cantrell, 1994).

Triads and SALTS are heavily dependent on the participation and assistance of volunteers from the elder community. Volunteers may conduct informal home security surveys, organize neighborhood watch groups, provide information and support to crime victims, or assist law enforcement agencies with record keeping (Cantrell, 1994). Involving older citizens in Triad's volunteer projects not only allows older people to make an impact on crime, but also allows law enforcement agencies to benefit from elders' valuable skills and experience.

Law Enforcement Gerontology

Recently, the notion of law enforcement gerontology (Rykert, 1994) is being mentioned. Law enforcement gerontologists are interested in: (a) working with elders to identify specific problems and develop means of limiting the risks of victimization, (b) alerting seniors about ongoing scams, and (c) involving elders in volunteer projects. Volunteering in projects gives elders a sense that they have some control over their life circumstances. Volunteering also helps law enforcement in their crime prevention efforts within the community.

In March 1993, Illinois became the first state to train officers as specialists in law enforcement gerontology. Several other states have followed their lead. In addition, the National Crime Prevention Institute in Louisville, Kentucky offers a 40-hour law enforcement gerontology course. The Institute's program addresses the demographics, myths, and facts of aging, the issue of family assaults and abuse, health care providers, guardianship, health care fraud, street crimes and traditional con games such as roof repairs and telemarketing schemes, legislative issues, and senior volunteer services (Rykert, 1994).

Despite these efforts, the police response to the special needs and problems of elders has been slow. This is regrettable though somewhat understandable. Elders are seldom victimized and commit few crimes; hence, police officers seldom encounter them. Moreover, police usually become involved in elder abuse situations only when a case that gets reported to adult protection service agencies is referred to them. In Miami-Dade County, Florida, for instance, the police are contacted any time second-party abuse, exploitation, or neglect is suspected by Adult Protective Service workers.

Attitudes of Elders Toward the Police

The research on elders' attitudes toward the police is mixed. There is a body of work arguing that those elders who have direct contact with the police hold generally favorable attitudes toward them (Acuri, 1981; Schack & Frank, 1978). These attitudes did not appear to be related to whether contact was in response to criminal or noncriminal events (Schack & Frank, 1978; Schack, Grissom, & Wax, 1980). Morello (1982), on the other hand, found that the greater the frequency of contact with the police, the less favorable were elders' attitudes towards them. Acuri (1981) has suggested that police indifference to elder problems is the root cause of elder dissatisfaction with police. Inversely, the police have done little to educate elders about the criminal justice system, an action that might serve to increase their confidence in it.

Delivery of Police Services to Elders

Logistical and Manpower Considerations

Metropolitan police departments, almost without exception, are strapped for resources to complete tasks expected of them. They respond to a wide range of calls for services. They also respond to the changing desires and needs of elected officials. Faced with the need to provide a myriad of services to multiple clients, police administrators are often pulled in diverse directions when deciding what strategies to develop and where to deploy officers. One thing is for sure, all other things being equal, geographical areas within major metropolitan areas exhibiting little need for police services receive less attention than areas manifesting high calls for service, high crime rates, and serious disorder problems. Disorder is a broad category. It includes such behaviors as public drinking, noisy neighbors, street corner gangs, street sale and possession of drugs, and commercial sex. It also refers to the poor physical condition of some neighborhoods. In these neighborhoods there are large amounts of uncollected trash, abandoned furniture and vehicles, and other manifestations of physical decay. These areas often have high rates of crime.

Police Decision Making

Police officers exercise a considerable amount of discretion in deciding how they will handle calls. Decisions to make an arrest, for instance, take into consideration offense seriousness, relationship between the offender and victim, offender and complainant demeanor, complainant desires, and the overall circumstances surrounding the situation to which the police officer has been summoned (Black, 1971; Harlow, 1985; Hindelang, 1976; Lundman, 1974; Piliavin & Briar, 1964; Reiss, 1971; Sherman, 1971, 1980; Smith, 1986; Smith & Visher, 1981; Sykes, Fox, & Clark, 1976; Visher, 1983).

Although much is known about the general exercise of police discretion, less is known about how this discretion affects different groups of people, including elders. Although police officers are believed to treat some groups, such as women and juveniles, more leniently when making arrests, little is known about how these arrests are resolved by the courts. If the courts treat them more harshly in terms of court filings, convictions, and longer sentences, is it because they are arrested only when committing more serious offenses—their lesser infractions tending to be overlooked (Langworthy & McCarthy, 1988)?

But what about older persons? Under what circumstances do citizens report elder crime to the police, and how do police departments handle these complaints? Do police officers treat elders more leniently at arrest? The little information available to answer these questions is somewhat contradictory. One study by Langworthy and McCarthy (1988) found that older offenders were less likely to be released by the police than younger suspects. Their data, however, were somewhat limited and thus subject to a series of caveats, including the observation that older and younger offenders were, in many other respects, treated similarly.

Ultimately, the exercise of police discretion may be influenced more by circumstances of an elder's offense than by age. Research has indicated that, where possible, police officers often prefer to establish order without making an arrest. If minor offenders appear to be cooperative, obedient to authority, and unlikely to repeat their offense in the near future, police may be less likely to arrest them than to take them home or notify some other agency. On the other hand, if police perceive the offender as unruly or antagonistic, they may regard this behavior as a rejection of police authority necessitating a formal arrest. Therefore, further research is needed on how older people react to the exercise of police authority. If older offenders tend to be respectful and submissive in their encounters with the police, they may benefit from police discretion, with fewer incidents of elder deviance resulting in arrest, and fewer elder arrests resulting in bookings (Alston, 1986).

Police Organization, Police Subculture, and Other Factors

Police departments are often viewed as emergency response agencies. In fact, much of their organization is geared to responding to calls for service as quickly as possible (Wilson & McLaren, 1977). In emergency situations, municipal police officers are often expected to arrive at the location of the call in less than three minutes. To accomplish these goals, police departments tend to emphasize centralization of command.

In responding to calls, police officers are expected to be able to handle conflicts, mediate disputes, and otherwise solve the problems found in the situations to which they are called, including making arrests when appropriate. Years ago, Egon Bittner (1970) put forward the notion of nonnegotiable coercive force as the primary reason most people call the police. Carl B. Klockars talks about this in terms of "Something ought not to be happening about which something ought to be done NOW!" (Klockars, 1985, p. 16). Police are called because they have the requisite resources to handle all manner of situations. This is what they are trained to do. This is what the department expects them to do.

In the course of "handling situations," police officers develop certain perceptions of what they should be doing. They develop perceptions of typical groups of people, typical actions committed by these people, and the typical police responses to these actions. Officers learn much of the information that shapes these perceptions informally and on the job during their first year on the police force. Other factors shaping police perceptions include local, state, and federal law, departmental policy, and local expectations of how people should treat others. Police responses to criminal and noncriminal calls from and about older persons are thus shaped by a number of external factors and expectations, including the common notion that the police department is primarily an emergency response agency.

Oftentimes, however, the types of problems experienced by elders cannot be resolved immediately. In many situations, the most helpful thing a police officer can do for an older person is to refer him or her to social service organizations that provide long-term, comprehensive assistance. Yet police officers appear to have relatively poor knowledge of community services and their potential value to older people. Furthermore, while it is possible to improve police officers' ability to make referrals and contacts, it may be much harder to persuade them that this is a legitimate police duty. Many police officers may see noncriminal, social service calls as intrusions into more important police duties such as apprehension of criminals and deterrence of crime. Therefore, they may deal with these calls as quickly as possible in order to be free for other work (Alston, 1986).

Police officers' focus on immediate action also may influence the type of referrals and contacts that they make. An Indiana study of elder abuse and neglect cases found that the 51 police officers included in the study tended to refer elder abuse and neglect calls to agencies that could provide immediate relief from the conflict at hand rather than referring them to agencies that could provide long-term, coordinated, and comprehensive care (Dolon & Hendricks, 1989). These officers ranked family conflict as the leading factor in abuse and neglect cases. The 55 visiting nurses/social service personnel interviewed, however, reported family conflict as the number two cause of abuse cases and the number eight cause in neglect cases. They reported inadequate support services, economic and physical dependency, mental health, stress, and living conditions ahead of family conflict as causes leading to elder abuse (Dolon & Hendricks, 1989). Although nurses and social services rated the police as helpful, the police seldom refer cases to social service providers, which may merely reflect the seriousness of the calls to which police respond (Dolon & Hendricks, 1989). Only 33% of police had any encounters with abuse and neglect cases; whereas, 69% of the nurses/social workers had had such experiences (Dolon & Hendricks, 1989).

The Future for Police and Elders

Traditionally, police departments are centrally organized and administered. The basic method of operation is largely "incident based" (Eck & Spelman, 1987, p. 4). In other words, police respond to incidents phoned into police departments. Using this method, police officers respond as quickly as possible, deal with the situation, write a report when necessary, and then move on to the next call for service. If a department's patrol zones are well organized with respect to criminal activities and calls for service, incident-based policing is able to dispatch police officers to different locations within reasonable periods of time. Whether it is equally effective in reducing crime levels is an entirely different question.

Incident-based policing is less well suited to responding to the special needs of certain groups of people than it is to responding to individual calls for assistance. In the case of elders, who may be dispersed throughout the city, their calls and needs may get lost in a myriad of other calls received within any particular patrol zone. Different zones differ in the typical calls for service received. Unless older persons constitute the typical call received from a zone, their needs, again, tend to be overlooked in favor of other priorities. Should the department decide that elders' needs in their city warrant the creation of a special group of officers who respond to criminal and noncriminal elder incidents citywide, dispatching these officers to elder calls could overcome, at least in part, some of the problems created by elder dispersion and the special problems in particular patrol zones. Several such units, including Milwaukee's Gray Squad and certain Triad and SALT initiatives, were the result of centralized organizational efforts. Creation of these units rests upon the initiative of police administrators working, perhaps, in collaboration with municipal government and with certain older activists. The continuation of such efforts is often dependent, however, on administrative support and the absence of more pressing organizational needs.

In assessing the future of elder issues within the context of delivering police services, there is reason for both doubt and hope. Given the emphasis on incident-based policing, it is doubtful whether municipal police departments will be able to give greater emphasis to elder issues and needs in the foreseeable future. Given the flood of demands upon city police departments to provide a wide range of services and given the low incidence of elder offenders and victims, it seems unlikely that significantly greater emphasis will be given to elders than those efforts currently underway. Although it would appear that the creation of specialized elder units in some departments indicates an increased police effort to reach this population, it is unknown at this point in time how successful these have been. Moreover, the quality of services rendered and the adequacy of the services as perceived by elders remains largely unmeasured.

The future of police–elder relationships is further complicated by the rapid growth of gated communities patrolled by private security guards. Due in part to real or perceived shortcomings in police services, older people in many communities are substituting private security services for traditional police protection. In recent decades, the number of private security guards has doubled and surpassed the number of police officers nationally. Private security currently outspends law enforcement by 73% (Blakely & Snyder, 1997). This trend toward private control of public safety and security may represent a movement away from public organization and collaborative efforts with the police, at least among the more affluent.

Although neither the current emphasis on incident-based policing nor the growth of the private security industry holds much promise for enhancing the relationship between police and elders, there are changes currently underway in the very philosophy of policing that promise more. These changes revolve around the notion of community-oriented policing. Delivering police services under the philosophy of community-oriented policing involves two major premises: partnerships and problem solving. As with incident-based policing, officers respond to calls for service. However, at the end of the call, police officers look for the underlying reasons for the call. If there are any, such as a physically deteriorating neighborhood, the officers, as part of their regular assignment, develop plans for tackling these problems. In tackling them, the police enlist people within the neighborhoods experiencing these problems in order to assist in providing the solution. They also enlist the assistance of other local government and private agencies where appropriate. By partnering with local citizens and other agencies, police officers are more likely to help eliminate the problem, thus reducing the calls for service to that location.

Community policing, although a philosophy, is best implemented in zones to which officers are permanently assigned. Being permanently assigned, officers are better able to become more aware of the people and their problems. This is particularly the case if their patrol zone was created with an eye for neighborhood integrity, that is, with an eye towards the existence of natural geographical boundaries and the presence of distinct groups of people and racial/ethnic populations. Being aware of local conditions and problems, officers are better able to build coalitions aimed at their solutions.

For elders living within a community-oriented policing zone, there is a greater likelihood that the problems affecting older individuals will become known to police officers. If the focus on local elder problems is driven by federal programs and national organizations and is merely trickling down to the local level, or if it is driven by departmental programs aimed at elders in general, elder problems may be overlooked at the community or neighborhood level. However, because community policing is, to a degree, decentralized, and because community police officers have been "empowered" to find unique solutions to local problems, these officers will have greater freedom to deal with the problems of elders in their neighborhoods than they would have under the philosophy of incident-based policing. Whether or not community policing is just a buzz word, funded by federal program dollars, or whether it is a truly new philosophy of policing, remains to be seen. If it persists, it bodes well for both the police and elders.

Conclusions

In recent years, law enforcement agencies and advocates for elders have initiated a number of programs designed to improve police response to the problems and needs of older people. At the core of many of these programs is an effort to increase police awareness of the demographics, myths, and facts of aging, including the current facts about elder victimization and abuse. Further research is needed to evaluate these programs for their quality and effectiveness.

Additionally, there is a continuing need to explore alternatives to centralized, incident-based delivery of police services. Community-oriented policing, with its emphasis on partnerships and problem solving, may be especially well suited to responding to the special needs of elders. By enlisting the assistance of elders, private organizations, and other public agencies, law enforcement agencies can improve both their awareness of the problems facing older people and their ability to offer long-term solutions.

References

Acuri, A. (1981). The police and the elderly. In D. Lester (Ed.), *The elderly victim of crime* (pp. 106–127). Springfield, IL: Charles C Thomas.

Alliance for Aging, Inc. (1999, January 13). Minutes from the meeting of the Area Agency on Aging advisory council, Miami, FL.

Alston, L. T. (1986). *Crime and older Americans.* Springfield, IL: Charles C Thomas.

Bittner, E. (1970). *The functions of police in modern society.* Rockville, MD: National Institute of Mental Health.

Black, D. (1971). The social organization of arrest. *Stanford Law Review, 23,* 1087–1111.

Blakely, E. J., & Snyder, M. G. (1997). *Fortress America: Gated communities in the United States.* Washington, DC: Brookings Institution.

Cantrell, B. (1994). Triad: Reducing criminal victimization of the elderly. *FBI Law Enforcement Bulletin, 63*(2), 19–23.

Dolon, R., & Hendricks, J. E. (1989). An exploratory study comparing attitudes and practices of police officers and social service providers in elder abuse and neglect cases. *Journal of Elder Abuse and Neglect, 1*(1), 75–90.

Eck, J. E., & Spelman, W. (1987). *Problem solving: Problem oriented policing in Newport News.* Washington, DC: U.S. Department of Justice, National Institute of Justice.

Gurnack, A. M., & Zevitz, R. G. (1993). Components of variation in elderly crime victim's perception of neighborhood safety: The role of specialized police services for seniors in Milwaukee, Wisconsin. *Police Studies, 16*(1), 20–27.

Harlow, C. (1985). *Reporting crimes to the police.* Bureau of Justice Statistics Special Report. Washington, DC: U.S. Government Printing Office.

Harpold, J. A. (1994). The FBI and the elderly. *FBI Law Enforcement Bulletin,* *62*(2), 10–11.

Hindelang, M. J. (1976). *Criminal victimization in eight American cities: A descriptive analysis of common theft and assault.* Cambridge, MA: Ballinger.

Klockars, C. B. (1985). *The idea of police.* Newbury Park, CA: Sage.

Langworthy, R., & McCarthy, B. (1988). Police disposition of arrests: An exploratory study of the treatment of the older offender. In R. Langworthy & B. McCarthy (Eds.), *Older offenders: Perspectives in criminology and criminal justice* (pp. 107–122). New York: Praeger.

Lundman, R. (1974). Routine arrest practices: A commonweal perspective. *Social Problems, 22,* 127–141.

Morello, F. (1982). *Juvenile crimes against the elderly.* Springfield, IL: Charles C Thomas.

Piliavin, I. M., & Briar, S. (1964). Police encounters with juveniles. *American Journal of Sociology, 70,* 206–214.

Reiss, A. (1971). *The police and the public.* New Haven, CT: Yale University Press.

Rykert, W. R. (1994). Law enforcement gerontology. *FBI Law Enforcement Bulletin, 62*(2), 5–9.

Schack, S., & Frank, R. (1978). Police service delivery to the elderly. *Annals of the American Academy of Political Science, 438,* 81–95.

Schack, S., Grissom, G., & Wax, W. (1980). *Police service delivery to the elderly.* Washington, DC: U.S. Department of Justice.

Sheriffs: Seniors, sheriffs, and police chiefs join to fight crime in 225 communities. (1996). *Aging, 367,* 36–37.

Sherman, L. W. (1971). The social organization of arrest. *Stanford Law Review, 23,* 1087–1111.

Sherman, L. W. (1980). *The manners and customs of the police.* New York: Academic Press.

Smith, D. (1986). The neighborhood context of police behavior. In A. J. Reiss, Jr. & M. Torny (Eds.), *Communities and crime* (pp. 313–341). Chicago: University of Chicago Press.

Smith, D., & Visher, C. (1981). Street level justice: Situational determinants of Police Arrest Decisions. *Social Problems, 29,* 167–177.

Sykes, R., Fox, J., & Clark, J. (1976). A socio-legal theory of police discretion (pp. 171–183). In A. Neiderhoffer & A. Blumberh (Eds.), *The ambivalent forces: Perspectives on the police* (2nd ed.). Hinsville, IL: Dryden Press.

Terry, W. C. III, Gibbons, S. B., & Rothman, M. B. (1988). *Policing Miami's housing projects for older persons: An evaluation.* North Miami, FL: Florida International University, Southeast Florida Center on Aging.

Visher, C. (1983). Gender, police arrest decisions, and notions of chivalry. *Criminology, 21,* 5–28.

Weith, M. E. (1994). Elder abuse: A national tragedy. *FBI Law Enforcement Bulletin, 62*(2), 24–26.

Wilson, O. W., & McLaren, R. C. (1977). *Police administration* (4th ed.). New York: McGraw Hill.

Zevitz, R. G., & Gurnack, A. M. (1991). Factors related to elderly crime victims' satisfaction with police service: The impact of Milwaukee's gray squad. *Gerontologist, 31*(1), 92–101.

Zevitz, R. G., & Rettammel, R. J. (1990). Elderly attitudes about police service. *American Journal of Police, 9*(2), 25–39.

Suggested Readings

Bureau of Justice Statistics. (1994). *National crime victimization survey: Elderly crime victims.* Washington, DC: U.S. Department of Justice, Office of Justice Programs, Bureau of Justice Statistics.

Cutshall, C., & Adams, K. (1983). Responding to older offenders: Age selectivity in the processing of shoplifters. *Criminal Justice Review, 8*(2), 1–8.

Hahn, P. H. (1976). *Crime against the elderly: A study in victimization.* Santa Cruz, CA: Davis Publications.

Lindquist, J. H. (1987). Issues in the criminal victimization of the elderly. In C. D. Chambers, J. H. Lindquist, O. Z. White, & M. T. Harter (Eds.), *The elderly: Victims and deviants.* Athens, OH: Ohio University Press.

Lindquist, J. H., White, O. Z., & Chambers, C. D. (1986). *Judicial disposition of elderly misdemeanor and felony defendants: Bexar County, Texas, 1973–1985.* Unpublished manuscript, Trinity College at San Antonio, TX.

Maguire, K., & Pastore, A. L. (1997). *Bureau of justice statistics sourcebook of criminal justice statistics, 1996.* U.S. Department of Justice, Bureau of Justice Statistics, Washington, DC: USGPO.

Malinchak, A. A., & Wright, D. (1978, March–April). The scope of elderly victimization. *Aging,* 10–16.

Quirk, D. A. (1991). An agenda for the nineties and beyond. *Generations, 15*(3), 23–26.

Wilbanks, W. (1985, April). *Are elderly felons treated more leniently by the criminal justice system?* Paper presented at the Third National Conference on Elderly Offenders, Kansas City, MO.

Chapter 2

Elders As Victims of Crime, Abuse, Neglect, and Exploitation

Rosalie S. Wolf

Concern about victims over time has changed in response to the evolution of legal concepts, the various approaches to ideas such as responsibility, and the need to "erect solid and unbreakable barriers between the unbridled power of the state and the citizen suspected of a crime" (Viano, 1985, p. 4). For the past 50 years, efforts have been underway to recognize the victim as deserving of compensation and a role in the criminal justice decision-making process. A wide array of programs has been established to make this possible but only recently have elders been included as a specific target group. The tendency in the past was to consider elders as dependent, vulnerable, and in need of protection. Blaming the victim was very much a part of the original (but flawed) construction of elder abuse as a manifestation of caregiver stress. This characterization, buttressed by societal prejudice against the aged and aging, had the effect of making old people into "legitimate or deserving" victims. As empirical data have become available, the myths and stereotypes have been slowly replaced by a more realistic appraisal of elder victims.

This chapter is divided into two sections: the first summarizes national crime survey data about elder victims of crime perpetrated by strangers (for the most part); the second section reviews information about elder victims of abuse, neglect, and exploitation perpetrated largely by family members in the home setting. From a historical, policy perspective these two issues developed along separate tracks: one was criminal justice; the other, public welfare. It became apparent in the last decade that although elder abuse was a public welfare matter and later taken over as an aging issue, it could also be viewed as a crime. Today, police officers, prosecutors, and health and social service providers realize that they all have an important role to play together in preventing victimization of elders whether perpetrated by strangers or by family members.

Elder Victims of Crime

Background

National interest in crime and older people first emerged as a social problem in the 1960s and "reached a height of public outrage in the mid-1970s" (Finley, 1983, p. 21). A set of assumptions was responsible for the deep concern about elder crime victims. The rate of victimization of elders was considered to be higher than that of younger persons; the physical and financial consequences, greater; the psychological impact, more profound; and the fear of crime, more prevalent (Finley, 1983). As part of a survey by Harris and Associates for the National Council on the Aging (1975), a national sample of persons 65 years of age and older was asked about the seriousness (very serious problem, somewhat a serious problem, hardly a problem) of 12 problems of daily living. Fear of crime/crime was first on the list in the "very serious" category, ahead of such problems as poor health, insufficient income, loneliness, etc.

With the publication of survey data results in the 1980s, higher crime rates and more severe consequences for elders were no longer valid assumptions (U.S. Department of Justice, Bureau of Justice Statistics, 1987). However, fear of crime as an age-related factor remained an overriding concern (Clemente & Kleiman, 1984; Finley, 1983; Ollenburger, 1981; Yin, 1985). Even a decade later, crime/personal safety was high on the agenda of older persons. It was among the top 10 topics recognized in the hundreds of local, state, and regional White House Conferences on Aging (WHCOA) (1995a). It also was in fourth place among a list of 17 issues that received the most public comments in response to a *Federal Register* request regarding the WHCOA agenda (1995b).

Prevalence—1987 BJS Report

A special report from the National Crime Survey (NCS) showed that violent crimes (rape, robbery, aggravated assault, and simple assault), household larceny, and burglary of elders were declining during this period, matching the trend for the U.S. population as a whole (U.S. Department of Justice, 1987). Moreover, persons 65 years and older had the lowest victimization rates of any age group, 12 years and older. They were only one-third as likely to be a victim of a violent crime (robbery, assault, rape) as the under 65 group. However, about 45% of the violent crimes against the elders were robberies (considered more serious than assault because it involves theft and force) compared to 18% for the younger age population. The report speculates that the higher proportion of elder robberies may be attributed to the belief among criminal offenders that older persons carry large amounts of cash with them and are less able or likely to defend themselves than younger persons.

The NCS found no measurable differences between the under and over 65 population in the proportion of persons who were physically attacked or injured, sustained serious or minor injuries, or received medical care or hospital treatment. However, a comparison of the 65 to 74 years and 75 years and older groups indicated that the latter were more likely to be injured and to receive medical care; although the small sample size precluded reporting this difference as statistically significant. The report also mentioned the "intangible effects of crime upon those who may be the most vulnerable physically and economically" (U.S. Department of Justice, 1987, p. 1).

Prevalence—BJS 1994 Report

Statistics on elder crime victims from a later BJS report (U.S. Department of Justice, 1994) continued to show a general decline in the crime victimization rates for violent crimes, personal theft, and household crime. In 1992, persons 65 years or older experienced about 2.1 million criminal acts: 4.0 per thousand persons or households compared to 64.6 for the 12–24 age groups, 27.2 for the 25–49 group, and 8.5 for the 50–64 year group. Higher rates of victimization of elders were generally associated with gender (male), age (young), race (Blacks), income (lower), marital status (separated or divorced), and place of residence (cities). In some instances, these associations depended on the types of crime. Although older men have in general higher victimization rates than women, older women have higher rates of personal larceny (such as purse snatching). So too, Whites have higher rates of personal larceny that do not involve contact between the victim and offender than Blacks. Differences in crime rates by type of crime, gender, and race have also been reported in an analysis of the FBI 1994 National Incident Based Reporting System data for South Carolina (McCabe & Gregory, 1998).

According to the 1994 BJS report, in comparison to the younger population, elders are particularly susceptible to crimes motivated by economic gain, including robbery, personal theft, larceny, burglary, and motor vehicle theft and least susceptible to violent crimes. Using BJS data from 1992–1994, Bachman, Dillaway, and Lachs (1998) examined the robbery and assault victimization experiences of older persons and how the incidents differed from that of younger persons. Younger men (less than 65 years) were twice as likely to experience a robbery victimization as younger women but among the over 65 population, there was no difference by gender. Bachman (1993) also compared national data from both the NCVS and Comparative Homicide File for the periods 1976–1980 and 1981–1990, and found no significant differences across the time period in the extent to which people under 65 years old were victimized by those known to them or by strangers. For the over 65 population, the percentage who reported an act of violence perpetrated by a relative more than doubled (3% to 8%), an increase that may be due to public attention given to elder abuse, neglect, and exploitation.

Consequences

As noted previously, not only had the early estimates of the prevalence of crimes against the older in relation to younger people been exaggerated but the beliefs about the consequences were also suspect. Writing on the effects of victimization, Yin (1985) specifies three types: financial loss, physical injury, and diminution of well-being. While he acknowledges that common sense would dictate that elder victims suffer more than younger victims in these three areas, study findings (Cook, Skogan, Cook, & Antunes, 1978) are equivocal. Yin states that the early researchers failed to distinguish between the seriousness of the victimization and the sufferings of the victim. In that context, older victims were found to suffer more than younger victims although the criminal acts that are involved are less serious. Victimization was found to have had no long-term effects on well-being (Lawton & Yaffee, 1980). However, later national crime victimization data (U.S. Department of Justice, 1994) did show that elder victims of violent crimes (9%) were more likely than younger victims (4%) to suffer a serious injury. When injured, almost half the older victims were hospitalized (two or more days) compared to one-quarter of the younger persons. These data differ from the earlier BJS report (U.S. Department of Justice, 1987) that found a significant difference with age only for those individuals 75 years and older.

Fear of Crime

Beginning in the late 70s, most of the attention with regard to crime and elders shifted from reports on prevalence to discussion about the fear of crime (Clemente & Kleiman, 1976; Gubrium, 1974 cited in Finley, 1983; Finley, 1983; Kennedy & Silverman, 1985; Lee, 1982; Liang & Sengstock, 1983; Norton & Courlander, 1992; Yin, 1985). Yin proposed a person–environment theory of fear made up of three components: personal vulnerability, environmental peril, and victimization experience (the interaction between the person and the environment). According to this theory, aged females and persons who perceive their health as poor would be more fearful as would persons living in urban areas and high crime neighborhoods and those who have been victimized, although findings on this last factor are more ambiguous. Elders' exposure to the mass media with its fixation on violence was proposed as a potential agent in generating fear but research has demonstrated it to be a non-factor. While differences in level of fear exist among elders with respect to age, health, race, etc., Yin reports that generally the disparity in level of fear between the young and old population is "not large."

Several years later, Ferraro and LaGrange (1992) found no evidence in a national sample of adults that older people were the age group most afraid of crime. In fact, it was the high level of fear reported by the younger respondents that surprised them. They attributed the inconsistencies in earlier studies to problems of measurement. Usually, single items measuring fear of crime were used, such as: How safe do you feel being out alone in your neighborhood at night? Is there any area within a mile of your home where you would be afraid to walk at night? How likely is it that a person walking around at night might get held up or attacked? Instead of these global measures, Ferraro and LaGrange used 10 types of victimization (being cheated, conned, swindled out of money, robbed, murdered, etc.) and examined each one separately and then together. In only one item of the 10, the fear of being approached on a street by a beggar or panhandler, did the fear of the older person exceed that of a younger person, and this condition was restricted to females. Even utilizing various methods and strategies to detect age effects in their data, the results still showed that the elders were not more likely to be afraid of crime than other age groups. With respect to property crimes, they were the least fearful. Work by Weinrath and Gartrell (1996) which examined age and gender interactions in two successive Canadian city surveys, disclosed that greater fear was associated with both recent and prior personal victimization (assault) than with property or household/neighborhood crime. Fear of crime among younger women increased as a result of these crimes, while among older women the same experiences were found to be "desensitizing." Researchers speculated that elders may have found the actual victimization less injurious than had been feared, have taken greater responsibility to avoid future crimes, or entirely denied the event.

Fraud

Although larceny offenses are included in the NCVS database, they represent a small percentage of the fraud and confidence schemes that are perpetrated on elders. Reporting rates for fraud are estimated at between 3% and 8%, the lowest of any major crime (Harshbarger & Scheft, 1993). Although persons of any age can fall for a con game, elders are thought to be particularly susceptible because they seem to be more trusting, more available at home or on the telephone, and perhaps more easily confused by the fast-talking con artist. Their assets may be more readily available as cash or certificates of deposits. Victims are often unaware that they have been swindled, too embarrassed to report to the family, or conclude that there is nothing that the police can do. It is true that these cases are difficult to prosecute because the perpetrators often do not live where they "work" and frequently change their names and identification, and the police lack the evidence to show a criminal intent to defraud. Some state statutes provide for enhanced penalties when the victim exceeds 60, 62, or 65 years. These can include, for example, ordering mandatory sentences and restitution, redefining various offenses as a class of felony or misdemeanor, and extending terms of imprisonment (Adams & Morgan, 1994).

Crime Prevention

The law enforcement community is increasingly aware of the growing older population and the need to address their vulnerability and fear. Almost every police agency conducts crime prevention programs that focus on fraud, con games, financial exploitation, personal safety in and outside the home, and home security. Police patrols function as crisis intervention teams ensuring the immediate safety of elders and then referring them back to the appropriate community agency. Some police departments have special units that help older victims complete identification forms and repair broken locks and windows. Others sponsor 24-hour hot lines, volunteer programs to assist elders through the criminal justice system, and projects that match police officers with isolated older persons (Police Executive Research Forum [PERF], 1993). The special needs of elders also have been recognized by some victim assistance programs that offer designated waiting areas, arrange for transportation, make home visits, provide escorts, and even station nurses at the court house.

One of the newest programs aimed at reducing the victimization of older persons is Triad, a cooperative, coordinated, multidisciplinary program of the International Association of Chiefs of Police, the National Sheriffs' Association, and the American Association of Retired Persons (AARP) with funding from the Department of Justice. The local Triads, formed by a sheriff, police chief, representatives of AARP or other older volunteers, are guided by a senior advisory group (SALT) of older persons and service providers. They help the law enforcement departments in determining the crime and public safety needs of older people and suggest services to meet those needs. Typical crime prevention programs might include expanded involvement in Neighborhood Watch, distribution of refrigerator cards with emergency medical information, dissemination of home security information, implementation of home safety inspections, training in coping with telephone solicitations and door-to-door salesmen, and courtwatch activities.

Under the 1994 Crime Act, several million dollars have been made available for training and technical assistance to law enforcement, crime prevention, victim assistance, consumer, protection, and senior citizen organizations to assist in preventing and intervening in telemarketing fraud schemes that target elders. The Act also dramatically increased the penalties for telemarketing fraud and supported a nationwide initiative to wipe out telemarketing operations in several metropolitan areas.

Elder Victims of Abuse, Neglect, and Exploitation

Community Settings

Background

The abuse and neglect of older persons as a public policy first surfaced not in criminal statutes but in the Social Security amendments of 1962 (DC Department of Public Welfare, 1967). The legislation allocated funds to the states for the purpose of providing an array of social, legal, and medical services (known as protective services) to meet the needs of adults who, because of physical or mental limitations, were unable to act in their own behalf or who were neglected or exploited. By 1978, most states had established adult protective services units (APS) in their public welfare (human services) departments or contracted with other public or private entities to provide the services.

Testimony about "parent battering" before a Congressional subcommittee on family violence that year (U.S. Subcommittee on Domestic and International Scientific Planning, 1978) and the media attention that followed awakened the nation to the problem of abuse, neglect, and exploitation by family members. Although mistreatment of older persons by intimate partners and close relatives had existed throughout history, the changes in values and expectations emanating from the civil rights, antiwar, and feminist movements of the 1960s and 1970s forced the country to recognize violence within family life. The Congressional hearings and investigations that followed documented the existence and severity of the problem (U.S. Select Committee on Aging, 1979, 1981), but it was not until 10 years later that national legislation in the form of an amendment to the Older Americans Act was passed. A limited amount of funds was made available to the states for preventive services, and a National Center on Elder Abuse established to provide technical assistance, training, and information dissemination. Since the state APS units were already handling these types of cases, a new service system was not needed. The construct "adults in need of protection" became "victims of elder abuse, neglect, and exploitation."

As an aging issue, elder abuse was viewed in the context of caregiving. The victim (usually a mother) was portrayed as very old, physically and/or cognitively under the care of a family member (usually a daughter) who, because of the burden of caregiving as well as other job and family responsibilities, was stressed out, angry, frustrated, and occasionally abusive or neglectful. This depiction of elder mistreatment was very closely related to the child abuse model. Both dealt with dependent victims, sometimes overly demanding, who required care and attention. Because no model statutes on elder abuse were proposed for the states to follow, the child abuse laws with mandatory reporting became the prototype for legislation dealing with elder abuse in three-fourths of the states.

The limitations of the child abuse model as an explanation of elder abuse soon became apparent. In the eyes of the law, elders have the right to make decisions for themselves unless the courts have ruled otherwise while children are not given that right. But even more significant is the fact that according to the Boston community survey (Pillemer & Finkelhor, 1988), mistreatment of elders by spouses or partners is more prevalent than abuse by adult children. The evidence that some forms of elder abuse qualified as family and intimate violence made it possible to incorporate elder abuse within the family violence framework as another public health and criminal justice issue. Although some people regret the "medicalization" and "criminalization" of the problem, the growing awareness and interest of the medical, legal, law enforcement personnel, and domestic violence advocates in elder abuse has helped to legitimate the movement to the degree that was not possible when elder abuse was regarded exclusively as a public welfare, social service, or even aging issue.

Abuse is generally categorized as physical, psychological (also called emotional abuse or verbal aggression), and financial or exploitation. Neglect is the refusal or failure to fulfill a caretaking obligation. Whether the behavior is labeled as abusive or neglectful may depend on how frequently the mistreatment occurs, its duration, intensity, severity, and consequences. Some confusion about the definitions prevails because of the differences in various state laws, particularly in how the manifestations are categorized. For example, isolating an elder may be considered an act of physical abuse in one state and emotional abuse in another. Lately, researchers (Hudson, 1994; Gebotys, O'Connor, & Mair, 1992) have suggested that it is the older person's perception of the behavior influenced by cultural norms that may be the salient factor in describing an action as abuse or neglect. Comparative studies have shown that certain groups take a broader view of what is abuse than others and thus are more apt to seek help, file a report, or press charges (Moon & Williams, 1993; Tomita, 1995; Hudson & Carlson, 1998).

Prevalence and Incidence

Unlike crime, which has been the subject of several national surveys, no national prevalence studies of elder abuse have been conducted.

Estimates of a 4% to 6% prevalence rate are based on the findings of five community-based studies, each carried out in a different country and employing various methodologies. A research team (Pillemer & Finkelhor, 1988) surveyed over 2,000 noninstitutionalized elders in the Metropolitan Boston area and found that 3.2% had experienced physical abuse, verbal aggression, and/or neglect since their 65th birthday. Financial exploitation was not part of the study. Spouse abuse (58%) was more common than abuse by adult children (24%), the proportion of victims was equally divided between males and females, and economic status and age were not related to the risk of abuse.

The questionnaire, with items on financial exploitation added, was used in a telephone survey of a national representative sample of elder Canadians (Podnieks, 1992). Four percent of the group reported having been mistreated: 2.5%, financially exploited; and smaller proportions, physically and verbally abused and/or neglected. Using questionnaires and clinical examinations, a Finnish geriatric team (Kivelä, Köngäs-Saviaro, Kesti, Pahkala, & Ijäs, 1992) found that 5.4% of the elders in their small, semi-industrialized town had been abused since they had reached retirement age. Several questions from the Boston study were added to a national representative sample survey in Britain (Ogg, 1993); 5% of persons 65 years and older reported having been recently verbally abused; 2%, physically abused, and 2%, financially exploited. The fifth report came from a population-based sample of 1,797 older persons living independently in Amsterdam, the Netherlands (Comijs, Pot, Smit, Bouter, & Jonker, 1998). It showed a one 1-year prevalence rate of 5.6%: verbal aggression, 3.2%; physical aggression, 1.2%, financial mistreatment, 1.4%, and neglect, 0.2%. Since the surveys were based on self-reports or limited to persons who could answer questions, or use the telephone, the percentages are probably an underestimation of the true prevalence.

Beginning in 1987, reports of elder mistreatment filed with the individual states have been compiled biennially to provide a national picture although adjustments have to be made to account for variation in state definitions and criteria (Tatara, 1993). From an estimated 117,000 reports, including self-neglect, in 1986, the total rose to more than 293,000 in 1996 (National Center on Elder Abuse, 1997). Of those, about 74,400 were substantiated cases of physical, emotional, financial abuse, and neglect (excluding self-neglect, which represents more than half the total). Much of elder mistreatment is thought to go unreported because it involves persons in intimate and family relationships who do not wish to make public disclosure of private matters, who may be fearful of repercussions, who do not know to whom to report, or who deny the maltreatment. Furthermore, physicians, social workers, and other human service workers who are in contact with elders may not be sufficiently trained in identifying the symptoms or in making the reports.

Using a nationally representative sample of 20 counties (National Center on Elder Abuse, 1998), the National Center on Elder Abuse and Westat, Inc. compiled the number of reports filed with the state protective service units and the number of cases seen by law enforcement agencies, hospitals, elder care providers, and financial institutions that met the definition criteria but would not have been reported. The national estimates revealed that 449,924 unduplicated older persons experienced abuse and/or neglect in domestic settings in 1996. Of this total number, 70,942 cases were reported and substantiated by APS agencies; the remaining 378,982 were estimated from the reports of community persons who had been trained in the identification and reporting of elder abuse as part of the incidence study. The study concluded that over five times as many unduplicated incidents of abuse and neglect were unreported as those that were reported and substantiated by APS agencies. Advocates for elder abuse victims estimated the unreported factor to be even larger because some isolated or homebound elders would not have come into contact with any of the elder care providers who were included in the study nor would they have reported the mistreatment to authorities.

Risk Factors

The causes of elder abuse are unknown; that is, there has been no research to date that links one factor or a group of factors to the mistreatment of an older person. The most that can be stated at this time is that there are certain factors (risk factors) that are associated with the problem. Over the years, a wide array of psychological, sociological, and gerontological reasons have been proposed as possible explanations of why family members mistreat their older kin (Wolf & Pillemer, 1989). The most likely explanations are stated to be (a) the victims' poor mental and/or physical state that increases their dependency on the abusers (caregivers) and/or decreases their ability to leave an abusive situation; (b) the abusers' dependency on the victims, primarily for financial support, especially housing; (c) the psychological state of the abuser (e.g., history of mental illness, substance abuse); and (d) family social isolation (Lachs & Pillemer, 1995). Among spouses, a history of violence in the marriage may be predictive of elder abuse in later life. Research in the past decade relating to dementia, care giving, the caregiver, stress, and elder abuse have cast further doubt about the caregiver stress model of elder abuse and neglect (Hamel et al., 1990; Homer & Gilleard, 1990; Nolan, 1993; Paveza et al., 1992; Steinmetz, 1988). Rather, studies point to the nature of the pre-morbid relationship between the elder and caregiver and the way these family members interact as the most predictive factor affecting the quality of the caregiving and the feelings of burden (Cooney & Mortimer, 1995). These factors have also emerged in Reis and Nahmiash's study (1998) to validate the indicators of an elder abuse screen. They identified three categories of indicators that discriminated between the abused and nonabused cases seen of a health and social service agency: (a) abuser's (caregiver) intrapersonal problems (e.g., has mental health, behavioral, and alcohol or other substance abuse difficulties); (b) abuser's (caregiver) interpersonal problems (e.g., has marital and family conflict and poor relationships generally and with the victim, is financially dependent on the victim); and (c) victim's (care receiver) shortage of social supports and past abuse. As noted in earlier work, the characteristics of the abuser rather than the victim are the most likely predictive factors of mistreatment (Bristowe & Collins, 1989; Wolf & Pillemer, 1989).

Consequences

Few empirical studies have examined the consequences of abuse on the victim's well-being, although clinical reports and case studies have documented the severe emotional stress experienced by victims. Depression, particularly, appears to be more often associated with abused elders than nonabused elders (Bristowe & Collins, 1989; Phillips, 1983; Pillemer & Prescott, 1989; Reis & Nahmiash, 1997).

Other conditions such as guilt, shame, fear, distrust, withdrawal, alienation, and post-traumatic stress syndrome have all been suggested as a response to abuse but the empirical evidence is lacking (Solomon, 1983; Booth, Bruno, & Marin, 1996; Baumhover & Beall, 1996). Comijs et al. (1998) asked 43 victims, who had been identified in a community survey, their reaction to the abuse. Most reported anger, disappointment, or grief. About one-quarter said that they had reacted aggressively themselves.

Little is known about the effect of mistreatment on an older victim's physical health. While emergency room utilization statistics have been used to document the very negative impact of domestic violence on the health of younger victims, this approach is not feasible for older persons because of the difficulty in distinguishing the effects of abuse from the concomitants of pathological aging. One research team (Lachs, Williams, O'Brien, Pillemer, & Charlson, 1998) combined data from an annual health survey of 2,812 elders with reports of elder abuse and neglect made to the local adult protective services agency over a 9-year period. They found that 48 persons in the large sample had been physically abused or neglected and 128 had been classified as self-neglect cases. When the mortality rate of the three groups was compared, by the 13th year following the initiation of the study, 40% of the nonreported (nonabused, nonneglected) group were still alive; 17% of the self-neglected elders, and only 9% of the physically abused or neglected elders. After controlling for all the possible factors that might affect mortality (e.g., age, gender, income, functional status, cognitive status, diagnosis, social supports, etc.) and finding no significant relationships, the researchers speculate that mistreatment causes extreme interpersonal stress that may confer an additional death risk.

Services/Prevention

Services for abused, neglected, and exploited elders are available through the states' adult protective service programs. Some programs are state-administered with regional and local offices. Other states have a county-based system with state supervision. Reports of elder mistreatment are received on special phone lines and are screened for potential seriousness. If mistreatment is suspected, an investigation by an APS worker is conducted. If the case is deemed an emergency, the investigation must be completed within a few hours of receipt of the call. On the basis of a comprehensive assessment that includes the physical, psychosocial, and environmental statuses of the victim, a care plan is developed that is intended to ensure safety and, at the same time, maximize autonomy of the elder. It might involve, for example, obtaining emergency shelter for the victim, admitting the victim to the hospital, arranging for home care and/or day care, calling the police, referring the case to the prosecuting attorney, or arranging for guardianship. In most states, once the initial situation has been addressed, the case is turned over to other community agencies for ongoing case management and services.

Community-based or state level coalitions have been organized across the country as a means of bringing together the various constituencies and professionals interested in the problem, particularly to promote public awareness, sponsor professional education, identify needs, and advocate for legislation. The very complex and multiple problems involved in some financial exploitation cases have led to the formation of financial abuse specialist teams (FAST). They include members from law enforcement, the public and private bar, banking, financial planning, real estate, prosecuting attorney's office, psychiatry, geriatrics, and adult protective services meeting together to determine the best way to proceed with a case that will increase the likelihood of successful prosecution/restitution/resolution.

Elder abuse cases are covered under protective services legislation that establishes the authority to receive reports of alleged abuse, investigate the cases, and provide services to alleviate or ameliorate the abuse. Nearly half of the protective services laws (Tatara, 1995) have provisions making elder abuse a misdemeanor or a felony with fines that range from $500 to $10,000 and imprisonment from 90 days to 10 years. About 20 states also explicitly designate elder abuse and/or neglect in their criminal code in order to increase the penalties and expedite trials. Some states also use domestic violence and mental health statutes in handling elder abuse cases. In a Delphi survey of judges, court administrators, lawyers, prosecutors, adult protective services workers, and social services personnel conducted by the American Bar Association (Stiegel, 1995), the respondents agreed that statutory remedies and better linkages between organizations involved in the problem were needed. Among the statutory reforms suggested were recovering attorneys' fees when an older abused person sues the abuser, permitting the prosecutor to try an alleged abuser even if the older person will not press charges, allowing a noncriminal or criminal court proceeding to continue even if the older person dies before it is concluded, and permitting judicial authority to issue injunctions and restraining orders in elder abuse/APS laws comparable to the authority provided in domestic violence laws. To promote better communication among organizations, they recommended the establishment of a special unit or staff with resources to handle abuse and exploitation within the Attorney General's office, cross-reporting between APS and law enforcement, and the appointment of prosecutors who specialize in elder abuse cases. These suggestions have already been implemented in some jurisdictions.

According to Heisler (1991), although traditional methods and approaches for dealing with elder abuse may have discouraged victims and service providers from turning to the criminal justice system for help, new awareness, laws, and procedures enable the system to play a stronger part in deterring further violence; particularly, if it is part of a community-wide, interdisciplinary effort. Involving the criminal justice system in elder abuse cases can stop the violence, protect the victim, protect the public, hold the perpetrator accountable, rehabilitate the perpetrator, communicate the societal intent to treat the conduct as a crime, and provide restitution to the victim. However, it may also have negative consequences. In situations where the abuser is the victim's sole source of care, the arrest, prosecution, and imprisonment of the abuser may leave the victim isolated or even lead to the victim's institutionalization.

Institutional Settings

Despite all the anecdotal information, media exposés, ethnographic studies, and license and certification reports on nursing homes, little is known about the incidence of abuse in institutional facilities. Four studies have examined abuse by staff in nursing homes, each representing a different approach to the problem. Pillemer and

Moore (1990) interviewed 577 nursing home personnel, of whom 38% were RNs or LPNs, to obtain information about the extent of abusive actions toward residents, those that they observed and those that they committed. Thirty-six percent of the sample had seen at least one incident of physical abuse in the preceding year by other staff members, and 10% admitted having committed at least one act of physical abuse themselves. A total of 81% of the sample had observed at least one incident of psychological abuse against a resident in the preceding year, and 40% admitted to having also done so.

A second study, carried out by the Office of the Inspector General, U.S. Department of Health and Human Services (1990), involved interviewing 232 persons who were directly or indirectly involved with nursing home care. State oversight agencies and resident advocates for nursing homes perceived abuse as a serious and growing problem, while nursing home administrators and industry representatives believed the problem to be minor. The most prevalent forms of mistreatment were physical neglect, verbal and emotional neglect, and verbal or emotional abuse. Although nursing home staff, medical personnel, other residents, and family or visitors could contribute to abuse, aides and orderlies were viewed as the primary abusers.

Paton, Huber, and Netting (1994), in an analysis of Long Term Care Ombudsman Program state reports from 1989–1990, found a total of 134,612 reports or complaints from 50 states and the District of Columbia, 28% of which dealt with resident care. Because only aggregate data were required in the annual reports, it was not possible to obtain national figures for the subcategories of abuse and neglect. Among 12 states that did record that type of data, abuse and neglect comprised 29% of resident care complaints.

The fourth study was based on 488 incidents of resident abuse prosecuted by Medicaid fraud control units from 1987 through 1992 (Payne & Cikovic, 1995). State Medicaid fraud control units are responsible for detecting, investigating, and prosecuting Medicaid fraud and resident abuse in nursing homes that accept Medicaid funding. Eighty-four percent of the reports involved physical abuse cases; 9%, sexual abuse; 3%, duty-related abuse; 1%, monetary abuse; and 2%, other. The perpetrators included all categories of nursing home personnel but nursing aides comprised the largest group (62%). Male employees were named in almost two-thirds of the incidents. Surprisingly, among the victims for which there were gender data, slightly more than half were males. Three hundred and thirty-five (335) offenders were convicted, with 295 receiving sentences. Sexual abuse was the incident most likely to result in a prison sentence.

From several of the studies, lack of adequate training of nursing home staff, especially those in direct contact with residents, emerged as an important causal factor. A content analysis of the Medicaid fraud incident reports indicated that the pressures of the job and lack of training played a role in the offender's choice to engage in abusive behavior. Pillemer and Moore (1990) found that the amount of staff-resident conflict and level of burnout were strongly related to physical abuse. Levels of burnout and resident aggression were predictors of psychological abuse. Using information gained in the latter study, a nursing home advocacy group in Philadelphia (CARIE) has designed an educational training program that helps staff deal with stress, burnout, and conflict (Hudson, 1992). With a very positive initial reaction from the staff, the training program has been made available to nursing homes here and abroad. Its impact on reducing the incidence of abuse and neglect is still under study.

Various legal processes have been instituted to reduce the potential for abuse and neglect in institutional facilities. In addition to the establishment of Medicaid fraud control units in the states, both the passage of the Nursing Home Reform Act of 1987, which includes the Resident Rights bill and federal standards of care, and, most recently, the institution of background checks and tracking systems on all employees are intended to improve the quality of care.

Summary

Newer data and better studies show that older persons are less likely to be victimized than younger people, particularly teenagers, and that younger rather than older people are more likely to fear crime. Nonetheless, elders are robbed and assaulted every day and live in fear of being a victim. Even if an elder has not personally experienced an act of violence, they are much more aware of crime and criminal activities than earlier generations through daily accounts of violence in the newspapers and its depiction on television and glorification in the movies. The most recent NCVS survey data indicate that elders do sustain more serious injuries than younger persons as a result of criminal attacks. Older people tend to be physically weaker, their bones more brittle, and their convalescence slower; thus, a relatively minor injury can cause serious, permanent damage. Many have limited incomes so that the loss of a small amount of money may have a more significant impact on them than on a younger person whose future lies before them. They also appear to be more often the target of unscrupulous home improvement programs, confidence schemes, and investment fraud.

Elders are also the victims of family violence that often is not reported to the criminal justice or social service systems. Twenty years of research into elder abuse has produced significant progress in understanding the nature and scope of the problem. Less weight is given to the caregiver stress theory and more to the interpersonal relationship between the elder and family member (perpetrator) and to the intrapersonal problems of the perpetrator. The states' adult protective service programs are the primary agencies for investigating and assessing abuse and neglect and developing care plans to resolve the situation. To this task they may bring a full array of social services and legal strategies but, given small services budgets in many locales, often only for a brief span of time and only for the victim, not the perpetrator. Although reasons are still obscure, the fact that older persons reported to a state agency as having been abused or neglected had three times the mortality rate of nonabused persons over a 13-year period raises some serious questions about the impact of the mistreatment and even the interventions.

Increasing penalties, community policing, and joint police–senior initiatives are recent efforts to reduce the crime rate and to give elders a greater sense of personal safety. With regard to elder abuse and neglect, the need is to educate the public and to train professionals about the problem, how to recognize the risk factors, and where to turn for help. A closer partnership among the mental health system, substance abuse programs, and elder abuse services is critical given the high prevalence of emotional problems and alcoholism in abusive families. Better understanding of the role of culture in defining abusive and neglectful behavior will be important in dealing with diverse populations. Research in recent years has helped to determine the extent of the problem and the characteristics of the victims and the perpetrators. Additional research is needed to understand why these violent acts occur and the best ways to prevent them.

References

Adams, W. E., & Morgan, R. C. (1984). Representing the client who is older in the law office and in the courtroom. *ElderLaw Journal, 2*(1), 1–38.

Bachman, R. (1993). The double edged sword of violent victimization against the elderly: Patterns of family and stranger perpetration. *Journal of Elder Abuse & Neglect, 5*(4), 59–76.

Bachman, R., Dillaway, H., & Lachs, M. S. (1998). Violence against the elderly: A comparative analysis of robbery and assault across age and gender groups. *Research in Aging, 20*(2), 183–198.

Baumhover, L. A., & Beall, S. C. (1996). Prognosis: Elder mistreatment in health care settings. In L. A. Baumhover & S. C. Beall (Eds.), *Abuse, neglect, and exploitation of older persons: Strategies for assessment and intervention* (pp. 241–256). Baltimore: Health Professions Press.

Booth, M. R., Bruno, A. A., & Marin, R. (1996). Psychological therapy with abused and neglected patients. In L. A. Baumhover & S. C. Beall (Eds.), *Abuse, neglect, and exploitation of older persons: Strategies for assessment and intervention* (pp. 185–204). Baltimore: Health Professions Press.

Bristowe, E., & Collins, J. B. (1989). Family mediated abuse of non-institutionalized elder men and women living in British Columbia. *Journal of Elder Abuse & Neglect, 1*(1), 45–64.

Clemente, F., & Kleiman, M. B. (1984). Fear of crime among the aged. In J. J. Costa (Ed.), *Abuse of the elderly: A guide to resources and services* (pp. 13–20). Lexington, MA: D. C. Health Co.

Comijs, H. C., Pot, A. M., Smit, J. H., Bouter, L. M., & Jonker, C. (1998). Elder abuse in the community: Prevalence and consequences. *Journal of the American Geriatrics Society, 46*, 885–888.

Cook, F. L., Skogan, W. G., Cook, T. D., & Antunes, G. E. (1978). Criminal victimization of the elderly: The physical and economic consequences. *Gerontologist, 18*(3), 338–349.

Cooney, C., & Mortimer, A. (1995). Elder abuse and dementia—A pilot study. *International Journal of Social Psychiatry, 41*(4), 276–283.

DC Department of Public Welfare. (1967). *Protective services for adults: Report on protective services prepared for the DC Interdepartmental Committee on Aging.* Washington, DC.

Ferraro, K. F., & LaGrange, R. L. (1992). Are older people most afraid of crime? Reconsidering age differences in fear of victimization. *Journal of Gerontology, 47*(5), S233–244.

Finley, G. E. (1983). Fear of crime in the elderly. In J. I. Kosberg (Ed.), *Abuse and maltreatment of the elderly: Causes and interventions* (pp. 21–39). Littleton, MA: John Wright-PSG.

Gebotys, R. J., O'Connor, D., & Mair, K. J. (1992). Public perceptions of elder physical mistreatment. *Journal of Elder Abuse & Neglect, 4*(1/2), 151–172.

Hamel, M., Gold, P. D., Andres, D., Reis, M., Dastoor, D., Grauer, H., & Bergman, H. (1990). Predictors and consequences of aggressive behavior by community-based dementia patients. *Gerontologist, 30*, 206–211.

Harshbarger, S., & Scheft, J. (1993). *Elderly protection project: Advanced law enforcement training manual* (3rd ed.). Boston: Office of the Attorney General.

Heisler, C. J. (1991). The role of the criminal justice system in elder abuse cases. *Journal of Elder Abuse & Neglect, 3*(1), 5–34.

Homer, A. C., & Gilleard, C. (1990). Abuse of elderly people and their careers. *British Medical Journal, 301*, 1359–1362.

Hudson, B. (1992). Ensuring an abuse-free environment: A learning program for nursing home staff. *Journal of Elder Abuse & Neglect, 4*(4), 25–36.

Hudson, M. F. (1994). Elder abuse: Its meaning to middle-age and older adults. Part II, pilot results. *Journal of Elder Abuse & Neglect, 6*(1), 55–81.

Hudson, M. F., & Carlson, J. R. (1998). Elder abuse: Its meaning to Caucasians, African-Americans and Native Americans. In T. Tatara (Ed.), *Understanding elder abuse among minority populations* (pp. 187–204). Bristol, PA: Taylor & Francis.

Kennedy, L. W., & Silverman, R. A. (1985). Significant others and fear of crime among the elderly. *International Journal of Aging and Human Development, 20*, 241–256.

Kivelä, S. L., Köngäs-Saviaro, P., Kesti, E., Pahkala, K., & Ijäs, M. L. (1992). Abuse in old age: Epidemiological data from Finland. *Journal of Elder Abuse & Neglect, 4*(3), 1–18.

Lachs, M., & Pillemer, K. (1995). Abuse and neglect of elderly persons. *New England Journal of Medicine, 332*, 437–443.

Lachs, M., Williams, C. S., O'Brien, S., Pillemer, K. A., & Charlson, M. E. (1998). The mortality of elder mistreatment. *Journal of the American Medical Association, 280*, 428–432.

Lee, G. R. (1982). Sex differences in fear of crime among older people. *Research on Aging, 4*(3), 284–298.

Liang, J., & Sengstock, M. C. (1983). Personal crimes against the elderly. In J. I. Kosberg (Ed.), *Abuse and maltreatment of the elderly: Causes and interventions* (pp. 40–67). Littleton, MA: John Wright-PSG.

McCabe, K. A., & Gregory, S. S. (1998). Elderly victimization: An examination beyond the FBI's index crimes. *Research in Aging, 20,* 363–372.

Moon, A., & Williams, O. (1993). Perceptions of elder abuse and help-seeking patterns among African-American, Caucasian American, and Korean-American elderly women. *Gerontologist, 33,* 386–395.

National Center on Elder Abuse. (1997). Understanding the nature and extent of elder abuse in domestic settings. Washington, DC: Author.

National Center on Elder Abuse. (1998). *The national elder abuse incidence study.* Washington, DC: American Public Human Services Association.

National Council on the Aging. (1975). *The myth and reality of aging in America.* Washington, DC: NCOA.

Nolan, M. (1993). Carer-dependent relationships and the prevention of elder abuse. In P. Decalmer & F. Glendenning (Eds.), *The mistreatment of elderly people* (pp. 199–209). London: Sage.

Norton, L., & Courlander, M. (1982). Fear of crime among the elderly: The role of crime prevention programs. *Gerontologist, 22,* 388–393.

Ogg, J. (1993). Researching elder abuse in Britain. *Journal of Elder Abuse & Neglect, 5*(2), 37–54

Ollenburger, J. C. (1981). Criminal victimization and fear of crime. *Research on Aging, 3*(1), 101–118.

Paton, R. N., Huber, R., & Netting, F. E. (1994). The long-term care ombudsman program and complaints of abuse and neglect. *Journal of Elder Abuse & Neglect, 6*(1), 97–115.

Paveza, G. J., Cohen, D., Eisdorfer, C., Freels, S., Semla, T., Ashford, J. W., Gorelick, P., Hirschman, R., Luchings, D., & Levy, P. (1992). Severe family violence and Alzheimer's disease: Prevalence and risk factors. *Gerontologist, 32,* 493–497.

Payne, B. K., & Cikovic, R. (1995). An empirical examination of the characteristics, consequences, and causes of elder abuse in nursing homes. *Journal of Elder Abuse & Neglect, 7*(4), 61–74.

Phillips, L. R. (1983). Abuse and neglect of the frail elderly at home: An exploration of theoretical relationships. *Journal of Advanced Nursing, 8,* 379–392.

Pillemer, K., & Finkelhor, D. (1988). Prevalence of elder abuse: A random sample survey. *Gerontologist, 28*(1), 51–57.

Pillemer, K., & Moore, D. W. (1990). Highlights from a study of abuse of patients in nursing homes. *Journal of Elder Abuse & Neglect, 2*(1/2), 5–30.

Pillemer, K., & Prescott, D. (1989). Psychological effects of elder abuse: A research note. *Journal of Elder Abuse & Neglect, 1*(1), 65–74.

Podnieks, E. (1992). National survey on abuse of the elderly in Canada. *Journal of Elder Abuse & Neglect, 4*(1/2), 5–58.

Police Executive Research Forum (PERF). (1993). *Improving the police response to domestic abuse.* Washington, DC: PERF.

Reis, M., & Nahmiash, D. (1997). Abuse of seniors: Personality, stress and other indicators. *Journal of Mental Health and Aging, 3,* 337–356.

Reis, M., & Nahmiash, D. (1998). Validation of the indicators of abuse (IOA) screen. *Gerontologist, 38,* 471–480.

Solomon, K. (1983). Victimization by health professions and the psychologic response of the elderly. In J. I. Kosberg (Ed.), *Abuse and maltreatment of the elderly: Causes and interventions* (pp. 150–171). Littleton, MA: John Wright-PSG.

Steinmetz, S. (1988). *Duty bound: Elder abuse and family care.* Newbury, CA: Sage.

Stiegel, L. (1995). *Recommended guidelines for state courts handling cases involving elder abuse.* Washington, DC: American Bar Association Commission on Legal Problems of the Elderly.

Tatara, T. (1993). Finding the nature and scope of domestic elder abuse with the use of state aggregate data: Summaries of the key findings of a national survey of state PAS and aging agencies. *Journal of Elder Abuse & Neglect, 5*(4), 35–57.

Tatara, T. (1995). *An analysis of state laws addressing elder abuse, neglect, and exploitation.* Washington, DC: National Center on Elder Abuse.

Tomita, S. K. (1995). An exploration of elder mistreatment among Japanese-Americans within a broad context of conflict: Conditions and consequences. *Dissertation Abstracts International.* (University Microfilms No. 9609796).

U. S. Department of Health and Human Services, Office of the Inspector General. (1990) *Resident abuse in nursing homes: Understanding and preventing abuse.* Dallas, TX: Author.

U.S. Department of Justice, Bureau of Justice Statistics. (1987). *Special Report Elderly Victims.* Washington, DC: DOJ.

U.S. Department of Justice, Bureau of Justice Statistics. (1994). *Selected findings from BJS Elderly Crime Victims.* Washington, DC: DOJ.

U.S. Select Committee on Aging. (1979). *Elder abuse: The hidden problem.* Washington, DC: Government Printing Office.

U.S. Select Committee on Aging. (1981). *Elder abuse: An examination of a hidden problem.* Washington, DC: Government Printing Office.

U.S. Subcommittee on Domestic and International Scientific Planning, Analysis, and Cooperation, Committee on Science and Technology. (1978). Washington, DC: Government Printing Office.

Viano, E. C. (1985). Victimology: An overview. In J. I. Kosberg (Ed.), *Abuse and maltreatment of the elderly: Causes and interventions* (pp. 1–20). Littleton, MA: John Wright-PSG.

Weinrath, M., & Gartrell, J. (1996). Victimization and fear of crime. *Violence and Victims, 11*(3), 187–197.

White House Conference on Aging. (1995a). *Official 1995 White House Conference on Aging Proposed Report: From Resolutions to Results Executive Summary.* Washington, DC: Author.

White House Conference on Aging (1995b). *Newsletter, 1*(3,4). Washington, DC: Author.

Wolf, R. S., & Pillemer, K. A. (1989). *Helping elder victims: The reality of elder abuse.* New York: Columbia University Press.

Yin, P. (1985). *Victimization and the aged.* Springfield, IL: Charles C Thomas.

Suggested Readings

Lawton, M. P., & Yaffe, S. (1980). Victimization and fear of crime in elderly public housing tenants. *Journal of Gerontology, 35,* 768–779.

Pillemer, K. (1986). Risk factors in elder abuse: Results from a case control study. In K. A. Pillemer & R. S. Wolf (Eds.), *Elder abuse: Conflict in the family* (pp. 239–263). Dover, MA: Auburn House.

U.S. Department of Justice, Office of Justice Programs. (1998). *National Institute of Justice research in brief: Preventing crime: What works, what doesn't, what's promising.* Washington, DC: DOJ.

Chapter 3

Elders As Perpetrators

Edith Elisabeth Flynn

F or the past two decades, the study of elders as perpetrators of crime has become a growing focal point of theoretical and empirical analysis for criminologists. This development is largely attributable to the rapidly changing age structure of the U.S. population, in which the number of elders, defined here as those aged 65 and older, has become the fastest growing age group (U.S. Bureau of the Census, 1996). Given this marked increase of elders relative to other age segments in the population, it is reasoned that, at a minimum, the number of older offenders will increase as well, even if their crime rates remain stable.

Age and Crime

Although the focus on older offenders is relatively recent, issues concerning the relationship between age and crime have long been among the most basic concerns of criminology. This is because the age distribution of crime is not only well documented in research and literature, but it is also one of the few undisputed facts in this challenging field of study (Farrington, 1986). National crime statistics, supported by victimization research, consistently show that crime is a young man's game. Most serious crimes are committed by young males between the ages of 14 and 24. Beyond this brief representation, age–crime curves show reliably that age is inversely related to criminal activity, with crime rates rising rapidly from the minimum age of responsibility, peaking during adolescence, and then decreasing quickly with entry into adulthood (Flynn, 1996). Next to age, gender is related to crime and is of great criminological interest. Not surprisingly, the female age-crime curve follows that of males, with crime peaking during the teenage years and decreasing rapidly thereafter. By the same token, females (at any age) are consistently less likely to commit crimes compared with males. In short, younger persons of any age outstrip older individuals in virtually all categories of crime.

Comparatively low levels of elder crime notwithstanding, it is imperative to study elder crime and older offenders for many reasons. First, elder crime, regardless of its prevalence or incidence, needs to be examined within the context of aging because it is likely to be, at least in part, a manifestation of underlying structural problems within society. Thus, a better understanding of elder crime can lead to enhanced understanding of the specific needs of elders as a whole. Second, the formulation of public policies for controlling elder crime and preventing it should be grounded in empirical knowledge, if the policies are to succeed. Third, the quality and fairness of recommendations and decisions made by social service providers, gerontologists, and criminal justice professionals are contingent upon their understanding of how age affects human behavior, including criminal behavior, and the way such behavior is perceived by them and society at large (McCarthy & Langworthy, 1988). And fourth, theoretical developments and research findings in this area may have applicability to the study of criminal behavior by other age groups.

This chapter explores elder crime in depth. Discussion topics include: (a) a review of key findings of recent research; (b) an analysis of patterns and changes in elder crime; (c) a presentation of relevant criminological and gerontological perspectives on elder crime; and (d) a discussion of elder crime patterns with a focus on the critical role played by mental health disorders and substance abuse in elder crime.

Research on Elder Crime

As noted earlier, the marked increase of elders in both absolute and relative numbers sparked a large number of highly publicized research efforts beginning in the early 1980s. Most were directed at estimating the extent of geriatric criminality and determining whether the share of elder crime had increased beyond their proportion in the population (Malinchak, 1980; McCarthy & Langworthy, 1988; Newman, Newman, & Gewirtz, 1984; Shichor, 1984, 1985). A majority of these research efforts pointed to increases in elder crimes and the fact that arrest rates for this population were higher than those of younger groups. A majority of scholars thought they were detecting a disturbing trend and an emerging social problem, in which elders would commit an increasing number of serious offenses, ranging from personal violence to property crime, to minor violations including vandalism, drunkenness, and driving offenses.

More recent research on old-age criminality found little evidence to support earlier predictions, or that a "geriatric crime wave" had, in fact, materialized (Covey & Menard, 1987; Inciardi, 1987; Long, 1992; Steffensmeier, 1987). Critiques of earlier research identified a number of methodological shortcomings. For example, earlier studies often ignored the small base levels of arrests among elders. Small increases in the raw numbers of elder arrests looked large when expressed as percentage changes. Increases in elder crime rates may simply reflect subtle, but pervasive changes in police and prosecutorial practices. Most importantly, in the absence of age-standardization techniques, the reported increases in elder crime could largely be a function of the pronounced growth of this specific segment in the general population.

Building on previous research, the more recent research efforts utilized more sophisticated analytical techniques applied to data covering considerably longer periods of time. As a result, they were able to clarify and refine the earlier findings. They also shed new light on the characteristics of elder crime. For example, Covey and Menard (1987) found that elders (aged 65 and over) were less likely to be arrested compared with younger persons for all crimes listed in the Uniform Crime Reports (UCR), irrespective of whether arrest rates or total arrests were considered. As far as types of crimes committed were concerned, the authors found larceny to be the most frequent offense for which both the young and the old were arrested. Analysis of crime patterns revealed interesting differences between the older and the younger population groups. After larceny, elders were most likely to be arrested for assault, followed by murder, robbery, auto theft, and rape. By contrast, after larceny, younger persons were most likely to be arrested for burglary, assault, auto-theft, robbery, rape, and murder. Finally, arrest rates for elders increased faster for property crimes, such as burglary, larceny, and auto theft compared with younger persons, while arrest rates grew faster for the young for crimes of violence, including homicide, aggravated assault, robbery, and rape.

Inciardi (1987) examined arrest rates of elders (defined as 60 years and older) computed over a period of 18 years (1964–1982). He observed significant decreases in the total arrest rates for this population. However, when arrest rates for specific crime categories were analyzed, the findings were startling and surprising. Specifically, elder arrest rates for violent crimes had increased from 9.1 to 16.0 per 100,000 older persons in the population, while arrests for property crime had increased even more, from 19.9 to 71.9 per 100,000. Inciardi attributed the decline of the aggregate arrest rate to pronounced decreases in arrest rates for victimless crimes, such as gambling, vagrancy, and disorderly conduct. He also noted that this finding was not unique to elders, but simply reflected a general national trend. Turning to property crimes, which had more than doubled for elders, Inciardi noted that the vast majority were attributable to the relatively benign category of larceny-theft. Finally, study data reflected a precipitous increase of "driving while intoxicated" (DWI) arrests, which had grown from 38.9 to 117.8 per 100,000 elders in the population.

Steffensmeier's exacting analysis of elder crime (1987) applied demographic age-standardization techniques to assess key questions concerning this population. After determining the basic crime patterns of elders (defined as 65 and over) he calculated changes in those patterns over a 20-year period (1964–1984). He also assessed changes in the magnitude and seriousness of elder crime by comparing rate increases (or decreases) with those of other age groups. Data analysis included the following interesting results. Criminal activity among elders had remained roughly the same over two decades. Actual crime levels and crime trends did not support any conjecture of a "geriatric crime wave." And, irrespective of the writings of some academics and the popular press, elders as a group had consistently lower levels of criminality than any other age group in the nation. Additional study details of interest include the following: (a) elder arrests had increased for larceny-theft and driving-while-intoxicated (DWI), but decreased significantly for disorderly conduct, public drunkenness, gambling, and vagrancy; (b) offense patterns in the larceny/theft category reflected particularly sharp increases for shoplifting; and (c) alcohol-related offenses (DWI and public drunkenness) accounted for an impressive 45% of total elder arrests.

Long's (1992) study of older offenders (defined here as 55 and over) analyzed UCR data from 1972 to 1989. Examining crime trends and patterns, she noted a decrease in total arrests for older persons even though that population segment had increased by 27% over the study period. Nonetheless, elder arrests did increase for crimes of violence and property offenses. After accounting for the 27% increase of older persons during the study period, Long computed an overall 50.6% increase in both offense types for older offenders. Again, property crimes accounted for much of that increase. However, since crimes committed by older offenders increased at lower rates compared with increases of offenses for all age groups, Long concluded that predictions of a coming geriatric crime wave had no basis in fact.

In summary, after being a nonissue for criminology for years, elder crime gained attention in the 1970s largely because of the marked increase of elders in U.S. society. The earliest studies predicted that elders would increasingly turn to crime and projected the emergence of yet another social problem. The topic resurfaced in the late 1980s, when scholars questioned the validity of the earlier assessments. All the comprehensive studies reviewed above agree that elder crime, while on the increase, should not be characterized as a "geriatric crime wave." They also note that while elder crime had increased for some offense types, it had decreased for others. In particular, elder property crime was found to have increased, and within that category, larceny/theft, DWI, and other relatively minor city and ordinance violations. By the same token, elder crime was found to have decreased in the "victimless crime" categories, such as disorderly conduct, gambling, vagrancy, and public drunkenness. It will be the task of this chapter to examine whether these crime trends and patterns have continued into the present, or whether they have changed in any material way.

Elder Crime: Recent Changes and Offense Patterns

Data Sources and Their Limitations

Estimates regarding the nature and the extent of elder crime are based primarily on the following sources: (a) the Uniform Crime Reports (UCR) collected annually on crimes known to the police and published by the Federal Bureau of Investigation (FBI); (b) the National Crime Victimization Survey (NCVS), collected annually by the Bureau of the Census, in cooperation with the Bureau of Justice Statistics; and (c) various self-report surveys and empirical studies conducted by criminologists and social scientists nationally and internationally. The Uniform Crime Reports divide offenses into two parts: Part I crimes also known as "Index Crimes" consist of major felony offenses and include murder and nonnegligent manslaughter, forcible rape, robbery, aggravated assault, burglary, larceny/theft, auto theft, and arson. Part II crimes are nonindex offenses. They include less serious crimes such as simple assault, forgery, fraud, embezzlement, vandalism, drunkenness, gambling, and so on. For analysis and comparison purposes, crime data are commonly expressed as crime rates. These rates are computed by dividing the number of reported crimes by the total population and multiplying by 100,000.

Official crime statistics, including the UCR, suffer from a number of methodological, reporting and record-keeping problems. For example, not all crimes are reported to police. As a result, the reports do not reflect the nation's true crime rates. The police, who provide the raw data for the UCR, report voluntarily. Reports vary in accuracy and are subject to vicissitudinous definitional interpretations. Politics, changes in police practices, and modernization of record-keeping and data processing have all been known to influence the accuracy of statistics (Sherman & Glick, 1984). Also, in case of multiple offenses committed in any one event, only the most serious crime is reported in the UCR. Perhaps worst of all, both the UCR and NCVS focus on "crime in the streets," not "crimes in the suites." As a result, much serious crime ranging from white-collar to organized crime goes unreported. The NCVS is specifically designed to assess the magnitude of the true crime rates, also known as the "dark figure of crime." It gauges the extent of victimization due to assault, burglary, larceny, rape, robbery, and auto theft. The surveys do not collect data on Part II crimes or on homicide because only crimes whose victims can be interviewed are measured. The NCVS provides a wealth of information on victim experiences, including the characteristics and numbers of offenders, crime events, and the extent of injuries and financial losses. But the NCVS is not without shortcomings either. They include problems with victim recollections, exaggerations or underreporting, telescoping of events in which victims transpose crimes that occurred earlier into the survey period. There are also interviewer and data processing effects. Finally, self-report studies, the final major data source, augment information on the amount and types of crime committed and on other issues. Methodological drawbacks include, but are not limited to, sampling bias, telescoping, and other internal and external threats to validity.

Nonetheless, they represent a useful alternative to official statistics, while supplementing information on the extent of crime in the country (Menard, 1987). For example, self-reports point to wide disparities between official crime data and actual rates of offending, especially as they relate to age, race, and gender (Adler, Mueller, & Laufer, 1995). Despite their shortcomings, the combination of data sources discussed above provides reasonably good estimates of the amount of crime committed, as well as the characteristics of crimes, criminals, and their victims.

Recent Trends of Elder Crime

In an effort to determine the relative frequency of criminal involvement by age and to assess patterns of offenses over time, multiyear

UCR statistics are analyzed. Table 3.1 presents the percent distribution of the U.S. population categorized by age and the relative contribution of these categories to the nation's arrest rate for the years of 1985 and 1995. It also reflects the change in the age composition and the arrest rates over the decade under analysis. As previously discussed, the highest arrest rates are consistently found in the younger age categories. Specifically, in 1985, the highest arrest rates occurred in the 25 to 29 age category, followed by the 19 to 21, 22 to 24, and the 16 to 18 age groups. By contrast, each of the three oldest age groupings (55–59, 60–64, and 65+) had the lowest arrest rates. Persons aged 65 and over had an arrest rate of 0.9%, even though this category represented 11.9% of the U.S. population. In 1995, the same data elements reflect subtle, but interesting changes. The 25 to 29 age group remained in the highest arrest category. But there is a shift in the younger and older population groups. Specifically, the 30 to 34 age group registered the second highest offense rate, followed by the 16 to 18, and 19 to 21 age group. In 1995, all three oldest categories registered declining arrest rates. Individuals aged 65 and over experienced a 22% decline in their arrest rates, even though this age group had increased by 8% to a total of 12.8% of the population during the decade.

The fact that elders contribute only modestly to the nation's arrest rate presents only a part of the picture. This is because the aggregate statistics of Table 3.1 do not differentiate between minor and major crimes. The next set of tables divides the arrest statistics into crimes of violence and property offenses to assess the relative seriousness of elder criminal activity.[1] Table 3.2 shows total arrests of older offenders by four age categories at two-year intervals from 1991 to 1995. Analysis of the data shows once again that elders, as a group, do not contribute in major ways to the nation's crime rate. Further, when considering directionality of change, the data reflect continuation of a remarkable stability in elder criminality, as previously noted by Steffensmeier (1987). More detailed analysis of violent crime trends by age category reveals a two-tenths of 1% increase for those aged 50 to 54. There is a one-tenth of 1% increase for persons 55

---

[1]Violent crimes include offenses of murder and nonnegligent manslaughter, forcible rape, robbery, and aggravated assault. Property crimes consist of burglary, larceny/theft, motor vehicle theft, and arson.

TABLE 3.1 Percentage Distribution of Total U.S. Population and Persons Arrested for All Offenses and Percentage Changes Between 1985 and 1995

Age group	1985		1995		Change between 1985–1995	
	U.S. population (%)	Persons arrested (%)	U.S. population (%)	Persons arrested (%)	In population (%)	In arrests (%)
12 & under	18.7	1.8	19	1.7	2	–6
13–15	4.6	7.2	4.3	8.2	–6	13
16–18	4.6	12.9	4.1	12.9	–11	0
19–21	5.1	14.4	4.1	11.6	–20	–19
22–24	5.4	13.3	4.2	10	–22	–25
25–29	9.2	17.5	7.2	14.5	–22	–17
30–34	8.5	11.9	8.3	14.3	–2	20
35–39	7.4	7.7	8.5	11.5	15	49
40–44	5.9	4.7	7.7	7.1	31	51
45–49	4.9	3	6.6	4	35	33
50–54	4.6	2.1	5.2	2	13	–4
55–59	4.7	1.5	4.2	1	–11	–33
60–64	4.6	1	3.8	0.6	–17	–4
65 & over	11.9	0.9	12.8	0.7	8	–22

Source: Sourcebook of Criminal Justice Statistics—1986, 1997. U.S. Department of Justice. Bureau of Justice Statistics. Washington, DC: USGPO 1987, 1997.

TABLE 3.2 Total Arrests, Distribution by Age

	UCR Arrests 1991				UCR Arrests 1993				UCR Arrests 1995			
	50–54	55–59	60–64	65 and up	50–54	55–59	60–64	65 and up	50–54	55–59	60–64	65 and up
Total	190,702	113,178	71,292	78,831	224,409	122,983	74,140	85,099	226,410	119,031	68,039	75,542
% Distrib.	1.8	1.1	0.7	0.7	1.9	1	0.6	0.7	2	1	0.6	0.7
Violent Crime	8,174	4,480	2,813	3,206	10,116	5,516	3,412	4,053	10,810	5,635	3,260	4,043
% Distrib.	1.5	0.8	0.5	0.6	1.6	0.9	0.5	0.6	1.7	0.9	0.5	0.7
Property Crime	20,705	13,447	9,518	14,288	22,419	12,459	8,445	13,978	20,487	10,650	6,451	10,380
% Distrib.	1.2	0.8	0.6	0.8	1.3	0.7	0.5	0.8	1.3	0.7	0.4	0.6
Crime Index Total	28,880	17,927	12,331	17,494	32,535	17,975	11,857	18,031	31,297	16,285	9,801	14,423
% Distrib.	1.3	0.8	0.5	0.8	1.3	0.7	0.5	0.7	1.4	0.7	0.4	0.6

Note: All percentages are based on the number of elder arrests divided by the total arrests for each category.

Source: Uniform Crime Reports for the United States, 1991, 1993, 1995. Federal Bureau of Investigation (Washington, DC: USGPO, 1992, pp. 223,224; UCR 1993, pp. 227, 228; and Table 38, pp. 218, 219.

to 59 years old. There is no increase for those aged 60 to 64, and a one-tenth of 1% increase for persons 65 years old and over. Property crime patterns reflect a modest increase of one-tenth of 1% for the 50 to 54 age group and a decrease by the same amount for those aged 55 to 59. Property crime decreased by two-tenths of 1% for persons in the age categories of 60 to 64, and 65 and over.

To further clarify crime trends, Table 3.3 charts arrest frequencies and percentages from 1989 to 1995 for the U.S. population as a whole, and for persons aged 65 and over. Analysis shows that total arrests for the population increased by 1.4% over the study period. By contrast, elder arrests decreased by 10%, even though elders' proportion had increased in the population as noted above. Index Crimes for the whole population declined by 4.5%.[2] For elders, Index

TABLE 3.3 Elder Arrests (65 years and over) for Index, Violent, and Property Crimes and Percentage Change (1989–1995), Total Population and Those Elders 65 and over

Year		Total arrests	Index crimes	Violent crimes	Property crimes
1989	U.S. Pop.	11,261,295	2,345,498	537,084	1,808,414
	65+	83,702	17,954	3,347	14,607
		0.7%	0.8%	0.6%	0.8%
1991	U.S. Pop.	10,743,755	2,277,306	556,669	1,720,637
	65+	78,831	17,494	3,206	14,288
		0.7%	0.8%	0.6%	0.8%
1993	U.S. Pop.	11,765,764	2,422,839	648,416	1,774,423
	65+	85,099	18,031	4,053	13,978
		0.7%	0.7%	0.6%	0.8%
1995	U.S. Pop.	11,416,346	2,239,934	619,230	1,620,704
	65+	75,542	14,423	4,043	10,380
		0.7%	0.6%	0.7%	0.6%
1989–1995	U.S. Pop.	1.4%	−4.5%	15.2%	−10.3%
%Change	65+	−10%	−20%	21%	−29%

Note: All percentages are based on the number of elder arrests divided by the total arrests for each category.

Source: Uniform Crime Reports, 1989, 1991, 1993, 1995. Washington, DC: U.S. Government Printing Office.

[2]Index Crimes include arson.

Crimes declined by an impressive 20%. But the picture is notably different for violent crime. Arrests for violent crimes increased by 15.2% for the population as a whole. For elders, arrests for violent crimes increased by 21%, thereby rising a bit faster compared with the population as a whole. In contrast, property crime shows a striking decline of 29% for elders, while it decreased by 10.3% for the total population. These data stand in contrast to Doyle's analysis of arrest rates for persons 65 and over, which determined a notable increase in elder property crime between the years of 1967 and 1992. Whether this discrepancy represents a trend reversal remains to be seen. The variance in the analytic time frames explains some of the differences in the study results. But the lion share of the substantial decreases in property, white collar, and related crimes shown in Table 3.5 is probably more likely attributable to such factors as the buoyant economy and unusually low unemployment rates. Although basic demographics and stiffer sentencing policies probably are paramount factors, the steady growth in the older prisoner population may be explained, at least in small part, by this rise in violent crime among the older population. In fact, older inmates (age 50 and over) have increased as a percentage of the prison population from 4.9% in 1990 to 6.8% in 1997, thereby registering a 38% growth (Flynn, 1998).

In summary, analysis of elder crime in the 1990s agrees with earlier findings that older persons do not significantly contribute to the nation's vexing crime problem. As reflected in Table 3.3, elder arrest rates for Index Crimes, violent crime, and property offenses remain very low. Elders also have the lowest arrest rates of any age segment in the population (Table 3.1). As a result, the present analysis differs from previous findings of increasing elder property crime.

Violent Crime

The present analysis establishes important variations from previous research findings on elder crime. To gain an even better understanding of the problem, specific patterns of offenses are now examined in greater detail. As already noted, violent crimes increased for older offenders in recent years. Table 3.4 compares arrests (and percentage changes) for each of the UCR Index Crimes for the total population

TABLE 3.4 Arrests for Violent Crimes and Percentage Changes for the Total Population and Persons Aged 55, 60, 65, and Over

	1989				1995				Percent Changes 1989–1995			
	Total Pop.	Age 55–59	Age 60–64	Age 65+	Total Pop.	Age 55–59	Age 60–64	Age 65+	Total Pop.	Age 55–59	Age 60–64	Age 65+
Murder/homicide*	17,975	220	170	205	16,701	207	104	149	−7%	−5.9%	−39%	−27%
Forcible rape	30,544	338	218	232	26,561	321	202	235	−13%	−5%	−7%	1.3%
Robbery	133,830	261	104	139	137,811	255	124	149	3%	−2.2%	19%	7.2%
Aggr. Assault	354,735	4,081	2,559	2,771	438,157	4,852	2,830	3,510	23%	19%	11%	27%
Other Assault	771,794	7,353	4,430	4,850	975,418	9,366	5,341	6,207	26%	27%	21%	28%

Note: Includes nonnegligent homicide.

Source: Sourcebook of Criminal Justice Statistics 1990, 1997. U.S. Department of Justice, Bureau of Justice Statistics. Washington, DC: USGPO.

with those of elders over a 7-year time span. (a) The data show that elders do not play a significant role in the national murder rate. In general, murder and nonnegligent homicide have decreased by 7% for the population as a whole over the study period. Elders in the 55 to 59 age category registered a more modest decline of 5.9%. Murder declined by a substantial 39% for those aged 60 to 64. Those 65 years old and over saw a decline of 27%. (b) Forcible rape decreased in a similar fashion. There was a reduction of 13% for the population as a whole. Rape declined 5% for elders in the 55 to 59 age category and by 7% for those aged 60 to 64. The small increase of 1.3% for those aged 65 and up has no significance given the small base level of arrests for this group. (c) Robbery increased by 3% in the total population. It decreased for those aged 55 to 59 by 2.2%. Once again, the percentage increases noted for the two older age categories can be safely ignored due to their small base levels of arrests on which they are computed. (d) However, the crime picture changes dramatically for aggravated assault.[3] Over the study period, this crime increased by 23% for the population as a whole. For those between the ages of 55 and 59, it increased by 19%. The next age category (60 to 64) saw an increase of 11%. And for those aged 65 and over, aggravated assault increased by an impressive 27%. (e) To complete the picture of elder violence, the category of "other assault" is included in this analysis even though this offense is not part of the FBI's Index Crimes.[4] Table 3.4 shows that assaults increased nationally by 26%. Similar increases are noted for elder Americans. There was a 27% increase for the 55 to 59 age category. Those between the ages of 60 to 64 saw an increase of 21%. The largest increase of 28% is noted for those aged 65 and over.

Property Crime and Related Offenses

Compared with previous studies of elder property crimes, the current analysis provides an expanded view of the subject. Table 3.5 shows

---

[3]Aggravated assault is defined as an unlawful attack by one person upon another for the purpose of inflicting severe or aggravated bodily injury. It is usually accompanied by the use of a weapon or by means likely to produce death or great bodily harm. Attempts are included.
[4]Assault is defined here as an unlawful physical attack or attempted physical attack upon a person. It is synonymous with "simple assault" and usually implies an attack without weapons resulting in minor injuries.

total arrests for property offenses and related crimes for older offenders (age 65 and over) and for the population as a whole. It also depicts elder arrests as a percentage of all arrests for each crime category as well as percentage changes in arrests from 1989 to 1995. Unlike earlier findings of increases in elder property crimes, the data show steep declines in most property crime categories with a few notable exceptions as discussed below.

Elder arrests decreased for 13 of the 17 crime categories featured in Table 3.5. Burglary declined by 16%, even though it increased by 38% for the total population. Auto-theft decreased by 25% for elders, while declining by 18% for the whole population. Arson decreased by 5%, yet it increased by 2% for the total population. Stolen property offenses (e.g., buying, receiving, possessing) decreased 20% for elders and only 10% for the rest of the population. Weapons offenses (e.g., carrying, possessing) decreased by 8% for elders. It increased for the total population by 4%. Vandalism declined by 10% for elders and 6% for the total population. Two crimes previously reported as having risen precipitously currently show equally dramatic decreases. Elder arrests for larceny/theft declined by 30%. By comparison, larceny/theft decreased by a more modest 7.2% for the total population. DWI declined 14% for elders. It decreased 23% for the total population. Elder arrests for disorderly conduct, drunkenness, vagrancy, and gambling declined by 29%, 40%, 37%, and 50% respectively. (The comparable percentage changes for the whole population in the same categories are −13%, −21%, −31%, and −9%.) Since such behaviors are mostly voluntary and rarely involve effective complainants, they are commonly referred to as "victimless crimes." It is noted that the impressive declines in arrests for these crimes continue a trend previously identified by Steffensmeier (1987). Sex offenses (which exclude forcible rape and prostitution) saw a small decrease of 0.2% for older persons, with a larger decrease of 13% for the total population.

The four categories reflecting growth in elder arrests are: liquor law violations, offenses against family and children, drug abuse, and white-collar crime. Elder liquor law violations increased by 13%, while they decreased by the same amount for the whole population. Offenses against family and children increased by 70% for elders and even more for the total population (79%). Drug abuse violations for elders increased by 11%. For the population as a whole it

TABLE 3.5 Arrests for Property, White Collar, and Related Crimes for the Total Population and Persons Aged 65 and Over and % Changes 1989–1995

Total Pop.	1989			1995			Percent Changes 1989–1995	
	Total Pop.	Age 65+	% of all arrests	Total Pop.	Age 65+	% of all arrests	Total Pop.	Age 65+
Burglary	356,717	513	0.1%	492,315	431	0.09%	38%	-16%
Larc./theft	1,254,220	13,816	1.1%	1,164,371	9,722	0.8%	-7.2%	-30%
Auto theft	182,810	190	0.1%	149,053	143	0.1%	-18%	-25%
Arson	14,665	88	0.6%	14,965	84	0.6%	2%	-5%
White Collar*	384,009	2,257	0.6%	423,642	2,365	0.6%	10%	5%
Stolen Prop**	141,763	316	0.2%	127,844	252	0.2%	-10%	-20%
Vandalism	247,802	742	0.3%	232,702	670	0.3%	-6%	-10%
Weapons***	180,670	1,300	0.7%	187,237	1,200	0.6%	4%	-8%
Sex Offense****	83,487	1,617	1.9%	72,272	1,613	2.2%	-13%	-0.2%
Drugs	1,075,728	1,668	0.2%	1,144,228	1,849	0.2%	6%	11%
Gambling	17,166	958	6%	15,676	480	3%	-9%	-50%
Family Off*****	58,525	341	0.6%	104,952	581	0.6%	79%	70%
DWI	1,333,327	16,520	1.2%	1,033,280	14,220	1.4%	-23%	-14%
Liquor Viol.	502,798	1,897	0.4%	435,311	2,152	0.5%	-13%	13%
Drunkenness	668,252	11,967	2%	527,200	7,153	1.4%	-21%	-40%
Disord. Cond.	646,097	4,430	0.7%	561,641	3,159	0.6%	-13%	-29%
Vagrancy	29,586	247	0.8%	20,521	156	0.8%	-31%	-37%

*Includes forgery, counterfeiting, fraud, and embezzlement
**Includes buying, receiving, possessing
***Includes carrying, possessing, etc.
****Except forcible rape and prostitution
*****Offenses against family and children

Source: Sourcebook of Criminal Justice Statistics 1990, 1997. U.S. Department of Justice. Bureau of Justice Statistics. Washington, DC: USGPO.

increased by 6%. White-collar crime (e.g., forgery and counterfeiting, fraud, and embezzlement) grew by 5% for older persons and 10% for the total population.

To better understand the patterns of elder criminality and their change over time, Table 3.5 charts elder arrests as a percentage of all arrests for each of the property, white-collar and related crime categories listed. Analysis shows that in 1989, the majority of elder arrests occurred in eight crime categories: gambling (6%), drunkenness (2%), sex offenses (1.9%), DWI (1.2%), larceny/theft (1.1%), and vagrancy (0.8%), disorderly conduct (0.7%), and weapons offenses (0.7%). For 1995, the rank-ordered percentages reflect continuity in patterns, with a few minor changes: gambling (3%) continues in the first place, sex offenses (2.2%) moved into the second position, no doubt reflecting a growing public awareness and resulting reduced tolerance for such offenses. The two alcohol-related offense categories, DWI (1.4%) and drunkenness (1.4%), are now tied in the third position. Vagrancy (0.8%) and larceny/theft (0.8%) follow, showing declining rates. To further highlight the fact that the bulk of elder crime gravitates principally toward minor property and alcohol-related offenses, Table 3.6 depicts past and present offense patterns for this population. The table features data developed for the present study and information generated for earlier time periods by other scholars (Shichor & Kobrin, 1978; Steffensmeier, 1987).

TABLE 3.6   Past and Present Patterns of Elder Criminality Showing Offense Categories with the Most Frequent Elder Arrests*

1965	1974	1984	1989	1995
drunkenness	drunkenness	DWI	gambling	gambling
dis. conduct	dis. conduct	drunkenness	drunkenness	sex offenses
other but	DWI	larceny/theft	sex offenses	DWI
traffic	vagrancy	other but	DWI	drunkenness
gambling	gambling	traffic	vagrancy	vagrancy
DWI		dis. conduct	larceny/theft	larceny/theft
vagrancy		gambling	weapons	family offenses
larceny/theft		vagrancy		

*Based on arrest data, reflecting varied methodological approaches.

Sources: Steffensmeier (1987); Shichor/Kobrin (1978); *Sourcebook of Criminal Justice Statistics* (1990, 1995).

Considering that the studies used varied methodologies to arrive at their results covering a time span of 30 years, there is a striking consistency in their findings. Specifically, the preponderance of elder criminality, past and present, revolves around a small number of offense categories. Three of these offenses, namely, gambling, drunkenness, and vagrancy, are essentially "victimless" crimes. Sex offenses, DWI, and offenses against the family are more serious in nature and are often tied to substance abuse. Arrests for larceny/theft, the final perennial, have fallen sharply in recent years.

In summary, despite inherent limitations in utilizing UCR data, the present analysis of specific patterns of offenses committed by elders does reflect an increase in recent years in violent crimes for this population. Specifically, while older persons age 65 and over do commit murder, forcible rape, and robbery, they do not play a significant role in the national crime rate for these offenses. By contrast, elder violence has increased sharply in the categories of aggravated assault (27%) and other assaults (28%). However, these increases are similar to the increases for these crimes in the population as a whole, which rose by 23% and 26%, respectively. While the rise in elder assaults gives cause for concern, the actual number of these offenses, on which the percentages change has been calculated, remains low. The analysis of property offenses contradicts earlier study findings and points to substantial decreases for a majority of such offenses, including larceny/theft. Elder crime has increased in four offense categories: liquor law violations, offenses against family and children, drug abuse, and white-collar crime. Finally, examining elder crimes of all types over several decades shows that the bulk of elder crime consists of relatively minor offenses, with the exception of sex offenses, DWI, and family violence. The remaining sections of this chapter focus on the relevant criminological and gerontological perspectives on elder crime and examine specific elder crime patterns within the parameters of mental health disorders and substance abuse.

Explaining Elder Crime

As previously noted, the relationship between age and crime has long been an issue of central concern for criminologists. The present analysis of national arrest rates unequivocally confirms that compared to the young, elders are the least contributors to the nation's crime problem. In spite of some speculation in the literature that elder crime may be underestimated because of either police and prosecutorial lenience, or increased public tolerance of elder eccentricities (including some crimes), a preponderance of studies note that age does not appear to affect arrest or prosecution decisions in any significant way (Doyle, 1997; Kercher, 1987; Krohn, Curry, & Nelson-Kilger, 1983; Petersilia, 1985). Since elder crime is uncommon, its very rarity requires explanation. The fact that crime decreases with age is known as the "aging-out effect." Its causes are multiple and include biological, individual, and social factors (Flynn, 1996). Biological and individual factors help account for declining crime rates because many criminal activities require good physical condition and mental development. For example, high levels of testosterone have consistently been tied to aggression and violence in young males. Physiology, individual and social factors are invariably tied to the dynamics of the human life cycle (Wilson & Herrnstein, 1985). As children enter their early teenage years, parental controls wane while peer influence heightens. Teens' proclivity to join peer groups (including gangs) for status, sex, alcohol, drugs, and money, provides the single best explanation for the rapid escalation of delinquency and crime during the teenage years. Most youths "mature out" of crime as they traverse the life course into adulthood with all its attendant responsibilities, which leaves the question of how to explain elder crime. Prevalent criminological theories provide some answers.

Theoretical Perspectives on Elder Crime

In their discussion of theoretical perspectives on elder crime, Akers, LaGreca, and Sellers (1988) eschew the need for special theories relating to this issue in view of the general applicability of the major criminological theories to this population. The key concepts and propositions of strain, control, social learning, and related major criminological perspectives are not age-specific. They have relevance for explaining elder crime, as they do for juvenile delinquency or crimes committed by middle-aged offenders. Since the nation's crime problem converges at the early stages of the life cycle, most criminological theories have been applied to and tested on youthful offender populations. Nonetheless, their holdings have been successfully applied to some forms of elder deviance, thus proving their explanatory power for crime at the end of the life cycle (Blumstein, Cohen, Roth, & Visher, 1986).

Of particular relevance for this discussion are seminal criminological writings on adolescent and elder crime, pointing to striking similarities between the two age groups (Moberg, 1953). For example, Wolk (1963) identifies the following shared characteristics, including a life in considerable flux: As youths mature, they must cope with the turmoil of physical and mental change, while elders must learn to adapt to declining physical and mental health. Self-concepts and traits are similar. Included are feelings of insecurity, inadequacy, egocentricity, lower tolerance for life's frustrations, and worries about the future and one's immediate survival. In a similar vein, Feinberg (1984) notes the following commonalities: Both age groups are exempted from certain work responsibilities. Time schedules are relatively unstructured. There is an emphasis on play and leisure as a way of life. Limited financial independence is accompanied by comparative freedom from family responsibilities. The focus is on consumption, not production. By the same token, youths and elders have less prestige and status compared to that enjoyed by working adults.

Feinberg (1984) also notes important differences between the young and old. Among the more important are the facts that youths can look forward to assuming economic, familial, and political roles. By contrast, elders can mostly anticipate their disengagement from such roles. Further, the young can expect and are expected to enter mainstream society, while elders particularly in the U.S. society, are expected to leave and not come back. With the passage of time, status, financial resources, and power of youths become stronger while those of elders tend to grow weaker.

Feinberg's writings resonate key elements of the gerontological theory of disengagement (Botwinick, 1973). The latter describes the disengagement of elders from their functional roles in society and suggests that such a development is satisfying to elders and functional for society when younger, more efficient workers increase productivity compared to work performed by older individuals. Disengagement theory has deservedly drawn much criticism. Aging and performance are highly heterogeneous processes. Therefore, assumptions about when aging begins are as fatally flawed as are statements about performance based on specific age categories.

It is essential to note here that Feinberg's discussion focuses primarily on the negative aspects of aging. This is because his purpose is to explain the atypical event—elder crime. Offsetting the negativism of this focus is a host of recent research on healthy aging, which indicates that a majority of elders navigate the shoals of old age with great success, in good health, and functional status lasting well into late life. For example, life expectancy at birth in the United States has increased from 47 years in 1900 to over 76 years today and is likely to reach 83 years by the year 2050 (Rowe, 1997). The collective findings point to a compression of morbidity in old age, with many chronic disorders ranging from arthritis, dementia, emphysema, hypertension, and stroke decreasing in prevalence. Most important for the present discussion is the finding that "89% of those aged 65 to 74 report no disability, and even after age 85, 40% of the population is fully functional" (Rowe, 1997, p. 367). The "new gerontology" is expanding its previously limited focus on age-related illnesses to the exploration of "healthy senescence," defined by Rowe as "the progressive nonpathological, biological, and physiological changes that occur with advancing age and that influence functional status as well as the development of disease." Advances in aging research furthermore indicate that lifestyle and other environmental influences can profoundly affect and modify outcomes of aging (Finch & Tanzi, 1997). Finally, previously held notions of mental decline and neuron death are false and not inevitable consequences of brain aging (Morrison & Hof, 1997).

In sum, the brief consideration of the prevailing theoretical perspectives on elder crime, coupled with the consideration of recent research findings of the "new gerontology" suggests the following: Elder deviance and crime may best be viewed as the product of the combined and varied effects of bio-psychosocial changes impacting individuals as they enter the older stages of the life cycle. Further, the difference between the majority of law abiding elders and the few who engage in deviance or commit crimes late in life may well be a function of an elder's social, psychological, and physiological coping resources. Major social resources include material assets, lifestyle, nutrition, and interpersonal and environmental support systems. Psychological resources encompass personality traits, skills, and intelligence, among others. Physiological resources include genetic variations which, in turn, influence longevity and susceptibility to major age-related illnesses.

The Role of Mental Disorders in Elder Crime

Cumulative technological advances in the neurosciences over the recent decades suggest that the behavioral and social sciences could benefit from expanding their conceptual bases to include data and findings from neurochemistry, neuropsychiatry, and other related scientific disciplines. A recent meta-analysis of a wide range of studies conducted over a period of 35 years noted that the relative incidence of neuropathology among violent offenders occurred at "many hundreds of times in excess of that found in the general population" (Pallone & Hennessy, 1998). Specifically, psychopathology ratios ranged from 32:1 for homicide offenders, to 21:1 for "habitual aggressive" offenders, to a low of 4:1 for "one-time aggressives." Befitting good science, the authors do not claim to have established sole causation between neuropathology and aggression. But they do observe that the sheer magnitude of their findings could not be written off as an artifact of chance.

There is long-standing evidence in American jurisprudence and in the criminological literature that organically based disorders, such as brain damage, cerebral diseases, epilepsy, and traumatic brain injuries can negatively affect human behavior (Hucker, 1984; Petrie, Lawson, & Hollender, 1982; Roth, 1968). As such, organic and functional mental disorders can play a contributory or even causative role in many kinds of antisocial conduct, including assaults and nonjustifiable homicide. Looking at older offenders, there is a scarcity of studies, and the few studies that do exist are characterized by contradictory findings. For example, estimates of prevalence of organic brain syndrome among elders range from 14% to 40% (Hucker & Ben-Aron, 1985; Whiskin, 1968). Among the reasons for these notable disparities in psychiatric assessments of the prevalence of organic and functional illnesses among elders are: (a) serious methodological flaws, especially in case of studies conducted decades ago; (b) the utilization of varied and vague diagnostic criteria; and (c) conclusions resting on insufficient numbers of cases studied. Pending establishment of the true prevalence of functional and organic brain diseases among elders, it is reasonable to assume that some elder offenders will have these disabilities. As a consequence, their criminal activities may be caused, wholly or in part, by seriously impaired judgments or a loss of control or restraint. It is essential, therefore, that mental health and criminal justice professionals explore the possibility that elder offenders may suffer from these impairments. The quality of justice and punishment is contingent upon the full consideration of extenuating circumstances such as diminished mental capacity.

The Role of Substance and Alcohol Abuse in Crime

Substance and alcohol abuse are two of the nation's most serious health and social problems. Research has clearly linked alcohol consumption and other substance abuse to homicide, assaults, and domestic violence, as well as to such offenses as drunken driving, liquor violations, and public drunkenness (Goldstein, 1989; U.S. Department of Justice, 1992). Nationally, the combined use of drugs and alcohol accounted for 18% of the alcohol-involved rapes and sexual assaults, 36% of the alcohol-involved robberies, 24% of the aggravated assaults in which the offender was drinking, and 15% of the simple assaults involving a drinking offender (U.S. Department of Justice, 1998). Studies of alcohol use by convicted offenders show that more than 36% of the 5.3 million convicted adults in jails, in prisons, or under probation/parole supervision had been drinking when they committed the offenses for which they were convicted. This amounts to just under 2 million convicted offenders nationwide on an average day, for whom alcohol was a factor in their crime (U.S. Department of Justice, 1998). While drugs exert varying deleterious psychophysiological effects on users, alcohol is known to reduce inhibitions and decrease coordination and mental functioning. Together, these substances exact a heavy toll in human life, causing serious injuries, illness, and even death. The pursuit of these substances inflicts enormous social costs by reducing the quality of life and overwhelming the nation's health care and criminal justice systems.

Alcohol Abuse and Elder Crime

The relationship between elder crime and alcohol abuse has been explored in a number of studies (Meyers, 1984). The FBI's newly developed National Incident-Based Reporting System (NIBRS) reports that in 1995, 8.6% of older Americans (defined as age 50 and over) were involved in alcohol-related violent incidents. This compares favorably with those in the age category of 30 to 39, which accounted for 37.9% of alcohol-related violence.[5] The previously discussed study by Shichor and Kobrin (1978) established that alcohol-related arrests, particularly those for DWI and public drunkenness, accounted for the majority of elder offenses. Prevalent theoretical explanations for elder alcohol abuse suggest a wide range of reasons: disengagement from mainstream society, the stress and strain of aging, social isolation, illness, and bereavement.

Analysis of the most recent data featured in this chapter (Table 3.5) suggests that alcohol-related crime has changed. In particular, the UCR data show a significant decline in DWI and drunkenness arrests for the population as a whole, including older Americans. Even more to the point, recently published data by the Department of Transportation and the FBI show that in 1995, elders (defined as those age 50 and older) were responsible for only 9% of DWI arrests, even though that age group accounts for 32.8% of licensed drivers (U.S. Department of Justice, 1998). The impressive decreases in DWI arrests no doubt reflect the influence of nationwide efforts to combat the problem. They include pressure groups such as Mothers Against Drunk Drivers (MADD); legislative lowering of permissible levels of blood alcohol concentrations in drivers; rigorous law enforcement, including random sobriety checks; accelerated prosecution; harsher punishment of convicted offenders; treatment; and education. It is generally thought that these efforts are probably

---

[5]The NIBRS represents the next generation of crime data from law enforcement agencies. Designed to replace the UCR, it collects information on 57 types of crimes. The 1995 data reported here were collected from law enforcement agencies in nine states.

most successful at curbing the so-called "social drinker." By contrast, the chronic alcoholic is not likely to be stopped by any of these tactics. Such problem drinkers tend to accumulate long histories of vehicular, criminal, and violent offenses. Recent statistical reports indicate that few older Americans fall into this category. In 1986, only 6.8% of persons 65 or older were involved as drivers/fatalities in alcohol-related accidents. By 1996, that percentage fell to 5.4%, the lowest of any age category listed (U.S. Department of Justice, 1998). In spite of the welcome decrease in alcohol-related crime among elders, Table 3.5 does indicate that elder arrests for DWI and drunkenness still account for 2.8% of all elder arrests for property, white-collar, and related crimes. This datum is exceeded only by gambling (3%) and approximated by sex offenses (2.2%). Also, on the negative side, elder arrests for "liquor violations" increased between 1989 and 1995, although the actual numbers of arrests are low.

Drug Abuse

The analysis of drug offenses committed by elders presented in this chapter (Table 3.5) not only indicates the seriousness of the nation's drug problem but also reflects an acceleration of drug use over the past 6 years. In 1989, elders made up 0.2% of all drug arrests. By 1995, elder drug arrests as a percentage of all arrests remained the same; however, percentage changes from 1989 to 1995 reflect an 11% increase for elder drug arrests, which is larger than the 6% increase in drug arrests for the population as a whole. Nonetheless, it should be noted that the actual number of elder drug arrests (N = 1,859 in 1995) is minuscule compared to drug arrests for the population as a whole (N = 1,144,228). In the absence of specific studies focusing on the relationship between elder substance abuse and crime, it is best to use a cautious approach in the interpretation of these findings. Certainly, substance abuse has proliferated in the population, including the elder population. Substance abuse affects the physical and mental health of the user and calls for treatment interventions. Some elder drug users are no doubt involved in a range of criminal activities. But the nature of the drug-crime relationship remains shrouded. At present, criminologists do not agree on a causal path. Does drug abuse lead to crime or does criminal behavior precede substance abuse? It could well be that substance abuse and crime derive from the same bio-psychosocial factors. Also, different drugs, such as heroin, cocaine, and methamphetamines, affect behavior, including crime, in different ways. In the interim and until further research provides better answers, criminologists agree that while drug abuse may not cause crime, it certainly enhances it considerably (Nurco, Hanlon, Kinlock, & Duszynski, 1988). In view of this discussion, it is premature to single out older drug users for responses above and beyond those afforded substance abusers in the general population. Ultimately, psychosocial–medical treatment and education are likely to provide the best answers.

Specific Patterns of Elder Crime

Criminal Homicide

Historically, elders have been consistently underrepresented among homicide offenders. The data presented in Table 3.4 confirm not only that elders continue to have low homicide rates but that they have registered significant declines. As such, they follow declines in the national homicide rate for the population as a whole. Between 1989 and 1995 those in the age category of 55 to 59 experienced a 5.9% decline. Those over age 60 saw an impressive 39% decrease, while homicide for elders 65 and over declined by 27%.

One of the few studies of older homicide offenders utilized FBI data to provide some interesting answers concerning this population (Wilbanks & Murphy, 1984). Among its most important findings is the observation that elders are affected (albeit to a lesser extent) by the same sociological factors that generate differential rates of homicide from state to state. Even though homicide rates vary considerably between states, the ratio of elder to nonelder rates is similar across all states and jurisdictions. The authors also noted variations in the incidence of homicide by race and sex, with older African-American males having the highest homicide rates and white females the lowest. This observation parallels Holinger's (1987) epidemiological study of violent deaths in the United States. It notes that the homicide rates for males of each racial category is higher than for females of the same category. In a similar vein, the rates for non-Whites are greater than for Whites. Holinger found the non-White factor so great in increasing the risk of homicide that, unlike suicide, the non-White female homicide rates are greater than those for White males (1987, p. 59). Hollinger's analysis yielded another interesting finding. He notes that suicide, homicide, and motor-vehicle accident rates seem to run parallel over time. And since homicides, motor-vehicle accidents, and nonmotor vehicle accidents correlate significantly with overt self-destructiveness, that is, suicide, the author suggests that self-destructiveness may play an important role in various forms of violent death in the population (1987, p. 135).

Prevalent theories for elder homicide include previously discussed biological changes due to the process of aging. Some cases clearly involve organic brain dysfunctions which, in turn, may lead to rigidity, suspicion, or low frustration tolerance with consequent aggression. Other factors include disengagement, financial strain, deteriorating health, and social isolation. Aday (1994) observes that for many elders the range of social interaction shrinks with time. As a consequence, the remaining interpersonal primary relationships become intense. Feelings of vulnerability and dependency are heightened. Either can easily deteriorate into conflict and violence. The fact that most older homicide offenders commit their crimes disproportionately against family members adds considerable validity to these explanations. Since older males and females are more likely to kill in domestic situations, it follows that the majority of such killings occur in their residences. In a vast majority of cases the weapon is a firearm (Goetting, 1992). And unlike younger felony offenders, elders are less likely to kill in connection with the commission of other felonies (McNamara & Walton, 1998). A recent analysis of elder homicides not only supports these findings, but sheds light on previously discussed situational and ethnic factors. Kratcoski (1990), examined 179 cases of nonjustifiable homicides by persons aged 60 and over and found that: in 81% of the cases the parties had been involved in an altercation; 89% of the victims and perpetrators were intimates; 82% of the offenders were male; 72% were African American; 74% of the deaths occurred in a private domicile; 9% of the perpetrators killed themselves after killing the victim; 44% of the offenders had consumed alcohol; 40% of the victims and offenders were under the influence of alcohol at the time of the killing; and 46% of the offenders had an extended history of alcohol abuse.

Although the prevention of homicide is difficult, there are usually a number of warning signs indicating risk and problem acceleration: social isolation, depression, deteriorating health of household members, alcoholism, and episodic violence. There is a great need for community recognition on the part of the helping professions, including mental health, social services, and as a last resort, criminal justice.

Suicide and Homicide-Suicide

Holinger's (1987) national study of suicide confirms well-known patterns and trends. Suicide rates for males are greater than for females at any age. White male suicides also increase with age. Although young females have the lowest rates, women between the age of 35 and 64 are consistently at highest risk for suicide. Looking at age and race, suicide rates are greater for whites than for nonwhites in most age groups. But younger, non-White age groups between the age of 15 and 44 have recently increased, and are now higher than those of older age groups. Males over 65 have the highest suicide rates in the nation. In 1992, the national suicide rate stood at 19 per 100,000 in the population, with elders committing disproportionately more suicides than any other age group. A recent study by Cohen and Eisdorfer (1996–1997) notes that Florida, with its large proportion of older Americans, has one of the highest suicide rates in the nation: 24 per 100,000 in 1993. Embedded in this trend is a newly emerging public health problem: homicide combined with suicide. Vastly understudied, the national homicide-suicide rate is pegged at 0.2 to 0.3 per 100,000 for all ages. Focusing on regional prevalence in Florida, Cohen and Eisdorfer (1998) determined a homicide-suicide rate of 0.4 to 0.9 per 100,000 for people aged 55 and over.

The typical homicide-suicide involves a Caucasian husband (or brother) who kills his wife (or sister) with a gun and commits suicide shortly thereafter. In most instances, the perpetrator is in a "caregiver" role. The victim is often in declining health and may suffer from such debilitating illnesses as Alzheimer's, Parkinson's, or cancer. Most commonly, the caregiver is likely to suffer from ill health and severe depression and to feel physically, emotionally, and financially exhausted from years of caregiving. He may also be faced with the prospect of separation and the heartbreak of having to place his loved one into a nursing home, with all the devastating emotional and financial implications that this act usually entails. But most of all, he is likely to be despondent about a future without hope and filled with pain. While some killings may be the result of a spouse's express wish to die, Cohen and Eisdorfer's study found that the women were not always willing victims. Medical records indicate that about two-thirds of the women killed had at least some evidence of defensive wounds or had expressed fears to neighbors and friends about their husband's talk of suicide (1998, p. 4). Guns are the preferred weapon, with most killings occurring in the home. Finally, homicide-suicides are not the exclusive domain of older White males. In her research in South Florida, Gibson (1998) found two-thirds of couples were Hispanic, with a mean age difference of 18 years between males and females. These couples' relationships were marred by fighting, violence, and separation.

The problem of homicide-suicides has opened up a myriad of legal and moral questions. At present, the criminal justice system of the United States makes no allowances for mitigating circumstances that may surround mercy killings. With the exception of Oregon, most states criminalize assisted suicide and prosecute those who defy the law. While grand juries sometimes refuse to indict, and jury nullification or prosecutorial discretion occasionally benefit mercy killers, the majority of perpetrators suffer the legal consequences of their actions (Wrightsman, Nietzel, & Fortune, 1998). Given the current haphazard nature of justice in this context, it may be time for legislatures to address this problem.

Perhaps the saddest aspect of the homicide-suicide phenomenon is that it is preventable. A recent publication of the Tallahassee Commission on Aging with Dignity (1997) proposes the following prevention strategies: (a) expand existing respite care to provide temporary relief for family caregivers; (b) create incentives for families who want to care for aging parents and other family members, but lack sufficient resources; (c) increase hospice and home health care for elders; and (d) adjust nursing home reimbursement rates so that those with high ratings receive higher compensation than those with lower ratings. Beyond these measures, Cohen (1998) suggests an interrelated process for family assistance, interventions involving assessment, and the development and implementation of a health care plan.

Sex Offenses

Society's image of the sex offender, including older sex offenders, is shrouded in myths and misperceptions. For example, there is the public image of the typical sex offender as a male stranger who stalks and preys upon female victims. The predator's motivation is invariably seen as entirely sexual. Older sex offenders, in turn, are often depicted as "dirty old men," who engage in predominantly nonviolent offenses such as exhibitionism, voyeurism, or pedophilia. Still other misperceptions include the often erroneous assumption by police and others that pedophiles who molest young males are homosexual. The reality, however, is quite different.

Sex offenders are highly complex in their motivation, activities, and the relationships to their victims. The vast majority of violent sex offenders are males assaulting females, with women accounting for a small percentage of offenders. An even smaller number of sex offenders involves victims and perpetrators of the same sex. A recent report by the U.S. Department of Justice (1997) notes that studies on crimes of rape and sexual assault revealed a high percentage of cases with child victims. In self-reported victimization surveys of the public, teenagers reported the highest per capita rates of exposure to rape and sexual assault. Further, self-reports of convicted rapists and sexual assault offenders indicate that two-thirds had violated victims under the age of 18. A full 58% of these inmates reported that their victims were aged 12 or younger. Information based on police reports shows that in 90% of the rapes of children under the age of 12, the child knew the offender. Age and type of sex offenses are clearly related, with arrestees for rape concentrated in younger age groups, while those arrested for other sex offenses (statutory rape and offenses against common decency) are more prevalent among older persons. As such, in 1995, persons 50 years old and over accounted for 5% of those arrested for rape and a full 10% of those arrested for other offenses. Age differences are particularly striking when looking at the characteristics of imprisoned sex offenders; less than 5% of incarcerated violent offenders are at least age 50, but about 7% of rapists and 12% of sexual assaulters are 50 and older.

The analysis of Table 3.4 shows that forcible rape declined by 13% between 1989 and 1995 for the population as a whole. Forcible rape for older offenders in the age categories of 55 and 59 also declined, but not as dramatically. By contrast, those aged 65 and over registered an increase of 1.3%. The "other" sex offense category featured in Table 3.5 shows a 13% decrease of such crimes for the population as a whole, but only a 0.2% decrease for those aged 65 and over.

Although the number of older sex offenders is relatively small compared with other age groups, the seriousness of this type of offense, coupled with rapidly decreasing public tolerance and harsher sentencing practices, has led to the accumulation of older sex offenders in the nation's prisons (Flynn, 1998). In many of the major state prison systems (such as Michigan, Georgia, and Florida) about one-third of older inmates aged 55 and older are sex offenders serving relatively long sentences. A study by Walters (1987) found that, relative to rapists and nonsex offenders, child sex offenders tend to be older, better educated, White, married, and prone to major affective disorders. In view of the findings, the author suggests that child sex offenders may have problems being passive in social situations, as well as with their psychosexual identity. However, the assumption that older pedophiles are more likely to play a passive and, therefore, less hurtful role may be premature. An analysis comparing younger and older sex offenders by Stevens (1995) revealed serious predatory behavior on the part of the older offenders, including sexual intercourse by physical force. The duration of offending behavior ranged from single events to 8 years and often included multiple victims. Among the major theories explaining sexual predations are mental and organic brain disorders, personality disorders, and alcoholism. In the absence of definitive studies, it is important that human service providers and criminal justice practitioners recognize that sex offenders do inflict serious physical and psychological damage on their victims. Few recover completely from their experiences. As a result, proper diagnosis and treatment of the offender should be mandatory. After imprisonment, extended community supervision and treatment are fast becoming the normative response to this type of offender.

Property Offenses and Shoplifting

Contrary to many previous studies of elder crime, an analysis of Table 3.5 shows that older offenders do not play a major role in the nation's property crime. Older Americans commit few burglaries, auto theft, arson, forgery, counterfeiting, fraud, or embezzlement. Beyond gambling offenses, it is noted that in 1995, 0.8% of older offenders were arrested for the crime of larceny/theft. Between 1989 and 1995, elder arrests in this category decreased by 30% compared with a much smaller decrease of 7.2% for the population as a whole.

Larceny/theft in general and shoplifting in particular are serious problems for the nation's merchants and retailers. A recent national report (Shoplifters Alternative, 1996) estimates that employee theft, shoplifting, administrative errors, and vendor fraud caused approximately $25.7 billion in retail losses in 1995. While the type of merchandise tends to determine the gender of the customer, analysis of arrestees showed that 55% were men and 44% were women. No gender information was noted for 1% of the arrestees. Of interest in the current discussion is the fact that slightly more than 60% of arrestees were adults, ages 18 and over. Of the arrestees, 52% were between the ages of 18 and 30, and 45% were between the ages of 31 and 65. Only a scant 3% were persons aged 65 and over. One third of juvenile offenders were between the ages of 13 and 17. This group stole disproportionately more in relation to their numbers in the population (7%). Among the adults, 41% were Caucasian. African Americans accounted for 29%, Hispanics for 44%, and Asian Americans for 1% of the arrestees. The most frequently stolen items included tobacco products, athletic shoes, brand-name apparel, designer jeans, intimate apparel, health and beauty aids, and video and compact disks.

At this point of the discussion the finding that elders are underrepresented among shoplifters should not come as a surprise. Elders do steal and engage in related property crimes, but they do so with less frequency than other age groups. Incidentally, kleptomania, defined as a recurrent failure to resist impulses to steal objects, is extremely rare at any age (Fishbain, 1987). Studies examining the motivational patterns of shoplifters have identified a wide variety of reasons for shoplifting: desire for profit or gain, economic hardship, psychosocial stress due to marital or family conflict, pleasure derived from risk taking, and perception of low risk of apprehension and prosecution (Ray, 1987). A detailed study of the influence of psychosocial factors by Yates (1986) provides valuable insight into the problem. The author noted three distinct categories of shoplifters. The first, most prevalent, group steals for profit or gain because of real needs or want. Individuals in this category are likely to be young, female, and single. They steal food or clothing for themselves or their offspring. They are also likely to engage in other criminal activities. A second, smaller group, characterized as "nonrational" shoplifters, consists of older, married females. Key motivating factors are not a lack of resources but depression and social isolation. Such persons are likely to have marital or family conflict. They suffer from illness and depression. Many had lived through traumatic childhoods. Otherwise law-abiding, they lack assertiveness, feel isolated, and alone. The final group engages in random thefts of useless articles for no apparent reason, needs, or want. Least prevalent, this group's thievery makes the least "sense" of all (Yates, 1986).

Feinberg's (1984) study focuses exclusively on elder shoplifters and clarifies a number of prevalent myths concerning this particular offender population. First, most elder shoplifters are not indigent. Most have financial resources, own their homes, and have white-collar or professional backgrounds. Consonant with the national data discussed above, elders do not steal need-based items such as food or drugs, but purloin clothing and/or cosmetics. Second, elder shoplifting can rarely be attributed to selective memory loss, since most abscond with multiple items. Third, elders do not shoplift because they are lonely, isolated, or crave attention. Most elder shoplifters do not live alone. A majority are married, and most have family or friends living in their immediate vicinity. Rejecting such commonly accepted explanations for elder shoplifting, Feinberg attributes such behavior to the previously discussed changes in the life cycle. As elders disengage from work, they are separated from mainstream society. The passage into one's advanced years brings on role disengagement, role transitions, and the need to learn new roles. Unfortunately, there are no road maps or guideposts to show the way (Feinberg, 1984). The statistics discussed in this chapter demonstrate that the vast majority of elders successfully navigate the passage into their senior years as law-abiding citizens. However, for a few the monumentality of change may well break down the traditional bonds of social control, and cause them to become involved in crime. Once such crime is shoplifting.

Conclusions

Given the marked increase of elders relative to other age segments in the population, elder crime has become a major concern for policy makers. The topic has also turned into a focal point of criminological scholarship. In the face of often contradictory findings concerning the criminal activities of elders, including predictions by some, of an impending geriatric crime wave, this chapter's detailed analysis of patterns and changes in elder crime demonstrates that elders, as a group, are least likely to be involved in crime in this nation. Specifically, data analysis shows that in 1995, those in the 25 to 29 age category recorded the highest arrest rates among any age group, while elders had the lowest arrest rates by far. From 1985 to 1995, individuals aged 65 and over saw a 22% decline in their arrest rates, even though this age group increased by 8% to a total of 12.8% of the U.S. population.

To assess the seriousness of the crimes elders do commit, the current study analyses crime trends and provides a detailed examination of elder involvement in Index Crimes, crimes of violence, property crime, and other related offenses. First, between 1989 and 1995, elder Index Crimes declined by an impressive 20%. They declined by 4.5% for the population as a whole. Second, contrary to previous study findings of significant elder involvement in property crime, this study shows a striking decrease of 29% in this offense category. By contrast, property crime declined by only 10.3% for the total population. Disaggregation of the property offense category for elders shows significant decreases in burglary (16%), auto theft (25%), arson (5%), stolen property (20%), vandalism (10%), weapons of-fenses (8%), gambling (50%), and vagrancy (37%). Larceny/theft, consistently identified in prior research as a major elder crime, shows a 30% decrease. For the total population, larceny/theft decreased by a more modest 7.2%.

In a similar vein, earlier studies identified elders as disproportion-ately involved in alcohol-related crimes. The data in this study indi-cate otherwise. Elder drunken driving (DWI) decreased by 14%, drunkenness by 40%, and disorderly conduct by 29%. These impres-sive decreases are no doubt attributable to the influence of sustained nationwide efforts to combat the problem, as well as to definitional changes in the latter categories.

In contrast to these encouraging findings, elder crime shows in-creases in four categories: family offenses (70%), liquor violations (13%), drug offenses (11%), and white-collar crime (5%). With the exception of liquor violations, these data are comparable to the increases noted for the total population.

Third, data analysis shows that elder crimes of violence do not quite follow the benign patterns set by Index Crimes and property offenses. Between 1989 and 1995, elder arrests for violent crimes increased by 21%. This increase exceeds the 15.2% growth recorded for the population as a whole. Disaggregation of the violent crime category shows that elders do not play a significant role in the na-tional murder rate. In fact, murder and nonnegligent homicide committed by those 65 years old and over, decreased by 27%. It decreased for the total population by 7%. Examination of the forcible rape and robbery rates committed by elders 65 and over, reveals only modest increases by 1.3% and 7.2%, respectively. For the total population, forcible rape decreased by 13%, while robbery increased by 3%. But little significance need be attached to these increases in view of the small base level of arrests for this age group in both categories. The one violent crime where elders give cause for concern is aggravated assault. Elder arrests for this Index offense increased by an impressive 27%. It increased 23% for the total population during the study period. Similar increases were recorded for the lesser, non-Index crime of "other assaults." It increased by 28% for those aged 65 and over, and by 26% for the total population. These data show that some elders are capable of violence and serious crime.

However, even in these categories their actual number remains relatively low.

Since elder crime is uncommon, its rarity requires explanation. Conceptually, lower arrest rates among elders are best explained by combining prevailing criminological theories with recent gerontological research findings. Taken together, they suggest that elder deviance and crime is best viewed as the product of the combined and varied effects of bio-psychosocial changes impacting individuals as they enter the advanced stages of the life cycle. Further, the difference between the majority of law abiding elders and the few who do commit crimes late in life is likely to be affected by an elder's social, psychological, and physiological resources.

In summary, there is no evidence of a geriatric crime wave. Most elders are law-abiding. As such, elders are best viewed as a stabilizing force in society and not as an emerging, new problem on the horizon of criminal justice. Though numerically small, some elders do engage in crime and violence and are quite capable of inflicting serious losses and harm. Data analysis indicates that elder offense patterns and motivations are remarkably similar to those operant for other age groupings. The increase observed in elder violence, especially in assaults, is worrisome, but not surprising. The fact is that elders are prone to experience the same personal, social, and environmental strains as persons in other age groups. Neither are they exempted from the vagaries of human passions. No one outgrows the capacity for the range of emotions so often tied to violent behavior. In fact, elder violence, when it does occur, correlates positively with personal privations, alcoholism, and lives characterized either by over-dependence in interpersonal relationships or by unstable social relationships. But there is no evidence in the data that elders become more violent with age. Finally, given the heterogeneity of older offenders, professionals in medicine, mental health, human services, and criminal justice need to individualize their approaches to treatment and prevention. No criminal activity, whether drunkenness, liquor violations, or sexual delinquency should be simply written off as "geriatric crime," since all such activities are amenable to treatment. Individual assessment of elder needs and the closest possible cooperation between the helping professions and criminal justice practitioners should be the focus of our approach to this particular offender population.

References

Aday, R. H. (1994). Aging in prison: A case study of new elderly offenders. *International Journal of Offender Therapy and Comparative Criminology, 38*(1), 79–91.

Adler, F., Mueller, G. O. W., & Laufer, W. S. (1995). *Criminology.* New York: McGraw-Hill.

Akers, R. L., La Greca, A. J., & Sellers, C. (1988). Theoretical perspectives on deviant behavior among the elderly. In B. McCarthy & R. Langworthy (Eds.), *Older offenders* (pp. 35–50). New York: Praeger.

Blumstein, A., Cohen, J., Roth, J. A., & Visher, C. A. (1986). *Criminal careers and "career criminals."* Washington, DC: National Academy Press.

Botwinick, J. (1973). *Aging and behavior: A comprehensive integration of research findings.* New York: Springer Publishing Co.

Cohen, D. (1998). Detection and treatment of depression in caregivers. *Home Health Care Consultant, 5*(6), 32–36.

Cohen, D., & Eisdorfer, C. (1996–1997). Homicide-suicide in older persons in the United States. *Newslink, 22*(4), 16–17.

Cohen, D., & Eisdorfer, C. (1998). Florida study finds elderly homicide-suicide rising. *Population Today, 26*(3), 4.

Covey, H. C., & Menard S. (1987). Trends in arrests among the elderly. *Gerontologist, 27,* 666–672.

Doyle, D. P. (1997). Aging and crime. In K. F. Ferraro (Ed.), *Gerontology, perspectives and issues* (2nd ed., pp. 347–359). New York: Springer Publishing Co.

Farrington, D. P. (1986). Age and crime. In M. Tonry & N. Morris (Eds.), *Crime and justice: An annual review of research* (Vol. 7, pp. 189–250). Chicago: University of Chicago Press.

Federal Bureau of Investigation. (1989). *Uniform crime reports.* Washington, DC: U.S. Government Printing Office.

Federal Bureau of Investigation. (1991). *Uniform crime reports.* Washington, DC: U.S. Government Printing Office.

Federal Bureau of Investigation. (1992). *Uniform crime reports.* Washington, DC: U.S. Government Printing Office.

Federal Bureau of Investigation. (1993). *Uniform crime reports.* Washington, DC: U.S. Government Printing Office.

Federal Bureau of Investigation. (1995). *Uniform crime reports.* Washington, DC: U.S. Government Printing Office.

Feinberg, G. (1984). A profile of the elderly shoplifter. In E. Newman, D. Newman, & M. Gewritz (Eds.), *Elderly criminals* (pp. 46–48). Cambridge: Oelgeschlager, Gunn, and Hain.

Finch, C. E., & Tanzi, R. E. (1997). Genetics of aging. *Science, 278,* 407–411.

Fishbain, D. A. (1987). Kleptomania as risk-taking behavior in response to depression. *American Journal of Psychotherapy, 41,* 598–603.

Flynn, E. E. (1996). Age and crime. In J. E. Birren (Ed.), *Encyclopedia of gerontology* (Vol. 1, pp. 353–359). San Diego: Academic Press.

Flynn, E. E. (1998). *Managing elderly offenders, A national assessment* (Monograph prepared for the National Institute of Justice). Washington, DC: National Institute of Justice.

Gibson, L. (1998). Providers could prevent murder/suicide in the elderly. *Medical Business, 4,* 13.

Goetting, A. (1992). Patterns of homicide among the elderly. *Violence and Victims, 7,* 203–215.

Goldstein, P. (1989). Drugs and violent crime. In N. A. Weiner & M. Wolfgang (Eds.), *Pathways to criminal violence* (pp. 16–48). Newbury Park: Sage.

Holinger, P. C. (1987). *Violent deaths in the United States. An epidemiologic study of suicide, homicide, and accidents.* New York: Guilford Press.

Hucker, S. J. (1984). Psychiatric aspects of crime in old age. In E. S. Newman, D. J. Newman, & M. Gewirtz (Eds.), *Elderly criminals.* Cambridge: Oelgeschlager, Gunn and Hain.

Hucker, S. J., & Ben-Aron, M. H. (1985). Elderly sex offenders. In R. Langevin (Ed.), *Erotic preference, gender identity, and aggression in men: New research studies* (pp. 211–223). Hillsdale, NJ: Erlbaum.

Inciardi, J. A. (1987). Crime and the elderly: A construction of official rates. In C. D. Chambers, J. H. Lindquist, O. Z. White, & M. T. Harter (Eds.), *The elderly: Victims and deviants* (pp. 177–190). Athens, OH: Ohio University Press.

Kercher, K. (1987). Causes and correlates of crime committed by the elderly: A review of the literature. In E. F. Borgatta & R. Montgomery (Eds.), *Critical issues in aging policy: Linking research and values* (pp. 254–306). Beverly Hills, CA: Sage.

Kratcoski, P. C. (1990). Circumstances surrounding homicides by older offenders. *Criminal Justice and Behavior, 17,* 420–430.

Krohn, M., Curry, L., & Nelson-Kilger, S. (1983). Is chivalry dead? An analysis of changes in police practices of males and females. *Criminology, 71,* 417–437.

Long, L. M. (1992). A study of arrests of older offenders: Trends and patterns. *Journal of Crime and Justice, 15,* 157–175.

Malinchak, A. A. (1980). *Crime and gerontology.* Englewood Cliffs, NJ: Prentice-Hall.

McCarthy, B., & Langworthy, R. (1988). *Older offenders.* New York: Praeger.

McNamara, R. P., & Walton, B. (1998). Elderly criminals in the United States. In D. E. Redburn & R. P. McNamara (Eds), *Social gerontology* (pp. 222–235). Westport, CT: Auburn House.

Menard, S. (1987). Short-term trends in crime and delinquency: A comparison of UCR, NCS and self-report data. *Justice Quarterly, 4*, 455–474.

Meyers, A. R. (1984). Drinking, problem drinking, and alcohol-related crime among older people. In E. S. Newman, D. J. Newman, and M. L. Gewirtz (Eds.), *Elder criminals* (pp. 51–65). Cambridge: Oelgeschlager, Gunn & Hain.

Moberg, D. (1953). Old age and crime. *Journal of Criminal Law Criminology and Police Science, 43*, 773–775.

Morrison, J. H., & Hof, P. R. (1997). Life and death of neurons in the aging brain. *Science, 278*, 412–419.

Newman, E. S., Newman, D. J., & Gewirtz, M. L. (Eds.). (1984). *Elderly criminals.* Cambridge, MA: Oelgeschlager, Gunn, and Hain.

Nurco, D. N., Hanlon, T. E., Kinlock, T. W., & Duszynski, K. R. (1988). Differential criminal patterns of narcotics addicts over an addiction career. *Criminology, 26*, 407–423.

Pallone, N. J., & Hennessy, J. J. (1998). Brain dysfunction and criminal violence. *Society, 35*(6), 21–27.

Petersilia, J. (1985). Racial disparities in the criminal justice system: A summary. *Crime and Delinquency, 31*, 15–34.

Petrie, W. M., Lawson, E. C., & Hollender, M. H. (1982). Violence in geriatric patients. *Journal of the American Medical Association, 248*, 443–444.

Ray, J. (1987). Every twelfth shopper: Who shoplifts and why? *Social Casework. The Journal of Contemporary Social Work, 68*, 234–239.

Roth, M. (1968). Cerebral disease and mental disorders of old age as causes of antisocial behavior. In A. DeReuck (Ed.), *The mentally abnormal offender.* Boston: Little, Brown.

Rowe, J. W. (1997). The new gerontology. *Science, 278*, 367.

Sherman, L., & Glick, B. (1984). The quality of arrest statistics. *Police Foundation Reports, 2*, 1–8.

Shichor, D., & Kobrin, S. (1978). Criminal behavior among the elderly. *Gerontologist, 18*, 213–218.

Shichor, D. (1984). The extent and nature of lawbreaking by the elderly: A review of arrest statistics. In E. S. Newman, D. J. Newman, & M. L. Gewirtz (Eds.), *Elderly criminals.* Cambridge, MA: Oelgeschlager, Gunn, and Hain.

Shichor, D. (1985). Male-female differences in elderly arrests: An exploratory analysis. *Justice Quarterly, 2*, 399–414.

Shoplifters Alternative. (1996). *Why do shoplifters steal?* Jericho, NY: Shoplifters Anonymous.

Steffensmeier, D. J. (1987). The invention of the "new" senior citizen criminal. *Research on Aging, 9,* 281–311.

Stevens, G. F. (1995). Grandfathers as incest perpetrators: Dirty old men or predatory offenders. *Journal of Crime and Justice, 18,* 127–141.

Tallahasse Commission on Aging with Dignity. (1997, November 13). *Aging advocate suggests use of tobacco settlement fund to overhaul caregiving system* [Pamphlet]. Tallahassee, FL: Author.

U.S. Bureau of the Census. (1996). *Statistical abstracts of the United States.* Washington, DC: U.S. Government Printing Office.

U.S. Department of Justice. (1992). *Drugs, crime and the justice system.* Washington, DC: U.S. Government Printing Office.

U.S. Department of Justice. (1997). *Sex offenses and offenders: An analysis of data on rape and sexual assault.* Washington, DC: U.S. Government Printing Office.

U.S. Department of Justice, Bureau of Justice Statistics. (1986). *Sourcebook of criminal justice statistics.* Washington, DC: U.S. Government Printing Office.

U.S. Department of Justice, Bureau of Justice Statistics. (1987). *Sourcebook of criminal justice statistics.* Washington, DC: U.S. Government Printing Office.

U.S. Department of Justice, Bureau of Justice Statistics. (1990). *Sourcebook of criminal justice statistics.* Washington, DC: U.S. Government Printing Office.

U.S. Department of Justice, Bureau of Justice Statistics. (1995). *Sourcebook of criminal justice statistics.* Washington, DC: U.S. Government Printing Office.

U.S. Department of Justice, Bureau of Justice Statistics. (1997). *Sourcebook of criminal justice statistics.* Washington, DC: U.S. Government Printing Office.

U.S. Department of Justice. (1998). *Alcohol and crime.* Bureau of Justice Statistics. Annapolis Junction, MD: NCJRS.

Walters, G. D. (1987). Child sex offenders and rapists in a military prison setting. *International Journal of Offender Therapy and Comparative Criminology, 31,* 261–269.

Wilbanks, W., & Murphy, D. D. (1984). The elderly homicide offenders. In E. S. Newman, D. J. Newman, & M. L. Gewirtz (Eds.), *Elderly criminals* (pp. 79–91). Cambridge, MA: Oelgeschlager, Gunn & Hain.

Wilson, J. Q., & Herrnstein, R. (1985). *Crime and human nature* (pp. 126–147). New York: Simon and Schuster.

Whiskin, F. E. (1968). Delinquency of the aged. *Journal of Geriatric Psychiatry, 1,* 242–262.

Wolk, A. (1963). The geriatric delinquent. *Journal of the American Geriatrics Society, 11*(7), 653–659.

Wrightsman, L. W., Nietzel, M. T., & Fortune, W. H. (1998). *Psychology and the legal system* (pp. 53–54). Pacific Grove, CA: Brooks/Cole.

Yates, E. (1986). The influence of psycho-social factors on non-sensical shoplifting. *International Journal of Offender Therapy and Comparative Criminology, 30,* 203–211.

PART II

Elders and the Criminal Court

Chapter 4

Elders in the Courtroom

William E. Adams, Jr.

This chapter discusses the impact of old age on the major participants in the criminal trial process. The participants in the process include the judge, jury, witnesses, defendant, and attorneys as well as other court personnel that assist with administrative functions (bailiffs, clerks, and court reporters). This chapter focuses on how age affects the experiences of the participants with active roles in the decision-making aspects of the trial compared to those with solely administrative responsibilities. It will also consider how the process can be improved for older participants, including courtroom access for those who have physical impairments. This review is hindered by the dearth of rigorous empirical studies of the trial process, both civil and criminal. Although there are arguably more studies about jurors than other trial participants, commentators have noted a lack of understanding about even what jurors do and how they think (Landsman, 1998).

The discussion of this topic is further complicated by the indeterminacy of what age is the appropriate marker for when one should be considered "older." The empirical research and scholarly commentary on older participants in criminal trials use different age ranges in designating who is older. This variability is also reflective of the disparity among numerous governmental policies and programs that use old age as a factor in determining status or eligibility. For example, the criminal justice system utilizes a number of different ages to designate who is older. The Uniform Crime Report identifies age 65 and older as the oldest age category. Federal and some state prison systems report age 45 and over as "older," whereas age 55 is sometimes referred to as "elderly" in other parts of the criminal justice system (Ellsworth & Helle, 1994). Thus, in this chapter, the age threshold for what constitutes "older" will vary according to the particular study under discussion.

The fact that an attorney, judge, or witness is older doesn't necessarily change the role that individual plays in the court system. A judge has the same duties and performs the same functions regardless of age. The same holds true for attorneys and witnesses. Similarly, the older defendant is bound by the same rules of procedure and evidence, and the same burden of proof is carried by the state to obtain a conviction of the accused, regardless of his or her age.

Recognition, however, that the roles of attorneys, judges, or witnesses do not change with age does not mean that others' perceptions of older persons in these roles are exempted from society's general ambivalence about age distinctions. In the criminal trial process as in society as a whole, advanced age can be seen by some as a sign of experience and perhaps wisdom, or it can cause concern about diminishing physical and mental abilities sometimes associated with the aging process. In addition, the influence that age exerts upon the perception of the participant in the criminal trial process may depend upon the participant's role. Thus, old age may be perceived more positively for a judge or an attorney than for a witness or defendant. Furthermore, the perception that a juror has diminished capacities because of age may influence the conduct of a particular trial. The attitude that judges have about juries in general (King, 1998) or particular jurors may influence the conduct of the trial, because judges have control over trial procedures. Thus, a judge with a distrust of the competency of jurors to process information may exclude more evidence, provide more extensive instructions, and solicit and answer more questions from jurors than judges who have more confidence in their jury panel (King, 1998).

It should also be recognized that the impact that age has on the perceptions of various criminal trial participants may be transcended by other factors such as shared professional memberships, educational level, race, age, gender, wealth, and other socioeconomic indicators. The legal system is both hierarchical and patriarchal in nature, and the courtroom itself exemplifies this most. The architecture of most traditional courthouses is meant to establish a sense of majesty and intimidation to those who enter. These themes are reflected in such architectural details as the tendency for most older courthouses to sit atop an imposing set of steps, to have oversized doors and other features, and to have the bench elevated above the litigants. In addition, the courtroom itself is separated with railings and gates in order to exclude those who are neither members of the bar nor participants in the case at hand.

Thus, it should not be surprising that the importance of status and other indicia of power and prestige may dwarf the role of age. Consequently, a judge is likely to feel that she has more in common with a young male attorney than an older witness or juror her age because of the pervasive impact of a shared educational and professional background as well as a likelihood that they share a similar economic status. Furthermore, the effect of race and gender in our society is also reflected in the legal profession and may have a more profound impact than age, particularly because the judiciary and bar are still disproportionately white and male.

Although traditionally many of the most revered lawyers and jurists were old when they were at the peak of their power, the profession itself excluded women and racial minorities from the bar until this century. Much scholarly commentary discusses the failure of the legal profession to overcome barriers to access for racial minorities and women, which arguably still exist inside and outside the courtroom (Burton, 1996; Costello, 1997; Fuchs Epstein, Saute, Oglensky, & Gever, 1995; Hernandez-Truyol, 1998; Resnik, 1997; Second Circuit, 1997).

In addition to these other variables, the impact of physical and mental disabilities requires special consideration. The need to accommodate physical or mental disabilities of the older person may vary depending upon which trial participant has the impairment. Thus, a judge or an attorney with a cognitive dysfunction may no longer be qualified to perform that role, whereas an older defendant or witness with the same disability may require accommodations in the courtroom, but not be disqualified from participating. Additionally, a majority of states require that jurors be mentally and physically sound (Fukurai & Butler, 1994). Criminal defendants, on the other hand, have a constitutional right to participate in their case to the extent possible. Although a mental disability probably would impact the credibility of a witness, it would not bar testimony as long as the witness meets the minimal capacity requirements for testifying, i.e., understanding the oath to tell the truth. For the attorney presenting the testimony of a person with a mental disability, the need to prepare the witness carefully and to ask clear and simple questions becomes even more important than for other witnesses.

In addition to these other factors, it should be noted there are particular legal implications concerning the participation of an older person as a juror. Because of the requirement that jurors represent a cross section of the community, the U.S. Supreme Court has found that procedures that result in systemic underrepresentation of certain groups from the jury selection process violate the Sixth Amendment rights of criminal defendants. The Court has recognized that blacks, Hispanics, and women are "cognizable classes" that may not be underrepresented, but it has not so recognized older persons at this point (Fukurai & Butler, 1994). A number of states permit older persons, usually defined as those age 65 or 70 and above, to voluntarily excuse themselves from jury service (Eglit, 1981; Fleming, 1988). The differential treatment ranges from complete exemptions to procedures that require older persons to ask to be excused from service. Although most courts have rejected defendant claims that such provisions violate their constitutional right to a representative jury, some courts have upheld such claims. At least one court has held that old age alone is not grounds for jury disqualification (*King v. Leach*, 1942).

Interestingly, more cases have involved procedures that cause underrepresentation of younger persons (usually dealing with procedures that have a discriminatory impact upon persons under 21, 25, or 30), and some courts have been willing to accept the argument that younger persons compose a cognizable group whose values and perceptions are such that their exclusion violates a defendant's right to have a jury representative of the community. Others have refused to recognize that young persons constitute such a cognizable group, however (Fleming, 1988). The United States Supreme Court has stated in dicta that states could confine selection of jurors to persons within certain ages (*Strauder v. West Virginia*, 1879).

The Older Judge

In discussing the impact of age on participants in the trial process, it may be true that the judicial role is the one least affected in a negative way. In some circumstances, advanced age may actually be perceived favorably. To the extent that age is considered an indicator of experience or wisdom, some may view the older judge more favorably than a judge who is much younger. This "advantage" has its limits even with judges, though, as a number of states have mandatory retirement statutes, with ages typically ranging from 70 to 75.

This situation exists despite the existence of other laws prohibiting age discrimination. The federal Age Discrimination in Employment Act was passed by Congress in 1967 to prohibit age discrimination in the workplace across the nation. The statute was amended in 1974 to cover employees of federal and state governments. Although this would seem on its face to cover judges, the statute contained exceptions for certain elected officials and political appointees who conduct policy making. In addition, the Act does permit some age distinctions to be made under specified circumstances. The courts have ruled in regard to other professions that mandatory retirement is legally permissible under this act as well as under the Equal Protection Clause of the U.S. Constitution. For example, the U.S. Supreme Court has refused to overturn mandatory retirement laws as applied to police officers (*Massachusetts Board of Retirement v. Murgia*, 1976) and foreign service officers (*Vance v. Bradley*, 1979).

State judges forced to retire pursuant to state laws also litigated the legality of such actions under the federal act and the Constitution. After disagreement in the lower federal courts, the U.S. Supreme Court held in *Gregory v. Ashcroft* (1991), that state laws mandating retirement for judges were a violation of neither the Age Discrimination Act nor the Equal Protection Clause of the U.S. Constitution. After ruling that it need only apply rational basis judicial review, because age is not a suspect class and judges do not have a fundamental right to be judges, the Court went on to find that Missouri could rationally believe that judges' physical and mental capacities would diminish with age and that the election process might be inadequate to determine that judicial performance had become deficient. The

Court also held that the authority of the state to determine qualifications for its important government officials is reserved under the Tenth Amendment and assured by the Guarantee Clause of Article IV, Section 4. It therefore concluded that the statutory exclusion for appointees at the policymaking level included judges.

These retirement laws persist despite the productivity of older judges in other systems that do not mandate retirement. The federal judicial system permits judges to continue to work as long as they wish, although they can take "senior" status (reduced caseload responsibilities) after age 65 once their age and years of service add up to at least 80 (Makar, 1997). One commentator has argued that old age is a benefit to a judge because being a judge requires "good judgment," which is "a function of age and experience" (Makar, 1997). He also notes that some of the nation's most distinguished appellate judges such as Holmes, Brandeis, and Learned Hand were productive into their 80s (Makar, 1997). It is certainly common for justices on the U.S. Supreme Court to remain on the Court well past age 65. Although the duties of appellate judges differ from those of trial judges, it is unlikely that the intellectually rigorous arguments over which they preside are less challenging than the duties of the latter. In fact, the assumption that age brings experience and wisdom may actually enhance the perceived authority of older trial judges with defendants, attorneys, and jurors. This potential advantage may be stronger for the judge than for any other participant in the courtroom, with the possible exception of the older attorney.

How advanced age affects a judge's performance is unclear. There have been few studies of judicial behavior, in part because of judges' reluctance to be studied. Even appellate judges, who write published opinions to justify their decisions, are the subject of surprisingly few descriptive studies that analyze their decision-making processes (Simon, 1998). There have been a few studies, however, that have attempted to determine whether the age of the judge affects how he or she perceives older defendants. At least one study of judges concluded that older judges are no more sympathetic to older defendants than are younger judges. The study found that while 59% of judges were sympathetic towards older persons, 20% were neutral and 22% were unsympathetic. The age of the judges was not found to affect their opinions (Feinberg & Khosla, 1985). The survey found that in sanctioning older shoplifters young judges were twice as likely to require performance of community service work by the defendant, whereas older judges used probation and economic penalties more often. Older judges, moreover, were found to be no more likely than their younger counterparts to agree with the statement: "The elderly are not shown enough respect in our society" (Feinberg & Khosla, 1985).

The Older Lawyer

Generally, the older lawyer is considered a distinguished member of the legal profession. Young attorneys are generally viewed as enthusiastic but lacking in skill and experience. The client may prefer the representation of an older attorney to that of a younger attorney, because the perception of age in the legal profession is that of experience, knowledge, sage advice, and wisdom. However, a jury comprised of a significant number of older people might "side with" a younger attorney because they like the younger lawyer (Posner, 1995), seeing in that younger lawyer their child or grand-child. Therefore, Posner (1995) posits, jurors may give young lawyers success in the courtroom incommensurate with the lawyers' years of experience.

As the attorney matures in practice and gains experience, the amount the attorney charges to handle a case increases. For example, an attorney hired out of law school to work as an associate for a large firm will usually bill at an hourly rate far lower than that of a partner (Collins & Tripoli, 1998). Further, the new associate may not even have any client contact, instead receiving all work assignments from the supervising partner. As the number of years of practice experience increases, so does the hourly rate at which the attorney bills, with senior partners of the firm generally paid the most. Therefore, in the legal system, the older lawyer is generally considered to be more knowledgeable, experienced, and successful compared to younger lawyers (Posner, 1995). Thus, being an older lawyer generally conveys a positive image.

Even though the legal profession puts great stock in older attorneys, it is possible that at some point, the older attorney may be held in diminished esteem, especially if the attorney develops obvious physical problems (American Bar Association [ABA], 1991). At that point, age can detrimentally affect others' perceptions of the attorney. An attorney who has a hearing impairment and cannot hear a witness answer, or who has a visual impairment and cannot see exhibits clearly, may be perceived as being "incompetent" and may even harm his or her client's case. In such cases, the attorney may choose to no longer practice in the courtroom, but still function very effectively in the office.

In the legal profession, attorneys who chose law as a second career often face employment problems (Tucker, 1994). They cannot command the same salaries as attorneys in the same age group who initially chose the legal profession (Tucker, 1994). Further, firms may be reluctant to hire someone age 55, for example, and recently graduated from law school, because normally that person will not practice law for the same number of years as a 25-year-old who graduated in the same class. Firms may see hiring the 25-year-old, normally at a lower initial salary, as a better investment.

On the other hand, clients may view a second-career lawyer as more experienced (Tucker, 1994) than a new lawyer. Plus, "second-career" lawyers, having had prior work experiences, can more quickly become functioning lawyers than those in their graduating class who have no work experience (Tucker, 1994). Nonetheless, in a poll of second-career law graduates, the responders specified that age operated as a limiting factor during their job search in the following ways:

- the older graduates were asked age-associated questions that younger graduates were not;
- the interviewers expressed concern about the older graduates' ability to cope with the work hours and pressure, their ability to cope with being supervised by younger attorneys, and their attitude about earning less than in their previous careers;
- the interviewers seemed more accepting of the younger graduates who possessed the same credentials as the older graduates; and
- the interviewers had concerns that the older graduates did not fit the image of the firm's attorneys (Tucker, 1994).

There is little written in the academic and professional literature about the older lawyer's place in the legal system. As noted at the outset, the role of the lawyer does not change by virtue of the lawyer's age. Instead, how the public and those involved in the judicial process perceive an older lawyer may be affected more by the lawyer's obvious physical capacities. Further, accommodations may have to be made for the older lawyer's physical limitations, if any exist.

The Older Defendant

One of the goals of the criminal justice system is to punish based on levels of responsibility. Thus, in American jurisprudence, juveniles are generally deemed to lack the same criminal responsibility as adults who commit the same acts and, consequently, are punished less severely. Whether older defendants should be treated differently by the criminal justice system is a more controversial issue. At least one legal commentator has argued that old age should be considered a potential defense similar to that of post-traumatic stress syndrome (Cohen, 1985). Under this theory old age could be considered as one of the excuse defenses, like insanity, intoxication, or duress. Unlike justification defenses, which cover acts that society deems to be not wrongful, such as self-defense, excuse defenses concede that the act is unlawful, but either do not hold the actor accountable or provide a lesser penalty than would be imposed absent the excusable circumstance (Dressler, 1989). Whether the old-age defense should be applied as a conclusive presumption of diminished responsibility, a rebuttable presumption, or simply a factor to be considered in mitigating punishment, is subject to debate. Alternatively, the old age defense might be treated as all of the above with its weight increasing as age increases.

Although interesting, this theory of old age as criminal excuse has not found much support, even in the academic literature, because the excuse defenses in general seem to vary from the predominant paradigm in American criminal jurisprudence, which is Kantian in nature, that is, the focus in criminal law should be "on the act and the actor's capacity to choose that act rationally and without coercion" (Lelling, 1998). Thus, an examination of factors related to the act beyond rationality and voluntariness are exceptions to the normal concerns of the criminal law.

To the extent that age is used as an excuse based upon a presumption of reduced rationality, the rationale would seem to be susceptible to charges of being reliant upon overgeneralizations about older persons. To the extent that it is applied to older persons who can demonstrate a decreased ability to engage in rational behavior, it is arguably an unnecessary surrogate for the true subject under inquiry, rationality.

Beyond the notion of old age as a defense, it is still worth considering how age affects the defendant as a participant in the criminal process. One study has indicated that older accused offenders are less likely to use due process protections than their younger counterparts (Feinberg, 1988). Yet another study found that older defendants charged with felonies were more likely to proceed to trial (Champion, 1988). In addition, there is debate within the scholarly literature about the disparate impact of various types of punishment upon older defendants. Long sentences or economic penalties may have a more serious impact upon an older person (Gewerth, 1988; James, 1992). There are also court access concerns for older persons with disabilities. This issue is the subject of the next section of this chapter.

Court Accommodations for Elders with Disabilities

In the courtroom, persons with disabilities are protected from discrimination by the Americans with Disabilities Act. This federal law requires that court services be made accessible to persons with disabilities. One commentator has suggested that courts should implement plans to guarantee the legally required access (Albrecht, 1994). In 1991, a number of legal and advocacy groups for elders and persons with disabilities convened to discuss better ways to serve both groups in the courts and recommended that judges and court professionals be educated about their needs. Pursuant to this recommendation, the National Judicial College developed a training program for the courts, which set as one of its objectives teaching court personnel to appraise each older person who appears in court as a witness, juror, defendant, or attorney as an individual (Albrecht, 1994).

The physical layout and conduct of proceedings can be changed in order to remove impediments to access to the courts and to support elders' roles in the process. Necessary accommodations may be only minor. For example, if an older witness or defendant has hearing problems, court administration should provide the person with appropriate amplification devices, such as headsets, or real-time visual transcription (ABA, 1991). Another alternative is to physically rearrange the courtroom to place the older person with hearing difficulty in a location closer to speakers such as the judge. Bailiffs can make sure people sitting in the gallery keep quiet to minimize any outside noise. Attorneys can be instructed to face the person when talking, keep their hands away from their mouths, and talk in a low pitch at a slow and even pace (ABA, 1991). The speaker should not stand with a light source behind him or her, and, instead, the court should have the light shine on the speaker's face (ABA, 1991).

Older people with vision impairments may need to have magnifying devices available. A judge can keep something as simple as a magnifying glass at the bench. Exhibits can be blown up large enough to accommodate many vision impairments. The typeface used for written materials and exhibits should be large and plain (ABA, 1991; Barnes, 1992). The witness needs adequate time to read the document or exhibit. Nonglare paper should be used. Lighting in the courtroom and chambers needs to be examined. Lighting should not cast shadows and should be bright enough to enable a person to see (ABA, 1991; Adams & Morgan, 1994). If there are windows in the courtroom, blinds, curtains, or window film should be used to eliminate glare. No one should be seated facing a window or looking into a light (Adams & Morgan, 1994). If a video is played, the monitor should produce a bright and clear picture. The defendant, witness, and jurors should all have clear views of the monitor. If necessary, multiple monitors should be used, or participants should be allowed to move to locations where they have a clear view of the monitor.

Older people with mobility impairments also need to be accommodated. The path to the counsel table, the witness box, or the jury box needs to be free of obstructions (ABA, 1991; Adams & Morgan, 1994). If the floor is carpeted, the pathway should be without seams, frays, or wrinkles. If the floor is tiled, the surface should be dry, free from obstruction, and made from a nonskid material. If the witness has a mobility impairment, the steps up to the witness box should be checked to assure access. If the steps are too steep, the court should consider having a seat in the well of the courtroom for the person to testify. If the person is concerned or embarrassed about limited mobility, or the attorney is concerned that the witness' physical frailty may somehow affect the jury's perception of testimony (see chapter 6), the attorney can seek a recess and ask for the jury to be removed before the person is called to testify, allowing the person to proceed to the stand in the absence of the jury (Adams & Morgan, 1994).

For a variety of reasons, it may be difficult for an older person to sit for extended periods of time. Back problems or arthritic conditions are more prevalent among older individuals. If so, the judge needs to be informed of this and call frequent recesses to allow such individuals adequate time to stand or move around. Frequent breaks may be needed to accommodate other physical conditions as well (ABA, 1991; Adams & Morgan, 1994).

The temperature of the courtroom is important. A room that is too warm will cause individuals to doze off during technical or dry testimony. A room that is too cold can make someone just as miserable. Because persons with circulatory conditions are prone to being cold (Spence, 1989), a lower temperature in the courtroom and chambers can inhibit their ability to communicate effectively.

Jurors' perceptions of elders may color the way they perceive the older defendant or witness and, thus, how they view the reliability of the older person's testimony (ABA, 1991; Yarmey, 1984; see chapter 6, this volume). When older persons suffer from diminished capacity, the reliability of their testimony may be questioned, resulting in their testimony being discounted, stricken, or, in the most extreme, the person being disqualified from testifying based on a lack of capacity (Adams & Morgan, 1994; Yarmey, 1984). Attorneys can take steps to reduce or eliminate such problems. Advanced age in a witness does not by itself diminish the value of that witness' testimony. If the witness forgets a fact during testimony, the attorney can repeat or rephrase the question, seek leeway from the court, seek a recess, or use documents to refresh the person's recollection.

Carefully preparing for testimony can increase the person's effectiveness (Adams & Morgan, 1994).

For individuals who have never had any dealings with the judicial process, including many older persons, it is helpful to have the basics explained. Prior to the start of the proceeding, the attorney calling the person as a witness should identify the participants, including the attorneys, bailiffs, the court clerk, the court reporter, and the judge; explain their roles; and describe the court procedures. Encouraging people to watch other proceedings in advance of their own, just to familiarize themselves with the process, can go far to eliminate their anxiety over their own cases (Adams & Morgan, 1994).

Clients and witnesses with demonstrable confusion or memory problems may have these problems for a number of reasons. The client may simply be very nervous or may have mental confusion or memory problems caused by depression, medication the client is taking, or an organic problem (Adams & Morgan, 1994; Spence, 1989). For example, a person in the early stages of Alzheimer's disease may be more alert and better able to function earlier in the day rather than later. To accommodate such a problem, the court can schedule proceedings to start early in the morning and end by midday. Mental health professionals can help by providing an assessment of the older person that determines the person's abilities (Adams & Morgan, 1994).

A solution that has been implemented in the Thirteenth Judicial Circuit of the state of Florida is the creation of the Elder Justice Center. The Elder Justice Center was established to make the court system user-friendly and easily accessible to elders who must undergo any type of legal process. The Center accommodates older people by providing ombudsmen, referrals to social and legal services, access to enhanced communications devices, large-print reproductions of standard court forms, and a variety of other services.

Conclusions

It is difficult to generalize about the effects of age on participants in the criminal trial system. In the first place, there has been a limited amount of research on elders in the justice system as a whole. There is even less on the courtroom, particularly in relation to criminal trials. As the population in general ages, this situation merits additional attention.

To the extent that age impacts participants in the system, the effect may vary according to the participant. Judges and attorneys may gain some advantage from advanced age because of the premium placed upon experience by defendants and jurors. As noted, however, mandatory retirement laws for judges indicate that advanced age can be a disadvantage even in a position where many older persons thrive.

In addition, to the extent that age is a variable influencing the perceptions and behaviors of attorneys and judges, it may be less important than other variables. For example, an older judge may relate to and understand a younger attorney better than an older juror or defendant because education, experience, and status may be more important variables than age. Similarly, as indicated by the study on judicial opinions, judges may not show any difference in attitude towards older defendants in their courtrooms. Moreover, while the Americans with Disabilities Act and the growth in advocacy for elders have led to increased awareness among criminal justice professionals of the need to make the court system accessible for elders with disabilities, the key variable here is not age, but disability.

Furthermore, to the extent that advocacy for elders in the legal system has grown, this growth has occurred primarily within the civil system. The criminal system has mostly refused to consider old age as a reason for differential treatment. As the number of older criminals increases, the prison system is being forced to consider the humanitarian and resource issues involved with housing older offenders (see chapters 11 and 12). Similarly, as the courts encounter larger numbers of older persons in the courtroom, they also may need to consider the issue of age more comprehensively. This may become necessary as a matter of law as well as a matter of practicality, whether it regards jury qualifications, trial procedures, or sentencing matters.

References

American Bar Association Commission on Legal Problems of the Elderly. (1991). *Court-related needs of the elderly and persons with disabilities.* Washington, DC: Author.

Adams, W. E., & Morgan, R. C. (1994). Representing the client who is older in the law office and in the courtroom. *Elder Law Journal, 2,* 1–38.

Age Discrimination in Employment Act, 29 U.S.C. §621–634.

Albrecht, J. (1994). Meeting the needs of the disabled and elderly in court. *Judges Journal, 33,* 10–16, 38.

Barnes, A. P. (1992). Beyond guardianship reform: A reevaluation of autonomy and beneficence for a system of principled decisionmaking in long term care. *Emory Law Journal, 42,* 633–760.

Burton, E. B. (1996). More glass ceilings than open doors: Women as outsiders in the legal profession. *Fordham Law Review, 65,* 565–572.

Champion, D. J. (1988). The severity of sentencing: Do federal judges really go easier on elderly felons in plea-bargaining negotiations compared with their younger counterparts? In B. McCarthy & R. Langworthy (Eds.), *Older offenders: Perspectives in criminology and criminal justice* (pp. 143–156). New York: Praeger.

Cohen, F. (1985). Old age as a criminal defense. *Criminal Law Bulletin, 21*(1), 5–36.

Collins, C., & Tripoli, L. (1998). Retired? You're hired! How some firms and partners play the practice endgame. *Of Counsel, 17*(2), 6–8.

Costello, M. A. (1997). Women in the legal profession: You've come a long way—or have you? *Detroit College of Law at Michigan State University Law Review, 1997,* 909–915.

Dressler, J. (1989). Exegesis of the law of duress: Justifying the excuse and searching for its proper limits. *Southern California Law Review, 62,* 1331–1386.

Eglit, H. (1981). Of age and the constitution. *Chicago Kent Law Review, 57,* 859–914.

Ellsworth, T., & Helle, K. (1994). Older offenders on probation. *DED Fed. Probation, 58,* 43–50.

Feinberg, G. (1988). The role of the elderly defendant in the criminal court: Full-dress adversary or reluctant penitent. In B. McCarthy & R. Langworthy (Eds.), *Older offenders: Perspectives in criminology and criminal justice* (pp. 123–156). New York: Praeger.

Feinberg, G., & Khosla, D. (1985, September). Sanctioning elderly delinquents. *Trial,* pp. 46–50.

Fleming, T. (1988). Age group underrepresentation in grand or petit jury venire. *American Law Reports, 4th series, 62,* 859–1018.

Fuchs Epstein, C., Saute, R., Oglensky, B., & Gever, M. (1995). Glass ceilings and open doors: Women's advancement in the legal profession, a report to the Committee on Women in the Profession, The Association of the Bar of the City of New York. *Fordham Law Review, 64,* 291–449.

Fukurai, H., & Butler, E. (1994). Sources of racial disenfranchisement in the jury and jury selection system. *National Black Law Journal, 13*, 238–275.

Gewerth, K. (1988). Elderly offenders: A review of previous research. In B. McCarthy & R. Langworthy (Eds.), *Older offenders: Perspectives in criminology and criminal justice* (pp. 14–31). New York: Praeger.

Gregory v. Ashcroft, 111 S. Ct. 2395 (1991).

Hernandez-Truyol, B. E. (1998). Las Olvidadas—gendered in justice/gendered injustice: Latinas, fronteras and the law. *Journal of Gender, Race and Justice, 1*, 353.

James, M. (1992). The sentencing of elderly criminals. *American Criminal Law Review, 29*, 1025–1044.

King, N. J. (1998). Why should we care how judges view civil juries? *Depaul Law Review, 48*, 419–422.

King v. Leach, 131 F. 2d 8 (5th Cir. 1942).

Landsman, S. (1998). Symposium: The American civil jury: Illusion and reality. Fourth Annual Clifford Symposium on Tort Law and Social Policy: Introduction. *Depaul Law Review, 48*, 197–200.

Lelling, A. E. (1998). A psychological critique of character-based theories of criminal excuse. *Syracuse Law Review, 49*, 35–97.

Makar, S. (1997). In praise of older judges: Raise the mandatory retirement age. *Florida Bar Journal, 71*, 48–50.

Massachusetts Board of Retirement v. Murgia, 427 U.S. 307 (1976).

Posner, R. (1995). *Aging and old age.* Chicago: University of Chicago Press.

Resnik, J. (1997). Gender matters, race matters. *New York Law School Journal of Human Rights, 14*, 219–236.

Second Circuit of the United States Courts of Appeals, Working Committees. (1997). Report of the Working Committees to the Second Circuit Task Force on Gender, Racial and Ethnic Fairness in the Courts. *Annual Survey of American Law, 1997*, 117–414.

Simon, D. (1998). A psychological model of judicial decision making. *Rutgers Law Journal, 30*, 1–142.

Spence, A.P. (1989). *Biology of human aging.* Englewood Cliffs, NJ: Prentice Hall.

Strauder v. West Virginia, 100 U.S. 303 (1879).

Tucker, M. (1994). Second-career lawyers: More thoughtful, more experienced, more realistic. *Law Hiring and Training Report, 14*(7), 2–4.

Vance v. Bradley, 440 U.S. 93 (1979).

Yarmey, A. D. (1984). Accuracy and credibility of the elderly witness. *Canadian Journal on Aging, 3*, 79–90.

Suggested Readings

Americans with Disabilities Act of 1990, 42 U.S.C.A. §12101 *et seq.*

Dressler, J. (1987). *Understanding criminal law.* New York: Matthew Bender.

Taeuber, C. M. (1992). *Sixty-five plus in America.* Washington, DC: U.S. Department of Commerce, Economics and Statistics Administration.

Chapter 5

Impact of the Criminal Justice Process on Older Persons

Sanford I. Finkel and Inez J. Macko

America's older population is growing at a rapid pace. According to the U.S. Census Bureau, at the beginning of the century, only *1 in every 25* Americans (3.1 million) was over the age of 65; by the middle of the next century, *one in five* Americans (80 million) will be over the age of 65. This chapter will primarily focus on the criminal justice system as seen through the eyes of older crime victims and their advocates, and, to a lesser extent, will focus on elder criminals. The experiences described in this chapter are derived from two sources: the clinical practice of the authoring psychiatrist, and from evaluations by the Council for Jewish Elderly's (CJE's) Crime/Victim Witness Assistance Program (CVWAP), established in 1984 by CJE. CJE serves people over 60 of all denominations and races and has annually assisted 125 to 200 crime victims between the ages of 60 and 102.

According to the Bureau of Justice Statistics, 5.7 of every 1,000 people over the age of 65 reported being victims of crime in the United States in 1997, homicides excluded. Of these, 77% were victims of *violent* crimes, including aggravated assault, battery, and strong-arm robbery (U.S. Department of Justice, 2000). Older crime victims are injured more often and more severely than others. They are: more likely to face someone armed with a gun; more likely to be victimized in or near their homes; and less likely to attempt to protect themselves (U.S. Department of Justice, 1994).

Psychological Impacts of Victimization

For many, the crime act itself stirs up anxiety and self-esteem issues. It may aggravate or restimulate latent family conflicts. Depressive symptoms such as insomnia, poor concentration, and low energy occur commonly, and the risk of developing a major depressive episode increases markedly. Some refuse to leave their home and/or limit their activities. Their functional level decreases and, in some cases, their health deteriorates shortly thereafter. Post-traumatic stress disorder is also common, and many victims suffer from flashbacks. Finally, some incur financial expense, such as a paid caregiver, as well as any financial loss due directly to the crime.

These behavioral health and psychosocial issues can profoundly affect the effectiveness of the older person as a witness. If they have depression, a low energy level, lack of interest, pessimism, and poor concentration, these can significantly lower the capacity to cooperate with the ASA, provide articulate answers at deposition or in court, or focus on the facts of the crime rather than their own shames ("I should have known better.") or self-pity ("Why me?"). Flashbacks and anxiety result in cognitive blocking and inability to focus on questions or facts, which, in turn, result in the judge/jury/attorneys questioning the veracity and reliability of the older victim.

Every attempt is made by the agency (CJE) to provide psychological and, if indicated, psychiatric services, to treat any psychiatric disorder, as well as to provide counseling and to help prepare the older person for the challenges of the judicial process. However, most older people going through this experience lack this type of support.

Further, the process itself causes additional stress and may intensify or re-create psychological symptoms. Cases may linger on, intensifying tension and flashbacks. Most alleged offenders do not confirm their guilt immediately, so the process is slow. ASAs may rotate, thereby necessitating a starting over process with the new ASA. Older people get discouraged and confused by the slowness of the process. One older victim complained: "It took a few seconds to rob me, and more than a year to get to justice. Something is wrong with the system."

In the meantime, the older person continues to age. Medical problems and sensory diminution may occur. Memory fades over time, so subsequent testimony may not be consistent with the initial testimony. In a long trial, "I don't remember," and "It could have been that way or not," weakens the testimony. Previously stated responses become meaningless if they cannot be reconfirmed. Further, sometimes the older victim can no longer recognize the perpetrator because of the latter's change of appearance, the older person's sensory changes, or the passage of time blurring the memory. The perpetrator's appearance may be different, for example, long hair to short hair, or from jail attire to street clothes. Both the ASA and PD pull out sections of previous testimony. Their attempts to refresh memory or confront contradictions has the effect of increasing anxiety and weariness, weakening the will of the older person to proceed. Dismissal of the case, particularly after a long delay, creates or intensifies the feelings of shame and inadequacy of older victims. They become self-critical of their poor performance and feel that they have let everyone down. Some believe that they never should have proceeded with prosecution in the first place and thus are getting what they deserve. This psychological state results in further withdrawal and regression, a fact not generally appreciated within the judicial system.

The Older Crime Victim Is Defeated

Elder victims of crime often feel helpless when enmeshed in the current judicial system.

For example, an 87-year-old woman, a diabetic, was attacked on the street and robbed of her handbag. Fortunately, or so it would seem, the police apprehended the robber. Within a short time she is asked to identify this man and does so without hesitation. Six weeks later, at the preliminary hearing, the prosecuting and defense attorneys ask her many questions. At this point, her memory isn't as clear as it was at the time of the assault, but even though she doesn't remember everything, she remembers the salient details. Another six weeks pass. Now, on the day of the trial, she is told to appear at 8 AM to testify. Seven hours later, and without an adequate lunch, she testifies. The room is dimly lit, both lawyers are yelling at her. The defense attorney is challenging her recollections and reliability, and the prosecuting attorney is upset because she does not remember as many details as she did six weeks earlier. There's no one there to help her, and she is feeling victimized again. She becomes anxious. Anxiety, of course, causes cognitive dysfunction, and so her recollections become labored and less clear. The judge is impatient and (she feels) ridicules her, telling the jury that her testimony is not consistent. She feels like a fool, like she is no good. The experience stirs up feelings of inadequacy and self-esteem problems that she hasn't had in a long time. In the end, her effort to testify doesn't matter anyway. Because the police didn't use the right language during the arrest, the alleged perpetrator goes free. The woman experiences posttraumatic stress syndrome and needs psychotherapy as a result. Two weeks later, one of her neighbors is robbed by the same man. Again he is apprehended, but the neighbor refuses to testify. She doesn't want to go through the experiences of her friend.

In fact, only 30% to 40% of older people who have crimes perpetrated against them will prosecute and, of those, only about half result in convictions. Thus, about 15% to 20% of crimes perpetrated against older people wind up going to trial and a conviction. With present odds of five to one against you, why bother? How can the current system encourage and attain a higher level of justice?

The Older Crime Victim Prevails

Not every situation results in disappointment and defeat, however. Some result in justice with excellent recovery.

A victim of attempted murder, an 80-year-old Caucasian, was hospitalized, injured by a cut throat. He demanded justice, so the court process began. He was determined that "the alleged offender was going to pay." He refused to go back to the scene of the crime to pick up his belongings. He left everything, including his clothes. The program was able to relocate the victim witness (V/W) to a secure building in another police district. However, the building had a telephone system that allowed you to enter, and the victim said that he could not afford a telephone. We and the police were concerned about his security. The police officers donated money for a phone, and the program paid basic service for one year. The police also provided transportation to and from the hearings which spanned many months, as well as the trial itself. Before he was prepared for court, he was given counseling, personal education on crime prevention, advocacy, and support. He had flashbacks the night before the hearings. The assistant state's attorneys (ASAs) were told that the victim was hard of hearing, had some knowledge of the court process, and knew who the players were. The ASA needed assistance on how to speak to a hearing-impaired and forgetful elderly person.

At the hearings, the public defenders were hostile, allowing the victim insufficient time to respond to questions. The ASAs and the agency advocated on his behalf and the judge interceded.

Nevertheless, the number of continuances grew for unknown reasons. This was wearing on him. He returned on multiple occasions to repeat, interpret, identify the alleged defender, and give testimony. He was told to look at the CJE advocate for assurance in the courtroom and, if the question was not clear, to ask for the question a different way. He was instructed to always take five breaths before responding to the question. The judge complimented him on the way he presented his testimony.

Although the friends of the alleged offender were sitting in the courtroom, he was not intimidated by their looks and remarks. A guilty conviction was handed down. At the sentencing, the V/W prepared a Victim Impact Statement (VIS) and presented it at court. The judge ruled guilty, and now the offender is spending several years in the penitentiary.

In the meantime, the Illinois Crime Victim Compensation Act (ICVCA) was sent an application to cover unpaid medical, hospital, lab, doctors, and other fees through the Illinois attorney general's (IAG's) office. It took about a year to be paid by the State comptroller's office after being approved by the State of Illinois court of claims. The long delay of financial remuneration is an additional detrimental component, one that is commonly ignored. In conclusion, in spite of obstacles, the victim received justice and made a complete recovery.

Older people also perpetrate crimes.

The Older Criminal "Wins"

Mr. A. B. is a 76-year-old single male with a long history of bipolar (manic-depressive) illness, manic type. When off of his mediation, he drinks heavily and becomes physically and verbally abusive. He is seen in a State Psychiatric Hospital following a second homicide. After the first episode he was also hospitalized after successfully pleading an insanity defense. He was hospitalized for several months, but all symptoms of mental illness disappeared while on anti-manic medication. The hospital could not justify keeping a patient without signs or symptoms of mental illness. Thus, he was released.

Always unhappy about the side effects of the medication, he discontinued it, and the old patterns returned several months later. This led once again to heavy drinking and homicide. However, he was quite wealthy and well-represented legally. Once again he successfully pleaded an insanity defense and was psychiatrically hospitalized. Within weeks he was again stable and the hospital was in a quandary of not wanting to release him, given his history and noncompliance pattern, but without psychiatric justification to keep him.

Thus, with excellent resources financially and legally and with articulation and expression of humiliation and remorse this individual was able to utilize the existing legal system to his benefit.

The Older Criminal Usually Loses, Though Sometimes Wins

Mr. C. D., age 79, had a long history of alcohol abuse but this had worsened considerably since his wife died two years ago. Their joint medical bills wiped out much of their savings, and he has no remaining friends. He commonly drinks whiskey all day and leaves his apartment very late at night. At times he also has been found to be shoplifting. Local police are sympathetic to his plight and don't want to prosecute him as a criminal, though he has been charged with disturbing the peace.

When found on the street semiconscious at 2:00 AM he is driven back home with comments such as "Sleep it off, Pops" or "You'd better start to take care of yourself, or you're going to get very sick." The result is that the pattern is uninterrupted, the problem continues with no meaningful referral, and the privileges of jail, hospitalization, or referral for intervention services bestowed on a younger offender with similar problems is not available to the older adult.

Those under 60 are 10 times more likely to commit a crime than those over 60 (Taylor & Parrott, 1988). In fact, both compare that over 11% of the population in Britain, only 1.9% of the sample remanded in custody were over the age of 65. Taylor and Parrott (1988) also discovered that older people in prison had a disproportionately high incidence of psychiatric disorders, including alcoholism and affective illness. In contrast, criminal activity on the part of elder schizophrenics was extremely low. This may be due to a decrease in delusions and hallucinations which occurs with aging, as a result of higher mortality rates, or institutionalization. Hucker and Ben-Aron (1984) found that demented elders had comparable rates for non-felon sex offenses, but otherwise older people with dementia appear underrepresented in the criminal population. It should be noted, however, that charges are rarely brought against demented elders who become physically aggressive and delusional and who injure family members and caregivers. Such behavior usually results in institutionalization rather than criminal prosecution.

Another extreme example of this relates to a case in which the first author was an expert witness. A 75-year-old woman with a benign brain tumor had become demented and aggressive. On her first day of admission to a nursing home, she murdered her 93-year-old roommate. No criminal charges were pursued, but the woman spent the duration of her days in a state psychiatric hospital.

Homicide/suicide are more common in late life (Cohen, Llorente, & Eisdorfer, 1998). A healthy spouse may kill a mate of many years who is suffering from a painful illness, a terminal illness, or dementia. These cases rarely are seen in the criminal justice system. Likewise, Hough and Mayhew (1983) found that older shoplifters are less likely to be prosecuted.

Interaction with the Police

Chicago is fortunate to have specifically designated police officers to handle older adult crime victims, including follow-up. Ninety percent of all referrals to CJE emanate from them. They accompany CJE staff on home visits and to situations in which they suspect potential physical abuse, drugs, guns, or other weapons. In so doing, they provide a degree of reassurance and structure to the older person, although some victims may fear retaliation. Nevertheless, the degree of police initiative and follow-up depends on the individual officer's attitude, knowledge, and judgment of the crime that was committed. The police are called upon to deal with a wide range of problems.

It is important to note that not every alleged episodes of victimization results in a police report. Many officers are astute at differentiating those who spuriously claim to be victims but who are not.

> Mrs. A. placed frantic calls to the police officer reporting that she had been victimized. She said that her possessions (jewelry, money, watches, etc.) had been taken by the man down the block, and she wanted the police to make an arrest. However, there was no arrest because the alleged victim had misplaced the items.

> Mrs. B. also made a frantic call complaining of theft. The items reported missing were found on the caller's shelf in a closet. Her children were called, and they came in from other cities and assumed the responsibility for her overall care and housing.

In both circumstances the police correctly identified forgetfulness or mild cognitive impairment and were helpful.

> In yet another circumstance, Mr. and Mrs. C. were playing with guns and bullets, shooting randomly into the sky. The neighbors were afraid of being hurt, or worse. This information was relayed to the police. Dressed in plainclothes (so as not to create worry and anxiety for the older adults or others in the neighborhood), they immediately went to meet the couple in the apartment building. (For the same reason, whenever possible, officers use an undercover car. This is a great concern for older adults who are crime victims.) They confiscated the pistols and bullets because they were not registered. The husband was livid and wanted his property back immediately, but did not pursue any action to have them returned.

> Mrs. G. is a 73-year-old African American woman. An out-of-state friend tried calling her for several weeks, but the caregiver would not

put the woman on the telephone. The friend called CJE for help, and a social worker performed an evaluation. Her findings revealed that the caregiver was a street person abusing the victim. The victim's family lived on the first floor but refused to be involved in or responsible for her well-being. The caregiver wanted the victim isolated from everyone. With police support, this caregiver was told to leave and was replaced with a different one. The special police officer makes frequent checks and monitors the situation. The older person improved cognitively and emotionally.

In all of these situations, the officers were available, responded promptly, evaluated the situation accurately, and acted in ways that were pragmatic and reassuring.

Police cooperation has been enhanced by the Chicago Alternative Policing Strategies (CAPS) started in 1993 in the city's 279 beats. The beats are of various sizes, based on the type and quantity of each crime. Studies were conducted on community policing, studying its philosophy, concepts, and practices for a five-year period before its adoption by the city of Chicago. The police work actively with community organizations, and the community-at-large to achieve this end, attending joint meetings, planning collaboratively, and implementing joint strategies that were developed in the partnership. This work also helps shape positive attitudes and better understanding of older people. This, in turn, allows the older person to feel more empathy and thus be more trusting.

Older people's perception of their own risk of being victims is at odds with reality. Women over 60 living in the inner city feel the most unsafe (60%, compared to 3% of men aged 16 to 30) but only 1.2% ever have experienced a crime perpetrated against themselves. Generally, crime rates against older adults are trending downward. Part of this decrease may be due to community policing, better personal education, reinforcement, practicing crime prevention, and efforts to address re-victimization. Agency/police collaboration can result in keeping someone safe and remaining in the community.

The police also play an important role as witnesses in court proceedings. There may be as many as six to eight officers on one case, for example, beat, tactical, receiving officer, detective.

Although the police are generally helpful, in this context there are notable exceptions.

Mr. and Mrs. H., Russian immigrants, both 85-years-old, were victims of a theft under $300. They did not understand the way our police system works and could not effectively communicate with the police. The police needed more information than was noted on the police report. An interpreter was hired and made an appointment to meet the investigating officer.

The police officer was uninterested and rushed the meeting. He restricted any attempts at advocacy. The older persons became frightened and discouraged. No supervisor was available. The older victims knew who had perpetrated the crime, where he lived, and wanted to know when he would be picked up and arrested! The Russian couple was so perplexed that they decided to drop the case. It never reached the courts, and they still see the alleged offender walking the streets. Further, they did not want to file a complaint against the officer and pursue it any further. The had lost respect for law enforcement.

Finally, the police work closely with community agencies in many cases, which are resolved with little or no additional intervention from the judicial system.

A thief knocked down an 80-year-old woman in the lobby of her building. She was found by her neighbors on the floor face-down. They called the police, who referred the case to the CVWAP. The victim knew there was someone in the lobby, but didn't pay attention. She went to her mailbox, put the key in the lock, and he came up behind her and made his move. Fortunately, she was not injured, but her upper plate was broken. She was assisted in repairing her plate and was given crime prevention information, followed-up for a month, and then the case was closed. She was not a repeat victim and now uses the "buddy" system whenever possible.

The Impact of Trial Attorneys

For most attorneys—whether for the plaintiff or defendant—it appears that there is little training and, too often, there is little empathy. For Public Defenders (PDs) and Assistant State's Attorneys, the caseload is so great that frustration and impatience occurs commonly. For the PDs there is little incentive to be empathetic or sensitive to the older victim's plight. Rather, having them appear as foolish and confused as possible may lend to the success of their case. Fortunately, the CJE representative tries to prepare the victim for what to expect. However, most communities do not have similar programs, and the older person often has little support in the current judicial system. This is especially true within the courtroom itself, and outside preparation may dissolve for the older person when confronted with anger, confrontation, and confusing questions amidst a context of unfamiliarity, sensory deprivation, and anxiety.

On the other hand, older criminals, particularly those with wealth and authority, may hire skillful attorneys who can assist them to avoid prosecution.

> Mr. H. I. was a long-time Mafia-associated figure. With clever attorneys he had been able to stay out of prison until his ninth decade. At that time he published autobiographical information for which he was called to testify under immunity. However, any mention of testifying resulted in a significantly and dangerously high increase in blood pressure, flushing and sweating and disorientation—he looked like a man ready to die. At all other times he was oriented, charming and articulate with intact memory and judgment. It was never clear how this sudden shift was brought about.
>
> This phenomenon occurred during interviews with him, as well as with other experts and, most importantly, his attorney. The attorney claimed, correctly and understandably, that his client did not have the mental competency to prepare for his trial or to testify. The subsequent report caused great concern on the part of the prosecuting attorney and judge and considerable delay to any resolution. The defendant's attorney maintained that the judicial process was making his very aged client very sick and family felt that this was unduly cruel punishment, particularly given that the charge was not related to a crime against property or person.

The Impact of the Judge, Bailiff, and Courtroom Milieu

The Role of the Judge

The judge sets the tone of his/her courtroom. Each courtroom has its own personality based on the presiding judge with its own degree of friendliness or lack thereof. Courtrooms also differ in structure, design, and environment. Some judges welcome older victims and are advocates, whereas others are hostile. The way a judge presents him or herself, for example, how he/she walks into the courtroom, has a profound effect on the older adult. If he/she appears calm and kind, the older adult is more relaxed. If, however, he/she projects a hard and cold demeanor, the older adult begins to worry and questions if he/she is going to receive "justice." Experience demonstrates that those judges who are able to communicate with the older adult victim receive clearer testimony. Those judges who are distant and have little compassion for the older adult crime victim receive very short answers and the older adult victim may lose focus on the proceedings.

Some judges expect the older victim to know the law and its procedures. They will "bark" at the victim/witnesses, causing them to become unsettled and upset, once again losing focus on the proceedings.

Mrs E. was a 63-year-old Russian-speaking woman who spoke very little English. An interpreter was provided for her by the court. She kept interrupting the proceedings because she believed that her case was not properly presented by the court interpreter. As she became progressively more distraught, the judge told the advocate to "sit down now!" The room became silent as the judge strongly outlined how court protocol would proceed. The older person became fearful and wanted to leave. Eventually, she was convinced to proceed, but with a different interpreter and advocate. Her facial expression and body language stiffened. She became taciturn, even secretive, and did not help her case. She left the courtroom in tears and said she would not return.

The rotation of judges also affects the older person. You may start out with a "good" judge and end up with a "bad" one for that session or for several sessions. Many older people become discombobulated and don't want to continue the process. The need to "connect" with the judge is of special concern to the older person, who feels secure in the alien judicial system if the parental figure is kind and interested.

Judges in a hurry stir up anxiety and franticness in many older people, making focusing and recollection more difficult. Some older people feel guilty that they are inconveniencing judges and are fearful of their wrath. Since we are seeking more productive outcomes from the criminal justice system, eliminating this rush might be helpful. To all involved, the judge that visibly pauses and evaluates the situation is a "good" judge.

> An 80-year-old C/V with a walker took too much time to approach the bench. He walked extremely slowly, as if he were just learning how to use his walker. He was starting to go to the PD's side rather than the victim's side or the ASA's side because he was concentrating on his walking. The judge was impatient and disrespectful. Instantly, the man became fearful and decided to drop the case.

When a case is held over for the afternoon session, whatever the cause, older people often suffer with the amount of time spent in court. Lunch breaks are short, and in some cases you have to leave the courthouse to obtain food. Older adults seem to have more energy and strength in the morning. They do learn patience, as cases may be held to 3:00 or 4:00 in the afternoon. However, many leave the courthouse exhausted, out of focus, and arrive home around 7:00 PM. Perhaps the court system should dedicate some courts as "older adults" courts with shorter hours.

The Courtroom Environment

In one of the older court buildings, courtrooms are small without enough bench seating for the older victims, the alleged offenders, or others. Conferences with the ASA and others are conducted in the hallway. Occasionally, one can meet in a conference room with other court personnel who enter and exit. The older person often stops talking for the distraction and waits until the door closes before continuing. The interior walls of the courthouse are a nondescript color and there is a small parking lot. In short, it is drab, overcrowded, and poorly lit, negatively affecting the older adult. By contrast, another courthouse is a newer structure, is handicapped accessible, has large courtrooms, is nicely decorated, and has ample seating and free parking. All of this contributes to a positive experience for the older adult person, placing him/her in a better frame of mind. Observation confirms that in courtrooms that are larger, well-lit, and have good air circulation, there is more likely to be active participation.

The older victim is also affected by the bailiff, court recorder, clerk of the court, and other court personnel. The bailiff organizes the courtroom and directs traffic. He/she makes sure the flow of people assembled maintain order, that is, attorneys, victims, witnesses, police. He/she also calls the court to order. Older adults seem to like this—how each bailiff maintains order differently, for example about not eating, chewing gum, drinking, and so on. There is a sense of structure that is reassuring.

The courtroom process stirs up curiosity. How does the transcription equipment work? How do the judge and clerk work together on each case? For some, an understanding of this process helps them focus and allows them a sense of structure.

Another threat (stressor) to the psychological well-being of the older victim is intimidation. This is a major concern for many victims, particularly if they are sitting with the alleged offender's family and friends. They become more fearful, and some express guilt. Some judges acknowledge victim intimidation and stop it. Other judges ignore it and proceed as if nothing is happening. This is another factor in trying to pursue "justice."

A caveat: The authors always advise the V/W to leave metal jewelry and other devices that carry metal at home so that the metal detector isn't set off, which, of course, enhances stress.

Ethnic, Gender, and Age Considerations

In Chicago, Russian immigrants are particularly vulnerable to crime. Many elders carry shopping bags made of light plastic material. They put their money and food stamps at the bottom of these bags, which become easy targets for criminals. Their experience in the former Soviet Union influences their attitude toward the police and the courts. Many are reluctant to get involved in any judicial process for fear of reprisal. While education and counseling often helps them proceed, there are still many exceptions.

Cases

An 82-year-old Russian immigrant who spoke no English was a victim of the "water department con game." A large amount of money was taken from his wallet, which was in his bedroom. He came to the CVWAP screaming because his rent money was taken. Through an interpreter we were able to calm him, and then help him file a police report. We contacted the landlord who verified the amount of rent and quickly returned the verification letter that we'd sent him. A check for a sizable amount of money was cut and sent to the landlord. Again, through the interpreter, we conveyed crime prevention tips to prevent further revictimization. As a result, he learned not to: carry large sums of money; leave his wallet on the dresser; and also not to open the door unless proper identification was slid under the door (this applying also to police officers). We described the current cons and scams to him. He changed his ways, and has not been revictimized. Communities must have such mechanisms to help older people. Unfortunately, the alleged offenders were not caught, due to the language differences, a vague description, and the victim's not being able to identify the truck they used.

A Japanese man and wife in their sixties were sitting in front of their house, which was located in a "hot spot" area. While there, a perpetrator ran up and grabbed the wife's purse, and a week later they were burglarized. A relative of theirs who was very upset about the incident and concerned for their safety made a police report. He spoke English, but the victims did not. They did not want to move even though they were afraid. It took time to convince them to move to senior housing and applications were sent to various sources. Crime prevention on "how not to be a victim" was relayed through the relative. Senior housing was located. The move was made, they are going on with their lives, but the alleged offenders were never caught.

A 70-year-old Chinese man who spoke no English, according to the interpreter, was out for his afternoon walk to the store. He was returning home, when a woman stopped him on the street asking for something. The victim did not understand her. Suddenly, she grabbed his bags and ran away with his pharmacy refills and groceries. The CVWAP paid for the emergency medicines. We gave the interpreter safety tips for the older adult, but he chose not to prosecute.

Those of foreign origin who speak little or no English generally prefer not to prosecute. They are overwhelmed by the crime experience itself, and feel the need to protect themselves from an even greater implosion of chaos and emotion.

The old-old, those over 80, are also less likely to proceed with the judicial process. They are more apt to fear reprisal, and are also more likely to have families who discourage their involvement with the judicial process. Their age, in the context of the length of the process, is also a deterrent.

Ageism

Are older people the victims of ageism? It is difficult to document the existence of ageism per se in the court system. After all, the same police, public defenders, and states attorneys are involved with younger people as well. However, sensory deficits, reduced energy, mild memory changes, and a sense of limited number of years to live all alter the older person's experience and make for increased stress. Further, the complex and sometimes quickened pace of the courtroom, as well as the slower pace of the process, pose additional stress on the older adult.

However, some episodes appear related to age.

A 68-year-old man was being harassed by the children in his neighborhood. He filed a complaint, and the process began. We went to court, and awaited the court call. He was a friendly man and understood what was happening. The ASA was prepared, but the PD looked at him, and began treating him as a "nothing," like a dottering, demented old man. The questions asked by the PD conveyed the message, "You don't know what you are talking about." He went through the process but complained about the pace of the process. He couldn't sleep the night before as he replayed the "court hearing" and his responses to various situations over and over again which increased his overall anxiety.

The Role of the Family

Generally, families are supportive and extremely helpful. They too are traumatized and outraged by the crime and pitch in to help their spouse/parent. Some urge their family member to pursue justice and proceed with the judicial process. It facilitates the older person's decision to move ahead. In some situations, however, family members may interfere and aggravate things, reprimanding or blaming the parent for the crime and may suggest a caregiver or even a nursing home placement as a solution. If children and grandchildren are opposed to proceeding, the older person is often too fearful to challenge them, being concerned about having their approval and support. In this context, they will refuse to file police reports or will not follow up with the criminal justice system process if a police report is made. The police and others in the judicial system rarely are of assistance in these circumstances.

Some crimes and abuse are perpetrated by family members themselves. Elder parents residing with an adult child on whom they are dependent are willing to take large amounts of psychological, financial, and even physical abuse without pressing charges. Some may be mentally ill and fearful of being in any environment away from their relative.

Mrs. M. N. is an 82-year-old woman with a long history of chronic schizophrenia, paranoid type. She required periodic hospitalizations. Her husband was a wonderful provider and protector. When he died suddenly, he left her with a seven-figure estate. Her son took her into his home, and then obtained power of attorney. Over the next few years he bought expensive cars and jewelry for girlfriends, and personal investments for himself which failed. Eventually a social agency was contacted to provide companionship when the son was away. Staff became aware that there was a problem, but by then the estate had been squandered. They contacted the State's Attorney and subsequently the son was imprisoned, and the mother was placed in a nursing home.

Mrs. O. P. was 77 and her son 45. They lived together in an apartment. The son had a history of drug and alcohol use. He had been in several treatment programs but would not complete them. The landlord asked them to move because of his uncontrolled outbursts. They moved to another apartment. The son was verbally and physically abusive to her. The police were frequently called to intercede. The police would arrest him, but she would have him released. The mother felt guilty about prosecuting, but the last occurrence was so devastating that she filed a complaint and followed through. Once again, the alleged offender denied everything, even when shown pictures of his mother's injuries (bruises to face, arms, back, chest, and a black eye). She had been less seriously hurt on numerous occurrences. Finally, the court system took over. The remedies that the ASA, PD, and judge agreed to were: (1) keep him in jail for a period of time so that he could receive treatment; and (2) that his release from jail be conditioned only on his completing the entire treatment plan.

The mother still wonders if she did the "right" thing. The authors had to educate her to the fact that she was a crime victim and under constant stress and fear as to what would happen the next time he lost control. The CVWAP prepares the older person for each court hearing, works with the ASA (who is kind, thorough, and tough), and the PD who realized the ongoing pattern. There is no one else who will assume this function. The mother keeps in touch with the program and advises of any changes in court dates. So far, staff have made most court dates because she needs advocacy and support. At the last court date, the son began looking better. The judge did not release him because he hadn't completed the rehab plan. This domestic violence case continues and demonstrates police, judge(s), ASA, and PD all collaborating effectively to protect the older person.

Not all victims of family abuse are women.

In one case the victim was a 66-year-old man, a widower who had remarried a woman in her 30's. Everything seemed fine for a while, until he retired. They subsequently became verbally abusive with each other, which proceeded to physical and financial abuse by the wife. Both parties did not want police intervention. The wife refused services, but the husband agreed to counseling.

One day he appeared at the CVWAP with injuries to his face, shoulder, arms, and hands. The authors assisted him in filing a police report, and a nurse was called to examine his injuries. He continues his counseling with a social worker. The authors also prepared him for court. He was hesitant about testifying and the authors had to convince him that it was necessary. The ASA requested an order of protection for him which was granted by the judge. The wife moved out, and eventually they were divorced. He would not pursue the financial abuse charges. However, his emotional state improved, and he believes he received justice.

Conclusions

Thus, with the rapid growth of older people imminent, particularly the old-old, there is an anticipation of a substantial increase in the number of crimes perpetrated against older people, as well as an increase in older criminals. For victims, while creative programs initiated by and with police and social service agencies allow a better level of intervention for older crime victims, the system is lacking in many ways. The process is a long one and doesn't factor in the impact of the judicial system on the older victim. Many elders suffer from psychiatric illness or self-esteem problems accentuated by the crimes which interfere with their effectiveness as witnesses and for which they receive minimal or no help. Sophistication of lawyers and judges on the needs of the older victim varies, and at worse, results in a dropped case with profound psychological and financial ramifications for the older victim. For non-English-speaking ethnic minorities and the very old, the system itself may feel as threatening as the crime. Their reluctance to pursue justice allows the perpetrator to remain at-large and free to continue unlawful and damaging activities. The justice system must focus on better education for professionals in the judicial arenas, as well as a pragmatic and helpful policy to assist the very old.

Specific Conclusions and Recommendations

1.   The elder crime victim is often frustrated by the complexity, attitudes, and pace of the criminal justice system. Sometimes they feel that they are more on trial than the perpetrator of the crime. A lack of rapport with police, attorneys, or judges often results in dropped cases because of a belief that they will never get justice here. The rotation of attorneys and judges also are a hindrance to successfully completed cases.

2.   Elders are often hesitant to report crimes. This may be especially true in the case of elder abuse. However, even when the perpe-

trator is external, the victim may be embarrassed and afraid to report crimes for fear of repercussions, as well as embarrassment in front of the family.

3. It is critical to be aware of sensory deficits and other medical problems when they exist and to adjust the proceedings and interventions accordingly.

4. Recommendations:

a. Courtrooms should establish hours geared to serving older people. This would include community courts which are easier to get to, thereby decreasing physical and fatigue factors.

b. There is a need for educational programs which begin in law school regarding the special needs and problems of older adults. There is often the feeling that defendants receive better legal services than the victims, which also discourages prosecution. The role of impatience is especially important to understand. Additional training is advisable for police, lawyers, judges, and other court personnel. This should result in better informed and thus more effective interventions.

References

Cohen, D., Llorente, M., & Eisdorfer, C. (1998). Homicide-suicide in older persons. *American Journal of Psychiatry, 155*(3), 390–396.

Hough, J. M., & Mayhew, P. (1983). *The British Crime Survey: First report.* London: HMSO.

Hucker, S. J., & Ben-Aron, M. H. (1984). Violent elderly offenders—A comparative study. In W. Wilbanks & P. K. H. Kim (Eds.), *Elderly criminals* (pp. 69–81). New York: Lanham.

Taylor, P. J., & Parrott, J. M. (1988). Elderly offenders: A study of age-related factors among custodially remanded prisioners. *British Journal of Psychiatry, 152,* 340–346.

U.S. Department of Justice, Office of Justice Programs, Bureau of Justice Statistics. (1994). *Elderly crime victims: National Crime Victimization Survey* [NCJ-147002]. Washington, DC: U.S. Department of Justice.

U.S. Department of Justice, Bureau of Justice Statistics. (2000). *Criminal victimization in the United States, 1997* [NCJ-174446, p. 175). Washington, DC: U.S. Department of Justice.

Suggested Readings

Aday, R. H. (1989). *Crime and the elderly: An annotated bibliography.* New York: Greenwood Press.

Alston, L. (1986). *Crime and older Americans.* Springfield, IL: Charles C Thomas.

Fattah, E. A., & Sacco, V. F. (1989). *Crime and victimization of the elderly.* New York: Springer-Verlag.

Jacoby, R., & Oppenheimer, C. (Eds.). (1991). *Psychiatry in the elderly.* Oxford: Oxford University Press.

McCarthy, B., & Langworthy, R. (Eds.). (1988). *Older offenders: Perspectives in criminology and criminal justice.* New York: Praeger.

Newman, E., Newman, D., Gerwitz, M., & Associates. (1984). *Elderly criminals.* Cambridge, MA: Oelgeschlager, Gunn, and Hain.

Taylor, P. J. (1998). Forensic psychiatry. *British Journal of Psychiatry, 153,* 211–278.

Chapter 6

The Older Eyewitness

A. Daniel Yarmey

Imagine the following scenario: a 75-year-old-woman robbed of her purse in broad daylight just after she leaves a bank tells the police:

> They stole my bank book, my credit cards, everything. Even my wrestling tickets. I lost $100 and change. It happened before I knew it. One guy came up behind me. I didn't see his face, but he was dark-skinned, 6' tall, skinny, about 17 years of age wearing a blue sweater with a big maple leaf crest. The other guy was running towards me. He was a short, fat, White kid, about 16 years old, and had a little thin moustache. He was wearing a black sweater and dirty blue jeans. I'll never forget his face.

The purpose of this chapter is to examine those factors beyond common knowledge about which the police, other legal officials, and potential jurors should be aware in their evaluation of the eyewitness testimony of older men and women (see Yarmey & Jones, 1982). First, what factors influence the accuracy and confidence of eyewitness recall and identification by older men and women? Second, is the eyewitness testimony of older persons given the same weight by the public (potential jurors) as that given the testimony of young and middle-aged adults?

Eyewitness testimony given at trial without any other corroborating evidence can lead to the conviction of an accused person in most jurisdictions. A simple in-court statement, such as, "I recognize the man in the blue suit sitting over there as the man who robbed me," can have a powerful effect on the trier of fact. Eyewitness testimony, next to an actual confession, has been described as the most incriminating evidence that can be introduced against a defendant (Brandon & Davies, 1973). When such reports are correct, they properly contribute to the conviction and appropriate punishment of dangerous felons. However, false identifications from lineups and photospreads are responsible for more convictions of innocent persons than all other causes combined (Huff, Rattner, & Sagarin, 1986).

The scientific investigation of eyewitness testimony can be traced back to the beginning of the 20th century (Sporer, 1982). Although the courts have been interested for several decades in what psychology has to offer the legal process, it wasn't until the late 1970s that social/cognitive psychologists gave serious attention to the legal applications of the scientific study of memory (Loftus, 1979; Yarmey, 1979). Eyewitness memory research has been conducted in laboratory settings, in simulated crime situations, in naturalistic field situations, and through archival analysis of police records (Bull & Carson, 1995). The results of this research have important implications for how the police and the courts understand the validity and reliability of eyewitness evidence (e.g., Cutler & Penrod, 1995; Memon, Vrij, & Bull, 1998; Ross, Read, & Toglia, 1994; Sporer, Malpass, & Koehnken, 1996; Thompson et al., 1998; Yarmey, 1990). As part of this research endeavor, there is a growing but still limited literature on the capabilities of older eyewitnesses (Bornstein, 1995; Yarmey, 1984a, 1996). As this chapter will show, older adults compared to young adults are less reliable eyewitnesses, on average, in selected situations. This conclusion, however, must be qualified by the fact that the cognitive and social processes that accompany adult aging, when applied to comparisons of performance of younger and older eyewitnesses, have not been extensively examined. Furthermore, the accuracy and credibility of reports from some older persons can be equal to or superior to some younger persons.

Eyewitness Memory

It is generally agreed that eyewitness memory is best understood in terms of three theoretical stages. First, there is the observation or acquisition stage in which information is perceived and encoded as memorial representations. Second, there is the retention or storage stage. This is the period of time that passes between the acquisition of selected information and its recollection. Third, there is the retrieval or narration stage in which an individual recalls and/or recognizes stored information. The accuracy and completeness of memory reports are influenced by factors that occur at any one or more of the three stages. Information cannot be accurately retrieved if it was not perceived. Information that is misperceived during the initial observation stage also will be incorrectly remembered. Information can be forgotten, altered, or supplemented by factors that occur during the retention stage. Finally, accurate and complete information may be available in memory but may not be accessible because of inappropriate questioning techniques.

Contrary to the opinion of many lay persons and officers of the court, personal experiences of an event are not recorded in memory similar to the workings of a videotape recorder (Loftus, 1979). Rather, memory is constructed and reconstructed from available bits and pieces of information into narrative wholes. Sometimes these constructions are reproduced relatively accurately, but they also can be faulty and incomplete. Witnesses may then fill in gaps and omissions in memory through the use of inferences about what "probably" must have happened. The challenge that faces the court is to distinguish between accurately remembered facts, and facts that are inferred or fabricated for whatever reasons.

Witness Characteristics and Witnessing Situations

Sensory and Perceptual Factors

When a crime occurs, men and women of all ages, cognitive skills, and intelligence levels, and each with his or her own unique personalities, are potential witnesses. Police officers and prosecutors do not have the luxury of selecting only those persons as witnesses who have superior observational abilities and communication skills. Whether or not witnesses are attentive, optimally aroused, and so on, are factors of potential importance to the eventual quality and quantity of eyewitness reports. The accuracy of these reports, however, can only be estimated after the fact, and analyzed in terms of average or group responses rather than specific individual behaviors. There is no typical witness just as there is no typical crime situation (Bekerian, 1993). Given this caveat, what can we say about the sensory and cognitive characteristics of the older eyewitness when a crime or accident is first observed?

As people age, their ability to perceive everyday life events is limited by gradual and insidious changes in sensory efficiency. In contrast to younger witnesses, older witnesses starting around the age of 50 years may fail to detect an event or make fine discriminations of details (Corso, 1981). Older witnesses may incorrectly perceive color, shape, depth, fine detail, or movement because of physical changes in vision, for example, increased rigidity of the iris and lens, increased opacity of the lens (Ivy, MacLeod, Petit, & Markus, 1992; Verrillo & Verrillo, 1985). Cataracts (or lens clouding) are present in approximately 25% of 70-year-olds (Corso, 1981). Older witnesses who experience a sudden change in illumination may have more difficulty during the adaptation period in seeing both central and peripheral events (Fozard, 1990). With aging the visual field shrinks, resulting in less sensitivity to peripheral signals. Rapid declines in both visual acuity and depth perception often occur between the ages of 60 and 80 years (Anderson & Palmore, 1974). With advanced age, hearing loss also is common, making it difficult in some circumstances for older persons to understand speech and conversations, especially when sounds are distorted by background noise or poor acoustics (Olsho, Harkins, & Lenhardt, 1985; Timm, 1985).

The perception of an event, however, is not dependent solely on receptor deficits. Some older persons fail to attend and properly comprehend an event because of cognitive changes that accompany adult aging (see Craik & Salthouse, 1992). Older persons are particularly handicapped when they must divide their attention between two or more tasks (Hartley, 1992). Research evidence suggests that age-related differences in short-term memory performance for adults up to their fifties compared with persons in their sixties and seventies is less than 10%, on average (Kausler, 1994). Although total recall performance has been found to decline significantly across research participants who ranged in age from 20 to 86 years, Delbecq-Derouesne and Beauvois (1989) found only a slight decline in short-term memory scores with the ratio of recall scores for the youngest adults to the oldest adults being 0.93. In contrast, a substantial age-related deficit in long-term memory scores was found with the oldest adult-young adult ratio being only 0.36. These findings support the conclusion that age-related differences in short-term memory are slight or nonexistent (Craik & Jennings, 1992).

It would be expected that if older adults, in contrast to young adults, acquire information more poorly, they would be inferior in subsequent event recall and person identification. The extent of impairment depends, of course, upon the individuals involved, and the particular situational factors present in any crime or accident. Senior citizens, in contrast to young adults, are judged more severely for identical everyday memory failures by younger persons (Erber & Rothberg, 1991). Because most crimes, especially those perpetrated by professionals, are short in duration, unexpected, committed in poorly lit conditions, and done in such a way as to minimize attention being focussed on the act or person, these factors have obvious implications for the accuracy of eyewitness testimony for all age groups.

Duration of Observation and Duration Estimation

The amount of time available for witnessing an event and a perpetrator determines the accuracy and completeness of memory performance. Short observation periods and rapidly changing events are particularly detrimental to older witnesses who require time to attend to fine visual details, and time to organize and integrate information (Pezdek, 1987). Moreover, when attention is focused on highly salient stimuli, such as a weapon, there is less time to attend to perpetrator characteristics and actions. However, the effects of weapon focus on subsequent identification performance are similar for both younger and older adult witnesses (O'Rourke, Penrod, Cutler, & Stuve, 1989).

In criminal situations witnesses's duration estimates of events often are important to the court because they permit placing of incidents into general and specific periods of time. Witnesses' credibility may be enhanced when they report that they spent a relatively long time examining the face and actions of the perpetrator. Older adults generally acknowledge that they would not be good eyewitnesses, on average (Yarmey & Jones, 1982), but believe that their credibility as witnesses depends upon how active and how powerful they appear (Yarmey, 1984b). In order to test the relationship between the accuracy of duration estimations and age of witnesses, Yarmey and Yarmey (1997) conducted a naturalistic field study. Two minutes after being stopped on the street by a young woman and engaged in a 15-second conversation, 603 citizens between the ages of 18 and 65 years old were asked to estimate the duration of their conversation. Consistent with other investigations (Loftus, Schooler, Boone, & Kline, 1987), women gave significantly longer overestimations (mean = 50.48 sec.) than did men (mean = 41.77 sec.). No significant relationship was found between age of witnesses and duration estimations. Men proved to be significantly more confident in the accuracy of their estimation than women, but the age of witnesses was not related to confidence in estimation. Over a hundred years ago, William James (1892) stated that the same space of time appears shorter as we grow older. However, James was referring to the appreciation of days, months, and years, rather than to seconds or minutes. It is likely that persons under and over the age of 65 judge the duration of short events in a similar manner (Fraisse, 1963).

Distance and Speed

Reports based on memory for distance between objects yield increasing underestimations with increasing distance (Radvansky, Carlson-Radvansky, & Irwin, 1995). Although young adults are superior to older adults in estimating both speed and distance (Storie, 1977), perceptual estimates in judging the speed of an oncoming vehicle are poor in an absolute sense for people of all ages. Older persons (mean age = 65) relative to younger persons (mean age = 22) tend to overestimate at lower speeds (15 mph), and underestimate at higher speeds (55 mph) (Scialfa, Guzy, Leibowitz, Garvey, & Tyrell, 1991).

Eyewitness Descriptions

Regardless of age, witnesses' descriptions of culprits, even from well-lit situations, are usually vague and general and should be accepted with caution (Yarmey, 1986). With few exceptions, accuracy of person descriptions declines with longer retention intervals (Flin, Boon, Knox, & Bull, 1992). Accuracy of descriptions depends, in part, upon the motivation, familiarity, expectations, and so on, of the eyewitness. Both older (mean age = 73) and younger (mean age = 20) persons are likely to make more recall errors when they witness a crime in an unfamiliar setting than in a familiar setting (Jung, Brimacombe, & Garrioch, 1998). However, although older and younger witnesses focus on many of the same central features of an event, they do not equally recall fine details of the perpetrator or the situation. Our studies of simulated crimes indicate that young adults (mean age = 21) were significantly superior to older adults (mean age = 70) in accuracy of recall for assailant characteristics, victim characteristics, environmental details, and for details of actions (Yarmey, 1982; Yarmey & Kent, 1980; Yarmey, Jones, & Rashid, 1984). When the results of these three studies are averaged, young adults were 20% more accurate in free recall, 13% more accurate in cued recall, and 15% more complete in their descriptions of the suspect. Similar differences in averaged performance were found between younger and older adults in recall of victim characteristics and situational factors (Yarmey, 1984b).

Qualitative differences in recall as a function of age of eyewitnesses also occur. In a study of memory for a simulated sexual assault (Yarmey et al., 1984), 80% of young witnesses ($n = 128$, mean age = 21) recalled the perpetrator carrying a knife in his hand, but only 20% of older witnesses ($n = 128$, mean age = 71) reported the weapon. Seventy-five percent of the older witnesses also had difficulty in discriminating a young girl (age 11) from a young boy, even though the girl wore her hair in a long pony tail. None of the young witnesses misidentified the girl as a boy. This study also suggested that older and younger witnesses may show differences in recall because of different interpretations related to the appearance of the assailant. That is, young witnesses recalled more details of the incident when the suspect had a well-dressed demeanor, whereas older witnesses remembered more information when the suspect had a poorly dressed demeanor. Interestingly, both younger and older men and women gave less complete descriptions of the suspect and situational context when the female victim dressed and acted in a more provocative manner than in a demure manner.

Witnesses typically give police few descriptors of the perpetrator, reporting on average between eight and ten characteristics (Tollestrup, Turtle, & Yuille, 1994; van Koppen & Lochun, 1997). Unfortunately, the more descriptors witnesses give, the less accurate and useful their reports become (Wells, 1985). Furthermore, the accuracy of eyewitnesses' descriptions of a perpetrator is not related to identification accuracy in a lineup (Pigott, Brigham, & Bothwell, 1990). There is general agreement in the research literature that witnesses' free descriptions of some suspects' characteristics, such as sex, hair color, and race, are relatively accurate (van Koppen & Lochun, 1997; Yarmey & Yarmey, 1997). However, recall of other characteristics such as age, height, and weight are highly error-prone (Flin & Shepherd, 1986; Yuille & Cutshall, 1986). Older witnesses, in contrast to younger witnesses, have been found to describe even fewer characteristics and are less accurate in recall for both physical characteristics and clothing characteristics (Brimacombe, Quinton, Nance, & Garrioch, 1997; van Koppen & Lochun, 1997).

Eyewitness memory studies show that men and women, regardless of age, generally are similar in memory performance. When sex differences are found, they are probably attributable to attention and gender-related information, and it is these differences which influence what people remember best (Loftus, Banaji, Schooler, & Foster, 1987). Because color blindness is 10 times more frequently found in males than females (Hurvich, 1981), one would expect this deficiency to influence eyewitness recall of color-related characteristics. Normal aging after age 50 also affects color vision, with blues looking darker and more readily confused with greens. Such changes in vision could account for certain types of errors in recall, such as older persons' poorer performance relative to young and middle-aged persons in describing hair color and eye color of a perpetrator (Yarmey, 1993).

In a study involving nearly 2000 men and women who visited a science museum and were shown a brief film clip of an assault, older women over 65 years of age proved significantly superior to their male counterparts in accuracy of recall. This study showed that recall performance improved from age 5 to 10 years up to the 26 to 35-year-old range and then began to fall, with the youngest and oldest age groups showing the poorest performance, especially older males

(Loftus, Levidow, & Duensing, 1992). Why older males proved inferior in memory in this study is uncertain.

Because most criminals are adolescent or young adults, research studies typically use young adults as perpetrators. It is reasonable to assume, because of their preferential interest, familiarity, and contact with older than younger individuals (Pratt & Norris, 1994), that memory of older adults would be better when describing a suspect closer to their own age group. List (1986) found that older adults (mean age = 68) shown a videotape of a shoplifting incident, portrayed by either a young adult woman or a middle-aged woman, were superior in memory for information relevant to the older actress than the younger actress. This finding could not be attributed to differential memorability of the two actresses. List (1986) suggested that the older adults best remembered the older shoplifter because she was more relevant to themselves, which would lead to more elaborate cognitive processing, and to higher memorability of this information.

Identification from Lineups and Photospreads

Properly constructed and administered, live lineups or photo arrays can be valid tests of memory processes. Lineup identifications are considered important for evidentiary purposes insofar as they reveal information that was not available in witnesses' recall. However, the U.S. Supreme Court in *U.S. v. Wade* (1967) stated that "The trial which might determine the accused's fate may well be not in court but at the pretrial confrontation." Eyewitness identification has been described in Britain as the Achilles heel of the criminal justice system (Devlin, 1976).

Recognition memory performance of older persons is more comparable to that of younger persons in contrast to other memory tasks, such as free recall and cued recall (Craik, Anderson, Kerr, & Li, 1995). However, traditional laboratory studies of recognition memory for faces still tend to show a slight but steady decline in performance with increased age (Bartlett, 1993). Some research on lineup identification with laboratory simulations of crimes has shown older witnesses (mean age = 73) and younger witnesses (mean age = 19) to be similar in performance (hit scores) in suspect-present lineups (Yarmey & Kent, 1980). However, older witnesses in contrast to younger witnesses do make significantly more false identifications in suspect-absent lineups (Yarmey et al., 1984). Innocent bystanders present at the scene of a crime also are at more risk of being falsely identified by older witnesses than by younger witnesses, especially if the innocent bystander has a "criminalistic" demeanor (Yarmey et al., 1984). The fact that older participants make significantly more false alarms than their younger counterparts has important implications for the reliability of eyewitness testimony. Although O'Rourke et al. (1989) found that witnesses 18 to 74 years of age differed in eyewitness identification, with a significant decline in performance after age 50, lineup identifications by older and younger witnesses were not differentially influenced by such factors as a robber's disguise, suggestive lineup instructions, lineup cues, or weapon presence.

One highly robust finding associated with identification accuracy is the cross-racial effect. The race of the witness and the race of the culprit when considered alone do not contribute much to identification accuracy (Cutler & Penrod, 1995). However, when both factors are involved in a culprit–witness confrontation, an interesting interaction effect emerges. Own-race recognitions are more accurate than other-race identifications (Bothwell, Brigham, & Malpass, 1989; Shapiro & Penrod, 1986). Brigham and Williamson (1979) have shown that older Afro-American participants demonstrated an own-race recognition memory bias, but older Whites did not (mean age = 72). Although there are several possible hypotheses underlying this effect, such as the role of differential familiarity and contact, prejudice or hostility, and so forth, none of these theories is recognized as providing a definitive explanation for the cross-racial effect at this time (Chance & Goldstein, 1996).

In addition to face identifications, witnesses may be asked to make speaker identifications for crimes committed in darkness, wearing of a mask or other facial disguise, obscene telephone calls, and so on (Yarmey, 1995). Because hearing loss is common with advanced age, especially for high frequency sounds, it would be expected that voice identification would show a steady decline with increasing age. With the exception of a study by Bull and Clifford (1984), who found that young adults between the ages of 21 and 40 were superior in voice-recognition accuracy to those over 40, there is no research on the older "earwitness." Research does indicate, however, that older adults in contrast to young adults have difficulty in remembering the source of their vocal information, such as whether they said some words or had imagined saying these words, and whether one person or another person had said some particular words (Hashtroudi, Johnson, & Chrosniak, 1989).

It is clear that research is needed to determine if there are procedures which can reliably improve the older eyewitnesses' memory without being leading or suggestive (Bornstein, 1995). It is probable that the older witnesses' descriptive recall would be facilitated by structured and supportive interview procedures (see discussion below). Because older witnesses are prone to make false identifications, it is possible that presenting photographs or lineup candidates one person at a time in a sequential manner, rather than in a many-person simultaneous procedure, would facilitate performance (Wells & Seelau, 1995). Such a procedure may lessen the workload on attentional resources and task demands on working memory of the older witness. However, a recent study by Searcy, Bartlett, and Memon (1998) indicated that although sequential presentations of lineup members reduced the false alarm rate relative to a simultaneous presentation, it did not disproportionately facilitate older witnesses' identification ability over their younger counterparts.

Older Eyewitnesses' Confidence in Their Memory

Older witnesses may or may not be different from younger witnesses in their confidence in lineup identifications. In contrast to my own research (see Yarmey, 1984b) which showed that older witnesses are less confident about their identifications than are younger witnesses, O'Rourke et al. (1989) and Adams-Price (1992) failed to find any significant age-related differences in confidence and accuracy of identifications. Similarly, Scogin, Calhoon, and D'Errico (1994) failed to find any significant confidence and accuracy correlations for young (ages 18 to 35, mean = 21), young-old (ages 59 to 74, mean = 68) and old-old eyewitnesses (ages 75 to 94, mean = 81). Recall performance declined across age groups but all groups performed poorly on lineup identifications. It is important to note that confidence judgments are highly malleable, regardless of age. Witnesses' confidence in the accuracy of their identification can be influenced by information they acquire after the crime, such as feedback and pretrial preparation (Wells, 1993; Wells & Bradfield, in press).

Senior citizens hold highly positive attitudes toward the police in North America (Sundeen & Mathieu, 1976; Yarmey, 1984b). Elders also are generally positive toward trial judges, prosecutors, and defense lawyers, but indicate difficulty in understanding defense lawyers (Yarmey, 1984b). These results suggest that older witnesses as a group are supportive of the key participants in the criminal justice system and would cooperate with them, if necessary (Yarmey, 1984b). However, if older persons are susceptible to pleasing authorities, or have been coached and given undue social support throughout the investigation, it is possible that their stated confidence at trial in having made an accurate identification could be untrustworthy.

Interviewing the Older Witness

As police are not present when most crimes occur, they are dependent on victims and bystander witnesses for information leading to the arrest and conviction of guilty persons. In an attempt to discover historical truths of who did what, where, when, how, and why, investigative interviews, when properly conducted, elicit facts without biasing or influencing the witness. The major purpose of investigative interviews is to obtain information that is as accurate, detailed, and complete as possible based upon witnesses' memory, while controlling those contextual or situational factors than can influence the validity of reports. Because memory is not like a video recorder, witnesses enter an interview situation with limited memorial information about a target event. Consequently, it is understandable why interview data are usually incomplete. Furthermore, some relevant information may be suppressed or not reported because it may be too embarrassing to describe, or may be assumed to be unimportant (Koehnken, 1995).

One way to improve eyewitnesses' recall would be to structure the investigative interview in an interviewee-friendly, memory-enhancing manner, such as the cognitive interview (Fisher, 1995; Fisher & Geiselman, 1992; Memon, Wark, Holley, Bull, & Koehnken, 1997). The cognitive interview is based on the theoretical principle that a memory is composed of a collection of features or details. The effectiveness of retrieval cues is related to the amount of overlap of the cue with the encoded witnessed event. Furthermore, there are several retrieval paths to memory for an event and information not accessible with one technique may be accessible with another. Following these principles of memory, witnesses are told: (1) to mentally reconstruct the physical and personal contexts that existed at the time of the witnessed event; (2) to report everything in detail without screening information that may be considered irrelevant or for which there is only partial memory; (3) to recall the event in different orders; and (4) to recall from a variety of different perspectives. Mello and Fisher (1996) found that recall for a videotape of a simulated crime by highly educated older witnesses (65 to 80) in contrast to educated younger witnesses (18 to 35) was significantly better when interviewed with the cognitive interview. Furthermore, the cognitive interview elicited significantly more information than did a standard interview for all witnesses.

Credibility of the Older Witness

There have been several recent studies that have examined how people, and in particular, mock jurors, perceive the credibility of older witnesses. The fact that jurors are influenced by characteristics of victims and witnesses is not extraordinary. Attitudes toward older adults are relatively more negative than attitudes toward younger and middle-aged adults (Slotterback & Saarnio, 1996). Increased negativity toward older adults appears to be associated with physical changes that occur in the process of aging, rather than to global assessments of supposed deficiencies. It is the process of aging, such as being perceived as more fragile, hard of hearing, slow moving, wrinkled, and so forth, that is judged negatively, not just old age. However, Slotterback and Saarnio (1996, p. 568) conclude that "negativity does not extend to all aspects of older adults nor will it be observed in all situations."

In the specific context of judging "the elderly as witnesses in court" the general public, police, lawyers, probation officers, and older persons differ in their perceptions of the older witness (Yarmey, 1984b). Yarmey found that all of the above groups ($n = 20$ in each group) were positive in general in their evaluative judgments of the older witness, with older participants (mean age = 71 years) most positive among all groups. Older participants indicated that older witnesses' evaluative worth (good–bad, honest–dishonest, worthless–valuable) was associated with their perceived activity (passive–active, fast–slow, sharp–dull) and potency (strong–weak, large–small, rugged–delicate), but not with their understandability (mysterious–understandable, predictable–unpredictable, simple–complicated). Police officers (mean age = 38), in contrast to the other groups, also were highly appreciative of the evaluative worth of the older witness. Police officers, lawyers (mean age = 48), and probation officers (mean age = 42) did not differ in their perceptions of the rated potency, activity, and understandability of the older witness. The general public (mean age = 32), in contrast, perceived the older witness as reliably less potent and less active. The public's evaluative ratings of the older witness were highly correlated with their ratings of understandability. Because the members of the general public in this study all qualified as potential jurors, it could be argued that jurors' trust in the testimony of the older witness is likely to be related to their understanding of older people. This study also showed that older adults judged prosecutors as more potent and more understandable than defense attorneys. Evaluations of trial judges and defense attorneys were reliably related to their perceived potency and understandability, whereas evaluations of prosecutors were correlated only with their perceived understandability. The activity of trial judges, prosecutors, and defense lawyers contributed very little to the older persons' evaluations of these groups. However, older persons' judged evaluative worth of these officers of the court was related to their understandability and perceived power.

Mock jurors are less likely to find a defendant guilty if an older person has been victimized and no other witnesses are present to corroborate his or her testimony (London, Nunez, & Jensen, 1998). When elders behave in ways that match the stereotype, they are treated more negatively than younger adults. However, when older persons contradict the stereotype and, for example, appear to be competent witnesses, there is a favorability bias over that of either their peers, or other young adults (Nightingale, 1992). Some older persons, particularly women, the uneducated, and individuals of low socioeconomic status, may be judged negatively for their speech styles. The use of powerless speech style in court, for example, frequent use of intensifiers (so, very), hedges (e.g., kinda, I think, I guess), hesitation forms (e.g., uh, well, you know), gestures, questioning forms (e.g., the use of rising question intonation in declarative contexts), and polite forms (e.g., sir, please, thank you), generally lowers witness credibility (Erickson, Lind, Johnson, & O'Barr, 1978). Also, if an older witness is difficult to understand as reflected by a quiet voice, a slow rate of speaking, or fragmented, weak speech style, he or she is likely to be perceived as having relatively low credibility (Brimacombe et al., 1997).

Studies of mock jurors' perceptions of older witnesses suggest that jurors probably enter the courtroom believing that older witnesses will be less accurate in their eyewitness memory than younger adults, but not any less honest than their younger counterparts (Brimacombe et al., 1997; Ross, Dunning, Toglia, & Ceci, 1989; Ross, Dunning, Toglia, & Ceci, 1990; Yarmey, 1984b). However, Brimacombe et al. (1997) also found that older persons are perceived to be less honest when they provide low-quality testimony. They suggest that when young adults evaluate the actual testimony of older adults, their judgments are not biased by negative stereotypes of seniors' eyewitness capabilities, but rather, by their weaker sounding testimony relative to younger adults. In other words, it is what the older (and younger) witness says, and how he or she says it, rather than any age-related stereotypes that determine the assessment of credibility.

Conclusions

Older adults, in contrast to young adults, have poorer vision and hearing, on average, which may impair eyewitness recall and identification in some situations. The effects of aging appear to be more detrimental to the completeness and accuracy of eyewitness recall than to eyewitness identification. However, certain factors involved in eyewitness testimony, for example, the accuracy and confidence in retrospective estimation of durations, the effects of weapon focus on subsequent identification performance, etc., have been shown to have similar effects across younger and older witnesses. When supportive and facilitative interview procedures are employed, the testimony of older (and younger) eyewitnesses can be highly accurate and useful to the courts. A negative stereotype exists toward the older adult, and when older witnesses match the stereotype, they may be judged less credible by jurors than younger witnesses. However, our understanding of the older eyewitness is based on relatively few studies. Much more experimental research about different eyewitness issues and situations and the capabilities of older eyewitnesses and their perceived credibility by jurors across heterogenous populations is needed before more definitive conclusions can be drawn.

Acknowledgment

The research conducted for this chapter was supported by a grant from the Social Sciences and Humanities Research Council of Canada.

References

Adams-Price, C. (1992). Eyewitness memory and aging: Predictors of accuracy in recall and person recognition. *Psychology and Aging, 7*, 602–608.

Anderson, B., & Palmore, E. (1974). Longitudinal evaluation of ocular function. In E. Palmore (Ed.), *Normal aging II, Reports from the Duke longitudinal studies, 1970–1973* (pp. 24–32). Durham, NC: Duke University Press.

Bartlett, J. C. (1993). Limits on losses in face recognition. In J. Cerella, J. Rybash, W. Hoyer, & M. L. Commons (Eds.), *Adult information processing: Limits on loss* (pp. 351–379). Toronto: Academic Press.

Bekerian, D. A. (1993). In search of the typical eyewitness. *American Psychologist, 48*, 574–576.

Bornstein, B. H. (1995). Memory processes in elderly eyewitnesses: What we know and what we don't know. *Behavioral Sciences and the Law, 13*, 337–348.

Bothwell, R. K., Brigham, J. C., & Malpass, R. S. (1989). Cross-racial identification. *Personality and Social Psychology Bulletin, 15,* 19–25.

Brandon, R., & Davies, C. (1973). *Wrongful imprisonment.* London: Allen & Unwin.

Brigham, J. C., & Williamson, N. L. (1979). Cross-racial recognition and age: When you're over 60, do they still "all look alike?" *Personality and Social Psychology Bulletin, 5,* 218–222.

Brimacombe, C. A. E., Quinton, N., Nance, N., & Garrioch, L. (1997). Is age irrelevant? Perceptions of young and old adult eyewitnesses. *Law and Human Behavior, 21,* 619–634.

Bull, R., & Carson, D. (1995). *Handbook of psychology in legal contexts.* New York: Wiley.

Bull, R., & Clifford, B. R. (1984). Earwitness voice recognition accuracy. In G. L. Wells & E. F. Loftus (Eds.), *Eyewitness testimony: Psychological perspectives* (pp. 92–123). Cambridge, MA: Cambridge University Press.

Chance, J. E., & Goldstein, A. G. (1996). The other-race effect and eyewitness identification. In S. L. Sporer, R. S. Malpass, & G. Koehnken (Eds.), *Psychological issues in eyewitness identification* (pp. 153–176). Mahwah, NJ: Lawrence Erlbaum Associates.

Corso, J. F. (1981). *Aging sensory systems and perception.* New York: Praeger.

Craik, F. I. M., Anderson, N. D., Kerr, S. A., & Li, K. Z. H. (1995). Memory changes in normal ageing. In A. D. Baddeley, B. A. Wilson, & F. N. Watts (Eds.), *Handbook of memory disorders* (pp. 211–241). New York: Wiley.

Craik, F. I. M., & Jennings, J. M. (1992). Human memory. In F. I. M. Craik & T. A. Salthouse (Eds.), *Handbook of aging and cognition.* Hillsdale, NJ: Erlbaum.

Craik, F. I. M., & Salthouse, T. A. (Eds.). (1992). *The handbook of aging and cognition.* Hillsdale, NJ: Erlbaum.

Cutler, B. L., & Penrod, S. D. (1995). *Mistaken identification: The eyewitness, psychology, and the law.* Cambridge: Cambridge University Press.

Delbecq-Derouesne, J., & Beauvois, M. F. (1989). Memory processes and aging: A defect of automatic rather than controlled processes? *Archives of Gerontology and Geriatrics* (Suppl. 1), 121–150.

Devlin, Honourable Lord Patrick (Chair). (1976). *Report to the secretary of state for the Home Department of the departmental committee on evidence of identification in criminal cases.* London: Her Majesty's Stationery Office.

Erber, J. T., & Rothberg, S. T. (1991). Here's looking at you: The relative effect of age and attractiveness on judgments about memory failure. *Journal of Gerontology: Psychological Sciences, 46,* 116–123.

Erickson, B., Lind, E. A., Johnson, B. C., & O'Barr, W. M. (1978). Speech style and impression formation in court setting: The effects of "power" and "powerless" speech. *Journal of Experimental Social Psychology, 14*, 266–279.

Fisher, R. P. (1995). Interviewing victims and witnesses of crime. *Psychology, Public Policy, and Law, 1*, 732–764.

Fisher, R. P., & Geiselman, R. E. (1992). *Memory-enhancing techniques for investigative interviewing: The cognitive interview.* Springfield, IL: Charles C Thomas.

Flin, R. H., Boon, J., Knox, A., & Bull, R. (1992). The effect of a five-month delay on children's and adults' eyewitness memory. *British Journal of Psychology, 83*, 323–336.

Flin, R. H., & Shepherd, J. W. (1986). Tall stories: Eyewitnesses' ability to estimate height and weight characteristics. *Human Learning, 5*, 29–38.

Fozard, J. L. (1990). Vision and hearing in aging. In J. E. Birren & K. W. Schaie (Eds.), *Handbook of the psychology of aging* (3rd ed., pp. 50–83). New York: Academic Press.

Fraisse, P. (1963). *The psychology of time.* New York: Harper & Row.

Hartley, A. A. (1992). Attention. In F. I. M. Craik & T. A. Salthouse (Eds.), *Handbook of aging and cognition* (pp. 3–49). Hillsdale, NJ: Erlbaum.

Hashtroudi, S., Johnson, M. K., & Chrosniak, L. D. (1989). Aging and source monitoring. *Psychology and Aging, 4*, 106–112.

Huff, R., Rattner, A., & Sagarin, E. (1986). Guilty until proven innocent. *Crime and Delinquency, 32*, 518–544.

Hurvich, L. M. (1981). *Color vision.* Sunderland, MA: Sinauer Associates.

Ivy, G. O., MacLeod, C. M., Petit, T. L., & Markus, E. J. (1992). A physiological framework for perceptual and cognitive changes in aging. In F. I. M. Craik & T. A. Salthouse (Eds.), *Handbook of aging and cognition* (pp. 273–314). Hillsdale, NJ: Lawrence Erlbaum Associates.

James, W. (1892). *Psychology, briefer course.* New York: Holt.

Jung, S., Brimacombe, C. A. E., & Garrioch, L. J. (1998, March). "Your place or mine?" The influence of crime settings on eyewitness performance. Poster presented at the meeting of the American Psychology-Law Society, Redondo Beach, California.

Kausler, D. H. (1994). *Learning and memory in normal aging.* New York: Wiley.

Koehnken, G. (1995). Interviewing adults. In R. Bull & D. Carson (Eds.), *Handbook of psychology in legal contexts* (pp. 215–233). New York: Wiley.

List, J. A. (1986). Age and schematic differences in the reliability of eyewitness testimony. *Developmental Psychology, 22*, 50–57.

Loftus, E. F. (1979). *Eyewitness testimony.* Cambridge, MA: Harvard University Press.

Loftus, E. F., Banaji, M. R., Schooler, J. W., & Foster, R. A. (1987). Who remembers what? Gender differences in memory. *Michigan Quarterly Review, 26*, 64–85.

Loftus, E. F., Levidow, B., & Duensing, S. (1992). Who remembers best? Individual differences in memory for events that occurred in a science museum. *Applied Cognitive Psychology, 6*, 93–107.

Loftus, E. F., Schooler, J. W., Boone, S. M., & Kline, D. (1987). Time went by so slowly: Overestimation of event duration by males and females. *Applied Cognitive Psychology, 1*, 3–13.

London, K., Nunez, N., & Jensen, B. L. (1998, March). *Examining three elderly stereotypes in various courtroom roles.* Poster presented at the meeting of the American Psychology-Law Society meeting, Redondo Beach, CA.

Mello, E. W., & Fisher, R. P. (1996). Enhancing older adult eyewitness memory with the cognitive interview. *Applied Cognitive Psychology, 10*, 403–419.

Memon, A., Vrij, A., & Bull, R. (1998). *Psychology and law: Truthfulness, accuracy and credibility.* New York: McGraw-Hill.

Memon, A., Wark, L., Holley, A., Bull, R., & Koehnken, G. (1997). Eyewitness performance in cognitive and structured interviews. *Memory, 5*, 639–656.

Nightingale, N. N. (1992, March). *Attitudes toward the elderly in the courtroom: Under what circumstances is there an age favorability bias?* Poster presented at the meeting of the American Psychology-Law Society meeting, San Diego, CA.

Olsho, L. W., Harkins, S. W., & Lenhardt, M. L. (1985). Aging and the auditory system. In J. E. Birren & K. W. Schaie (Eds.), *Handbook of the psychology of aging* (2nd ed., pp. 332–377). New York: Van Nostrand Reinhold.

O'Rourke, T. E., Penrod, S. D., Cutler, B. L., & Stuve, T. E. (1989). The external validity of eyewitness identification research: Generalizing across subject populations. *Law and Human Behavior, 13*, 385–395.

Pezdek, K. (1987). Memory for pictures: A life-span study of the role of visual detail. *Child Development, 58*, 807–815.

Pigott, M. A., Brigham, J. C., & Bothwell, R. K. (1990). A field study on the relationship between quality of eyewitnesses' descriptions and identification accuracy. *Journal of Police Science and Administration, 17*, 84–88.

Pratt, M. W., & Norris, J. E. (1994). *The social psychology of aging.* Cambridge, MA: Blackwell.

Ross, D. F., Dunning, D., Toglia, M. P., & Ceci, S. (1989). Age stereotypes, communication modality, and mock jurors' perceptions of the child witness. In S. J. Ceci, D. F. Ross, & M. P. Toglia (Eds.), *Perspectives on children's testimony* (pp. 37–56). New York: Springer-Verlag.

Ross, D. F., Dunning, D., Toglia, M. P., & Ceci, S. J. (1990). The child in the eyes of the jury: Assessing mock jurors' perceptions of the child witness. *Law and Human Behavior, 14*, 5–23.

Ross, D. F., Read, J. D., & Toglia, M. P. (Eds.). (1994). *Adult eyewitness testimony: Current trends and developments.* Cambridge: Cambridge University Press.

Scogin, F., Calhoon, S. K., & D'Errico, M. (1994). Eyewitness confidence and accuracy among three age cohorts. *Journal of Applied Gerontology, 13,* 172–184.

Searcy, J. H., Bartlett, J. C., & Memon, A. (1998). Relationship of post-event narratives, lineup conditions and individual differences to false identification by young and older eyewitnesses. Unpublished manuscript. University of Texas at Dallas.

Shapiro, P. N., & Penrod, S. D. (1986). Meta-analysis of facial identification studies. *Psychological Bulletin, 100,* 139–156.

Slotterback, C. S., & Saarnio, D. A. (1996). Attitudes toward older adults reported by young adults: Variation based on attitudinal task and attribute categories. *Psychology and Aging, 11,* 563–571.

Sporer, S. L. (1982). A brief history of the psychology of testimony. *Current Psychological Reviews, 2,* 3230–340.

Sporer, S. L., Malpass, R. S., & Koehnken, G. (Eds.) (1996). *Psychological issues in eyewitness identification.* Mahwah, NJ: Lawrence Erlbaum Associates.

Sundeen, R. A., & Mathieu, J. T. (1976). The urban elderly: Environments of fear. In J. Goldsmith & S. S. Goldsmith (Eds.), *Crime and the elderly* (pp. 51–66). Toronto: Lexington Books.

Timm, H. W. (1985). Eyewitness recall and recognition by the elderly. *Victimology: An International Journal, 10,* 425–440.

Tollestrup, P. A., Turtle, J. W., & Yuille, J. C. (1994). Actual victims and witnesses to robbery and fraud: An archival analysis. In D. F. Ross, J. D. Read, & M. P. Toglia (Eds.), *Adult eyewitness testimony: Current trends and developments* (pp. 144–160). Cambridge: Cambridge University Press.

United States v. Wade, 388 U.S. 218, 1967.

van Koppen, P. J., & Lochun, S. K. (1997). Portraying perpetrators: The validity of offender descriptions by witnesses. *Law and Human Behavior, 21,* 661–685.

Verrillo, R. T., & Verrillo, V. (1985). Sensory and perceptual performance. In N. Charness (Ed.), *Aging and human performance* (pp. 1–46). New York: Wiley.

Wells, G. L. (1985). Verbal descriptions of faces from memory: Are they diagnostic of identification accuracy? *Journal of Applied Psychology, 70,* 619–626.

Wells, G. L. (1993). What do we know about eyewitness identification? *American Psychologist, 48,* 553–571.

Wells, G. L., & Bradfield, A. L. (in press). "Good, you identified the suspect:" Feedback to eyewitnesses distorts their reports of the witnessing experience. *Journal of Applied Psychology.*

Wells, G. L., & Seelau, L. (1995). Eyewitness identifications: Psychological research and legal policy on lineups. *Psychology, Public Policy and Law, 1,* 765–791.

Yarmey, A. D. (1979). *The psychology of eyewitness testimony.* New York: Free Press.

Yarmey, A. D. (1982). Eyewitness identification and stereotypes of criminals. In A. Trankell (Ed.), *Reconstructing the past: The role of psychologists in criminal trials* (pp. 205–225). Stockholm, Sweden: Norstedt & Soners.

Yarmey, A. D. (1984a). Age as a factor in eyewitness memory. In G. L. Wells & E. F. Loftus (Eds.), *Eyewitness testimony: Psychological perspectives* (pp. 142–154). New York: Cambridge University Press.

Yarmey, A. D. (1984b). Accuracy and credibility of the elderly witness. *Canadian Journal on Aging, 3,* 79–90.

Yarmey, A. D. (1986). Verbal, visual, and voice identification of a rape suspect under different levels of illumination. *Journal of Applied Psychology, 71,* 363–370.

Yarmey, A. D. (1990). *Understanding police and police work: Psychosocial issues.* New York: New York University Press.

Yarmey, A. D. (1993). Adult age and gender differences in eyewitness recall in field settings. *Journal of Applied Social Psychology, 23,* 1921–1932.

Yarmey, A. D. (1995). Earwitness speaker identification. *Psychology, Public Policy, and Law, 1,* 792–816.

Yarmey, A. D. (1996). The elderly witness. In S. L. Sporer, R. S. Malpass, & G. Koehnken (Eds.), *Psychological issues in eyewitness identification* (pp. 259–278). Mahwah, NJ: Lawrence Erlbaum Associates.

Yarmey, A. D., & Jones, H. T. (1982). Police awareness of the fallibility of eyewitness identification. *Canadian Police College Journal, 6,* 113–124.

Yarmey, A. D., Jones, H. T., & Rashid, S. (1984). Eyewitness memory of elderly and young adults. In D. J. Muller, D. E. Blackman, & A. J. Chapman (Eds.), *Psychology and law* (pp. 215–228). Chichester, UK: John Wiley & Sons.

Yarmey, A. D., & Kent, J. (1980). Eyewitness identification by elderly and young adults. *Law and Human Behavior, 4,* 359–371.

Yarmey, A. D., & Yarmey, M. J. (1997). Eyewitness recall and duration estimates in field settings. *Journal of Applied Social Psychology, 27,* 330–344.

Yuille, J. C., & Cutshall, J. L. (1986). A case study of eyewitness memory of a crime. *Journal of Applied Psychology, 71,* 292–301.

Suggested Readings

Radvansky, G. A., Carlson-Radvansky, L. A., & Irwin, D. E. (1995). Uncertainty in estimating distances from memory. *Memory and Cognition, 23,* 596–606.

Scialfa, C. T., Guzy, L. T., Leibowitz, H. W., Garvey, P. M., & Tyrrell, R. A. (1991). Age differences in estimating vehicle velocity. *Psychology and Aging, 6,* 60–66.

Storie, V. J. (1977). *Male and female car drivers: Differences observed in accidents* (Rep. 761). Crowthorne, Berkshire, England: TRRL. Cited in D. M. Thompson, Eyewitness testimony and identification tests, in N. Brewer & C. Wilson (Eds.) (1995). *Psychology and policing* (pp. 119–154). Hillsdale, NJ: Erlbaum.

Thompson, C. P., Herrmann, D. J., Read, J. D., Bruce, D., Payne, D. G., & Toglia, M. P. (Eds.) (1998). *Eyewitness memory: Theoretical and applied perspectives.* Mahwah, NJ: Lawrence Erlbaum Associates.

Chapter 7

The Suggestibility of Older Witnesses

Brian H. Bornstein, Christy J. Witt, Katie E. Cherry, and Edith Greene

R esearch focusing on the accuracy of older eyewitnesses has primarily addressed their ability to describe details of a crime and their ability to recognize the crime's perpetrator. In general, they tend to perform somewhat worse than younger adults with respect to describing a crime's details, and they are also more likely to make false identifications (Yarmey, 1996; this volume). However, the magnitude of any age difference depends in part on how memory is tested. For example, older witnesses are disadvantaged more on tasks requiring free recall than on those merely requiring recognition of either event details or faces (Bornstein, 1995).

One of the most heavily investigated factors regarding eyewitness memory is the effect of giving witnesses misleading information after an event has occurred (Loftus, 1992). Loftus and her colleagues have demonstrated that participants' reported memory for an event is negatively influenced by false information concerning the event that is suggested to them after the event has taken place (Loftus, Miller, & Burns, 1978). A typical misinformation effect experiment has participants witness some event, such as an automobile accident

(Loftus et al., 1978). In subsequent questioning about the event, misleading information is implied to some participants (e.g., that there was a stop sign rather than a yield sign). When tested on their recognition memory for the event, misled participants are more likely than control participants to identify the picture containing the misleading information. In other words, they are less likely to report what they actually saw, showing a greater tendency to report something that was merely suggested to them afterward.

Are older adult witnesses more suggestible than younger adults? There are reasons to suspect that they would be. The misinformation effect can be explained in terms of "source monitoring," which refers to judgments about the origin, or source, of information, as opposed to remembering the information itself (Johnson, Hashtroudi, & Lindsay, 1993). According to Lindsay and Johnson (1989), the misinformation effect reflects a failure of source monitoring. Specifically, an eyewitness acquires information about an event from two sources: by observing the event itself, and from subsequent suggestion. When witnesses then falsely remember a piece of information as part of the event, rather than as a suggestion, they have committed a source monitoring error (Belli, Lindsay, Gales, & McCarthy, 1994; Lindsay & Johnson, 1989).

The source-monitoring approach is particularly relevant to studying memory in older eyewitnesses because of the effect of aging on this specific type of memory task. Compared to young adults, older persons have difficulty remembering the source of information (e.g., Hashtroudi, Johnson, & Chrosniak, 1989; Schacter, Kaszniak, Kihlstrom, & Valdiserri, 1991). Cohen and Faulkner (1989) applied these findings to an eyewitness situation by showing participants a film of a kidnapping, and then presenting them with a narrative containing misleading details. When tested on their memory of the film, older participants (M age = 70) were significantly more likely than younger participants (M age = 35) to have been misled by suggestive information that was in the narrative. Loftus, Levidow, and Duensing (1992) also found a tendency for older participants (over age 65) to be more suggestible than younger adults when remembering details of a videotaped crime, which is consistent with older adults' impaired ability to discriminate between different sources of information.

However, a recent study by Coxon and Valentine (1997) suggests that older witnesses may not be at such a disadvantage. They compared the suggestibility of children (M age = 8), young adults (M age = 17), and older adults (M age = 70). All participants watched a videotape of a kidnapping, following which they answered a number of questions about the video. For half of the participants, four of these questions contained misleading information (e.g., they were asked "Which arm was the kidnapper wearing her watch on?" when she had not actually been wearing a watch). The other (control) participants did not receive any misleading information. All participants were then asked 20 specific questions about the video, four of which assessed whether they accepted the misinformation.

Overall memory performance (i.e., total questions answered correctly) was worse in both older adults and children than in young adults. However, on the questions testing for misinformation acceptance, older participants in the control condition answered an average of 66% of the questions correctly, as opposed to 50% in the misled condition; whereas the figures for the young adults were 77% (control) versus 52% (misled). Not only were the older adults not more suggestible than young adults, but they were actually *less* suggestible: They were the only age group not to show a statistically significant misinformation effect.

Individual differences in educational attainment and verbal ability among the older adult samples may have contributed to these discrepant findings. Previous research in the cognitive aging literature has demonstrated that the magnitude of age-related deficits in performance on a variety of cognitive tasks tends to be smaller for higher ability older people who are well educated and socially active, relative to their lower ability counterparts (Cherry & LeCompte, 1999; Cherry & Park, 1993). Coxon and Valentine's (1997) participants were relatively highly educated (M education = 14 yrs), whereas the participants used by Loftus et al. (1992) were much more diverse (Cohen & Faulkner, 1989, do not provide demographic data on their older group).

The present study compares younger and older adult witnesses' susceptibility to misinformation. Previous research on the misinformation effect has not measured the relationship between the effect and individuals' perceptions of their own memory abilities. Such perceptions, and general knowledge of one's own memory processes, are referred to as "metamemory." In order to examine the relationship between metamemory and the misinformation effect in the present study, participants also completed a questionnaire that assessed their perception of their memory functioning. Although older persons tend to perceive their memories as being faulty, the correlation between self-assessment of memory abilities and actual memory performance is relatively low (Zelinski, Gilewski, & Thompson, 1980). We therefore predicted that there would be a negligible relationship between participants' self-assessed memory functioning and whether or not they were susceptible to misinformation, for both younger and older adults.

Method

Participants

A total of 80 people participated in the study. There were 40 undergraduates from Louisiana State University (M age = 20.3, SD = 1.6, Mdn = 20.0) and 40 older adults (M age = 69.0, SD = 5.3, Mdn = 70.0). Of the younger adults, 32 were female and 8 were male; of the older adults, 26 were female and 14 were male. Younger adults participated in the study in exchange for class credit. Older adults were volunteers from the community and were paid \$5.00 for their participation.

Participants' education level was classified as high school, some college education, bachelor's degree, or post-graduate education. Nearly all undergraduate participants were in the "some college" category; of the older adults, 87.5% had had some college education, and 65% had at least a bachelor's degree. Thus, the two groups were comparable in terms of education, with the older adults being perhaps slightly better educated on average.

Most participants rated their health (OARS, Duke University, 1975) as good to excellent. Three older adults and two younger adults rated their health as fair; no participants rated their health as poor. The Gardner and Monge (1977) 30-Point Word Familiarity Survey was given as a measure of verbal ability. The older adults' mean verbal score (M = 21.18, SD = 5.72) was significantly higher than the younger adults' score ($M = 12.53$, $SD = 3.86$), $t(78) = 7.93$, $p < .001$), a typical finding in the cognitive aging literature (e.g., Salthouse, 1988). All participants possessed at least 20/30 corrected binocular acuity, assessed with a standard Snellen eye chart.

Design

Age (young vs. old) was factorially crossed with two information conditions (control vs. misled). Twenty participants were tested in each between-group condition.

Materials and Procedure

Participants were tested in small groups of up to four individuals. During the orientation task, a slide of a woman was presented briefly (5 sec), followed by four questions concerning details of the slide. The witnessed event consisted of 22 slides of an accident in which a pedestrian is hit by a car. The slides were the same as those used by Loftus et al. (1978), and the basic procedure was also very similar. Participants were told to study the slide sequence in preparation for a memory test. The series of slides, presented for three seconds each, depicts a red automobile approaching an intersection at which half of the participants saw a stop sign and half saw a yield sign as the critical slide. The critical slide appeared as the ninth slide. Following this critical slide, the car turns right and then hits a pedestrian as he attempts to cross the street.

Immediately following the slide presentation, participants answered 20 questions concerning details of the events depicted in the slide series. As one of the questions, half of the participants were asked: "Did another car pass the red sports car while it was stopped at the *stop* sign?" The remaining participants were asked: "Did another car pass the red sports car while it was stopped at the *yield* sign?" The participants were randomly assigned to conditions in such a way that half of the participants were exposed to information that was consistent with what they had seen during the slide presentation (the *control* condition), whereas the other half were given information that was inconsistent with what they had seen during the slide presentation (the *misled* condition).

The participants then engaged in a 20-minute filler activity, which consisted of completing a demographic questionnaire and the vocabulary test. Afterward, they completed a forced-choice recognition test containing 10 pairs of slides, in which one slide had previously been presented during the first part of the study while the other slide had not. Each slide pair was presented for 8 seconds and was counterbalanced for left/right side presentation. The critical slide pair (i.e., the intersection with the stop and yield signs) appeared in position 6 for all participants.

Following the forced-choice recognition task, participants completed the Memory Functioning Questionnaire (Gilewski, Zelinski, & Schaie, 1990), a self-assessment measure of metamemory. The MFQ contains 64 items related to memory functioning that are rated on a 7-pt scale (e.g., "How well do you remember things that occurred last month?"). It consists of 4 subtests, measuring the general frequency of forgetting, the seriousness of forgetting in various situations, retrospective functioning (i.e., current compared to prior functioning), and frequency of mnemonics usage.

Results

Analyses of variance were performed on the data using age (young, old) and information condition (control, misled) as independent variables. Accuracy on the critical slide was scored as either 0 (incorrect) or 1 (correct).

Detail Questions

Twenty questions, which did not pertain to participants' susceptibility to misinformation, tapped their overall memory for details in the slides. A main effect of age was obtained for this overall score, $F(1, 76) = 6.57$, $p < .01$. The younger adults ($M = 15.3$, $SD = 1.7$) were more accurate on these questions than the older adults ($M = 14.3$, $SD = 1.8$). No other main effects or interactions were observed, $Fs(1, 76) < 1.35$.

Forced-Choice Recognition Test

A marginal main effect of information condition was found for the overall score on the forced-choice recognition test, $F(1, 76) = 3.33$, $p < .07$, with participants in the control condition answering slightly more questions correctly ($M = 9.05/10$, $SD = 0.88$) than participants in the misled condition ($M = 8.65/10$, $SD = 1.08$). No other main effects or interactions were observed, $F(1, 76) < 1.87$.

Critical Slide Recognition

Performance on the critical slide is shown in Figure 7.1. There was a main effect of information condition on recognition of the critical slide, $F(1, 76) = 5.29$, $p < .02$. Ninety percent of participants in the control condition were correct on this item, compared to 70% of participants in the misled condition. This finding indicates that we did obtain a misinformation effect across all participants. There was no main effect of age $F(1, 76) = 0.33$, nor was the interaction of age and information condition significant $F(1, 76) = 2.97$.

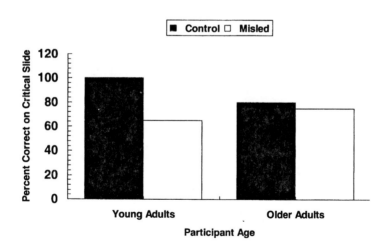

FIGURE 7.1 Percentage of older and younger participants giving the correct answer on the critical (misinformation) slide.

With regard only to the younger adults, a significant difference was found between those in the control condition (100% correct) compared to those in the misled condition (65% correct), $F(1, 38)$ = 10.23, $p < .005$. Considering only the older adults, however, this difference was not found. Older adults in the control condition (80% correct) were not significantly more accurate on the critical slide than older adults in the misled condition (75% correct). Thus, a statistically significant misinformation effect was found for the younger but not for the older participants.

Individual Differences and Memory Performance

Education

There was no significant correlation between participants' education level and either their total recognition score, $r = .06$, or their accuracy on the critical slide, $r = .00$. Likewise, neither measure of participants' memory performance was significantly correlated with their verbal ability, $rs < .1$.

Memory Functioning Questionnaire

Table 7.1 shows the mean MFQ scores for both age groups. A main effect of age was found for the subtest of metamemory questions concerning retrospective functioning, $F(1, 76) = 34.52$, $p < .001$. Younger participants ($M = 23.8$, $SD = 4.1$) scored higher on this subset of questions than the older adults ($M = 17.4$, $SD = 5.5$). There were no age differences for the other three components of the MFQ, $F(1, 76)s \leq 1.65$.

The four subtests of the metamemory questionnaire were highly intercorrelated. However, the metamemory subtest scores were correlated with neither participants' performance on the detail questions nor their accuracy on the critical slide in the forced-choice recognition test. The first subtest of metamemory questions, concerning the general frequency of forgetting, was correlated with the overall score on the forced-choice recognition test, $r = 0.23$, $p < .05$ for all participants. Broken down by age, this correlation was significant for older, $r = 0.35$, $p < .05$, but not for younger participants.

TABLE 7.1   Mean Scores (and Standard Deviations) on the Four
Subtests of the MFQ, As a Function of Participant Age

Subtest	Age	
	Younger adults	Older adults
1. General frequency of forgetting	166.2	163.1
	(25.0)	(23.8)
2. Seriousness of forgetting	75.4	80.3
	(22.8)	(23.0)
3. Retrospective functioning[a]	23.8	17.4
	(4.1)	(5.4)
4. Mnemonics usage	25.5	22.5
	(9.5)	(11.0)

Note. The number of items on the different subtests was: 33 on Subtest 1; 18 on Subtest 2; 5 on Subtest 3; and 8 on Subtest 4. For the younger adults, responses on Subtests 1 and 4 were correlated, $r = 0.39$, $p < .01$. For the older adults, responses on Subtest 1 were correlated with responses on Subtest 2, $r = 0.46$, $p < .005$, and on Subtest 4, $r = 0.46$, $p < .005$. Additionally, responses on Subtest 2 were correlated with responses on Subtest 4, $r = 0.34$, $p < .05$, for the older adults.
[a]The difference between older and younger adults on this subtest was statistically significant, $p < .001$.

Discussion and Implications

Despite research showing that aging is associated with source monitoring deficits (Hashtroudi et al., 1989), the effect of misleading suggestions was not greater in older participants than in younger adults. In fact, older witnesses failed to demonstrate a misinformation effect, while the effect was detected in younger witnesses. The absence of a misinformation effect in older participants is largely due to their poorer performance in the control condition (80% correct, vs. 100% for younger participants); yet it was nonetheless the case that older participants in the misled condition actually did somewhat better than their younger counterparts (75% vs. 65% correct).

Although some previous research has found an enhanced misinformation effect in older witnesses (Cohen & Faulkner, 1989; Loftus et al., 1992), the present results are consistent with other research that has failed to find such an effect (Coxon & Valentine, 1997).

Older participants in the present study had high verbal ability and were relatively highly educated, supporting the interpretation that older witnesses with a relatively high level of cognitive functioning appear not to be especially suggestible (cf. Coxon & Valentine, 1997). Although education level was not correlated with participants' eyewitness memory performance, both groups of participants were relatively homogeneous in terms of education. Because cognitive decrements in aging are related to education (Cherry & LeCompte, in press; Cherry & Park, 1993), future research on the suggestibility of older witnesses needs to compare older witnesses who differ in overall ability level. In general, older eyewitnesses—even those with relatively high cognitive functioning—do indeed tend to remember less information than younger witnesses (Coxon & Valentine, 1997). However, there is a lack of conclusive evidence to suggest that age exacerbates the negative influence of various factors on eyewitness memory, such as the presence of a weapon (O'Rourke, Penrod, Cutler, & Stuve, 1989) or misinformation.

Older participants were somewhat more likely to report problems in memory functioning. However, consistent with previous research (e.g., Zelinski et al., 1980), participants' metamemory evaluations were not correlated with their actual performance, in this case whether or not they demonstrated a misinformation effect. This lack of a relationship between memory performance and metamemory was observed for both age groups, though older adults who reported more frequent forgetting did tend to recognize fewer slides correctly. It is important to point out that although the metamemory questionnaire used in the present study covered various aspects of memory functioning, it did not specifically address participants' beliefs about their memory abilities in an eyewitness context. It is possible that those more specific beliefs would differ for older and younger adults, and also that they would correspond to eyewitnesses' actual memory performance. Additional research that addresses this issue is called for.

The present findings have significant implications for how older witnesses should be treated. Jurors—as well as older adults themselves—tend to hold negative stereotypes about older eyewitnesses, encompassing their general abilities both to remember event details and to recognize perpetrators (Bornstein, 1995; Yarmey, this volume). In addition, Ross, Dunning, Toglia, and Ceci (1990, Expt. 3) found that mock jurors specifically believe older witnesses are more susceptible to misleading information than young adult witnesses. Although there does appear to be a "kernel of truth" in the stereotype concerning older witnesses' ability to describe details of a crime (Yarmey, this volume), the findings of the present study provide no support for the perception that older witnesses—at least those who are highly educated—are also more suggestible than younger witnesses. In evaluating the testimony of eyewitnesses, both jurors and law enforcement officials should attend to the possible influence of post-event information; but they do not need to be more concerned with its effect on older witnesses than with its effect on the adult population at large.

Acknowledgment

We are grateful to Elizabeth Loftus for providing the slides for the experiment.

References

Belli, R. F., Lindsay, D. S., Gales, M. S., & McCarthy, T. T. (1994). Memory impairment and source misattribution in post-event misinformation experiments with short retention intervals. *Memory & Cognition, 22,* 40–54.

Bornstein, B. H. (1995). Memory processes in elderly eyewitnesses: What we know and what we don't know. *Behavioral Sciences and the Law, 13,* 337–348.

Cherry, K. E., & LeCompte, D. C. (1999). Age and individual differences influence prospective memory. *Psychology and Aging, 14,* 60–76.

Cherry, K. E., & Park, D. C. (1993). Individual difference and contextual variables influence spatial memory in younger and older adults. *Psychology and Aging, 10,* 379–394.

Cohen, G., & Faulkner, D. (1989). Age differences in source forgetting: Effects on reality monitoring and on eyewitness testimony. *Psychology and Aging, 4,* 10–17.

Coxon, P., & Valentine, T. (1997). The effects of the age of eyewitnesses on the accuracy and suggestibility of their testimony. *Applied Cognitive Psychology, 11,* 415–430.

Duke University Center for the Study of Aging and Human Development (1975). *OARS: Multidimensional Functional Assessment Questionnaire.* Durham, NC: Duke University.

Gardner, E., & Monge, R. (1977). Adult age differences in cognitive abilities and educational background. *Experimental Aging Research, 8,* 337–383.

Gilewski, M. J., Zelinski, E. M., & Schaie, W. (1990). The Memory Functioning Questionnaire for assessment of memory complaints in adulthood and old age. *Psychology and Aging, 5,* 482–490.

Hashtroudi, S., Johnson, M. K., & Chrosniak, L. D. (1989). Aging and source monitoring. *Psychology and Aging, 4,* 106–112.

Johnson, M. K., Hashtroudi, S., & Lindsay, D. S. (1993). Source monitoring. *Psychological Bulletin, 114,* 3–28.

Lindsay, D., & Johnson, M. K. (1989). The eyewitness suggestibility effect and memory for source. *Memory & Cognition, 17,* 349–358.

Loftus, E. F. (1992). When a lie becomes memory's truth: Memory distortion after exposure to misinformation. *Current Directions in Psychological Science, 1,* 121–123.

Loftus, E. F., Levidow, B., & Duensing, S. (1992). Who remembers best? Individual differences in memory for events that occurred in a science museum. *Applied Cognitive Psychology, 6,* 93–107.

Loftus, E. F., Miller, D., & Burns, H. (1978). Semantic integration of verbal information into a visual memory. *Journal of Experimental Psychology: Human Learning and Memory, 4,* 19–31.

O'Rourke, T., Penrod, S., Cutler, B., & Stuve, T. (1989). The external validity of eyewitness identification research: Generalizing across subject populations. *Law and Human Behavior, 13,* 385–395.

Ross, D. F., Dunning, D., Toglia, M. P., & Ceci, S. (1990). The child in the eyes of the jury: Assessing mock jurors' perceptions of the child witness. *Law and Human Behavior, 14,* 5–23.

Salthouse, T. A. (1988). Effects of aging on verbal abilities: Examination of the psychometric literature. In L. L. Light & D. M. Burke (Eds.), *Language, memory, and aging* (pp. 17–35). New York: Cambridge University Press.

Schacter, D. L., Kaszniak, A. W., Kihlstrom, J. F., & Valdiserri, M. (1991). The relation between source memory and aging. *Psychology and Aging, 6,* 559–568.

Yarmey, A. D. (1996). The elderly witness. In S. L. Sporer, R. S. Malpass, & G. Koehnken (Eds.), *Psychological issues in eyewitness identification* (pp. 259–278). Mahwah, NJ: Erlbaum.

Zelinski, E. M., Gilewski, M. J., & Thompson, L. W. (1980). Do lab tests relate to self-assessment of memory ability in young and old? In L. W. Poon, J. L. Fozard, L. S. Cermak, D. Arenberg, & L. W. Thompson (Eds.), *New directions in memory and aging* (pp. 519–544). Hillsdale, NJ: Erlbaum.

Suggested Readings

Loftus, E. F., Loftus, G. R., & Messo, J. (1987). Some facts about "weapon focus." *Law and Human Behavior, 11*, 55–62.

Ross, D. F., Read, J., & Toglia, M. P. (Eds.) (1994). *Adult eyewitness testimony.* New York: Cambridge University Press.

Sporer, S. L., Malpass, R. S., & Koehnken, G. (Eds.) (1996). *Psychological issues in eyewitness identification.* Mahwah, NJ: Erlbaum.

Chapter 8

Elders and Jury Service: A Case of Age Discrimination?

Pamela Entzel, Burton D. Dunlop, and Max B. Rothman

Participation in the jury process has important implications for older people. Jury service is many elders' only opportunity to play a direct role in the criminal justice system. Even more important, however, jury service provides older people with a unique opportunity to participate in the democratic process. Like voting, jury service places political power in the hands of the citizenry, creating an avenue for participatory self-government.

Furthermore, elders' participation in the jury system has important implications for the functioning of the jury system and judgment of the criminally accused. Older people, by virtue of their life experiences, can bring to the jury room values and approaches to deliberations that may have unsuspected importance in any given case. Most significantly, perhaps, the American tradition of trial by jury contemplates an impartial jury drawn from a cross-section of the community that includes older as well as younger people.

This chapter examines various factors influencing the nature and extent of elders' participation in the jury process, including laws, policies, practices, and perceptions that can have the effect of keeping older potential jurors from reaching jury panels. In particular, this chapter discusses age-based exemptions, excusals, and peremptory challenges, as well as their legal and ethical implications. Many of these topics, such as the constitutionality of age-based peremptory strikes, have begun to draw attention only recently and promise to gain visibility as the size of the elder population grows.

Representation of the Elder Population in the Jury System

Little or no empirical data are available to indicate the relative rates at which older people participate in the jury process. Courts in many states do not collect or record age-specific information on summoned jurors who decline service, report for service, or ultimately progress to jury panels. However, there is anecdotal information to suggest that older people serve on juries in relatively large numbers. For example, a number of states have recently changed their jury selection systems—broadening the pool of potential jurors from registered voters to those with a driver's license—in response to concerns that juries had been, among other things, "too old" (Miller, 1999).

If older people are, in fact, overrepresented on juries, this may be due, in part, to their relative availability. Compared to younger people, a larger number of older people do not hold full-time jobs, making them less likely to seek and obtain work-related excusals (American Bar Association [ABA], 1991). Similarly, because they are not as likely as younger people to be supporting minor children, older people generally do not have the child-care concerns that often prevent younger people from serving as jurors (although many elders do serve as caretakers of their parents or spouses, creating a potential conflict with jury service).

On the other hand, however, there are a number of reasons to suspect that a relatively large proportion of the elder population does not participate in the jury process. As discussed below, in many states, older people are either exempt or excused from jury duty on the basis of advanced age. Others may be exempt, excused, or even disqualified for reasons relating to illness or disability (Bleyer, McCarty, & Wood, 1994). Furthermore, older potential jurors who report for jury duty when summoned may be stricken from the venire based on stereotypes about older people. According to the ABA (1991, p. 102), attorneys may strike older prospective jurors based on the notion that "older persons are stubborn, indecisive, or cantankerous and will incorporate those attitudes when deciding guilt or innocence." Thus, clearly there is a need for empirical research on the representativeness of the jury system with respect to older people. In particular, research is needed on the comparative representation of various elder subgroups. Because the oldest-old (age 85 and over) may be especially vulnerable to elimination from the jury process due to illness, disability, or negative perceptions of elders and aging, the older juror population may include a disproportionate number of young elders (age 65 to 74) and relatively few of the oldest-old.

Elders' Perceptions of Jury Service

In a recent study of jury accessibility for older persons, Dunlop and Collett (1999) conducted a survey of Florida residents age 65 and over who had been summoned for jury duty. Surveying older potential jurors who reported for jury duty when summoned as well as older potential jurors who did not report, Dunlop and Collett found that each of these two groups overwhelmingly agreed that jury service is an important opportunity to participate in the democratic process. Despite their overall positive attitude regarding the value of jury service, however, study participants who did not report for jury duty expressed less interest in actually serving on a jury and more negative attitudes toward courts than those who reported for service. Interestingly, those who did not appear for duty also perceived that they possessed a greater familiarity with the courts than those who did appear, even though the latter group, overall, had more experience with jury service. These findings suggest that a significant number of older citizens who are summoned for jury duty may be reluctant to report not because they do not value their right to serve as jurors, but because of generally negative perceptions of the jury process.

In addition to having more negative attitudes toward jury service, older people in the Florida survey who did not report for service were also, on average, less educated, older, and more likely to have disabilities than those who did report. Moreover, a majority of respondents who did not report for jury duty indicated that they likewise would not report if requested to do so in the future; and the dominant reason given had to do with age or health/disability or a combination of the two. According to Dunlop and Collett, these findings may reflect an assumption among many older people who do not serve on juries that courts cannot accommodate them due to their age, illness, or disability.

Jury Service Exemptions and Excuses for Older People

In 21 states, older potential jurors who choose not to report for jury service are entitled to an exemption by virtue of their age (Bleyer, McCarty, & Wood, 1995). Most states that offer age-based exemptions limit eligibility to individuals over age 65 or 70, although Wyoming uses a cut-off of age 72 (Code of Civil Procedure, 1999). Nevada raised its qualifying age from 65 to 70 in 1997 and at the same time added a new exemption for individuals age 65 and over who live 65 or more miles from the court (State Judicial Department, 1999).

In New Jersey, older people are not automatically exempt from jury service but may be excused from service on age-related grounds. An excuse differs from an exemption in that an excuse is granted on an individual basis by the court, while an exemption is available to all eligible jurors who claim it (see Bleyer et al., 1994). Under New Jersey law, prospective jurors age 75 or older may be excused from jury duty on the basis of age (Court Organization and Civil Code, 1999).

California takes yet another approach, limiting special privileges for older jurors to those age 70 and over who have certain physical or mental disabilities. Unlike younger people, California residents age 70 and over who request to be excused from jury service on disability-related grounds cannot be required to provide verification of their disability (Judicial Administration Rules, 1999).

States with age-based exemption or excusal provisions do not prohibit older people from serving on juries, but merely provide that no person over a certain age should be required to serve unless willing to do so. Older people in these jurisdictions are given an option not to serve, which they alone may exercise (see Bleyer et al., 1994; Campaigne & Guarino, 1995). Despite the voluntary language of age-based exemptions and excuses, however, case law provides numerous examples of older potential jurors who were summarily excluded from the jury process without their knowledge or request (see e.g., *People v. McCoy*, 1995; *United States v. Bearden*, 1981; *Williams v. State*, 1976). In a 1976 case, for example, an Alabama jury commission clerk admitted to improperly excluding all persons over the age of 65 from the jury roll pursuant to an age-based exemption that Alabama then had in place (*Williams v. State*, 1976). Similarly, in a more recent case, *People v. McCoy* (1995), a California appellate court found that officials at the trial court level had routinely excused potential jurors age 70 and over regardless of whether they had requested to be excused. According to the California court (*People v. McCoy*, 1995, p. 601):

> [A]pparently a routine practice had developed among certain staff members to be more lenient with individuals 70 and older. Most persons in that age group who requested excusal were excused, regardless of the nature of their excuse. Others in that age group were excused even without a request.

Rationales for Relieving Older People from Jury Duty

Little information is available to explain why older people have been singled out for special exemptions and excuses relieving them from jury duty. Wishman (1986) has suggested that the ease with which older people are excused from jury service may reflect an assumption of senility or other disability in individuals beyond a certain age. Lending support to this notion, states have argued (and courts have agreed) that exemptions are reasonable in light of increased rates of "infirmities" among older people (see e.g., *Fox v. State*, 1989). Moreover, the California rule of court waiving the need to verify disability-related excuses when such excuses are proffered by individuals over age 70 would appear to rest on a presumption of disability in people of that age group.

Alternatively, the disparate treatment of older people during the initial stages of the jury process may reflect a desire to spare them the inconvenience that jury service might entail. For example, Nevada's exemption of individuals age 65 and over who live 65 or more miles from the court may suggest an intent on the part of the legislature to ease the burden jury service might present to older people who lack transportation or for whom travel of this distance would represent a hardship.

However, both of these rationales are flawed inasmuch as they rely upon broad assumptions about older people. Due to such factors as improved education and economic status, an increasing number of older Americans are staying healthy and active later in life. Thus, age is becoming a less and less accurate indicator of an individual older person's competence or ability to serve on a jury. Moreover, blanket exemptions based upon age often will produce arbitrary results, enabling qualified and capable potential jurors to avoid jury service for no reason other than their date of birth. The arbitrariness inherent in tying jury service exemptions to advanced age is underscored by the variability among states in the age at which older individuals become exempt from service. Depending on where he or she lives, an older person may become eligible to avoid jury duty on the basis of age at age 65, 70, 72, or 75.

The American Bar Association recommends the elimination of automatic exemptions for older people, favoring the use of tailored assessments of juror excuses over rigid reliance on age (Bleyer et al., 1994). Likewise, the Florida Supreme Court Commission on Fairness has just recommended to the Florida Legislature that the age exemption there be raised from 70 to age 85, or better still, be eliminated altogether. In place of the automatic age exemption, the Court urges that a judge trained in disability issues should rule on each juror excuse on a case-by-case basis (Dunlop & Collett, 1999). Individual assessments are the norm in states that do not categorically exempt older people from jury duty. In these states, the majority, older potential jurors who do not feel able to serve due to illness, disability, lack of transportation, or other reason still may request an excuse based on undue hardship (Bleyer et al., 1994). Thus, the need for categorical exemption or exclusion of all people over a certain age is highly questionable and should be addressed at federal and state court levels.

Furthermore, while some older people do have health, transportation, or other needs that might make it difficult for them to serve on juries, many of these needs can and should be met by the courts. Instead of readily excusing older potential jurors who would be unduly burdened by jury duty, courts should make reasonable changes in policies, practices, and procedures to allow older people to serve on juries with greater ease and efficiency. More older people might be encouraged to participate in the jury process if courts simply improved transportation to the courthouse, provided more appropriate and comfortable waiting areas, and explained to jurors exactly what is expected of them (Scott, 1982).

Similarly, many older people with disabilities are nonetheless capable of serving as jurors and might be encouraged to do so if courts provided reasonable accommodations. Courts are required by law to make reasonable efforts to ensure jury service accessibility for persons with disabilities. According to Title II of the Americans with Disabilities Act (ADA), public entities are prohibited from discriminating against individuals on the basis of disability. Title II covers state court programs and services, including jury service. It requires that courts ensure access to jury service by making reasonable changes in policies, practices, and procedures that promote effective communications and by increasing physical access to courthouse facilities for persons with disabilities (Bleyer et al., 1995).

In their statewide study of courtroom accessibility in Florida, Dunlop and Collett (1999) found that a large majority of the courts surveyed indicated that they were capable of accommodating elders with disabilities through the provision of staff assistance and facility accessibility. However, when it came to more complex and less frequently requested accommodations, such as making spoken or written information available in alternative formats, for example, real-time transcriptions or braille, the courts clearly had less experience. Some courts participating in the study reported that they were capable of providing these services but that because they were so rarely requested, the courts saw no need to advertise their availability. This finding suggests that the availability of jury duty exemptions and age-related excusals for older people may create a self-fulfilling prophesy. That is, some older prospective jurors may automatically seek to be relieved from jury duty because they perceive that the accommodations they would need are not available. This tendency may reduce the numbers and visibility of older jurors with disabilities, leading the court to surmise that there is no need to provide or advertise accommodations (an invidious version of "out of sight, out of mind"). This failure to advertise, in turn, may lead to additional exemption requests.

Age-Based Peremptory Challenges

In addition to triggering blanket exemptions from jury service, advanced age often serves as the unspoken basis of peremptory challenges. During jury selection, each side or party is allotted a fixed number of such challenges, which they may use to strike prospective jurors suspected of leaning to the other side (Abramson, 1994). Unlike challenges for cause, peremptory challenges require no justification or explanation. An attorney may peremptorily strike a member of the venire based on a mere hunch, without giving any reason (Abramson, 1994). In the last two decades, however, the U.S. Supreme Court has declared it unconstitutional to use peremptory challenges to eliminate jurors for reasons based upon race (*Batson v. Kentucky*, 1986) or gender (*J. E. B. v. Alabama*, 1994); and the Connecticut Supreme Court has extended the U.S. Supreme Court's logic to outlaw the use of peremptory challenges to eliminate jurors of a particular religion (*State v. Hodge*, 1999). Despite the unconstitutionality of race-, gender- and, perhaps, religious-based peremptory challenges, however, striking prospective jurors on the basis of age remains a valid and generally accepted practice. Indeed, attorneys exercising peremptory challenges often openly acknowledge their age-based discrimination (Amar, 1995; see e.g., *Currin v. State*, 1988; *Hernandez v. State*, 1991; *People v. McDonald*, 1988; *State v. Smith*, 1990; *United States v. Garrison*, 1988).

Moreover, in defense of peremptory strikes that are alleged to reflect improper race- or gender-based motives, attorneys frequently offer and courts routinely accept explanations based upon age (Raphael & Ungvarsky, 1993). For example, in *State v. Smith* (1990), where the defense challenged the prosecution's use of peremptory strikes to eliminate four black members of the venire, the prosecution explained that two venirepersons were struck because they were the same age as the defendant and that the other two were struck because they were "old." One of the older prospective jurors was in her fifties, and the other was in her sixties. The court upheld the prosecutor's strikes even though the prosecutor had failed to strike a White venireperson who was over 60 years old. This and other similar cases (see e.g., *Currin v. State*, 1990; *Thompson v. State*, 1990; but see *People v. McDonald*, 1988) reflect a willingness on the part of courts to accept age-based discrimination even while purporting to scrutinize motions for discrimination on other grounds.

When they are not being used as a guise for striking potential jurors on the basis of race or gender, age-based peremptory challenges often are used to eliminate older people from the venire based upon preconceived notions of how they will judge a given case. Often these preconceived notions are based not upon information about individual prospective jurors, but upon hunches, intuition, and stereotypes about aging and older people (Abramson, 1994; Olczak, Kaplan, & Penrod, 1991). Abramson (1994, p. 146) writes, "Lawyers have always relied on hunches, intuition, and their ideas about stereotypes" to identify undesirable jurors. For example, attorneys may strike older members of the venire based on the notion that older people are "stubborn, indecisive, or cantankerous" (ABA, 1991, p. 102).

According to law professor Nancy Marder (1995), attorneys may learn to rely on stereotypes borrowed from fellow litigators and trial manuals offering jury selection advice. A survey of trial manuals reveals numerous examples of jury selection "wisdom" rooted in sweeping generalizations about older people. The Honorable Walter E. Jordan (1980) advises that older jurors are less susceptible to presentation of new ideas and information than the young. Similarly, Adkins (1968/1969, p. 39) writes, "People in their 30's are least likely to have prejudices against others, those over 50 being the most prejudiced." Wenke (1988) suggests that older jurors generally are more tolerant of human frailty and more sympathetic to the injured than younger jurors. They also "tend to have more respect for authority and more prejudices than younger jurors," being especially prejudiced against "single persons and the young" (Wenke, 1988, p. 87). Finally, with respect to complex defenses, F. Lee Bailey recommends "jurors who are between 28 and 55 years of age" because "[t]hey will tend to be most alert and receptive" (Bailey & Rothblatt, 1971, p. 105).

Other, somewhat more recent manuals caution attorneys against using such stereotypes to forecast juror verdict preferences. Abbott (1987, p. 50), for example, warns that "[p]utting reliance on a single variable, such as occupation or any of the demographic variables of age, sex, and race is hazardous." Bennett and Hirschhorn (1993, p. 270) write, "Age stereotyping should be avoided by lawyers. Lumping jurors into positive or negative categories based solely on age can be as shortsighted as analyzing them based only on gender or race." Likewise, Belote (1986, p. 18) maintains that "contrary to conventional wisdom, demographic characteristics such as race, age, and sex rarely differentiate between plaintiff's and defendant's jurors."

A number of factors suggest that the latter pieces of advice, which counsel against prejudging jurors on the basis of advanced age, are more helpful and reliable than the former. First, lawyers who rely upon age-based stereotypes to identify unfavorable jurors run the risk that the stereotypes are false, in which case the lawyer's misplaced reliance may do his or her case more harm than good. As trial experts Hans and Vidmar (1986, p. 76) explain:

> False stereotypes can easily develop and even flourish under typical voir dire and challenge procedures. Attorneys are usually forced to exercise their peremptories on the basis of only limited information about prospective jurors. They never receive feedback on their choices, since those challenged jurors are eliminated. On the other side of the coin, the jury renders its verdict as a group. Attorneys thus seldom learn whether their hunches are correct.

Similarly, Alan Dershowitz has noted that among attorneys involved in jury selection "[t]en years of accumulated experiences may be 10 years of being wrong" (Hunt, 1982, p. 82). Therefore, jury selection wisdom rooted in popular stereotypes of older people should be viewed with a healthy dose of skepticism and put to the test of empirical research. In three scientific experiments, Olczak et al. (1991) found that trial lawyers who relied on stereotypes to predict juror verdict preferences did not accurately select jurors favoring their side. In fact, a number of scientific studies have found correlations between demographic characteristics and verdict preferences to be only negligible, with information regarding jurors' attitudes revealing far more about their preexisting biases (Hans & Vidmar, 1986; Marder, 1995, notes 156–57).

Second, even if a stereotype contains a kernel of truth with respect to older people in general, a prosecutor or defense attorney has no way of knowing whether an individual older juror is typical of elders generally. Older people in the United States are an extremely heterogenous group, varying in terms of race, ethnic origin, living arrangements, educational attainment, health status, and socioeconomic status. Indeed, although age does indicate length of exposure to life, it says very little about the nature of a juror's life experiences (Bennett & Hirschhorn, 1993). Due to the divergence of experience within a cohort over the course of a lifetime, older people actually have less in common than members of younger age groups (Ferraro, 1997). Consequently, peremptory challenges based solely on advanced age will tend to yield mixed results at best.

Third, in situations where generalizations about older people do indeed fit an individual older juror, this individual may nevertheless take the juror role seriously and try to put his or her predispositions aside. Numerous empirical studies measuring the relative contributions of juror characteristics and trial testimony to jury verdicts have found testimony to be the key determinant of trial outcomes (Diamond, 1990). According to sociologist Michael Saks (cited in Abramson, 1994, p. 171), "with few exceptions . . . verdicts are far more heavily influenced by the evidence and the arguments presented than by the jurors' personal characteristics."

Finally, regardless of how an older person might decide a given case, jury deliberation is a complex group process, the dynamics of which cannot be predicted (Marder, 1995). It is virtually impossible to predict which jurors will be the most instrumental in pushing the final verdict through and which will be the most resistant (Treger, 1992). Moreover, there is anecdotal evidence to suggest that the roles older jurors play during jury deliberation are as varied as the jurors themselves. For example, one criminal district court judge remarked, "There was a little old lady on one of my juries who, when polled, said she really hadn't decided guilt or innocence but just wanted to go along with whatever the other jury members wanted" ("Grandma, Stay Home!" 1980, p. 134). In contrast, Hahn (1993) describes a case in which, after 9 days of intense and argumentative deliberation, exasperated younger jurors ultimately deferred to a 57-year-old juror out of a general respect for elders.

Recognizing the limitations of relying upon common stereotypes to predict the verdicts of older jurors, growing numbers of lawyers are turning to social scientists and the theory of scientific jury selection (SJS) for more empirical guidance (Treger, 1992). Scientific jury selection involves the use of phone surveys, mock trials, or some combination of these two research methods to draw correlations between a potential juror's characteristics (e.g., age and reading habits) and his or her attitudes in a given case (Diamond, 1990; Treger, 1992). This information is then used to develop profiles of undesirable juror "types" to be eliminated from the jury venire through the exercise of peremptory challenges. Empirical research shows that the utilization of survey-based "scientific" selection methods yields slightly better results than using conventional intuition-based strategies (Sahler, 1996). Nevertheless, the predictive value of most SJS models is still quite low (Abramson, 1994; Diamond, 1990; Treger, 1992).

Little information is available on the attitudes that scientific jury consultants correlate with advanced age, perhaps due in part to the commercialization of jury studies (Fulero & Penrod, 1990). Ultimately, however, like the use of stereotypes, the use of SJS to evaluate older prospective jurors starts from the premise that older individuals will vote according to their age-group affiliation. Abramson (1994, p. 174) writes, "Scientific jury selection, as currently practiced, is not possible without the use of peremptory challenges based largely on inferences about a prospective juror from the person's group background." Thus, whether an attorney decides to strike an older juror on a hunch or on the basis of surveys and polls, he or she is drawing inferences from the juror's age, raising many of the issues discussed above.

Legal Implications of Age-Based Distinctions in the Jury Process

The use of age-based exemptions, excusals, and peremptory challenges to eliminate older potential jurors from the jury process raises a number of legal issues. In particular, the use of age-based peremptory challenges raises issues concerning older prospective jurors' equal protection rights. As mentioned above, courts have recently curtailed the exercise of peremptory challenges, finding challenges based upon race, gender, and religion to violate the Equal Protection Clause of the Fourteenth Amendment. This trend is stirring debate regarding the constitutionality of peremptory challenges based upon age (see Amar, 1995). Because age-based distinctions do not trigger heightened judicial scrutiny under traditional equal protection analysis, however, the use of age to differentiate among potential jurors may withstand Supreme Court review (Amar, 1995). As long as state actors can provide a "rational basis" for striking older prospective jurors on the basis of age, age-based peremptories are likely to be upheld.

In addition to raising questions concerning the rights of potential jurors, however, age-based exemptions, excusals, and peremptory challenges have implications for the rights of the accused. Under the Sixth Amendment, defendants are entitled to a jury drawn from a fair cross-section of the community. This does not mean that every jury must contain representatives of all groups in a community, but only that no group should be systematically and intentionally excluded during the jury selection process. One might argue that elimination of older people from the jury process through either age-based exemptions or peremptory challenges reduces the representativeness of the jury panel and thus runs counter to the fair cross-section ideal. The American Bar Association recommends the elimination of all automatic exemptions for older people on these grounds (Bleyer et al., 1994).

In order to establish a prima facie violation of the fair cross-section provision, however, it must first be shown that the group whose underrepresentation is challenged is a cognizable one, meaning a group with basic similarities that make it distinctive and identifiable (*Barber v. Ponte*, 1985; *Duren v. Missouri*, 1979; *Taylor v. Louisiana*, 1975; *Willis v. Zant*, 1983). And courts have been reluctant to recognize older people as cognizable group for Sixth Amendment purposes. In *Williams v. State* (1976), where evidence showed that all persons over the age of 65 had been excluded from the jury pool, an Alabama court found this group to be sufficiently "identifiable" for its exclusion to warrant reversal of the defendant's conviction.

However, a majority of courts that have considered the issue have rejected the cognizability of older potential jurors (*Barber v. Ponte,* 1985). For example, in *State v. Haskins* (1982), the Connecticut Supreme Court rejected arguments that older people share basic similarities in attitudes, ideas, or experiences, which could not be adequately represented if they were excluded from the jury selection process. Similarly, a California court refused to recognize persons over age 70 as a distinctive group where an expert witness testified that this group shares unique attitudes and beliefs not common to other groups but did not specify what these attitudes might be other than political conservatism (*People v. McCoy,* 1995).

In rejecting the argument that people over age 65 constitute a sufficiently cohesive group, one court noted, "The age parameters of the group are too arbitrary, and its supposed distinctive characteristics are too general and ill-defined" (*Brewer v. Nix,* 1992, p. 1113). Other courts cite perceived slippery slope problems in conferring cognizability upon age groups. For example, one court argues, "[I]f the age classification is adopted, surely blue-collar workers, yuppies, Rotarians, Eagle Scouts, and an endless variety of other classifications will be entitled to the same treatment. These are not the groups that the court has traditionally sought to protect from underrepresentation on jury venires" (*Barber v. Ponte,* 1985, p. 999).

Interestingly, these arguments conflict with many of the assumptions and rationales underlying age-based exemptions and peremptory challenges. For the purposes of exempting or challenging older jurors on the basis of age, legislators, attorneys, and judges often tend to treat older people as a homogenous group. In contrast, in the context of challenges to the underrepresentation of older people on jury panels, courts tend to emphasize the diversity of the elder population and the arbitrariness of age-based categories.

Ethical Implications of Age-Based Distinctions in the Jury Process

Ultimately, whether age is an appropriate tool for differentiating among potential jurors may be more of an ethical than an empirical or legal issue. Age discrimination in the jury process raises a number of ethical questions, not the least of which is whether state-sanctioned age discrimination in the criminal justice system ever can be justified. Some critics fear that differentiating among potential jurors on the basis of advanced age sends a harmful message to older people, signaling to them that they are not full and equal members of the community. Arguing against the use of peremptory challenges to strike individuals from the jury venire on the basis of group member-ship, Marder (1995, p. 1084) writes, "The individual thus singled out not only is declared unfit based on a stereotype, but also is excluded from performing a public duty." This practice, Marder (1995, p. 1084) continues, casts a stigma on the excluded individual and "undercuts notions of equality that are fundamental to a democ-racy." By this same logic, age-based jury duty exemptions and excu-sals, which relieve older people of what for other citizens is a civic obligation, also may send the wrong message to the elder community. Exemptions and excuses that are tied to advanced age may suggest to some older people that their participation in the jury process is not needed or valued as much as that of younger people.

The use of age-based distinctions in the jury process also may send the wrong message to the general public. Blanket jury exemptions for all older people reinforce negative stereotypes regarding elders' capabilities. Furthermore, reliance upon stereotypes about older people to identify favorable and unfavorable jurors during the jury selection process signals to the public that judging individuals on the basis of stereotypes, which is unacceptable in other walks of life, is acceptable in the courtroom (Marder, 1995).

Finally, to differentiate among jurors on the basis of age may have the negative effect of fostering cynical views of the criminal justice system. For example, when older potential jurors are stricken from the jury venire, they may leave with negative perceptions of the fairness of their justice system and doubts about whether that system can be fair to them (Marder, 1995). More generally, however, wide-spread use of stereotypes, polls, and surveys in attempts to predict juror behavior and influence trial outcomes may gradually erode public confidence in the jury system (Abramson, 1994; Marder, 1995; Sahler, 1996). The premise of these practices—the invidious idea that jurors inevitably bring with them a set of attitudes and biases built into their race, gender, and age, which compromises their ability to render an impartial verdict—may foster the idea that each juror represents his or her own brand of justice reflective of his or her social group (see Abramson, 1994). Furthermore, the misguided notion that jurors' attitudes and biases influence the verdict as much, if not more, than evidence presented at trial may give the impression that lawyers can outsmart the legal system by figuring out the demographics of justice and manipulating it during jury selection (Abramson, 1994).

In a move with potential implications for the use of age-based distinctions in the voir dire process, three states, Florida, Illinois, and Rhode Island, have adopted ethical rules that explicitly bar attorneys from discriminating against jurors (Charlow, 1997). However, only one of these three states, Florida, has included age among the prohibited grounds of discrimination (Fla. Rules of Professional Conduct, cited in Charlow, 1997). Moreover, none of these rules expressly mentions discrimination in the guise of peremptory challenges (Charlow, 1997). The only ethics rule to date that expressly bars discriminatory peremptory challenges is a District of Columbia rule that addresses peremptory strikes based upon "race, religion, national or ethnic background, or sex," but not age (D.C. Rules of Professional Conduct, cited in Charlow, 1997). Nevertheless, some argue, discriminatory peremptory challenges fly in the face of the tenets enunciated by the American Bar Association Model Rules of Professional Conduct (Charlow, 1997), creating a conflict that is likely to gain attention as the size of the elder population increases.

Conclusions

More research is needed on factors influencing the likelihood that older potential jurors will decline jury service, report for service, or ultimately progress to jury panels. In particular, there is a present need for critical evaluation of rationales underlying age-based exemptions and excusals from jury duty. Whether they represent purposeful discrimination against older people or benign attempts to relieve elders of the burdens of jury duty, age-based exemptions and excusals inevitably reduce the diversity and representativeness of jury panels and thus undermine the fair cross-section ideal. Moreover, even the most benign motives may be insufficient to justify the categorical exemption of all older potential jurors, as these exemptions may ultimately do more harm than good. The availability of exemptions and excusals based upon age may stigmatize older people and create a disincentive for courts to provide accommodations that would enable more older people to participate in the jury process.

Additionally, there is an immediate need for critical assessment of the widespread practice of striking older members of the venire solely because of their age. Recent court rulings outlawing the use of peremptory challenges to strike potential jurors on the basis of race, gender, and religion raise obvious questions regarding the constitutionality of peremptory challenges based upon age. Moreover, regardless of the legality of striking older members of the venire, this practice raises numerous ethical questions, including whether age-based discrimination is ever appropriate in the courtroom.

Finally, more research is needed on how actors in the criminal justice system perceive older jurors and how these perceptions shape the experiences of older people in the jury process. Anecdotal information suggests that stereotypes about aging and older people drive many of the laws, policies, and practices that keep older potential jurors from reaching jury panels. Interestingly, however, especially in the context of the Sixth Amendment right to a jury drawn from a fair cross-section of the community, where generalizations about older people might support arguments to include more older people on jury panels (cognizability), courts tend to reject age-based distinctions and view older people as individuals.

Ultimately, despite their widespread acceptance, stereotypes and age-based distinctions are inexact and often inappropriate criteria for differentiating among potential jurors. Because one's competence or ability to serve on a jury is ultimately an individual rather than a group or class matter, the practice of exempting or excusing older potential jurors on the basis of age will inevitably produce arbitrary results. Furthermore, stereotypes and generalizations about older people appear to be very poor predictors of how older jurors will decide a given case. Individual attitudes, beliefs, and behaviors comprise far more reliable predictors of a juror's verdict proclivities (Rothman, Dunlop, & Rambali, 1999).

References

Abbott, W. F. (1987). *Analytic juror rater.* Philadelphia: American Law Institute–American Bar Association.

Abramson, J. (1994). *We, the jury: The jury system and the ideal of democracy.* New York: Basic Books.

Adkins, J. C. (1968/1969, December/January). Jury Selection: An Art? A science? Or luck? *Trial, 5,* 37–40.

Amar, V. D. (1995). Jury service as political participation akin to voting. *Cornell Law Review, 80,* 203–259.

American Bar Association. (1991). *Court-related needs of the elderly and persons with disabilities: Recommendations of the February 1991 conference.* Washington, DC: Author.

Bailey, F. L., & Rothblatt, H. B. (1971). Successful techniques for criminal trials. Rochester, NY: Lawyers Co-operative.

Barber v. Ponte, 772 F. 2d 982 (1st Cir. 1985).

Batson v. Kentucky, 476 U.S. 79 (1986).

Belote, F. G. (1986). Jury research: Spotting jurors who can hurt. *American Bar Association Journal of the Section of Litigation, 12*(4), 17–20.

Bennett, C. E., & Hirschhorn, R. B. (1993). *Bennett's guide to jury selection and trial dynamics in civil and criminal litigation.* St. Paul: West Publishing.

Bleyer, K., McCarty, K. S., & Wood, E. (1994). *Into the jury box: A disability accommodation guide for state courts.* Washington, DC: American Bar Association.

Bleyer, K., McCarty, K. S., & Wood, E. (1995). Jury service for people with disabilities. *Judicature, 78*(6), 273–275.

Brewer v. Nix, 963 F. 2d 1111 (8th Cir. 1992).

Campaigne, C., & Guarino, G. A. (1995). Jury. *American Jurisprudence, 2d ed., 47,* 699–986.

Charlow, R. (1997). Tolerating deception and discrimination after Batson. *Stanford Law Review, 50,* 9–64.

Code of Civil Procedure, 1 Wyo. Stat. Ann. §§11-104 (Lexis 1999).

Court Organization and Civil Code, 2B N.J. State §20-10 (Lexis 1999).

Currin v. State, 535 So. 2d 221 (Ala. Crim. App. 1988).

Diamond, S. (1990). Scientific jury selection: What social scientists know and do not know. *Judicature, 73*(4), 178–183.

Dunlop, B. D., & Collett, M. E. (1999). *Jury service accessibility for older persons and persons with disabilities in Florida: Full report.* Tallahassee, FL: Florida State Supreme Court.

Duren v. Missouri, 439 U.S. 357 (1979).

Ferraro, K. F. (Ed.). (1997). *Gerontology: Perspectives and issues* (2d ed.). New York: Springer.

Fox v. State, 779 P.2d 562 (Okla. Crim. App. 1989).

Fulero, S. M., & Penrod, S. D. (1990). Attorney jury selection folklore: What do they think and how can psychologists help? *Forensic Reports, 3*, 233–259.

Grandma, stay home! (1980, February). *American Bar Association Journal, 66*, 134.

Hahn, E. A. (1993, October 4). Truth—and consequences—of 'juror bonding.' *New Jersey Law Journal*, S26.

Hans, V. P., & Vidmar, N. (1986). *Judging the jury.* New York: Plenum.

Hernandez v. State, 808 S.W. 2d 536 (Tex. Ct. App. 1991).

Hunt, M. (1982, November 28). Putting jurors on the couch. *The New York Times Magazine*, pp. 70–72, 78, 82, 85–86, 88.

J. E. B. v. Alabama ex rel. T. B., 511 U.S. 127 (1994).

Jordan, W. E. (1980). *Jury selection.* Colorado Springs, CO: McGraw Hill.

Judicial Administration Rules, 6 Cal. Rules of Court Appx. Div. I §4.5 (Lexis 1999).

Marder, N. S. (1995). Beyond gender: Peremptory challenges and the roles of the jury. *Texas Law Review, 73*, 1041–1138.

Miller, S. L. (1999, April 4). Verdict mixed on new jury selection system. *The Miami Herald*, p. 1L.

Olczak, P. V., Kaplan, M. F., & Penrod, S. (1991). Attorneys' lay psychology and its effectiveness in selecting jurors: Three empirical studies. *Journal of Social Behavior and Personality, 6*(3), 431–452.

People v. McCoy, 40 Cal. App. 4th 778, 47 Cal. Rptr. 2d 599 (Cal. Ct. App. 1 Dist. 1995).

People v. McDonald, 530 N. E. 2d 1351 (Ill. 1988).

Raphael, M. J., & Ungvarsky, E. J. (1993). Excuses, excuses: Neutral explanations under Batson v. Kentucky. *University of Michigan Journal of Law Reform, 27*, 229–275.

Rothman, M. B., Dunlop, B. D., & Rambali, C. (1999). The older juror. In W. F. Abbott & J. Batt (Eds.), *A handbook of jury research* (pp. 9-1–9-19). Philadelphia: American Law Institute–American Bar Association.

Sahler, D. (1996). Comment: Scientifically selecting jurors while maintaining professional responsibility: A proposed model rule. *Albany Law Journal of Science and Technology, 6*, 383.

Scott, J. N. (1982). Sitting, waiting, not knowing: Taking the delay out of discovery. *The Judges' Journal, 3*, 16–19.

State Judicial Department, 1 Nev. Rev. Stat. Ann. §6.020 (Lexis 1999).

State v. Haskins, 188 Conn. 432, 450 A. 2d 828 (Conn. 1982).

State v. Hodge, 248 Conn. 207, 726 A. 2d 531 (Conn. 1999).

State v. Smith, 791 S.W. 2d 744 (Mo. Ct. App. 1990).

Taylor v. Louisiana, 419 U.S. 522 (1975).

Thompson v. State, 390 S. E. 2d 253 (Ga. Ct. App. 1990).

Treger, T. L. (1992). One jury indivisible: A group dynamics approach to voir dire. *Chicago-Kent Law Review, 68,* 549–580.

United States v. Bearden, 659 F. 2d 590 (5th Cir. 1981).

United States v. Garrison, 849 F. 2d 103 (4th Cir. 1988).

Wenke, R. A. (1988). *The art of selecting a jury.* Los Angeles: Parker & Sons.

Williams v. State, 342 So. 2d 1325 (Ala. Crim. App. 1976).

Willis v. Zant, 720 F.2d 1212 (11th Cir. 1983).

Wishman, S. (1986). *Anatomy of a jury: The system on trial.* New York: Random House.

PART III

Elders and Imprisonment

Chapter 9

Sentencing the Older Offender: Is There an "Age Bias"?

Darrell Steffensmeier and Mark Motivans

A bundant empirical literature on various aspects of aging now flourishes within sociology and the social sciences more generally (Riley, Foner, & Waring, 1988). In criminology there also is an abundance of empirical research on both the age–crime and the age–victimization relationships (Steffensmeier & Allan, 1995). There also is some research that focuses specifically on elders—as victims, offenders, and incarcerated inmates (Fattah & Sacco, 1989; McCarthy & Langworthy, 1992; Newman, Newman, & Gewirtz, 1984; Steffensmeier, 1987; Wilbanks & Kim, 1984). Yet, in spite of its centrality and in contrast to other core variables such as race and gender, very little is known about the overall effects of age on judicial decision making in the handling of criminal defendants. There is in particular a virtual absence of empirical research that tests the widely held assumption that "there is an obvious propensity on the part of judges to be more lenient with elderly criminals" (Champion, 1987, p. 12).

The assumption that the older offender "gets off easier" is based largely on anecdotal impressions of lawyers and judges (Alston, 1986; Feinberg & Khosla, 1985; Kalvern & Zeisel, 1966), the statistical observation that the percentage representing elders among all persons arrested for crimes in the United States is much larger than the percentage representing elders among all persons convicted or incarcerated (Wilbanks, 1988), and the findings from a few studies which show that older offenders—particularly older shoplifters and older sex offenders—receive more lenient treatment than their younger counterparts (Champion, 1987; Cutsall & Adams, 1983; Wilbanks & Kim, 1984; Curran, 1984; Wilbanks, 1988).[1] Unfortunately, these studies blur any clear-cut conclusions because of shortcomings such as small sample size and the failure to simultaneously adjust for the effects of other case characteristics, including prior record and offense seriousness, that prior research shows also influence sentencing outcomes.

A recent analysis by Steffensmeier, Kramer, and Ulmer (1995) has helped clarify the overall effects of age on sentencing. They found a nonlinear or inverted U-shaped relationship when the full range of adult ages are included, from the late teens to young adulthood through middle and old age. The curvilinearity was due largely to the more lenient sentencing of youthful offenders (ages 18 to 20) as compared to young adult offenders (ages 21 to 29), the peak ages for receiving the harshest sentences. Very young offenders aged 18 to 20 receive sentences on par with offenders in their 30's, whereas offenders in their 50's and older receive the most lenient sentences. The age-sentencing relationship becomes strictly linear from about age 30 into old age. It appears that judges see youthful offenders as more impressionable and more likely to be harmed by imprisonment than young "adult" offenders, while they see older offenders as less dangerous and less risky prospects for release into the community (Steffensmeier et al., 1995). Previous sentencing studies typically masked these judicial preferences by treating age as a continuous or linear variable and thus "flattening out" its inverted U-shaped effect. That is, the more lenient treatment for the

---

[1]Note also that age is used frequently as a control variable in sentencing studies. When it is treated as a continuous variable and a linear effect is assumed, the age effect tends to be small or negligible (e.g., Myers & Talarico, 1987). As shown by Steffensmeier et al. (1995) and consistent with our analysis here, this anomalous finding in most statistical studies is due to the curvilinearity of the age-sentencing relationship and stems largely from the more lenient sentencing of youthful (ages 18 to 20) as compared to young adult offenders (ages 21 to 29).

youngest of the adult offenders tended to cancel out the remaining age effect occurring across the mid-twenties, thirties, forties, and into advanced age.

Our analysis here extends the research by Steffensmeier, et al. (1995), but focuses more explicitly on older defendants. We use two sources to examine whether such defendants receive similar or distinct sentences: (1) statewide data from Pennsylvania courts for the years 1991–1994; and (2) nationwide data from U.S. federal courts for the years 1992–96. As we describe below, both the Pennsylvania court data and the federal court data are exceptionally well suited for assessing whether decisions concerning sentence outcomes are age-driven, including whether the older offender is the beneficiary of especially lenient treatment.

Theoretical Expectations

Prior sentencing research suggests that judges are guided by three focal concerns in reaching sentencing decisions (Steffensmeier, Ulmer, & Kramer, 1998), and that they typically have limited time and limited information about defendants when rendering their sentencing decisions. The three focal concerns are the offender's blameworthiness and the degree of harm caused the victim, protection of the community, and practical implications of sentencing decisions. Blameworthiness is associated with offender's culpability and having the punishment fit the crime. Judges' views of blameworthiness are influenced mainly by offense severity and offender's criminal history but also may be swayed by defendant attributes such as gender or biographical factors such as prior victimization at the hands of others. Protection of the community draws on similar attributions but focuses more on the need to incapacitate the offender or to deter would-be offenders. Third, practical constraints and consequences come into play in sentencing decisions—including the offender's "ability to do time," health condition, special needs, the costs to be borne by the correctional system, and the disruption of ties to children or other family members. Also, judges are likely to be concerned about the impact of offender recidivism on the court's standing in the public's eye and on their judicial careers.

The focal concerns and their interplay are complex, and judges rarely have complete information about cases or defendants. To reduce uncertainty, judges may rely not only on the defendant's present offense and prior criminal conduct, but also on attributions linked to the defendant's social position, as indicated by the attributes of gender, race, social class, and age (Steffensmeier, Kramer, & Streifel, 1993; Ulmer, 1997). On the basis of these attributions or pieces of information, judges may project behavioral expectations about whether the offender is likely to be a good or bad risk for rehabilitation, poses special organizational considerations, and so on. As we spell out below, although three plausible patterns can be conjectured regarding the age-sentencing relationship, the interplay between the sentencing focal concerns and the "perceptual shorthand" associated with defendant's age suggests greater leniency for elderly defendants.

No Age Differences

Because the American criminal justice system places heavy emphasis upon the ideals of treating criminal defendants impartially and equally, it is reasonable to expect that judges will sentence strictly on the basis of what defendants have allegedly done, not on who they are or on how old they are. Older offenders should receive sentences as severe (or as lenient) as younger offenders convicted of identical offenses and with similar prior records. This view is buttressed by the bulk of research on sentencing which has established the overwhelming importance of legally relevant variables such as offense seriousness and prior record in sentence outcomes (Myers & Talarico, 1987; Kramer & Steffensmeier, 1993).

Older Offenders Sentenced More Harshly

Because judges may believe that older offenders "should know better" and therefore are more culpable than younger people, it also is plausible to assume that they will impose harsher sentences on older defendants. Or, judges may hold that the older person who violates the law is hopelessly incorrigible and society has no choice but to lock him up. Also, because many older offenders may have been given a "break" at earlier stages of police or court processing, it may be that only the most serious older offenders actually reach the sentencing stage (Fattah & Sacco, 1989). In effect, earlier leniency in the system may lead to what looks like harsh treatment by the sentencing judge.

Older Offenders Sentenced More Leniently

In spite of the preceding arguments, drawing from the literature on sentencing and on the sociology of age roles, we expect that older offenders will receive more lenient sentencing outcomes than their younger counterparts, net of other factors. This expectation is grounded in four main considerations that are likely to shape judges' sense of fairness and the playing out of the focal concerns noted above. These considerations—age-differentiated severity of imprisonment, practicality, future criminality, and relative dangerousness—overlap but each is distinct enough to be treated separately.

Differential Severity of Punishment

Doing time in jail or prison may be perceived as harder on older than younger offenders because of the perception that punishments are disproportionately felt. Time for older offenders is more likely to be seen as a diminishing, exhaustible resource wherein the future becomes increasingly valuable. A year of imprisonment given to an offender in his fifties or sixties takes a considerably larger proportion of that person's remaining years than the same punishment assigned to a 25-year-old offender (Sherwin, 1990). Also, older offenders may be seen as being more vulnerable to aggression from younger offenders, and in other ways may adapt less well to prison conditions.

Practicality

Judges also may conclude that sending older offenders to prison is financially costly, burdensome to correctional officials, and poses special problems for prison staff (e.g., special diets, medications, assorted health problems). The costs to society (or the state) of incarcerating older offenders are potentially much greater than for younger offenders due to special physical and psychological needs of the aged and the greater probability of death in prison (Adams, 1995).

Future Criminality

Judges (and other court officials) may believe that older persons are better able to reform themselves and that they are less likely to possess the pervasive criminal tendencies or physical skills that characterize younger offenders. Older persons are also less likely to be seen as part of a crime-generating peer group, and their criminal behavior is more likely to be seen as idiosyncratic. For example, the criminal activities of older offenders may be explained away as resulting from forces outside their control, such as extreme environmental circumstances or health problems associated with advanced age. It generally appears that older offenders are viewed as less likely to transgress in the future, have a good many "escape hatches" for crime, and receive a good deal of forgiving. Older offenders also may be more astute at swaying the sentencing judge toward a lenient sanction by showing remorse or rehabilitation (Steffensmeier, 1986).

Relative Dangerousness

Judges are likely to see the older offender as posing a lower risk of danger to the community than the younger offender. The decline in physical prowess and pugnacity accompanying advanced age leads to the expectation that older persons are less aggressive and less capable of using force to harm or threaten someone. In other areas of sentencing research, the general rule is well-established that the severity of the sentence is a function of the degree of actual or threatened physical harm in the offense (Steffensmeier, 1980). Older offenders are seen as less dangerous and the general community is simply less frightened by them. Releasing them back into the community (as compared to releasing younger offenders) is less likely to result in recidivating behavior that reflects badly both on the court and the sentencing judge.

Pennsylvania Data

The Pennsylvania data offer some of the richest information available in the country for analyzing judges' sentencing decisions regarding the decision to imprison, the length of the prison term, and age differences in sentence outcomes. Enacted in 1982 and applying to all offenders convicted of a felony or serious misdemeanor, the purpose of the Pennsylvania guidelines was to establish sentencing standards in the form of a sentencing matrix for each combination of offense severity and criminal history (Kramer & Scirica, 1986). First, the Pennsylvania guidelines system standardized the calculation and presentation of the defendant's prior record to the court, improved the likelihood that information about prior record is collected and recorded accurately, and ensured that sentencing judges are informed of the defendant's prior record and conviction-offense gravity score. The provision of criminal history information at sentencing is haphazard in many states; even when prior record information is collected, it may not be presented to, or considered by, the court. Thus, the Pennsylvania data are more likely to reflect accurately the impact of prior record on sentencing than is true of sentencing statistics from most other jurisdictions.

Another advantage of the Pennsylvania data is that the guidelines sentencing structure is a comparatively "loose" one that permits significant judicial discretion (Tonry, 1987). Also, the Pennsylvania criminal code endorses several sanction philosophies (for deterrence and incapacitation as well as for rehabilitation and retribution), so that there is considerable leeway for case characteristics to affect the sentences imposed, both within and across crime categories. Finally, the large number of cases (roughly 210,000, including 7,000 elders) enables a comprehensive and in-depth analysis of age effects on sentencing. Small sample size has prevented most prior research on the issue of age bias in sentencing from adequately controlling for the role of severity and type of offense in sentencing, and from considering the full range of ages, including whether curvilinear effects exist.

The data for this study are based on the monitoring system developed by the Pennsylvania Commission on Sentencing. Each sentence given for a separate transaction must be reported to the Commission. Besides age, independent variables include a combination of legally prescribed variables, offender characteristics such as gender and race, and contextual factors such as caseload size and mode of conviction (plea vs. trial). The legally prescribed variables include the severity of the convicted offense (severity) and criminal history score (history). We used the most serious conviction offense as defined by the Pennsylvania crimes code and a 10-point scale developed by the Commission ranking each statutory offense on the scale. To measure criminal history, we used a weighted, 7-category scale also developed by the Commission. The criminal history score measures the number and severity of the defendant's past convictions.

In the interest of parsimony and to ensure adequate sample size, we simplified the age categorizations into five age groups: late teens, 18 to 19; young adult, 20 to 29; middle-aged, 30 to 39 and 40 to 49; and older age, 50+ (broken out further into 50 to 59, 60+). Our analysis revealed that the curvilinear age relationship described earlier prevails in the data here—youthful offenders (ages 18 to 19) are sentenced more leniently than young adult offenders (ages 20 to 29) but more harshly than older offenders (50+). Because our interest centers on the older offender, we focus on the sentencing outcomes of defendants aged 50 to 59 and 60+.

Table 9.1 provides a breakdown of the kinds of offenses for which older persons are convicted, in comparison to younger age groups. The figures in the left side of Table 9.1 refer to the percentage that older offenders (either 50+ or 50 to 59 and 60+) contribute to total convictions for each offense. These percentages indicate how much crime older persons commit relative to other age groups. For example, persons age 50+ committed 4.3% of all homicides; broken out further, the 50 to 59 group committed 2.9%, and the 60+ group, 1.6% of all homicides. The profile-percent figures in the right side of the column show the types of crimes for which older persons are convicted. For each age grouping, this column reflects the percentage among all elder convictions of those convicted for each of the crime categories and nine offense groupings (summing these percentages will equal 100%). For example, of all convictions among the 50+ group, only 1.2% were convicted for homicide; broken out

TABLE 9.1 Percentage of Elderly Among Total Criminal Convictions and Profile of Elderly Offenders (1991–1994, Pennsylvania)

| | | Age | | | | | |
| | | 50+ | | 50–59 | | 60+ | |
Offense type	N	Percentage of total	Profile (%)	Percentage of total	Profile (%)	Percentage of total	Profile (%)
Total offenses	209856	3.3	100.0	2.3	100.0	1.0	100.0
Violent offense	26987	3.6	14.4	2.6	14.7	1.0	13.6
Homicide	1871	4.3	1.2	2.9	1.1	1.6	1.4
Assault	24955	3.6	13.1	2.6	13.5	1.1	12.2
Kidnapping	161	3.1	0.1	3.1	0.1	—	—
Sexual assault	5338	12.0	9.4	7.0	7.8	5.0	12.9
Rape	1562	4.7	1.1	2.8	0.9	2.0	1.4
Indecent assault	3776	15.1	8.3	8.7	6.9	6.6	11.5
Serious property	24627	1.0	3.5	0.8	4.3	0.2	1.7
Robbery	8856	0.7	0.7	0.6	1.1	0.1	0.4
Burglary	14968	0.9	0.9	0.8	2.6	0.1	0.6
Arson	803	5.1	0.6	3.2	0.5	2.0	0.7
Theft/fraud	62449	3.0	27.2	2.2	28.6	0.8	24.1
Felony theft	15081	2.6	5.7	2.0	6.4	0.6	4.3
Misd. theft	24676	1.6	5.9	1.3	6.8	0.3	3.9
Felony retail theft	6206	6.0	5.4	4.0	5.2	2.1	5.9
Misd. retail theft	6215	5.8	5.2	3.6	4.7	2.2	6.4
Felony forgery	5092	2.5	1.8	2.1	2.2	0.4	0.9
Misd. forgery	275	1.8	0.1	1.1	0.1	0.7	0.1
Misd. bad check	4904	4.2	3.0	3.2	3.1	1.2	2.6
Serious drug	19877	2.6	5.6	1.9	13.1	0.7	10.7
Minor drug	33081	1.9	12.3	1.6	6.5	0.3	3.6

(continued)

TABLE 9.1   (continued)

Offense type	N	50+		50–59		60+	
		Percentage of total	Profile (%)	Percentage of total	Profile (%)	Percentage of total	Profile (%)
Miscellaneous	17642	3.7	9.5	2.5	9.1	1.3	10.4
Weapons	1324	3.3	0.6	2.7	0.7	0.7	0.4
Corrupt organization	124	9.7	0.2	4.1	0.1	5.8	0.3
Involuntary manslaughter	674	7.4	0.7	4.4	0.6	3.2	1.0
Catastrophe	194	4.6	0.1	2.2	0.1	2.7	0.2
Criminal mischief	1600	2.2	0.5	1.7	0.6	0.6	0.4
Criminal trespassing	3350	1.4	0.7	0.9	0.7	0.5	0.7
Administration of justice	3978	2.2	1.3	1.7	1.4	0.5	0.9
Prostitution	1659	0.9	0.2	0.6	0.2	0.4	0.3
Firearms violation	4739	7.5	5.2	4.8	4.8	2.8	6.1
Other misdemeanor	16839	6.3	15.5	3.8	13.3	2.6	20.4
Other felony	3016	6.1	2.7	4.4	2.7	1.9	2.7

further, the profile percentages for homicide are 1.1% among those 50 to 59 and 1.4% among those 60 and over.

Specifically, we find:

• 3% of the total offenders convicted in Pennsylvania trial courts are 50+ years old. Of these, 2% are between the ages of 50 and 59 and 1% are age 60 or older

- Types of conviction offenses for older offenders are generally consistent with findings from analyses of elder arrest statistics (Steffensmeier, 1987):

    - Theft/fraud offenses comprise the largest number of convictions for offenders age 50+ (n = 1873) and make up the highest profile percentages for each age group (50+, 50 to 59, 60+)
    - Retail theft (felony and misdemeanor) represents the largest percent of total convictions within the theft/fraud category
    - While offenders in the 50+ age group are convicted of 12% of the total sex-related offenses, most of the sex-related offenses in this age group are less serious, misdemeanor offenses (e.g., indecent assault)
    - Older offenders (50+) comprise only a small proportion of serious property and drug convictions relative to the other age groups

- Profile percentages of the 50 to 59 age group show this group to be more prevalent in drug, theft/fraud, serious property, and violent offenses than the 60+ group. The 60+ group is most prevalent in misdemeanor offenses, retail theft, indecent assault, and miscellaneous offenses (firearms violation) relative to the 50 to 59 group

Findings

The bivariate analysis revealed that offense severity and prior record have large effects on sentence outcomes and thus are important statistical controls for estimating age effects. We also found that age is related to sentence outcomes—older defendants are treated more leniently than their younger counterparts. But the latter also have higher prior record and offense gravity scores. At issue here, therefore, is whether the "age advantage" persists when these and other variables known to influence sentencing are taken into account.

Because sentencing is a two-stage process, involving first a decision about whether to imprison and second, if incarceration is selected, a decision about the length of sentence, we employ two dependent variables: incarcerated versus not incarcerated (in/out decision) and length-of-prison term. Logistic regression is used to analyze the in/out or probation/prison decision and ordinary least squares (OLS) regression to analyze the length-of-term decision. Because the sample size is so large in our models, statistical tests must be interpreted with caution. We judge the relative importance of the substantive effects of the independent variables according to probability differences in the likelihood of incarceration and differences in months for sentence length.[2]

Our analysis first compares nondrug with drug cases and then collapses the offenses into three offense groupings (violent, property, drugs) and compares age effects across them. We also explore age effects for several offenses which have a comparatively high elder involvement (e.g., retail theft). Lastly, we go beyond the Pennsylvania data to assess whether the patterns observed here also hold when federal sentencing practices are examined.

Probation Versus Imprisonment Decision

Table 9.2 displays the results of the models estimating the effects of age on sentencing while controlling for the effects of the other variables. The models are presented separately for four groupings of offenses: total nondrug, violent, property, and drug. The reference category for all comparisons is young adult offenders (ages 20 to 29) who generally receive harsher sentence outcomes than other age groups. The results for the in/out decision are displayed on the left and those for the length-of-term decision are on the right side of the table.

For the total nondrug sample, we find that the older the defendant, the more likely he/she is to receive probation and the less likely he/she is to be imprisoned. This greater leniency toward older offenders remains consistent (i.e., about the same magnitude) across the violent and property-offense subgroupings of the nondrug total.

---

[2]The formula for converting odds ratios to probability effects is $[(\text{odds ratio})/(\text{odds ratio}+1)]-.5$

TABLE 9.2   Effects of "Elderly" on Sentence Outcomes in Pennsylvania, by Type of Offense

| | In/out decision (prob. diff.) | | | | Length of term (mos. length difference) | | | |
Age	Total nondrug	Violent	Property	Drug	Total nondrug	Violent	Property	Drug
20–29*	—	—	—	—	—	—	—	—
30–39	−.04	−.05	−.05	−.04	−1.0	−.19	−2.0	−.28
40–49	−.08	−.17	−.09	−.08	−2.6	−.70	−3.4	−1.1
50–59	−.13	−.21	−.15	−.14	−5.1	−.90	−6.0	−2.1
60+	−.26	−.37	−.29	−.15	−10.6	−1.9	−11.9	−2.0

*Age 20 to 29 is the reference group, meaning that the other age groups are compared with the age 20 to 29 group.

In approximate terms, older defendants aged 50 to 59 are about 5% less likely to be incarcerated than 30 to 49-year-olds, and about 15% less likely than 20 to 29-year-olds. The age effect is even larger when defendants age 60 and over are considered. They are about 30% less likely to be incarcerated than 20 to 29-year-olds. Notably, the age advantage in sentencing leniency is larger for nondrug offenses than drug offenses. The latter is consistent with age-based expectations that the softening effects on punishment severity stemming from a perception of lesser danger and greater rehabilitative potential among older offenders apply less to older drug offenders.

Sentence Length

Turning next to the sentence-length decision, the findings generally parallel those reported for the probation versus imprisonment decision. For the sample as a whole, we find that older defendants—and especially those over age 60—receive shorter sentences than their younger counterparts. Sentence lengths for the total nondrug group are incrementally more lenient with growing age. The age advantage is fairly substantial for property offenses (about 5 to 6 months),

198 • **ELDERS AND IMPRISONMENT**

whereas it is small or trivial for violent and drug offenses (less than 2 months). Note also that the greater leniency typically extended to those 60 and over, the oldest criminal defendants, does not materialize among drug offenders (i.e., the sentence lengths imposed on them are identical to those imposed on the 50 to 59 age group). In sum: older defendants are treated more leniently than their younger counterparts; however, the age advantage is stronger for property than violent or drug offending. Notably, the oldest defendants (age 60+) receive the shortest sentences—but again, the difference is smaller for drug offending and negligible when they are compared to the 50 to 59 age group.

Select Offenses

Because our data include sufficient numbers of older offenders convicted of particular crimes, we also can examine whether they receive especially lenient treatment for crimes like shoplifting as some writers have suggested (Cutsall & Adams, 1983; Wilbanks & Kim, 1984). Table 9.3 compares the sentence outcomes of older defendants to their younger counterparts for selected offenses in which elder involvement is relatively high.

TABLE 9.3 Effects of "Elderly" on Sentence Outcomes in Pennsylvania for Select Offenses (Forgery, Theft, Retail Theft, Drug Sales)

	In/out decision (prob. diff.)				Length of term (mos. length difference)			
Age	Forgery	Theft	Retail theft	Drug sales	Forgery	Theft	Retail theft	Drug sales
20–29[*]	—	—	—	—	—	—	—	—
30–39	−.02	−.09	−.03	−.04	−.70	−3.30	−.30	−.49
40–49	−.08	−.08	−.09	−.06	−.97	−.34	−.94	−.15
50–59	−.03	−.11	−.19	−.08	−2.34	−2.56	−2.77	−.05
60+	−.29	−.21	−.28	−.18	−10.80	−4.28	−2.73	−1.16

[*]Age 20 to 29 is the reference category.

The findings echo those reported above. Older defendants—especially those 60 and over—are less likely to be imprisoned and they also receive somewhat shorter prison terms if incarcerated. Across all four offenses, defendants aged 60+ are about 20% to 30% less likely to be imprisoned than young adults aged 20 to 29. Notably, the age advantage is smallest in the case of drug sales/distribution (about 18% less likely to be imprisoned). Older offenders also receive shorter prison sentences across the three property offenses (about 5 months) but the age advantage is trivial for drug sales/distribution (about one month). Note also that the age advantage is greatest among those 60 and over who, on average, receive shorter sentences than any other age group, including 50- to 59-year-olds.

U.S. Federal Sentencing Data[3]

To test further our Pennsylvania findings, we also examined age effects on sentencing practices involving male defendants in U.S. federal courts for the 1993–96 period. Following passage of the 1984 Sentencing Reform Act, a uniform set of guideline ranges determined by the combined consideration of the offender's criminal history and offense conduct is now applied by the federal court system in sentencing all criminal cases (Katzenelson & Conley, 1997; Wilkins & Steer, 1993). Thus, similar to Pennsylvania, the federal guidelines system structures but does not eliminate judicial discretion. The sentencing court, once it determines a defendant's final offense level and criminal history, has discretion to impose a sentence from any point within the applicable range or, in unusual circumstances, to depart above or below the range (Katzenelson & Conley, 1997; Wilkins & Steer, 1993).

We conducted separate analyses of drug and nondrug cases because drug convictions comprise almost 40% of all federal cases. The results, partitioned for drug and nondrug cases, are displayed

---

[3]Compared to other datasets on sentencing outcomes, the federal data entail unusually rigorous controls for prior record (i.e., 6-point scale) and offense seriousness (i.e., 43-point scale), along with information on defendant characteristics and contextual factors which prior research suggests might influence sentence outcomes.

TABLE 9.4   Effects of "Elderly" on Sentence Outcomes in U.S. Federal Courts for Nondrug and Drug Cases (1993–1996)

	Nondrug offenses		Drug offenses	
Age	In/out (prob. diff.)	Length of term (in months)	In/out (prob. effect)	Length of term (in months)
20–29*	—	—	—	—
30–39	−.07	−.14	−.04	−.08
50+	−.11	−3.13	−.08	−1.06

* Age 20 to 29 is the reference category.

in Table 9.4. The elder breakdown is only for ages 50 and over because of the small number of federal cases involving offenders age 60+. The findings parallel those found for the Pennsylvania. Older offenders (50+) are less likely to be imprisoned and they also receive shorter sentences than their younger counterparts. Relative to young-adult defendants, for example, older federal defendants convicted of nondrug offenses are about 11% less likely to be imprisoned; and, on average, they receive sentences that are about 3 months shorter. For drug cases, the differences persist but age effects are smaller—older defendants are about 8% less likely to be imprisoned and receive prison sentences about one month shorter. Thus, both the Pennsylvania and the federal data show that the age advantage in sentencing outcomes is diminished in drug cases.

Summary and Implications

These findings generally support the age bias model that we articulated earlier. Older offenders are somewhat less likely to be imprisoned than younger offenders; and if imprisoned, older offenders receive somewhat shorter prison terms. This age advantage is greater in cases involving property and violent offending than in drug cases. Importantly, these patterns were reflected in both Pennsylvania and federal sentencing practices.

However, an exception to this age advantage occurs in drug cases—where older defendants receive sentences roughly on par with other age groups (i.e., somewhat more lenient than young adults but almost identical to the 30 to 39 and 40 to 49 age groups). Also, the especially lenient treatment of offenders age 60+ does not materialize in drug cases (i.e., receive sentences essentially identical those received by 50- to 59-year-olds). The fact that the age advantage is diminished for drug-type offenses suggests that judges are as likely (or nearly so) to attribute stability of disposition to commit future drug-law violations to older as compared to younger drug offenders. Judges also may be particularly disparaging of the corrupting leverage of older drug traffickers whose offense behavior departs too far from age-linked expectations to justify leniency. However, an important caveat here is that our findings of a diminished age advantage in drug cases must be interpreted cautiously in view of the small number of older persons convicted of drug offenses. Such a small number can contribute to highly unstable estimates. Nonetheless, it is consistent with our theoretical expectations as outlined earlier.

The finding that the age advantage is largest in property offending cases is also consistent with expectations that older defendants are more likely to receive favorable outcomes when the courts are responding to defendants charged with minor crimes, on grounds that older persons committing serious crimes depart too far from traditional age-graded expectations, and, consequently, preferential treatment ceases. Also, the effects of age-based expectations (e.g., lesser aggression and strength of older persons) in softening the "dangerous" label associated with criminal behavior is likely to apply more to property than violent offending since the latter so strongly confirms the attribution.

Finally, there is an ongoing debate within law and criminal justice about whether age differences in sentencing outcomes, that is, the more lenient sentencing of older offenders, constitute warranted or unwarranted disparities (Sherwin, 1990; Acker, 1990; Pertierra, 1995). On the one hand, in view of the emphasis on equality before the law in our justice system, it is reasonable to expect that judges will sentence strictly on the basis of what defendants have allegedly done, not on who they are or on how old they are. Older offenders should receive sentences as severe (or as lenient) as younger offenders convicted of identical offenses and with similar prior records.

This view is buttressed by the bulk of research on sentencing which has established the overwhelming importance of legally relevant variables such as offense seriousness and prior record in sentence outcomes. Indeed, our findings also show that these legal variables are by far the most important determinants of sentence severity. On the other hand, to the extent that the age-linked considerations described earlier are seen as legitimate antecedents of judicial decision making, an overall pattern of more lenient outcomes for older offenders may still be defined as warranted and ought not necessarily be construed as age "bias." That is, it's appropriate for judges to use age as a basis for projecting behavioral expectations about whether the offender (1) is a good or bad risk for rehabilitation, (2) is a potential danger to the community, (3) is more or less blameworthy and deserving of punishment, and (4) poses special correctional costs. Whatever is advocated, these two positions represent conflicting views of "fairness" and constitute value judgments not easily resolvable, if at all, by empirical inquiry.

Conclusions

It is widely assumed that senior citizens who face criminal penalties are an advantaged group. Our findings confirm this conventional wisdom and show, in particular, that offenders 60 and over receive sentences that are especially lenient relative to other age groups. A partial caveat to this overall pattern is that older persons convicted of drug offenses receive sentences roughly on par with their younger counterparts. Apparently, judges are more uncertain about the "reform capabilities" of older drug offenders relative to older defendants convicted of committing violent or property offenses. Judges also seem to view older drug offenders (i.e., traffickers) as especially degenerate and a threat to society.

We interpret the overall more lenient sentencing of older defendants as consistent with the "age bias" model described earlier, which emphasized the interrelationship between judges' sentencing concerns (blameworthiness, protection of the community, and practicality or organizational demands) and age-linked attributions with regard to levels of dangerousness, propensity for crime, and ability to do time in prison. At issue from a policy perspective, is whether the statistically observed age disparities are warranted or unwarranted? To the extent that these age-based considerations reflect "real" differences in crime propensity or blameworthiness, they can be viewed as legitimate antecedents of judicial decision making. It is more debatable, but it can be plausibly argued that even factors such as the "costs" to the justice/correctional system of jailing older offenders are legitimate considerations in judges' sentencing.

References

Acker, J. R. (1990). On confusing justice with mercy: A reply to Professor Sherwin. *Prison Journal, 80,* 128–130.

Adams, W. E., Jr. (1995). The incarceration of older criminals: Balancing safety, cost, and humanitarian concerns. *Nova Law Review, 19,* 465–486.

Alston, L. T. (1986). *Crime and older Americans.* Springfield, IL: Charles C Thomas.

Champion, D. (1987). Elderly felons and sentencing severity: Intergenerational variations in leniency and sentencing trends. *Criminal Justice Review, 12,* 7–14.

Cutsall, L., & Adams, K. (1983). Responding to the older offender: Age selectivity in the processing of shoplifters. *Criminal Justice Review, 6,* 7–32.

Curran, D. (1984). Characteristics of the elderly shoplifter and the effects of sanctions on recidivism. In W. Wilbanks & P. Kim (Eds.), *Elderly criminals* (pp. 123–141). New York: University Press of America.

Fattah, E., & Sacco, V. (1989). *Crime and victimization of the elderly.* New York: Springer-Verlag.

Feinberg, G. D., & Khosla, D. (1985, September). Sanctioning elderly delinquents. *Trial,* pp. 46–50.

Kalvern, H., & Zeisel, H. (1966). *The American jury.* Chicago: University of Chicago Press.

Katzenelson, S., & Conley, K. (1997). *Guideline sentences in the ninth circuit.* Washington, DC: United States Sentencing Commission.

Kramer, J. H., & Scirica, A. J. (1986). Complex policy choices—the Pennsylvania commission on sentencing. *Federal Probation, 50,* 15–23.

Kramer, J. H., & Steffensmeier, D. (1993). Race and imprisonment decisions. *Sociological Quarterly, 34,* 357–376.

McCarthy, B., & Langworthy, R. (Eds.). (1992). *Offender perspectives in criminology and criminal justice.* New York: Praeger.

Myers, M. A., & Talarico, S. M. (1987). *The social contexts of criminal sentencing.* New York: Springer-Verlag.

Newman, E., Newman, D., & Gewirts, M. (Eds.). (1984). *Elderly criminals.* Cambridge, MA: Oelgeschlager, Gunn, and Hain.

Pertierra, C. J. (1995). Do the crime, do the time: Should elderly criminals receive proportionate sentences? *Nova Law Review, 19,* 793–819.

Riley, M. W., Foner, A., & Waring, J. (1988). Sociology of age. In N. Smelser (Ed.), *Handbook of sociology* (pp. 243–290). New York: Macmillan.

Sherwin, R. (1990). Employing life expectancy as a guideline in sentencing criminal offenders: Toward a humanistic proposal for change. *Prison Journal, 80,* 12–16.

Steffensmeier, D. (1980). Assessing the impact of the women's movement on sex-based differences in the handling of adult criminal defendants. *Crime and Delinquency, 23,* 344–356.

Steffensmeier, D. (1986). *The fence: In the shadow of two worlds.* Totowa, NJ: Rowman and Littlefield.

Steffensmeier, D. (1987). The invention of the new: Senior citizen criminal. *Research on Aging, 9,* 281–311.

Steffensmeier, D., & Allan, E. (1995). Gender, age, and crime. In J. Sheley (Ed.), *Handbook of Criminology.* Wadsworth.

Steffensmeier, D., Kramer, J., & Streifel, C. (1993). Gender and imprisonment decisions. *Criminology, 31,* 411–446.

Steffensmeier, D., Kramer, J., & Ulmer, J. (1995). Age differences in sentencing. *Justice Quarterly, 12,* 583–602.

Steffensmeier, D., Ulmer, J., & Kramer, J. (1998). The interaction of race, gender and age in criminal sentencing: The punishment cost of being young, black and male. *Criminology* (November).

Tonry, M. (1987). Sentencing guidelines and their effects. In A. von Hirsch, K. A. Knapp, & M. Tonry (Eds.), *The Sentencing Commission and Its Guidelines* (pp. 16–46). Northeastern University Press.

Ulmer, J. (1997). *Social worlds of sentencing: Court communities under sentencing guidelines.* Albany, NY: SUNY Press.

Wilbanks, W. (1988). Are elderly felons treated more leniently by the criminal justice system. *International Journal of Aging and Human Development, 26,* 275–288.

Wilbanks, W., & Kim, P. (1984). *Elderly criminals.* New York: University Press of America.

Wilkins, W., & Steer, J. (1993). The role of sentencing guideline amendments in reducing unwarranted sentencing disparity. *Washington and Lee Law Review, 50,* 63–88.

Suggested Readings

Albonetti, C. (1991). An integration of theories to explain judicial discretion. *Social Problems, 38,* 247–266.

Goetting, A. (1983). The elderly in prison: Issues and perspectives. *Journal of Research in Crime and Delinquency, 20,* 291–309.

Chapter 10

The Older Prisoner: Social, Psychological, and Medical Considerations

John J. Kerbs

The United States imprisons its citizens at a rate that is now second only to Russia (Mauer, 1997). As of mid-1998, America's jails and prisons held 1,802,496 persons, a rate of imprisonment of 668 persons per 100,000 U.S. residents 18 years of age and older (Gilliard, 1999). This rate is more than twice that in 1995 (313). On average, 1,475 inmates were added each week to this nation's jails and prisons between mid-1997 and mid-1998 (Gilliard, 1999).

As the number of imprisoned adults rises, there is increasing concern about the growing number of older prisoners (Aday, 1994b; Benekos & Merlo, 1995; Chaneles, 1987). Even though many Americans hold stereotypes of adult inmates as "aggressive young men," prison administrators have found that "the 'graying' of America is indeed reflected in the prison population" (Morton, 1992, p. 2). Recent statistics indicate that older prisoners (OPs) represent the fastest growing age group in prison (Ellsworth & Helle, 1994, p. 43). In light of this expansion and the need to plan for America's graying prison population, this chapter summarizes the best available information on OPs including: (a) the growing number of older inmates in federal and state prisons; (b) the demographic characteristics of older prisoners; (c) the older prisoner's health needs, that is, physical, mental, and social health needs; and (d) accompanying service delivery issues.

The Growing Number of Older Inmates in Federal and State Prisons

Definitional Issues Concerning Age

Although a significant number of criminologists have reviewed the problems associated with trying to define a cutoff point beyond which one is considered old in criminological research, no clear consensus has emerged (Fattah & Sacco, 1989; Forsyth & Gramling, 1988; Newman, 1984). Governmental programs often recognize age 65 as the cutoff because retirement and social security benefits are tied to this age, but many criminologists and criminal justice systems usually consider "55 and over" as old (Newman, 1984). Still, other criminologists (Morton, 1992) advocate for even lower cutoffs (age 50 and older). Because extant research varies in age-related cutoffs used to define populations under examination, this chapter specifies age categories where appropriate.

The Growing Number of Older Prisoners

In 1998, OPs age 50 or older represented about 7% of the total federal and state prison population. The most recent data from Camp and Camp (1991–1998) indicate that the number of OPs more than doubled from 34,845 in 1991 to 83,667 in 1998 (see Table 10.1). Given these rising figures, many predict the day will come soon when correctional nursing homes become commonplace. Some experts have suggested ironically that states will need to rename prisons as "Centers for the Treatment of Old Folks" (Rosefield,

TABLE 10.1   Number of Prisoners Age 50 and Older in Adult
Correctional Agencies on January 1

Correctional agency	1991	1992	1993	1994	1995	1996	1997	1998
State[a]	28,948	35,032	37,058	41,309	45,226	50,896	62,272	69,994
Federal[b]	5,897	6,554	7,244	9,169	10,055	12,108	11,271	13,673
Total[c]	34,845	41,586	44,302	50,478	55,281	63,004	73,543	83,667

[a]Figures represent the aggregate of all inmates 50 years of age and older in adult correctional agencies (i.e., prisons) on January 1 of each column year.
[b]Figures represent the aggregate of all inmates 50 years of age and older in the Federal Bureau of Prisons (FBOP) on January 1 of each column year.
[c]Totals for each year reflect the aggregate of federal and state prison populations. Please see Camp and Camp (1991–1998) for qualifications of data presented in Table 10.1.

1993) or "old age homes for felons" (Zimbardo, 1994). While such commentary appears extreme, the Federal Bureau of Prisons (FBOP) and a few states are well on their way towards having enough OPs to open correctional nursing homes. As of January 1998, the five states with the largest numbers of incarcerated inmates 50 years of age and older were Texas (9,126), California (8,659), Florida (4,403), New York (3,928), and Ohio (3,346); although these numbers are large, the FBOP clocked in with a total of 13,673 OPs in this age category (Camp & Camp, 1998).

By the year 2000, Chaneles (1987) projected, the United States will have approximately 125,000 inmates over age 50, with 40,000 to 50,000 over age 65. These projections appear realistic, given prevailing federal and state sentencing statutes (Benekos & Merlo, 1995; Ditton & Wilson, 1999; Turner, Sundt, Applegate, & Cullen, 1995) which emphasize determinate sentences,[1] long-term mandatory minimum sentences,[2] sentencing guidelines,[3] truth in sentencing (TIS)

---

[1]Determinate Sentencing—Determinate sentencing laws fix prison sentences, but allow for reductions via good-time or earned-time credit systems (Ditton & Wison, 1999).
[2]Mandatory Minimum Sentencing—These statutes required that offenders be sentenced to a specified amount of prison time (Ditton & Wison, 1999).
[3]Sentencing Guidelines—Such guidelines are established by sentencing commissions at the state and federal level to create a range of sentence lengths for specified offenses and offender characteristics (e.g., prior criminal history) (Ditton & Wison, 1999).

strategies,[4] and "three-strikes" sentencing strategies.[5] With respect to three-strikes strategies, the best available data indicate that 22 states and the federal government have enacted such policies (M. Mauer, personal communication, July 6, 1998). Many of these laws included "strikes" for nonviolent and drug-related crimes (Turner et al., 1995). Although it remains unclear whether these statutes have functioned as general deterrents leading to meaningful reductions in crime (Irwin & Austin, 1994; Petersilia, 1992; Steffensmeier & Harer, 1993; Turner et al., 1995; Visher, 1987; Zimring & Hawkins, 1991), academics and policy makers have noted that these statutes are responsible, in part, for both: (1) the rising incarceration rates; and (2) the rising number of OPs (Irwin & Austin, 1994; Benekos & Merlo, 1995; Turner et al., 1995).

Additionally, these laws have led to a "stacking effect" whereby OPs grow in both *number* (as seen in Table 10.1) and *proportion* due to sentencing statutes that hold young inmates longer, often into their golden years, without hope of parole (Zimbardo, 1994). In short, a substantial number of today's younger inmates will age in place and become tomorrow's OPs, that is, OPs who may or may not gain parole and/or release. The proportional stacking effect is visible in the rising average percentage of inmates (federal and state combined) who were 50 years of age and older as of January 1 for 1990 (4.9%), 1992 (5.7%), 1994 (5.9%), 1996 (6.6%), 1997 (6.8%), and 1998 (7.2%) (Camp & Camp, 1998). The initial elevations (in the early 90s) were probably due more to stiffer sentencing statutes requiring longer mandatory minimums (i.e., determinate sentences, mandatory-minimum sentences, sentencing guidelines, and TIS strategies) than to the "three strikes" statutes implemented thus far.

Finally, this stacking effect appears to be specific to OPs who are 50–64 years of age; Beck (1997) noted that the percentage of inmates 65 years of age and older did not significantly change between 1979 and 1991. The proportion of inmates 65 years of age and older is

[4]Truth In Sentencing (TIS)—These sentencing laws require prisoners to serve a substantial proportion (around 85% in many cases) of their court-ordered prison sentence. In comparison to determinate sentencing strategies, TIS laws often restrict or eliminate parole eligibility and good-time credits (Ditton & Wison, 1999).
[5]Three-Strikes Sentencing—These laws require life sentences (often without potential for parole) for recidivists.

probably stagnant at this point because cohorts of inmates (mostly younger inmates) sentenced on three-strikes statutes are yet to mature into this age bracket. Thus, inmates now sentenced via three-strikes statutes will age in place over the coming decades; and policy makers can expect to see consistently rising federal and state-level incarceration rates for the oldest of old inmates.

Demographic Characteristics of Older Prisoners

The Demography of Older Inmates in Prison

Nationally, the majority of OPs are non-Hispanic Whites; nevertheless, the OP population includes disproportionate numbers of African Americans, Latinos, and Native Americans. Additionally, most OPs over age 55 are male (about 95%); but the number of female OPs, like male OPs, is increasing annually (Florida Department of Corrections, 1993; Goetting, 1983; Kratcoski & Pownall, 1989; Merianos, Marquart, Damphousse, & Herbert, 1997). Educationally, the vast majority of OPs enter prison without high school diplomas and the average OP has a 7th-grade education (Goetting, 1983; Tobin & Metzler, 1983; Wilson & Vito, 1986). In terms of their marital status, about 34% of all OPs, as compared to 22% of all younger inmates, are married (Goetting, 1984).

Older inmates of state prisons are incarcerated for the gamut of offenses, but most are serving time for violent convictions such as homicide, and they are more likely serving time for violent crimes than are their younger counterparts (Goetting, 1984; Tobin & Metzler, 1983; Wilson & Vito, 1986). Beyond these findings, our knowledge of the demography of OPs is sketchy because most research fails to tease out differences involving intersections of age, gender, and race.

Older Inmate Typologies

Researchers in the early 1980s developed a number of typologies for OPs. Fry (1987); Goetting (1983, 1984); Metzler (1981); Morton

(1992); Tobin and Metzler (1983); and Teller and Howell (1981) provided detailed discussions of typologies. One of the original typologies identified two distinct types of OPs: (a) those incarcerated for the first time; and (b) those incarcerated more than once (Teller & Howell, 1981). Metzler (1981) saw three types: (a) those incarcerated at a young age for the first time who grew old in prison, (b) those incarcerated for the first time as older adults who are growing old in prison, and (c) multiple recidivists with multiple incarcerations. The most refined typology to date (Goetting, 1984) uses a four-category scheme developed from a national study of 11,397 state inmates in 1979. Of the total sample, 248 prisoners were 55 years of age or older, and each of these older inmates fell into one of the following four categories: (a) 41.38% were "old first offenders" who experienced their first incarceration at age 55 or older, (b) 2.32% were "oldtimers" who came into prison prior to age 55 and had served more than 20 continuous years, (c) 45.6% were "career criminals" who represented recidivists, excluding oldtimers, and (d) 10.68% were "young short-term first offenders" who came in prior to age 55 but had served fewer than 20 continuous years.

The heterogenous nature of OPs clearly demonstrated by this typology raises a few key policy issues. First, the largest proportion (45.6%) of OPs are career-criminal recidivists who represent valid public-safety concerns. Both the number and proportion of career criminals in prison will increase due to shifts towards determinate sentencing, TIS strategies, and recidivist statutes that provide long, mandatory minimums for repeated felony convictions, again often without options for parole (Irwin & Austin, 1994; Merianos et al., 1997; Petersilia, 1992; Turner et al., 1995). The second largest proportion (41.38%) of OPs experienced their first incarceration as older citizens. In contrast to these two groups, the smallest category consisted of "oldtimers" who grew old in prison as a result of a long-term incarceration. Although members of this group constituted only 2.32% of the older sample in 1979, they will undoubtedly grow in number and proportion as three-strikes legislation and longer mandatory-minimum sentences exert their effect (Benekos & Merlo, 1995; Turner et al., 1995). One study of New Jersey's prison system found that "nine out of ten inmates in their 30s will not have a chance at parole until they are at least 50 years old" (*Corrections Today*, 1990, p. 138).

The Older Prisoner's Health Needs (Physical, Psychological, and Social)

Most extant research has focused on younger inmates, which limits our current understanding of the often largely invisible OP population. Still, there is some information that can help concerned professionals, correctional staff and policy makers who wish to know more about this population.

The Older Prisoner's Physical Health

Some literature suggests that the health of the typical OP tends to deteriorate rapidly during incarceration (Rubenstein, 1984). This rapid decline (or accelerated biological aging) may be due, in part, to three factors: (a) unhealthy lifestyles prior to incarceration; (b) unhealthy lifestyles fostered in prison; and (c) harshness and stress of prison life, which exacerbates the aging process (Fattah & Sacco, 1989). Consequently, "the inmate population is generally considered to have aged roughly 10 years beyond the average citizen" (Rosefield, 1995, p. 4). In other words, a typical 50-year-old inmate would be physiologically similar to an average 60-year-old person outside of prison. On the other hand, Fattah and Sacco (1989) have argued that prison can potentially slow the aging process for those who lived destructive lifestyles and/or in substandard conditions prior to their incarceration.

A substantial proportion of OPs are likely to have serious health problems. Some studies have found that the average OP has three chronic health conditions and many have a history of alcohol abuse (Chaiklin & Fultz, 1985; *Corrections Today*, 1990; Wilson & Vito, 1986). Rosefield (1995) reported on one unpublished study of inmates over age 60 in a prison hospital that found an average of 2.4 medical conditions requiring seven to ten prescription medications per OP.

Even though most research on the OP's health is based on small and nonrandom samples, the specific health conditions experienced by aging inmates are worthy of review. In a survey of 31 OPs from two prisons in Florida, among whom 80% reported one or more medical problems and 60% claimed two or more (Vega & Silverman, 1988), 45% claimed to have significant cardiovascular illness. Other chronic medical problems (e.g., diabetes, arthritis, circulatory, and pulmonary diseases) were noted by inmates, and these problems were congruent with those found by Chaiklin and Fultz (1985), who studied the 12 oldest offenders in Maryland's prison system. Unfortunately, most prison hospitals are designed for acute care rather than the care of chronic illnesses (Alston, 1986). This situation raises policy questions addressed later in this chapter.

The Older Prisoner's Psychological Needs and Characteristics

Prisons are generally considered to have "deleterious effects caused by the 'dehumanizing' and 'depersonalizing' characteristics of [the] institutional environment" (Fattah & Sacco, 1989, p. 88). This caustic environment can lead to a rapid deterioration of the mental health of any prisoner, but perhaps more so for OPs (Fattah & Sacco, 1989). Psychologically, prison and the stress associated with prison may be more harmful to the OP than the younger prisoner because OPs are: (a) more sensitive to environmental prison stress (Silverman & Vega, 1990); and (b) more likely to put on a "facade of adjustment . . . which results from a denial and suppression of their feelings [regarding stress and anger]" (Vega & Silverman, 1988, p. 153).

Although no consensus exists in the literature regarding the psychological profile of OPs, Rubenstein (1984) found, from the literature of the 1970s, numerous studies that collectively suggest OPs are: (a) more introverted and neurotic than their younger counterparts; (b) more neurotic and experience more anxiety, apprehension, concern with physical functioning, and despondency than the general population; (c) more insecure and fearful of authority, correctional officers, the future, illness, pain, and young Black inmates; and (d) less active and more likely to have lower expectations, that is, they felt helplessness, as if they should give up. On the other hand, some studies have documented that OPs psychologically adjusted to prison better than younger inmates, because the former were less likely to be depressed and to experience psychic pain compared to their younger counterparts (Teller & Howell, 1981). Fattah and

Sacco (1989) also noted that prison might decrease loneliness for those who had few friends prior to incarceration.

Studies with such positive results, however, are few in number and the preponderance of research since 1980 documents poor psychological adjustment to prison life. For example, one researcher examined 248 OPs in Florida and found that "mental health concerns arose from the 24.2% who described life as dull, the 25.4% who listed their present life satisfaction as poor, and the 34.7% who reported they were not happy" (McCarthy, 1983, p. 65). Almost 30% felt lonely "quite" often and 39% said they were "sometimes" lonely. Although this study used a relatively large sample, the results remain tentative as McCarthy did not specify the study's sampling methodology. Aday (1994a) conducted the most recent psychological investigation, using a case-study research design to examine 25 OPs experiencing their first incarceration in a maximum-security reception center in the Southeast. On average, OPs were 68-years-old and their first reactions to prison late in life were often characterized by depression, family conflict, fear of dying in prison, and thoughts of suicide. Nonetheless, even with these problematic psychological characteristics, it is not clear if these characteristics are the effects of prison life or reflect preexisting states.

The Older Prisoner's Social Needs and Characteristics

Anytime someone enters prison, that person's social ties to those on the outside become strained and difficult to maintain. Incarceration contributes to the weakening of relationships between inmates and their respective families and friends (Aday & Webster, 1979; Rubenstein, 1984). Because OPs are not immune to this situation, they often become isolated. Some withdraw into a lonely and introverted existence, which is clearly documented in the literature (Eysenck, Rust, & Eysenck, 1977; McCarthy, 1983). Aging inmates who do not have external support cope more poorly in prison than those who maintain external support systems (Rubenstein, 1984). Complicating matters, an aging inmate's external support system may be tenuous because friends and relatives also tend to be older and prone to disability, death and illness, which restricts or eliminates visitation and even communication (Vega & Silverman, 1988).

For example, Wilson and Vito (1986) examined aging inmates (over age 49) in a medium security prison and found that many complained of not receiving regular visits from family and friends. Contact via phone and letters from family members was more frequent, but still limited. On average, they received only one phone call and/or letter every 1 to 2 weeks. Of the 25 first-time OPs examined by Aday (1994a), 11 reported *never* receiving visits from family members, seven received visits on at least a monthly basis, and the remaining seven reported visits of once or twice per year. Most of these inmates also stayed in touch with their families through mail and phone, but six "never made or received calls." Surprisingly, most of these OPs were positive about their family relationships: 15 said that they were *very satisfied*, two reported being *fairly satisfied*, and only eight said they were *not very satisfied*.

Other studies have found that career criminals (recidivists) have less stable family lives with higher incidences of divorce as compared to older offenders experiencing their first incarceration late in life (Rubenstein, 1984). Vega and Silverman (1988) found that aging inmates in two of Florida's prisons were partially "estranged" from their families. A majority (57%) of the OPs did not receive family visitors and only 10% had regular visits from friends. Finally, 90% indicated that they communicated with relatives by phone or mail.

Given issues surrounding disrupted communication with contacts outside of prison, one must wonder if aging inmates develop extensive internal ties with inmates and guards. Rubenstein (1984) indicated that they do. However, the literature on this issue documents mixed findings. Wiegand and Burger (1979) stated that "the aged in the institution [i.e., prison] are primarily loners. They do not join into groups" (p. 49). Reed and Glamser (1979) examined the social patterns of 52 male OPs in one prison and found that about 66% belonged to one or more organizations (e.g., Alcoholics Anonymous, American Legion, and Seventh Step). Although affiliation with prison organizations was found to be common, personal friendships were uncommon because many older inmates believed that confiding in a fellow inmate would be viewed as a weakness that could put them in danger. In stark contrast to the findings of Reed and Glamser (1979), Vega and Silverman (1988) found that 93% of OPs sampled formed friendships within prison. Congruent with the findings of Wiegand and Burger (1979), Wilson and Vito (1986), on the other hand, found that many OPs were "socially isolated" and only a few believed they had or could foster close friendships in prison. They reported, overall, very little involvement in prison programs.

The sample limitations noted for research regarding the physical and psychological characteristics of OPs are applicable to the research discussed in this section. Thus, the findings reviewed for the OP's social needs should be viewed as tentative as well due to the overreliance on nonrandom, small, and otherwise potentially unrepresentative samples.

Additional Aspects of the Older Prisoner's Psychosocial Adjustment to Prison

As previously discussed, OPs often seem to experience multiple problems, including but not limited to, adverse psychological outcomes, educational deficits, poor health and health care, and social support problems. These problems do affect the older inmate's ability to adjust to prison. Research by Sabath and Cowles (1988) found that low levels of education, poor health, and infrequent family visits led to poor adjustment in prison because these factors reduce the OP's ability to fill time with activities (i.e., recreation, social events, and work).

Adding to this complex mix of difficulties are the conditions of confinement, which also affect the OP's psychosocial adjustment to prison. Over the past two decades, U.S. prisons have changed in fundamental ways, and the proliferation of prison gangs represents one of the most detrimental changes over time. Gangs have effectually eroded the OP's quality of life (Hunt, Riegel, Morales, & Waldorf, 1993). Conflict between the generations also exists. In the past, aging inmates were afforded a higher status due to their advanced age and experience with crime; however, this has changed. Younger prisoners no longer respect OPs; indeed, they appear to disrespect them now (Hunt et al., 1993).

These changes mean that "victimization and fear of victimization by younger, stronger inmates is a serious problem for [OPs]" (Vito & Wilson, 1985, p. 18). Their fear can become so pronounced that some OPs restrict their activity by choosing to: (a) stay inside prison units and avoid the prison yard; or (b) only venture outside units in groups of two or more (Wilson & Vito, 1986). Unfortunately, the strongest predictor of an inmate's mental health (i.e., psycho-physiological disturbances) is his or her level of fear regarding other prisoners (McCorkle, 1993).

Although OPs appear to live in fear at times, they rarely act out. Compared to their younger counterparts, OPs are easier to supervise and less likely to escape, violate prison rules, and/or receive disciplinary reports (Goetting, 1984; Rubenstein, 1982, 1984; Wilson & Vito, 1986). OPs are so well-behaved that many prison officials view them as having a "stabilizing" or "calming" effect on younger inmates; thus, OPs are seen as "good insurance against future Atticas" (Krajick, 1979, p. 35 as cited in Vito & Wilson, 1985, p. 19). Interestingly, some empirical research supports this view (Mabli, Holley, Patrick, & Walls, 1979).

Of course, generalizing this stereotype of well-behaved OPs to all aging inmates is dangerous and inappropriate because some elders are "old and ornery" according to McShane and Williams (1990), who examined a group of 179 aging inmates 50 years of age and older. They discovered that about 9.5% ($n = 17$) of these inmates were "serious" disciplinary problems and 32% ($n = 57$) fell into a minor disciplinary category, whereas all others did not have disciplinary histories. Their most common rule violation was failing to obey orders, followed by possessing contraband and creating disturbances; but most OP rule violations were nonviolent. This same study also found that OPs with serious institutional disciplinary problems appear to be those who: (a) had served more time, (b) were serving longer sentences, and (c) had the longest times between visits from external contacts. Thus, three-strikes legislation and sentencing statutes that extend the average length of incarceration for many inmates may exacerbate the disciplinary problems of OPs.

The Institutional Dependency of Older Prisoners

The latest policy shifts that lead to longer terms of confinement for many OPs cause criminal justice professionals to increasingly fear that such statutes will create a population of inmates who may be difficult to decarcerate due to "institutional dependency"—a.k.a., "institutional neurosis," and "prisonization" (Alston, 1986; Fattah &

Sacco, 1989). Alston (1986) noted that institutional dependence, in its most pronounced form, occurs when "the individual gives over control of his[/her] life to the institution and ceases to participate in life outside its walls" (p. 216).

This condition is serious because inmates can become overly dependent upon the institution, making successful reintegration to the community more difficult. Aging inmates may be more prone to institutional dependence for several reasons. In addition to having lost social ties to the external community, OPs are more likely to have served longer sentences and thus have become more accustomed to the prison environment. In addition, the inmate's own "declining health and diminishing job skills can also encourage dependence on the protective environment of prison" (Alston, 1986, p. 216). Certain subgroups of OPs appear to be particularly prone to institutional dependency, including unmarried OPs, those first incarcerated at an early age, and recidivists (Fattah & Sacco, 1989).

The Health Needs and Characteristics of Older Female Prisoners

Unfortunately, we know little about older women in prison beyond their proportional representation in some studies. All of the studies previously reviewed (except Kratcoski & Babb [1990]) failed to examine older female inmates, leaving gender differences largely unexplored. The literature contains extremely little information on this very small category of prisoners (Rubenstein, 1984), and a similar dearth of research exists that explicitly examines the intersection of age, ethnicity, gender, and race. In one of the only published studies on female OPs, Kratcoski and Babb (1990) studied the psychosocial adjustment of 442 inmates between 50 and 84 years of age in multiple state and federal prisons. The sample had a mix of males (80%) and females (20%) and 23% of the sample was non-White. Gender differences were present. Twice as many of the women compared to the men (50% versus 25%) said they never had visitors. This may be due to the greater incidence of separation and divorce among women, as compared to men, in the sample, and the typical placement of female inmates into isolated, rural facilities. Additionally, female OPs were less likely than the men to participate in sporting and recreational programming, including card games, other games, and television. Furthermore, female OPs were less likely to interact with other inmates even though they were also less likely to view them as violent or aggressive. Finally and significantly, more female than male OPs reported being in poor or terrible health (47% versus 25%). Depression and worry were the two most persistent health problems experienced by aging female inmates.

Kratcoski and Babb (1990, p. 278) concluded that "most of the adjustment problems of older inmates . . . [were] primarily related to the type of institution structure in which they . . . [were] housed rather than to the gender of the inmates." Remote prisons and/or restrictive policies exacerbated the adjustment problems of both female and male OPs; however, the former are typically located in more isolated and remote high-security facilities.

Service Delivery Issues for Older Prisoners

The problems facing OPs are fairly clear, but we need more research because past studies have serious sampling problems that limit our capacity to competently inform policy for them. Past research has relied heavily upon nonrandom, small, and otherwise potentially unrepresentative samples. Future studies should emphasize and employ random sampling methodologies (hopefully at the state or national level); this would allow the results to be generalizable to large groups of OPs and not just those in a given prison and/or prison hospital.

Even though sampling problems limit our ability to form sound conclusions regarding the needs of OPs, it appears that they are, on average, medically challenged by chronic health problems; additionally, many OPs experience a variety of social and psychological problems. Unfortunately, most states do not appear to be prepared to work with these individuals. Aday (1994b) noted that "most states do not have any specific written policies which address aged or infirm inmates" (p. 48).

Although the presence of chronic health conditions among older prisoners appears to be the norm, most prison hospitals are geared towards the acute-care needs of younger inmates (Alston, 1986). Ninety percent of the 600 prison hospitals in the United States fail to "meet basic standards of care established by the medical profession" (Lundstrom, 1994, p. 166). This is a legal issue: all inmates have the right of access to medical care via *Estelle v. Gamble* (1976). Hence, prisons must do a better job of addressing both acute and chronic health problems by supplying a full array of services—acute care, dental, general medical, nutritional, and long-term care services (Kratcoski & Pownall, 1989). Clearly, substantial funding increases will be required to raise basic standards of care for OPs.

Not only is obtaining access to basic health care an issue for many OPs, access to other services also appears to be problematic. A 1990 survey of correctional health-service administrators in all 50 states and the District of Columbia (Aday, 1994b) showed that in 17 states there were no geriatric facilities or special programs for OPs. This raises serious concerns. According to the law, OPs have not only the right to appropriate medical treatment, but also rights to: (a) a reasonably safe environment, (b) appropriate treatment, (c) special education, (d) access to programs and resources, and (e) due process (American Correctional Association, 1992; Rosefield, 1995).

With respect to safety, most prison systems are only starting to develop policies, procedures, and programmatic options to increase the safety and decrease the victimization of OPs; in the meantime, direct victimization and fear of victimization by younger inmates are profound problems for OPs (Wilson & Vito, 1986). Interestingly, New Mexico recently went on record as indicating that the victimization of OPs was one of their most pressing problems in responding to the needs of aging/infirm inmates (Aday, 1994b) and at least one state (West Virginia) has created a protective custody section for OPs.

Educational and special education programming (now designed for younger inmates) needs to be redeveloped to meet the older inmate's developmental stage in life. GED programs and vocational training programs (the two main options available in prisons) hold little appeal for most in their sixth and seventh decades of life. Moreover, OPs receive little rehabilitation in prisons because "rehabilitation, as a correctional objective, is often dismissed in the case of . . . [OPs] on the grounds that it is neither feasible nor desirable" (Fattah & Sacco, 1989, p. 123). This leads prison administrators to allocate resources largely to younger inmates. Consequently, OPs rarely gain access to counseling, educational, and/or vocational prison programs (Sabath & Cowles, 1988; Wiegand & Burger, 1979; Wilson & Vito, 1986).

Although it is of concern that these programs are of little relevance to aging inmates due to their structure and content (Aday, 1994b), it is even more disturbing to hear that prison staff: (a) actively discourage OPs from attending such programs, or (b) openly deny them access to such programs (Goetting, 1983; Wiegand & Burger, 1979) simply because some correctional staff feel that "you can't teach an old dog new tricks" (Wiegand & Burger, 1979). In short, correctional staff are sometimes unwilling to refer OPs to the limited number of openings in educational programs (e.g., GED programs) because their preference is to offer courses to younger prisoners. Even though GED programming is probably more appropriate (developmentally speaking) for younger inmates, it is not at all clear that OPs are provided with equal access to programming compatible with their respective interests and needs—for example, college, continuing education, counseling to deal with grief and loss, walking programs, and sporting activities exclusively for OPs.

Beyond the availability of programs, the issue of physical access to programs and facilities must be addressed. Clearly, the physical facilities of most prisons are not structurally designed for OPs to: (a) minimize falls; (b) permit OPs with mobility limitations or assistive devices barrier-free access to bathrooms and other facilities; or (c) allow for short walks to access meals, medical services, social services, and other needed services (Adams, 1995; Aday, 1994b; Morton, 1992; Zimbardo, 1994). The implication of this situation is obvious: existing prisons will need to be retrofitted for physically challenged OPs. Retrofitting for equal access is essential (not optional) in light of the 1998 U.S. Supreme Court Decision (*Pennsylvania Department of Corrections v. Yeskey*), which found that Title II of the Americans with Disabilities Act of 1990 unambiguously extends to state prison inmates.

Greater attention to the OPs' psychological needs is also critical. Prison counseling programs are "geared to rehabilitate younger inmates, rather than coping with issues such as chronic illness or death" (Aday, 1994b, p. 53). More programming is needed to address issues concerning chronic illness, death and dying, depression, grief, institutional dependence, isolation, loss, and other concerns pressing older inmates. Programmatic needs are clear and present, but the capacity to address these needs is limited by the lack of adequate staff. This problem stems from the absence of staff training programs, as well as the absence of proper staff screening protocols to determine who should work with OPs in the first place (Aday, 1994b).

Even though OPs possess certain legal rights noted previously, in practice their rights appear to be largely illusory (i.e., rhetorical). The failure of prisons to safeguard these rights has led academics, legal scholars, and correctional practitioners to warn policy makers about the possibility of individual and class-action lawsuits against prison facilities (Booth, 1989; Dugger, 1988; Goetting, 1985; Lundstrom, 1994; Morton, 1992). Aggressive efforts are needed to avoid litigation by correcting programmatic and structural deficiencies in prison that differentially and adversely affect OPs. It remains unclear, at this time, whether the motivation for this correction is adequate in 1999 to foster substantive reforms. Still, it is clear that prison systems and correctional staff are not immune to litigation. In 1997, 30,336 lawsuits were filed against agencies or staff in 47 jurisdictions; moreover, 148 class-action lawsuits across 29 jurisdictions were in effect January 1, 1998. Such numbers will probably increase as OPs test the courts with suits related to medical care and the ADA of 1990.

Conclusions

The older prisoner's physical, psychological, and social needs are complex and require gerontologically informed service delivery systems. If we are to create such service delivery systems, we must first answer the question of why we, as a society, should care about the cultivation of elder-friendly prisons which meet the needs of this vulnerable population. Many voters, criminal justice professionals, and policy makers, to be sure, argue that these OPs have "nothing coming to them" because many have committed heinous crimes involving horrible outcomes including, but not limited to, loss of life.

Unfortunately, such arguments are counterproductive, inhumane, and legally compromised. Inmates are sent to prison *as* punishment and not *for* punishment; the loss of liberty associated with incarceration is often devastating for OPs who face their potential mortality in prison, and we should not punish them further via medical, psychological, and/or social neglect. Such pervasive correctional neglect and indifference to the OP's special needs is ethically wrong and legally suspect in relation to civil rights, due process, issues of fairness, and human rights. If prisons fail to use their administrative discretion in meaningful ways towards the goal of addressing the OP's needs, then they are opening themselves up to losing their discretion via consent decrees, court orders, and judicial interventions aimed at assuming administrative control of prisons. Given the current level of negligence in various states around the country, there appears to be a window of opportunity for litigation to advance the OP's access to needed services. Hence, the American Civil Liberties Union and other organizations engaged in prison advocacy work would do well to focus some of their attention on the best interests of the older inmate.

Acknowledgments

This work is supported by the National Institute on Aging Training Grant, T32-AG0017. The author would like to thank Dr. Burton Dunlop, Dr. Ruth Dunkle, Dr. Sheila Feld, Dr. Phillip Fellin, Dr. Max Rothman, and Dr. Patricia Welch for their assistance with the development of this chapter.

References

Adams, W. E., Jr. (1995). The incarceration of older criminals: Balancing safety, cost, and humanitarian concerns. *Nova Law Review, 19,* 465–486.

Aday, R. H. (1994a). Aging in prison: A case study of new elderly offenders. *International Journal of Offender Therapy and Comparative Criminology, 38,* 79–91.

Aday, R. H. (1994b). Golden years behind bars: Special programs and facilities for older inmates. *Federal Probation, 58*(2), 47–54.

Aday, R. H., & Webster, E. C. (1979). Aging in prison—The development of a preliminary model. *Offender Rehabilitation, 3,* 271–282.

Alston, L. T. (1986). *Crime and older Americans.* Springfield, IL: Charles C. Thomas.

American Correctional Association. (1992). *Working with special needs offenders; Book 1.* Washington, DC: Author.

Beck, A. J. (1997). Growth, change, and stability in the U.S. prison population, 1980–1995. *Corrections Management Quarterly, 1*(2), 1–14.

Benekos, P. J., & Merlo, A. V. (1995). Three strikes and you're out: The political sentencing game. *Federal Probation, 59*(1), 3–9.

Booth, D. E. (1989). Health status of the incarcerated elderly: Issues and concerns. In S. Chaneles & C. Burnett (Eds.), *Older offenders: Current trends* (pp. 193–214). New York: Haworth Press.

Camp, G. M, & Camp, C. G. (1991). *The corrections yearbook 1991: Adult corrections.* South Salem, NY: Criminal Justice Institute.

Camp, G. M, & Camp, C. G. (1992). *The corrections yearbook 1992: Adult corrections.* South Salem, NY: Criminal Justice Institute.

Camp, G. M., & Camp, C. G. (1993). *The corrections yearbook 1993: Adult corrections.* South Salem, NY: Criminal Justice Institute.

Camp, C. G., & Camp, C. M. (1994). *The corrections yearbook 1994: Adult corrections.* South Salem, NY: Criminal Justice Institute.

Camp, C. G., & Camp, C. M. (1995). *The corrections yearbook 1995: Adult corrections.* South Salem, NY: Criminal Justice Institute.

Camp, C. G., & Camp, C. M. (1996). *The corrections yearbook: 1996.* South Salem, NY: Criminal Justice Institute.

Camp, C. G., & Camp, C. M. (1997). *The corrections yearbook: 1997.* South Salem, NY: Criminal Justice Institute.

Camp, C. G., & Camp, C. M. (1998). *The corrections yearbook: 1998.* South Salem, NY: Criminal Justice Institute.

Chaiklin, H., & Fultz, L. (1985). Service needs of older offenders. *Justice Professional, 1*(1), 26–33.

Chaneles, S. (1987). Growing old behind bars. *Psychology Today, 21*(10), 47–51.

Corrections Today. (1990). The aging prison population: Inmates in gray. *Corrections Today, 52,* 136.

Ditton, P. M., & Wilson, D. J. (1999). Truth in Sentencing in State Prisons. *Bureau of Justice Statistics Bulletin.* Washington, DC: U.S. Department of Justice—Office of Justice Programs.

Dugger, R. L. (1988). Graying of America's prisons: Special care considerations. *Corrections Today, 50*(3), 26–30, 34.

Ellsworth, T., & Helle, K. A. (1994). Older offenders on probation. *Federal Probation, 58*(4), 43–50.

Estelle v. Gamble, 97 S. Ct. 285, 1976.

Eysenck, J. B. G., Rust, J., & Eysenck, H. J. (1977). Personality and the classification of adult offenders. *British Journal of Criminology, 17*(2), 169–179.

Fattah, E. A., & Sacco, V. F. (1989). *Crime and victimization of the elderly.* New York: Springer-Verlag.

Florida Department of Corrections. (1993). *Status report on elderly inmates.* Tallahassee, FL: Author.

Forsyth, C. J., & Gramling, R. (1988). Elderly crime: Fact and artifact. In B. R. McCarthy & R. H. Langworthy (Eds.), *Older offenders: Perspectives in criminology and criminal justice* (pp. 13–13). New York: Praeger.

Fry, L. J. (1987). Older prison inmate: A profile. *Justice Professional, 2*(1), 1–12.

Gilliard, D. K. (1999, March). Prison and jail inmates at midyear 1998. *Bureau of Justice Statistics Bulletin.* Washington, DC: U.S. Department of Justice—Office of Justice Programs.

Goetting, A. (1983). Elderly in prison: Issues and perspectives. *Journal of Research in Crime and Delinquency, 20*(2), 291–309.

Goetting, A. (1984). Elderly in prison: A profile. *Criminal Justice Review, 9*(2), 14–24.

Goetting, A. (1985). Racism, sexism, and ageism in the prison community. *Federal Probation, 49*(3), 10–22.

Hunt, G., Riegel, S., Morales, T., & Waldorf, D. (1993). Changes in prison culture: Prison gangs and the case of the Pepsi Generation. *Social Problems, 40*(3), 398–409.

Irwin, J., & Austin, J. (1994). *It's about time: America's imprisonment binge.* Belmont, CA: Wadsworth Publishing Company.

Krajick, K. (1979). Growing old in prison. *Corrections Magazine, 5,* 32–46.

Kratcoski, P. C., & Babb, S. (1990). Adjustment of older inmates: An analysis of institutional structure and gender. *Journal of Contemporary Criminal Justice, 6*(4), 264–281.

Kratcoski, P. C., & Pownall, G. A. (1989). Federal Bureau of Prison programming for older inmates. *Federal Probation, 53*(2), 28–35.

Lundstrom, S. (1994). Dying to get out: A study on the necessity, importance, and effectiveness of prison early release programs for elderly inmates suffering from HIV disease and other terminal-centered illnesses. *Brigham Young University Journal of Public Law, 9*(1), 155–188.

Mabli, J., Holley, C. S. D., Patrick, J., & Walls, J. (1979). Age and prison violence: Increasing age heterogeneity as a violence-reducing strategy in prisons. *Criminal Justice & Behavior, 6*(2), 175–186.

Mauer, M. (1997). *Americans behind bars: U.S. and international use of incarceration, 1995.* Washington, DC: The Sentencing Project.

McCarthy, M. (1983). The health status of elderly inmates. *Corrections Today, 45*(Feb), 64–65.

McCorkle, R. C. (1993). Fear of victimization and symptoms of psychopathology among prison inmates. *Journal of Offender Rehabilitation, 19*(1/2), 27–41.

McShane, M. D., & Williams, F. P., III (1990). Old and ornery: The disciplinary experiences of elderly prisoners. *International Journal of Offender Therapy and Comparative Criminology, 34*(3), 197–212.

Merianos, D. E., Marquart, J. W., Damphousse, K., & Hebert, J. L. (1997). From the outside in: Using public health data to make inferences about older inmates. *Crime & Delinquency, 43*(3), 298–313.

Metzler, C. (1981). *Senior citizens in Massachusetts state correctional facilities from 1972–1979.* Massachusetts: Massachusetts Department of Corrections.

Morton, J. B. (1992). *Administrative overview of the older inmate.* Washington, DC: National Institute of Corrections.

Newman, D. J. (1984). Elderly offenders and American crime patterns. In E. S. Newman, D. J. Newman, & M. L. Gewirtz (Eds.), *Elderly criminals* (pp. 3–16). Boston: Oelgeschlager, Gunn and Hain, Publishers, Inc.

Pennsylvania Department of Corrections v Yeskey, 118 S. Ct. 1952 (1998).

Petersilia, J. (1992). California's prison policy: Causes, costs, and consequences. *Prison Journal, 72,* 8–36.

Reed, M. B., & Glamser, F. D. (1979). Aging in a total institution: The case of older prisoners. *Gerontologist, 19*(4), 354–360.

Rosefield, H. A. (1993). The older inmate: "Where do we go from here?" *Journal of Prison and Jail Health, 12*(1), 51–58.

Rosefield, H. A. (1995). *The Leon and Josephine Winkelman Lecture: Geriatric Prisoners.* Ann Arbor, MI: The University of Michigan, School of Social Work.

Rubenstein, D. (1984). The elderly in prison: A review of the literature. In E. S. Newman, D. J. Newman, & M. L. Gewirtz (Eds.), *Elderly criminals* (pp. 153–168). Boston: Oelgeschlager, Gunn and Hain, Publishers, Inc.

Sabath, M. J., & Cowles, E. L. (1988). Factors affecting the adjustment of elderly inmates to prison. In B. R. McCarthy & R. H. Langworthy (Eds.), *Older offenders: Perspectives in criminology and criminal justice* (pp. 178–196). New York: Praeger.

Silverman, M., & Vega, M. (1990). Reactions of prisoners to stress as a function of personality and demographic variables. *International Journal of Offender Therapy and Comparative Criminology, 34*(3), 187–196.

Steffensmeier, D., & Harer, M. D. (1993). Bulging prisons, and aging U.S. population, and the nation's violent crime rate. *Federal Probation, 57*(2), 3–10.

Teller, F. E., & Howell, R. J. (1981). Older prisoner: Criminal and psychological characteristics. *Criminology, 18*(4), 549–555.

Tobin, P., & Metzler, C. (1983). *Typology of older prisoners in Massachusetts state correctional facilities, 1972–1982.* Boston: Massachusetts Department of Corrections.

Turner, M. G., Sundt, J. L., Applegate, B. K., & Cullen, F. T. (1995). "Three strikes and you're out" legislation: A national assessment. *Federal Probation, 59*(3), 16–35.

Vega, M., & Silverman, M. (1988). Stress and the elderly convict. *International Journal of Offender Therapy and Comparative Criminology, 32*(2), 153–162.

Visher, C. A. (1987). Incapacitation and crime control: Does a "lock 'em up" strategy reduce crime? *Justice Quarterly, 5,* 513–543.

Vito, G. F., & Wilson, D. G. (1985). Forgotten people: Elderly inmates. *Federal Probation, 49*(1), 18–23.

Wiegand, N. D., & Burger, J. C. (1979). Elderly offenders on parole. *Prison Journal, 59*(2), 48–57.

Wilson, D. G., & Vito, G. F. (1986). Imprisoned Elders: The experience of one institution. *Criminal Justice Policy Review, 1,* 399–421.

Zimbardo, P. G. (1994). *Transforming California's prisons into expensive old age homes for felons: Enormous hidden costs and consequences for California's taxpayers.* San Francisco: Center on Juvenile and Criminal Justice.

Zimring, F. E., & Hawkins, G. (1991). *The scale of imprisonment.* Chicago: University of Chicago Press.

Suggested Readings

American Correctional Association. (1995). *1995 Directory of juvenile and adult correctional departments, institutions, agencies and paroling authorities.* Laurel, MD: Author.

Americans with Disabilities Act of 1990, 42 U.S.C.A. §12101 *et seq.* (1993).

Goetting, A. (1984). Prison programs and facilities for elderly inmates. In E. S. Newman, D. J. Newman, & M. L. Gewirtz (Eds.), *Elderly criminals* (pp. 169–176). Boston, MA: Oelgeschlager, Gunn and Hain, Publishers, Inc.

Rubenstein, D. (1982). The older person in prison. *Archives of Gerontology and Geriatrics, 1,* 287–296.

Chapter 11

Arguments and Strategies for the Selective Decarceration of Older Prisoners

John J. Kerbs

America's correctional crisis is gaining speed as jail and prison populations continue to swell. In 1998, U.S. jails and prisons housed over 1.8 million inmates and expanded by 1,475 prisoners per week on average (Gilliard, 1999). Despite this substantial and rapidly growing census, most prison systems operated at or above capacity in 1997 (Camp & Camp, 1998; Mumola & Beck, 1997). To be exact, 23 states and the Federal Bureau of Prisons operated above 105% of their rated capacities. In January of 1995, the National Prison Project of the American Civil Liberties Union reported that 28 states and the District of Columbia were under consent decree or court order to decrease overcrowding either throughout their entire state system or within at least one of their major prison facilities. By 1998, court orders concerning population limits affected 141 institutions nationwide (Camp & Camp, 1998). Although there is no expectation that this situation will change without major policy shifts, the selective decarceration of older prisoners (OPs) represents one potential solution to overcrowding in prisons.

As Lundstrom (1994, p. 158) noted: "it's no longer a question today of whether or not somebody is going to be released—the question is who." Nine states have already enacted statutes implementing emergency release programs designed to legally release inmates (over 2,000 in 1996) as a measure to control inmate population levels (Camp & Camp, 1998). Other states debate the issue of "who" should be released, showing a renewed interest in using scarce prison space primarily for high-risk offenders in an effort to reduce overcrowding. This strategy, dubbed "selective incarceration" (Culbertson & Schnieders, 1984, p. 399), has a flip side: "selective decarceration," which the literature often neglects, but the prison industry silently condones and implements as wardens and parole boards try to ameliorate prison overcrowding.

This chapter analyzes the growing debate about whether older prisoners (OPs) should be released into community-based alternatives to prison. Generally speaking, there are two schools of thought regarding the correctional handling of OPs. The first advocates a reformist position, arguing that prisons do not meet their various needs; hence, prison officials should retrofit physical facilities and retool programming to better accommodate their needs (Aday, 1994a, 1994b; Anderson & McGehee, 1991, 1994; Kratcoski & Pownall, 1989; Morton, 1992; Rosefield, 1995). Although release programming for OPs may be part of the overall argument being made, it is not a *primary* emphasis for reformists.

The second school of thought on this issue is a bit more controversial. It primarily advocates for the selective decarceration of OP's (Adams, 1995; Lundstrom, 1994). The remainder of this chapter examines the arguments and strategies for the selective decarceration of OPs (50 years of age and older).

The Arguments for Selective Decarceration

The main arguments for decarcerating OPs revolve around financial considerations, criminological issues regarding recidivism, programmatic deficiencies, and legal liabilities. These arguments will be discussed in turn.

Financial Considerations

At present, it costs three times more (on average) to keep OPs in prison as compared to younger inmates; this is largely due to health care cost differentials between younger and older inmates. Although the cost of incarcerating younger inmates is about $21,000 per year on average, the cost of incarcerating prisoners over age 50 is around $60,000 per year. For those 60 years of age and older, the cost rises to $69,000 per year (Zimbardo, 1994).

High health care costs for OPs result from the serious, chronic, and complex nature of their health problems. The average OP has three chronic health conditions (*Corrections Today*, 1990). These conditions can result in high medical fees and frequent visits and in-patient stays at nearby community hospitals (Chaiklin & Fultz, 1985). In Michigan, for example, 69% of prisoners 65 years of age and older used off-site hospital and specialty health care services during a 1-year period (2/95 through 1/96) (Michigan Department of Corrections, 1996a, 1996b). States like Michigan often outsource medical services for OPs, because most prison hospitals are designed for acute care and not chronic care services (Alston, 1986). Furthermore, when community treatment is needed, guards must provide continuous and expensive supervision.

The ultimate price of current "get-tough" sentencing statutes (e.g., three-strikes statutes that mandate life sentences with and without opportunities for parole) may be significant tax increases as federal and state governments struggle to raise the "hundreds of billions of dollars" needed to care for the resulting increases in the numbers of imprisoned OPs (Zimbardo, 1994, p. 4). The financial implications of such figures worry correctional administrators as their prison populations age. A recent survey of 50 states and the District of Columbia found that nearly 50% of all states viewed their most pressing problem in responding to the needs of aging/infirm inmates as medical costs (Aday, 1994b).

Although projected costs for OPs are high, some of the costs are potentially avoidable. Morton (1992) noted that some health problems can become so debilitating that many OPs " . . . are not considered security risks [in prison]" (pp. 11–12). Thus, less expensive community-based alternatives to prison *may* provide sufficient correctional supervision while maintaining public safety at profound cost savings. As Table 11.1 shows, the corrections-budget costs for keeping OPs in prison are much higher than those for any community-based alternative to prison, including nursing homes, which cost around $41,000 per year (far less than the $60,000 to $69,000 required to imprison an OP for a year). The financial gravity of such figures becomes apparent when one considers the following: the total number of federal and state inmates serving life sentences (with the option of parole), natural life sentences (without access to parole), and terms of 20 years or more reached 273,307 prisoners as of January 1, 1998 (Camp & Camp, 1998).

To be fair, the true cost of community-based alternatives to prison has yet to be carefully calculated for OPs. Most financial figures for community-based options (except nursing homes) do not account for costs associated with the older offenders' increased morbidity and associated health care needs. Nonetheless, it is reasonable to assume that substantial savings can be achieved by circumventing the extra layer of correctional costs associated with prison placements (which are certainly more expensive than community-based supervision) and the added correctional supervision required when OPs require treatment in the community.

TABLE 11.1 Average Correctional Department Costs for Various Supervision Options

Supervision option	Yearly costs	Daily costs
Regular parole (regular number of visits & contacts)[a]	$1,689.95	$4.63
Intensive parole (greater number of visits & contacts)[a]	$2,865.25	$7.85
Parole with special programming (e.g., substance abuse)[a]	$3,401.80	$9.32
Parole with electronic supervision[a]	$3,952.95	$10.83
Halfway house (DOC operated)[a]	$17,895.95	$49.03
Prison for general inmate population[a]	$20,261.15	$55.51
Nursing home[b]	$41,000.00	$112.33
Prison for OPs: 50 to 60 years old[c]	$60,000.00	$164.38
Prison for OPs: over age 60[c]	$69,000.00	$189.04

[a]Figures for 1997 taken from Camp & Camp (1998).
[b]Figures taken from *The Cash Crunch* (1998).
[c]Figures taken from *Corrections Today* (1990).

Criminological Considerations Regarding Recidivism

Perhaps the single best argument and basis for the selective decarceration of aging inmates is their lower recidivism rate. Since the mid-1800s, the criminological and sociological literature has documented (via quantitative, ethnographic, and self-report studies) the inverse relationship between age and criminal involvement (Shover, 1985). This inverse relationship has been called one of the "brute facts of criminology" and "no fact about crime is more widely accepted" (Hirschi & Gottfredson, 1983, p. 552). It also extends to known criminals who, as they age, desist from crime as evidenced by the recidivism literature on paroled inmates (Grant & Lefebvre, 1994; Hoffman & Beck, 1984; Steffensmeier & Harer, 1993; Zimbardo, 1994). In short, recidivism rates among adults "tend to be lower in each succeeding age group" (Fattah & Sacco, 1989, p. 16), and "the older a person is at his or her first offense, the less likely that person is to commit repeat offenses" (Alston, 1986, p. 132). Finally, the inverse relationship between age and recidivism is not diminished when controlling for relevant (alternative) explanatory variables such as the potential effects of an inmate's prior criminal history (Hoffman & Beck, 1984).

The specific rates of recidivism show dramatic declines across the life span as studied so far. Zimbardo (1994) quoted one Bureau of Justice Statistics report as follows:

> While an estimated 21.8% of those 18 to 24 years old at release return to prison within the first year, 12.1% of those 25 to 34 at release, 7.1% of those aged 35 to 44, and 2.1% of those aged 45 and over do so within the first year. . . . Through 7 years after release, nearly half (49.9%) of those aged 18 through 24 at release will have returned to prison, compared to 12.4% of those 45 and over at release. (pp. 9–10)

The potential reasons for this inverse relationship include: (a) The Burn-Out Hypothesis, (b) decline in physical capacity to commit crimes, (c) decreased social interactions, (d) redirection of aggressive tendencies from an outward to inward orientation, (e) advanced internal inhibitions with age, (f) successful rehabilitation, and (g) lower detection rates (Fattah & Sacco, 1989).

Beyond the reason(s), the fact remains that recidivism rates (defined in various ways across different studies) decrease as age increases. This research lends support to selective decarceration policies and procedures based, at least in part, on the inmate's age; it also raises questions about incarceration policies and whether more older felons past their fifth decade of life should be diverted to community-based alternatives to prison in the first place. Given that OPs have much lower recidivism rates than their younger counterparts, the selective decarceration of OPs can open up bed space for younger inmates who represent relatively greater threats to public safety.

Programmatic Deficiencies

The third argument for the decarceration of OPs concerns both the physical structures of prisons and access to programs and needed services. Prisons, in short, are not designed for OPs with age-related disabilities and chronic health problems. Although many OPs have limited mobility due to traumatic injury and/or illness, most prisons are not structurally designed to: (a) minimize falls; (b) permit barrier-free access to bathrooms and other facilities; or (c) allow for short walks to access meals, medical care, and other needed services (Adams, 1995; Aday, 1994a, 1994b; Morton, 1992). Of course, retrofitting prisons for inmates with disabilities would further increase their incarceration costs; and correctional administrators have been slow to make prisons "user friendly" for them.

Beyond the problem of physical access to programs and services, there is the more fundamental issue of service availability. Even though many OPs have health conditions requiring *chronic care*, most medical facilities in prison are designed for *acute care* needs and treatment; moreover, the vast majority of all prison hospitals in this country fail to meet the basic standards of care established by the medical profession (Lundstrom, 1994). Hence, the typical OP's health problems stand a good chance of going untreated. In addition, the older inmates' unique psychosocial needs often go unattended since most counseling, educational, recreational, and vocational programs are oriented towards healthy young inmates

(Adams, 1995; Aday, 1994a, 1994b; Morton, 1992; Vega & Silverman, 1988; Zimbardo, 1994).

Perhaps the biggest obstacle to service provision for OPs is the presence of ageism in prison systems (Goetting, 1985). In short, prisons neglect and discriminate against OPs by denying them access to, or failing to provide access to, relevant services and treatment. For a full review of such discrimination, please see chapter 10 of this volume.

This is not to say that we do not know how to engage OPs with and without disability in prison settings. Numerous academics and practitioners have written about how to retrofit programming to accommodate an aging clientele (Aday, 1994b; Anderson & McGhee, 1991, 1994; Dugger, 1988; Morton, 1993, 1994; Kelsey, 1986; Rubenstein, 1982; Vito & Wilson, 1985). Indeed, a few model prison programs do an excellent job of adapting to meet the OP's special needs (Anderson & McGhee, 1991, 1994). Unfortunately, these programs are few in number (Aday, 1994b), and so the majority of OPs are programmatically neglected as they live within the general prison population.

Legal Liabilities

The final rationale for release is based on ethical and legal considerations regarding the inability of prisons to protect the OP's rights. Prisoners retain many of the same rights enjoyed by those outside of prisons, including the right to: (a) a reasonably safe environment, (b) appropriate treatment, (c) special education, (d) access to programs and resources, and (e) due process (American Correctional Association, 1992; Rosefield, 1995). Finally, the Eighth Amendment of the U.S. Constitution prohibits the "cruel and unusual punishment" of any offender.

Although all OPs retain these rights, few actually benefit from them. Creating a reasonably safe environment, for example, may require the placement of OPs into age-segregated units. Aday (1994b) found that 17 states do not have the capacity to place (some) OPs in such units, and most states only have a limited capacity to permit age-segregated placements. OPs living in the general prison population can experience economic, physical, psychological, and sexual victimization (Bowker, 1982); hence, victimization and fear of victimization by younger inmates is a problem for them (Wilson & Vito, 1986). The advancement of three-strikes legislation could be expected to exacerbate this victimization. Lundstrom (1994) found studies which indicated that young offenders serving long sentences "often turn [their] anger into exploitative behavior towards elderly prisoners" (p. 164). Of course, none of this bodes well for the OP given that over 273,000 federal and state inmates are serving life sentences (with and without the option of parole) and/or 20+ year terms as of January 1, 1998 (Camp & Camp, 1998).

With respect to the right to treatment, the right of access to medical care was confirmed in *Estelle v. Gamble* (1976); consequently, correctional systems must supply a full range of medical services—acute care, chronic care, dental care, and nutritional services (Kratcoski & Pownall, 1989). Fairly recent publications indicate that the rights confirmed by *Estelle v. Gamble* (1976) remain largely illusory or rhetorical because " . . . 90% of the country's 600 prison hospitals do not meet basic standards of care established by the medical profession. . . . As a result [of understaffing and overcrowding], inmates are dying from ailments that go unattended or are treated improperly" (Lundstrom, 1994, p. 166).

With respect to an OP's right of access to special education, prison programs, and resources (as discussed in chapter 10), research by Wiegand and Burger (1979) and others (Aday, 1994b; Goetting, 1983, 1985; Sabath & Cowles, 1988; Wiegand & Burger, 1979; Wilson & Vito, 1986) clearly demonstrated that OPs have been systematically: (1) denied access to existing programs; and (2) not given access to prison programs specific to their needs. The dearth of relevant programming is a serious problem. Recreational programs are often oriented towards highly active and physically taxing sports that are more popular with and suitable to younger inmates. Vocational training also has less appeal for OPs who are much less likely to reenter the workforce. Finally, deficits are seen in prison counseling programs, which are designed to rehabilitate young inmates, not to counsel OPs dealing with chronic illness or death (Aday, 1994b).

Given all of the above, it is clear that there are multiple legal foundations of individual and class-action litigation relating to the failure of prisons to safeguard the rights of older inmates. Moreover, both the Rehabilitation Act of 1973 and the Americans with Disabilities Act (ADA) of 1990 specify that those with physical and/or mental disabilities have the legal right to *equal access* to programs, services, and other activities (Morton, 1992). Given the structural and programmatic barriers to "equal access" for OPs, the next wave of court-ordered consent decrees may be linked to the ADA of 1990 (see, for example, the U.S. Supreme Court decision of *Pennsylvania Department of Corrections v. Yeskey* (1998), which found that Title II of the Americans with Disabilities Act of 1990 unambiguously extends to state prison inmates).

As of 1990, 17 states said they did not have geriatric facilities or special programs for OPs (Aday, 1994b). Among those states that did have special facilities, these facilities typically helped only some OPs with basic medical needs. These states also lacked specialized counseling and recreational and/or vocational programming, which raises additional "equal access" issues and the possibility of future litigation (Booth, 1989; Dugger, 1988; Goetting, 1983, 1984, 1985; Kalmanoff, 1982; Lundstrom, 1994; Morton, 1992).

Approaches for Selective Decarceration of Older Prisoners

This section discusses various approaches to the selective decarceration of older inmates. However, this review is not exhaustive of all possibilities and many states may have new approaches not covered here.

Before turning to specific strategies, certain general issues and principles need to be addressed. First, it is important to realize that not all OPs will be suitable candidates for early release (i.e., selective decarceration). Older inmates are a heterogeneous group with varying offense and sentence histories that mandate a certain degree of case-by-case selectivity even though their relative risk of recidivism (compared to their younger counterparts) is very low. Policy initiatives aimed at decarceration must pay special attention to public safety issues by promoting proper risk-assessment protocols that weigh carefully a number of salient factors, including the OP's recent behavior in prison, medical history, presenting offense, sentencing history, time served, and other factors related to the risk of recidivism and danger to the community.

Certainly, some OPs (regardless of their offense histories) can become medically compromised to the point of moderate or severe disability; this may nullify their potential threat to society and argue for their release, with the provision that they receive medical care in the community (not deinsitutionalization without medical follow-up). Sentence histories may also influence efforts to decarcerate some OPs. For example, inmates who have served 20 or more continuous years of time in prison may develop an "institutional dependency" upon prison because they have served long sentences (see chapter 10 for discussion of institutional dependence). Such continuous time in prison can advance survival skills needed in prison while diminishing life skills required to survive outside of prison. The rising number of "lifers" as a result of three-strikes convictions has led academics and criminal justice professionals to fear that the United States may be creating a group of inmates who are almost impossible to release due to institutional dependence. Specific attention will be needed to decarcerate certain subgroups of OPs known to be particularly prone to institutional dependency (e.g., those unmarried, those first incarcerated at an early age, and recidivists when compared to late offenders) (Fattah & Sacco, 1989).

Given the special needs of the average OP, it is not clear whether community-based alternatives to prison are ready to take OPs and provide them with quality support services. In short, the community-service infrastructure may be inadequate to stabilize older releasees with an integrative and fully thought-out array of supports. Basic services (e.g., counseling, housing, and transportation) and governmental supports (e.g., Medicare, Medicaid, Social Security, Supplemental Security Income, etc) may need augmentation. Moreover, the literature has indicated that community-based programs are often incapable, unwilling, or less willing to take older multiproblem inmates with health-related and work-related limitations, as compared to their younger and often healthier counterparts (Chaneles, 1987; Goetting, 1983; Wiegand & Burger, 1979). This situation indicates the need for more training and resources to foster placements and care programs that are free of discrimination. Legally speaking, there are numerous acts (as discussed previously) which prohibit such discrimination, and these acts can provide sound foundations for litigation aimed at ameliorating discriminatory policies and procedures. Additionally, employers who discriminate against older releasees, based upon their age, also face liability under the Federal Age Discrimination Employment Act of 1967, which makes it unlawful for employers to discriminate, based upon age, against those between 40 and 70 years of age.

The remainder of this discussion examines the various approaches to decarceration.

Sentencing Reform

The time is right to reevaluate and reform existing sentencing statutes. More specifically, we need to reexamine all life statutes (i.e., life sentences with and without the possibility of parole), three-strikes statutes, statutes that promote long-term mandatory minimums, and laws which eliminate parole options and/or the capacity to grant good time. Such statutes prematurely foreclose on the opportunity for selective decarceration in cases that represent relatively low risks of recidivism. Other concerns also exist. With respect to three-strike statutes, many jurisdictions go against public opinion by including strikes for nonviolent and drug-related crimes that "the public does not feel are among the most serious offenses" (Turner, Sundt, Applegate, & Cullen, 1995, p. 25). Numerous jurisdictions are implementing these statutes despite the fact that "throw away the key" strategies "have been unsuccessful in achieving meaningful reductions in crime . . . " (Turner et al., 1995, p. 33). Paradoxically, while these statutes are purported to increase public safety, they may profoundly impede this goal by holding inmates too long, thereby multiplying the number of low-risk offenders (i.e., OPs) in prison; this fills costly and limited correctional bed space which might be more efficiently used for inmates with a higher risk of recidivism. In short, these statutes may run counter to public sentiments, fail to achieve meaningful reductions in crime, result in increased costs to taxpayers, and impede public safety.

To correct this situation, various avenues should be pursued. First, policy makers and politicians must stop promoting three-strikes (recidivist) legislation which promotes "life" sentences without access to parole for those who have aged into a low-risk bracket for recidivism. Second, three-strikes statutes should be modified on three levels: (a) restrict viable strikes to violent offenses only; (b) put "a reasonable time limit on the inclusion of prior convictions as applicable 'strikes' " (Zimbardo, 1994, p. 12); and (c) eliminate juvenile convictions as possible "strikes." Finally, legislation is needed to retroactively alter prior three-strikes convictions to permit parole after the offender serves a "reasonable" mandatory minimum (probably no more than 10 years). We also need to look beyond three-strikes legislation to the inflexible sentencing strategies embodied in determinate sentencing systems, truth-in-sentencing strategies, and anything else that severely restricts and/or eliminates access to parole (such sentence strategies are discussed in the next section of this chapter). All of this could be done retroactively via legislation that permits earlier access to parole for past and present convictions.

Parole Reforms

Sentencing trends around the country have led to long mandatory-minimum sentences and three-strikes sentences, which often block an inmate's access to parole for protracted periods of time. Policy makers and legislators have promised "truth in sentencing" which often means that "good time" (sentence reductions for good behavior in prison) and access to parole hearings are restricted and/or eliminated at both the federal and state level. Truncating access to parole limits one of the key structural avenues to the selective decarceration of OPs who are, behaviorally speaking, good candidates for release. Within prisons, most OPs are well-behaved and they rarely violate prison rules and regulations (Goetting, 1983; Rubenstein, 1982, 1984). Accordingly, they usually receive low-security classifications (Kratcoski & Pownall, 1989) in the least-restrictive level because most do not pose significant safety threats to guards and/or other prisoners.

Given their model behavior and low risk of recidivism, one must ask: should they be paroled to community-based alternatives to prison? If the answer is yes, then several modifications must be made to the way parole boards currently operate. First, OPs should have more frequent access to parole board hearings, including the option for parole board hearings following the diagnosis of a terminal illness, which would allow qualifying OPs to be released to family or hospice care (McCarthy, 1983). A number of states have passed such parole review laws (Rosefield, 1995). They allow parole when there is a diagnosis of a terminal illness. Others permit parole for inmates who have both served a minimum amount of their sentence and reached a particular age, for example, 60 years. This allows for safeguards against "automatically" releasing OPs without proper risk assessments. All states should expand and implement parole board review laws to cover both terminal and physically disabling diseases that render OPs harmless to society.

Beyond efforts to create more frequent parole reviews, something must be done to address the use of discriminatory parole criteria. Even though OPs are good candidates for parole based upon their relative risk of recidivism (which should be the main issue), they may be poor candidates because they may not have: (a) histories of participation in prison programs, which parole boards consider to be indicative of an inmate's personal commitment to reform; (b) sound employment plans—often required by parole boards—as a result of advanced age and/or health problems; (c) viable incomes, because of inadequate employment plans and/or a failure to arrange for another source of monetary support, e.g., General Assistance, Social Security, Supplemental Security Income; and/or (d) the ability to return to their families and friends, which creates problems with residential plans required by parole boards.

There are a number of reasons, however, why these criteria may be inappropriately applied to OPs. The assumption that OPs have a poor attitude toward reform as evidenced by their failure to engage in "meaningful" prison activities, for example, is biased against OPs (Virginia Parole Board, 1992). Such biased criteria can include the OP's participation in work and in counseling, educational, and/or vocational programming—the same developmentally inappropriate programming which prison staff discourage OPs from attending! Parole boards should waive criteria involving an OP's participation in programs unless the board can prove that relevant, developmentally appropriate and accessible programs are available to them.

Mandated employment plans should also be waived because many OPs will be at a disadvantage in the job market due to their felony convictions and advanced age. For those who can work, employment plans should be pursued upon release; however, parole boards and parole officers should be flexible on this requirement as OPs approach their retirement years (Roberg & Webb, 1981). "Inmates above 50 years of age or below 65 . . . are in a twilight zone. They are not old enough to qualify for the benefits that accrue to those of retirement age, such as Social Security, and not young enough to compete for most jobs with younger men who have longer employment records" (Roberg & Webb, 1981, p. 166).

Matters can become very complicated if inmates are over age 65 and unable to financially support themselves via Social Security and/or other mechanisms. Because of their incarceration histories, some long-term OPs may not have contributed to the Social Security system and so they may be ineligible for benefits. Others may have contributed to the system; however, they may not be fully vested and/or they may not have had better paying jobs, resulting in low monthly Social Security incomes which are inadequate to cover living expenses. This is especially problematic for groups who historically have been denied equal access to higher paying jobs—e.g., African Americans who are overrepresented among OPs (Roberg & Webb, 1981). The implications of this situation are fairly straightforward: unless special efforts are made, parole boards are unlikely to release OPs without employment or the financial means to cover living expenses and housing costs (Fattah & Sacco, 1989).

Still, there are multiple ways of economically stabilizing and housing unemployed and underemployed OPs in the community. First, some OPs will be eligible for Social Security and Medicare upon release; hence, caseworkers can help them to certify or recertify for Social Security so that they can draw incomes upon discharge and receive Medicare benefits (Morton, 1992). If ineligible for Social Security and/or Medicare, caseworkers can help OPs apply for Supplemental Security Income and Medicaid (Dobelstein, 1990). These financial and medical arrangements help states shift part of their costs to the federal government (a potential benefit for states willing to decarcerate OPs). Moreover, most community-based alternatives will be cheaper than prison placements; so a state can expect to reduce housing costs even if it still has to cover community residential costs in supervised release programs. Even the most complex cases (e.g., involving terminally ill and indigent OPs) can be maintained more efficiently in the community (Lundstrom, 1994) if a state department of corrections pays for case management services to shift financial liabilities to General Assistance, Medicaid, Medicare, Social Security, Supplemental Security Income, and so on.

On a closing note, residential plans for parole also can be complex for OPs, especially "oldtimers" and "career criminals" who have lost their support networks during long or multiple incarcerations. In such cases, residential options like halfway houses and independent living arrangements can be viable alternatives.

Reintegration Programs

Reintegration programs prepare release plans and assist inmates with their return to the community by setting the stage for employment, financial assistance, and housing. These programs are for inmates who are not necessarily ill or physically infirm, but who pose a low risk for recidivism as "pre-parole" or "parole" candidates. The most famous "model" reintegration program for OPs is probably the Project for Older Prisoners (POPS) which was originally designed and implemented by Jonathan Turley in 1989 at Tulane University's Law School (Lundstrom, 1994). Since 1989, offices have been opened at other law schools in various states. These programs are small and staffed with law students who volunteer their time, lowering costs significantly. To achieve the OP's reintegration, POPS uses a 4-step protocol: (a) identify low-risk/high-cost inmates; (b) assign OPs to law students who conduct extensive risk assessments, including interviews and background checks; (c) develop residential and employment/financial plans; and (d) prepare reports for parole/pardon board reviews.

Thus far, POPS has been popular in the professional literature, which commends POPS for effectively maintaining public safety while decarcerating older inmates (Lundstrom, 1994; Roth, 1992), a development which bodes well for the expansion of POPS-like programs. Given this apparent success, POPS should be critically evaluated as a potential model for states looking to implement relatively inexpensive (volunteer-based) approaches to the OP's decarceration. Moreover, this model appears to hold promise for use in other disciplines/fields outside of law. Schools of social work, for example, could easily staff such programs with Master's level interns.

Compassionate Release Programs

One of the options of last resort for debilitated and/or dying inmates is the compassionate release program that accelerates parole while providing case management services to stabilize released inmates in the community. Such programs allow for the release of inmates who "are no longer a threat, even though they may have a considerable amount of time left on their sentences" (Rosefield, 1993, p. 57). Many of these programs exist in the United States, and they typically accelerate parole releases in medical cases with poor or terminal prognoses (Morton, 1992). Although release protocols differ from state to state, parole boards typically use their discretionary powers to release inmates after: 1) conducting a thorough review of the medical issues involved; and 2) conducting an assessment to determine if the person represents a threat to public safety. Given the inmates' costly and intensive medical and social service needs, caseworkers coordinate a mix of resources (e.g., General Assistance, Medicaid, Medicare, Social Security, Supplemental Security Income, etc.) to cover food, housing, and health costs.

These programs are purported to be both efficient and effective. New York is just one state that reportedly saves millions each year via compassionate release (Lundstrom, 1994). Still, a well-detailed assessment of the efficiency and effectiveness of these programs is yet to be published—even though a 1990 survey found that 22 states had compassionate release programs (Morton, 1992). Future studies are needed to fill this void and fully evaluate the costs, effectiveness, efficiency, and quality of care associated with these programs. In the meantime, compassionate release programs appear promising and should be pursued within all states and the Federal Bureau of Prisons (Morton, 1992).

Pardons and Clemency

Although governors do not often use their discretionary powers, pardons and clemency represent two viable approaches for the OP's release. To be sure, many politicians have promoted stiffer penalties; but some governors have also circumvented those same penalties by invoking their discretionary powers to pardon offenders and/or grant clemency (Benekos & Merlo, 1995). Still, governors rarely grant pardons or clemency because released inmates who recidivate become political liabilities. To discourage the governor's use of pardons and clemency, some states like Washington have passed legislation mandating that governors report twice each year on the status of inmates released via pardons or clemency and that such reports continue for at least 10 years or as long as the offender lives (Benekos & Merlo, 1995).

If pardons and clemency are to remain as viable mechanisms for selective decarceration, laws should be revised so that governors do not have to report the status of each release. Although this removes part of the political liability created by potential recidivism, the public need not worry about a governor's use of unbridled discretion because checks and balances are often in place to assure against inappropriate releases. As a case in point, clemency in Louisiana requires *both* the parole board's and governor's approval (Wikberg & Foster, 1990).

Decarceration via Community-Based Alternatives to Prison

The early release and parole of aging inmates will be successful only if there are community-based programs to attend to their needs. Numerous community-based options should be expanded specifically for OPs. These options include, but are not limited to, the following: (a) community-corrections programs which are legislatively authorized to run statewide in 24 states (Harris, 1996); (b) day treatment programs; (c) intensive and regular parole programs; (d) nursing homes; and (e) residential treatment programs. For those requiring more extensive supervision than provided via ordinary parole, any of the above community-based alternatives could be linked with electronic tethers to provide uniquely safeguarded supervision (Lundstrom, 1994). Tethers should only be used when necessary, however, because they will render the OP ineligible for federal benefits—for example, Medicare and Social Security (Roth, 1992).

Special efforts should be made to develop community-based alternatives for those OPs who are the most overrepresented in state and federal prisons—African American OPs. These clients are not easy to decarcerate because virtually all of them (close to 100% according to Roberg & Webb, 1981) live in poverty and are, thus, financially dependent upon others. Thus, community programs will need protocols to financially stabilize impoverished OPs.

Of course, many OPs of all races seeking release would be living in poverty. While some federal acts (e.g., the Job Training and Partnership Act and the Older Americans Act of 1965 with subsequent amendments) may provide small pockets of money for programs to help, these acts are financially limited and will probably need budgetary augmentation to assure that released OPs have access to community counseling, employment services, in-home services, nutritional services, meal services, and senior centers.

Other Options

The suggestions noted above are limited and each jurisdiction should consider the most effective and efficient options available given the constraints of their respective correctional systems. Many states are probably using very innovative solutions that are not well-documented. It would be useful to identify states that might be doing the best job of diverting and decarcerating by looking at those states with the lowest rates of incarceration for OPs. These states may have solutions which could be shared with other jurisdictions.

Conclusions

The strategies noted above can maintain public safety when used with risk-assessment protocols that allow for the selective targeting and decarceration of OPs at low-risk of recidivism. These strategies are worth pursuing because they save tax dollars, improve public safety, and provide OPs with a less restrictive and more humane correctional environment that maintains public safety while meeting the OP's programmatic needs. Although prisons are largely inadequate to advance this goal, community-based alternatives to prison seem best-suited to this mission because they permit access to existing community resources.

Solutions to problems presented by America's aging prison population are available. The time is right to release OPs: selective-decarceration does make sense—criminologically, ethically, financially, legally, medically, and socially. Although we have approaches to slow and/or eliminate the graying of our prisons, only time will tell if we are willing to initiate multilevel interventions that will achieve this goal. The political feasibility of sufficiently funding these interventions is, unfortunately, in question. As a society, we seem more inclined to fund and build prisons rather than to establish and maintain community-based alternatives to prison. Consequently, while we have answers, we may not have the sociopolitical motivation to decarcerate even the most low-risk OP, and future generations may find themselves stuck with enormous expenses that siphon money from education, health care, and social services.

Acknowledgments

This work is supported by the National Institute on Aging Training Grant, T32-AG0017. The author would like to thank Dr. Burton Dunlop, Dr. Ruth Dunkle, Dr. Sheila Feld, Dr. Phillip Fellin, Dr. Max Rothman, and Dr. Patricia Welch for their assistance with the development of this chapter.

References

Adams, W. E., Jr. (1995). The incarceration of older criminals: Balancing safety, cost, and humanitarian concerns. *Nova Law Review, 19*, 465–486.

Aday, R. H. (1994a). Aging in prison: A case study of new elderly offenders. *International Journal of Offender Therapy and Comparative Criminology, 38*(1), 79–91.

Aday, R. H. (1994b). Golden years behind bars: Special programs and facilities for older inmates. *Federal Probation, 58*(2), 47–54.

Alston, L. T. (1986). *Crime and older Americans.* Springfield, IL: Charles C. Thomas.

American Correctional Association. (1992). *Working with special needs offenders; Book 1.* Washington, DC: Author.

Americans with Disabilities Act of 1990, 42 U.S.C.A. §12101 *et seq.* (1993).

Anderson, J. C., & McGehee, R. D. (1991). South Carolina strives to treat elderly and disabled offenders. *Corrections Today, 53*(5), 124, 126, 127.

Anderson, J., & McGehee, R. D. (1994). Incarceration alternatives: A special unit for elderly offenders and offenders with disabilities. *Forum on Corrections Research, 6*(2), 35–36.

Benekos, P. J., & Merlo, A. V. (1995). Three strikes and you're out: The political sentencing game. *Federal Probation, 59*(1), 3–9.

Booth, D. E. (1989). Health status of the incarcerated elderly: Issues and concerns. In S. Chaneles & C. Burnett (Eds.), *Older offenders: Current trends* (pp. 193–214). New York: Haworth Press.

Bowker, L. H. (1982). Victimizers and victims in American correctional institutions. In R. Johnson & H. Toch (Eds.), *The pains of imprisonment* (pp. 63–76). Beverly Hills, CA: Sage.

Camp, C. G., & Camp, C. M. (1998). *The corrections yearbook: 1998.* South Salem, NY: Criminal Justice Institute.

The cash crunch: The financial challenge of long-term care for the baby boomer generation: Hearing before the Special Committee on Aging, United States Senate, 105th Cong., 2d Sess. (1998).

Chaiklin, H., & Fultz, L. (1985). Service needs of older offenders. *Justice Professional, 1*(1), 26–33.

Chaneles, S. (1987). Growing old behind bars. *Psychology Today, 21*(10), 47–51.

Corrections Today. (1990). The aging prison population: Inmates in gray. *Corrections Today, 52,* 136.

Culbertson, R. G., & Schnieders, E. (1984). Life cycle costs for correctional services in Michigan. *University of Detroit Journal of Urban Law, 61*(3), 391–400.

Dobelstein, A. W. (1990). *Social welfare: Policy and analysis.* Chicago: Nelson-Hall Publishers.

Dugger, R. L. (1988). Graying of America's prisons: Special care considerations. *Corrections Today, 50*(3), 26–30, 34.

Estelle v. Gamble, 97 S. Ct. 285, 1976.

Fattah, E. A., & Sacco, V. F. (1989). *Crime and victimization of the elderly.* New York: Springer-Verlag.

Federal Age Discrimination Employment Act of 1967, 29 U.S.C. §621 *et seq.* (1982).

Gilliard, D. K., (1999, March). *Bulletin: Prison and jail inmates at midyear 1998.* Washington, DC: U.S. Department of Justice, Bureau of Justice Statistics.

Goetting, A. (1983). The elderly in prison: Issues and perspectives. *Journal of Research in Crime and Delinquency, 20,* 291–309.

Goetting, A. (1984). Elderly in prison: A profile. *Criminal Justice Review, 9*(2), 14–24.

Goetting, A. (1985). Racism, sexism, and ageism in the prison community. *Federal Probation, 49*(3), 10–22.

Grant, B. A., & Lefebvre, L. (1994). Older offenders in the correctional service of Canada. *Forum on Corrections Research, 6*(2), 10–13.

Harris, M. K. (1996). Key differences among community corrections acts in the United States: An overview. *The Prison Journal, 76,* 192–238.

Hirschi, T., & Gottfredson, M. (1983). Age and the explanation of crime. *American Journal of Sociology, 89,* 552–584.

Hoffman, P. B., & Beck, J. L. (1984). Burnout: Age at release from prison and recidivism. *Journal of Criminal Justice, 12,* 617–623.

Job Training and Partnership Act of 1986, 29 U.S.C. §1501 *et seq.* (1992).

Kalmanoff, A. (1982). Double trouble: The alienation of disabled inmates. *Corrections Today, 44*(6), 34, 36, 38, 39, 41.

Kelsey, O. W. (1986). Elderly inmates: Providing safe and humane care. *Corrections Today, 48* (May), 56.

Kratcoski, P. C., & Pownall, G. A. (1989). Federal Bureau of Prison programming for older inmates. *Federal Probation, 53*(2), 28–35.

Lundstrom, S. (1994). Dying to get out: A study on the necessity, importance, and effectiveness of prison early release programs for elderly inmates suffering from HIV disease and other terminal-centered illnesses. *The Brigham Young University Journal of Public Law, 9*(1), 155–188.

McCarthy, M. (1983). The health status of elderly inmates. *Corrections Today, 45* (Feb), 64–65.

Michigan Department of Corrections. (1996a). *The elderly in Michigan prisons: Michigan Department of Corrections—1996.* Lansing, MI: Author.

Michigan Department of Corrections. (1996b). *White Paper: Elderly Prisoners.* Lansing, MI: Author.

Morton, J. B. (1992). *Administrative overview of the older inmate.* Washington, DC: National Institute of Corrections.

Morton, J. B. (1993). Training staff to work with elderly and disabled inmates. *Corrections Today, 55*(1), 42, 44–47.

Morton, J. B. (1994). Training staff to work with special needs offenders. *Forum on Corrections Research, 6*(2), 32–34.

Mumola, C. J., & Beck, A. J. (1997). *Prisoners in 1996.* Washington, DC: US Department of Justice, Office of Justice Programs, Bureau of Justice Statistics.

Older Americans Act of 1965, P.L. 89–73, 79 Stat. 218, (codified as amended in scattered sections of 42 U.S.C.A., §3001 *et seq.*).

Pennsylvania Department of Corrections v Yeskey, 118 S. Ct. 1952 (1998).

Rehabilitation Act of 1973, 29 U.S.C. §301 *et seq.* (1982).

Roberg, R. R., & Webb, V. J. (1981). *Critical issues in corrections: Problems, trends, and prospects.* St. Paul, MN: West Publishing Company.

Rosefield, H. A. (1993). The older inmate: "Where do we go from here?" *Journal of Prison and Jail Health, 12*(1), 51–58.

Rosefield, H. A. (1995). *The Leon and Josephine Winkelman lecture: Geriatric prisoners.* Ann Arbor, MI: The University of Michigan, School of Social Work.

Roth, E. B. (1992). Elders behind bars. *Perspectives on Aging, 21*(4–5), 25–29.

Rubenstein, D. (1984). The elderly in prison—A review of the literature. In E. S. Newman, D. J. Newman, & M. L. Gewirtz (Eds.), *Elderly criminals* (pp. 153–168). Boston: Oelgeschlager, Gunn, and Hain, Publishers, Inc.

Rubenstein, D. (1982). The older person in prison. *Archives of Gerontology and Geriatrics, 1*(3), 287–296.

Sabath, M. J., & Cowles, E. L. (1988). Factors affecting the adjustment of elderly inmates to prison. In B. R. McCarthy & R. H. Langworthy (Eds.), *Older offenders: Perspectives in criminology and criminal justice* (pp. 178–196). New York: Praeger.

Shover, N. (1985). *Aging criminals.* Beverly Hills, CA: Sage Publications.

Steffensmeier, D., & Harer, M. D. (1993). Bulging prisons, and aging U.S. population, and the nation's violent crime rate. *Federal Probation, 57*(2), 3–10.

Turner, M. G., Sundt, J. L., Applegate, B. K., & Cullen, F. T. (1995). "Three strikes and you're out" legislation: A national assessment. *Federal Probation, 59*(3), 16–35.

Vega, M., & Silverman, M. (1988). Stress and the elderly convict. *International Journal of Offender Therapy and Comparative Criminology, 32*(2), 153–162.

Virginia Parole Board. (1992). *Parole guidelines: Procedural manual (January 1,1992).* Virginia: Author.

Vito, G. F., & Wilson, D. G. (1985). Forgotten people: Elderly inmates. *Federal Probation, 49*(1), 18–23.

Wiegand, N. D., & Burger, J. C. (1979). Elderly offenders on parole. *Prison Journal, 59*(2), 48–57.

Wikberg, R., & Foster, B. (1990). Long-termers: Louisiana's longest serving inmates and why they have stayed so long. *Prison Journal, 80*(1), 9–14.

Wilson, D. G., & Vito, G. F. (1986). Imprisoned elders: The experience of one institution. *Criminal Justice Policy Review, 1*(4), 399–421.

Zimbardo, P. G. (1994). *Transforming California's prisons into expensive old age homes for felons: Enormous hidden costs and consequences for California's taxpayers.* San Francisco: Center on Juvenile and Criminal Justice.

PART IV

An International Perspective

Chapter 12

Elders and the Criminal Justice System in England

Judith Phillips, Anne Worrall, and
Alison Brammer

> In popular imagery, the elderly are often associated
> with victimisation; crime is perceived to be an age
> war, with young offenders preying on innocent el-
> derly victims.
>
> R. Mawby—*The Victims of Crime: A New Deal*

There is very little interest in England in the role of elders in criminal justice. Such material as exists is concerned almost exclusively with the vulnerability of elders as actual or potential victims of crime or with their (in)competence as dispensers or watchdogs of criminal justice. There has been virtually no research undertaken on elders as perpetrators of crime or on their experiences of punishment. Yet there has been a steady increase in the numbers of elders in prison (Home Office, 1997a) and the treatment of geriatric prisoners is becoming a matter requiring discussion and policy development (Codd, 1995).

The relationship between age and criminal behaviour has been constructed almost exclusively as a problem of youth. Indeed, there has been no attempt even to define what constitutes the older criminal. Many research studies—and even official statistics—seem content to group all offenders over 25 together. The reason for this, of course, is that the population of offenders is markedly younger than the population at large. The vast majority of offenders grow out of crime by the age of 25, and it is not unreasonable, therefore, to consider anyone over that age to be older.

So, in talking about elders and criminal justice, we are talking about at least three very different groups of people, who may have little in common. First, we may consider elders as dispensers or watchdogs of justice. These are likely to be highly respectable, frequently well-educated and affluent elders, whose involvement in criminal justice is either professional (judges, lawyers, psychiatrists, etc.) or voluntary and altruistic—or at least, part of their perceived civic duty—such as magistrates, prison Boards of Visitors (BoV), and so on. Second, we may consider victims of crime, who, at least according to media images, are likely to be frail, vulnerable, probably struggling financially and living in poor conditions, terrorized by local youth and the fear of crime. Third, we need to consider older criminals, who may actually not be all that old—just older than the average criminal. Such criminals may be aging recidivists, long-term prisoners, older first offenders or older "first caught" offenders (the latter group including such differing offenders as retired social workers and priests charged with offenses of sexual abuse decades ago and older war criminals who have evaded capture for decades).

Given these disparate groupings, one wonders whether it makes sense at all to talk of elders in relation to criminal justice as though they shared some common characteristics and experiences. However, given the dearth of research in England in any of these areas, it is perhaps important to highlight these groups and suggest an agenda for future research. This is the purpose of this chapter.

Elders As Magistrates and Board of Visitors Members

Dignan and Wynne (1997) studied the composition of a bench of magistrates in the north Midlands. In line with earlier studies, they found that 80% of the bench were aged over 50 and only 5% under 40. Their study also confirmed that benches are dominated by the middle classes, with high proportions of magistrates being in managerial or professional employment and almost a third of female magistrates being unemployed outside the home.

Worrall's (1994) study of prison BoV members found that 68% of respondents were over 50 years of age and only 7% were under 40 (Sandiford, 1998). For both sexes (54% male, 46% female), the single most common age category was between 50 and 60. More women than men under 50 were members of boards, whereas the situation was reversed for members over 60. In terms of occupation, 42% of the men described themselves as retired (compared with 10% of the women). Of the women, 30% described themselves as housewives or voluntary workers. Pen portraits of BoV members suggest similar personal characteristics and backgrounds as magistrates, with younger men and women joining only if they are in managerial or professional jobs that allow time off for public duties.

Martin and Godfrey (1994) found that BoVs lacked credibility with prisoners because they were too old, too middle class and generally unrepresentative of the community. Descriptions included shopkeepers, a cross between magistrates and social workers, the wrong people, upper class, ex-colonels and successful self-made businessmen . . . professional people who have time . . . middle-aged . . . financially in a position to do it (Martin & Godfrey, 1994, p. 361).

Judges and Magistrates

The retirement age for senior judges is 75; for circuit judges it is 72 (with a possible extension to 75); and for magistrates and stipendiaries, 70 (Griffiths, 1991). The average age on appointment is 52 or 53, with 60 the average age of all those in office, rising to an average of 65 in the Court of Appeal and 68 in the House of Lords (Griffiths, 1991, p. 33). In 1991, only one judge out of 550 (ranging from circuit judges to the House of Lords) was black. At the same time, the proportion of female judges was a little higher but still only numbering two Lord Justices, two High Court Judges, and 19 circuit judges.

Elders As Witnesses

There is increased incidence of mental incapacity with old age. One in five people over 85 suffer from dementia, which may affect a person's capacity and thus competence and credibility as a witness to a crime. Questions concerning the credibility of older witnesses have arisen before the Registered Homes Tribunal, a body with jurisdiction to hear cases concerning registration of residential and nursing homes in the United Kingdom. In pronouncing judgment, the tribunal has on occasion made comments suggesting that the evidence of elder, incapacitated adults is unreliable. One such case was Mitchell v. West Sussex County Council (1991) Decision 162, where the tribunal described an older woman with dementia as "muddled in her use of expressions . . . she had mood swings, was emotionally immature, and the tribunal felt unable to rule out the possibility of imagination playing a part." The Pigot report (Home Office, 1989) suggested that special measures for child evidence should be extended at the discretion of the court to vulnerable adult witnesses. It has been suggested that the use of video recorded interviews, that are currently in use in children's cases, could be extended to cases involving vulnerable adults. One example where this was permitted is the case of a pensioner who recorded her evidence, including cross-examination, on video as she was not sure she would survive to see the trial (Dyer, 1992).

The recent Home Office report, *Speaking up for Justice*, published in June, 1998, focuses on witnesses who are subject to intimidation, are victims in rape and serious sexual offenses, and who are vulnerable (Home Office, 1998). The problems experienced by those with learning difficulties largely prompted the inclusion of the term "vulnerable" adult. Its definition, however, extends the term to cover a potentially wide group of individuals that may include elders. The definition suggested entails that the court should make available special measures to assist the witness if it is required by reason of significant impairment of intelligence and social functioning/mental disability or other mental or physical disorder, or physical disability. The court may exercise discretion to make measures available where the witness would be likely to suffer emotional trauma or would be likely to be so intimidated or distressed as to be unable to give best evidence without the assistance of special measures. In exercising its discretion, the court must take into account the age, culture, and ethnic background and relationship to any party to the proceedings (among other factors). These recommendations would require legislation for implementation. In a case where, for example, an older woman has been assaulted by her son and giving evidence is likely to be traumatic for her, then the court could exercise its discretion to make special measures available to enable her to give best evidence. These measures could include use of live CCTV links to enable the witness to give evidence outside the courtroom, being accompanied by a supporter if desired, use of screens in court, and submission of video recorded interviews with police or social workers as the witness's evidence in chief. It is notable that, in the conclusion to the report, the stated reason for the exclusion of elders as a group within the main focus of the report was due to a lack of literature found on their experiences as witnesses (Home Office, 1998, p. 195).

Elders As Victims of Crime

Age is an important predictor in homicide victimization. The age group most at risk of homicide is children under the age of 1, with 44 offenses per million population in 1996. The next most "at risk" group is males between 16 and 49, with between 20 and 28 offenses per million population. Males and females over the age of 50 are among the lowest "at risk" groups, with six to seven offenses per million population (Home Office, 1997b).

The 1996 British Crime Survey (Mirrlees-Black, Mayhew, & Perry, 1996) found that 1% of interviewees aged over 60 had been victims of contact crime (i.e., violence) in the preceding year (Table 4.1, p. 29). This compares with 3.9% of interviewees aged 30 to 59 and 13.2% of interviewees aged 16 to 29. Table 12.1 breaks this down into categories of violence. In all, 3% of victims of violence were over 60—compared with 39% between 30 and 59, and 58% between 16 and 29.

Contrary to popular belief, the British Crime Survey (1996) also found that fear of crime and perception of risk of victimization

TABLE 12.1   The Proportion of Victims of Violence Who Were Over 60

Offense	Men 60+ (%)	Women 60+ (%)
Domestic violence	< 1	1
Mugging	3	7
Stranger violence	4	1
Acquaintance violence	1	1

Source: The 1996 British Crime Survey.

were less for those over 60 than for younger interviewees for most categories of crime. However, in relation to their perception of risk of mugging, for example, those over 60 still overestimated their risk, whereas younger age groups tended to underestimate their risk. When it comes to general worry about crime, those over 60 appear to worry less than average about most categories (burglary, mugging, rape, theft of cars, and theft from cars). Men over 60 are slightly more worried about mugging than younger men (though much less so than women over 60) and women over 60 are much less worried about rape than younger women. They are also less worried about theft of cars and theft of articles from inside cars than either younger women or all men.

Mawby (1988) argues that elders may constitute a "high-harm" group. Although they may not be a "high risk" group, the impact of victimization may be greater than for younger groups. Although they do not perceive themselves to be at high risk, they do see themselves as being particularly vulnerable once they have been victimized. The crimes which elders are most likely to experience are "household" crimes, especially vandalism. They are more likely than younger victims to be victimized by more than one offender (i.e., a group) and, perhaps most significantly, they are less likely than younger victims to know their offenders. The actual crime appears to be less important in terms of impact than the experience of being victimized by several unknown (usually young) offenders. In terms of response, Victim Support and the police identify elders as most in need of victim services (Corbett & Maguire, 1988) and elders themselves are more appreciative of Victim Support than are younger victims (Mawby, 1988).

Elders are constructed as vulnerable and unable to protect themselves. They are marginalized and not considered full members of society. Along with children, they are subject to idealized perceptions as victims of crime. Although they are less at risk than other groups, the media reports their victimization in a graphic fashion. "The elderly then become victims of a moral panic which in reality bears little relation to their actual risk of crime. In this way, the elderly become victims, not only of crime from time to time, but of media reporting" (Walklate, 1989, p. 78).

Elder Abuse

Research is needed in the United Kingdom to establish rates of incidence and prevalence in elder abuse (Ogg & Bennett, 1992). This is a difficult task, however, when there is such divergence of opinion about what should be included in definitions of elder abuse (Brammer & Biggs, 1998). A survey by Ogg and Bennett (1992) found that 1 in 20 older people reported some kind of abuse, with the highest prevalence for verbal abuse. The survey excluded older people in institutions and those too ill or disabled to participate; arguably these are groups who may be more vulnerable to abuse and might have increased the prevalence rates found.

Elder abuse is not conceptualized in legal terms, is not a clearly defined offense, and has no satisfactory working definition (Brammer & Biggs, 1998). A recent independent report, Longcare, about events in two residential homes for adults with learning disabilities in Buckinghamshire has called for a new offense to be introduced in criminal law for a specific arrestable offense of causing harm or exploitation of a vulnerable adult, that will carry a maximum penalty of 10 years imprisonment (Buckinghamshire County Council, 1998).

Abusive situations may, however, include behavior which is covered by the criminal law. This would include offenses under the Offenses Against the Person Act 1861, Sexual Offenses Act 1956, and the Theft Act, and range from common assault to grievous bodily harm, rape, murder, theft, and fraud. The criminal law is most likely to be relevant where abuse takes the form of a positive act, though in limited circumstances where a duty of care has been assumed, criminal liability may arise from breach of that duty (Brammer, 1996). The case of *R v Stone* [1977] I QB 354 illustrates this. A 67-year-old man, of below average intelligence, partially deaf and blind, together with his partner provided a home for his 61-year-old sister, who was anorexic. The sister's health declined to such a point that she was bedridden. The appellants were aware of her condition. She eventually died from toxaemia from infected bedsores. Consequently, the appellants were convicted of manslaughter on "the basis that since she had become infirm, they had assumed the duty of caring for her. They could have discharged this duty either by providing care for her themselves or by summoning help" (Brammer & Biggs, 1998, p. 293).

Criminalizing Elder Abuse

It is also argued that use of criminal law is inappropriate because perpetrators are themselves victims of the situation, for example, careers subject to an excessive degree of stress (Griffiths et al., in Decalmer & Glendenning, 1993). Phillipson and Biggs (1995) argue that criminalization of abuse and neglect in this country should be avoided, based on commentaries on the U.S. experience (Formby, 1992) which suggest that as abuse often arises out of ignorance, criminal sanctions will have no deterrent effect and further, their existence may make victims less likely to report abuse by a caregiver.

Under common assault, established under Offenses Against the Person Act 1861—normally the victim must initiate proceedings, not the police. A common law exception to this was established in respect of elderly and infirm people in the case of Pickering v Willoughby (1907). This case involved an older woman who had suffered a number of strokes and was assaulted by her niece who had moved in to live with her. The court held that her great nephew could initiate proceedings on behalf of the victim on grounds that, "if the person assaulted is so feeble, old, and infirm as to be incapable of instituting proceedings, and is not a free agent but under the control of the person committing the assault, the information may be laid by a third person." Under this exception, the police could initiate action on behalf of older victims. Victims may be reluctant to become involved with criminal proceedings, a familiar argument, advanced in the context of domestic violence. Dawson and Faragher (1979) argue that the problem of getting victims of domestic violence to cooperate with the police has been exaggerated, and many victims are willing to cooperate (Pahl, 1985).

Domestic Violence

There is an overlap between domestic violence and elder abuse. Certain abusive relationships among older couples can be described as graduated domestic violence. It is an area that has received least attention in terms of research. As McCreadie (1996) states, "There is almost a curious hiatus in the literature as, despite the findings about the extent of abuse between older spouses and partners, the domestic violence literature has barely concerned itself with older people and the elder abuse literature has barely concerned itself with domestic violence." It is an omission which would support the development of a "family violence" approach as advocated by Kingston and Penhale (1995). Domestic Violence units are being established throughout the country, many of which include elder abuse cases within their ambit of inquiry.

Regrettably, because elder abuse is not statutorily recognized in this country, there is no easily accessible data which would quantify criminal cases of elder abuse. Abuse may take place within the residential sector as well as in domestic settings; indeed, its incidence there may be higher, and the residents older and more vulnerable (Glendenning, 1993). Where abuse is discovered, the usual course will be for the Registration and Inspection unit to take action, which may include an administrative process to force closure of the home. Short of that, and in less serious cases where concerns center on reduced standards of care, it is possible to bring a prosecution in the Magistrates court for breach of the Registered Homes Act Regulations 1991 (Brammer,1994). It is an offense to carry on a home in respect of which an individual's registration has been cancelled. Under an obvious loophole in the legislation, however, there is no automatic bar to that individual seeking registration in respect of another home.

Elders As Perpetrators

> Biology has another impact [apart from gender] on
> the likelihood of offending and it's a blunt one:
> crime is largely a function of age.
>
> Moir & Jessel—*A Mind to Crime*

> Crimes of the elderly are largely related to alcohol,
> and such socially defined offenses as vagrancy—
> although there is, perhaps not surprisingly, a cluster
> of senior males involved in embezzlement, at a time
> in their career when opportunities for making off
> with major sums begin to present themselves.
>
> Moir & Jessel—*A Mind to Crime*

Croall (1998) points out that young people's crime is more visible and public than older people's crime. White-collar, professional, and organized crime requires skill, experience, and a certain level of financial success. Con men, racketeers, and tax evaders peak in the 50 to 59 age group. There is evidence that older shoplifters are less likely to be reported.

In 1994, the peak age for known offending for males was 18 (at 9% of the population) and for females it was 14 years (at 2% of the population). In contrast, offending drops to about 1% of the male population between 40 and 50 and to below 0.5% by the age of 60. Female offending drops to below 0.5% by the age of 40 and to virtually nothing by 60 (Home Office, 1995). It should be noted that the gender difference in offending narrows from about 9:1 at the age of 18 to below 2:1 by the age of 40 and almost 1:1 over the age of 60.

A rationalization for the crime committed in old age is often sought, locating it in psychiatric and psychological discourses—homelessness, alcohol abuse, psychiatric disorder (Taylor & Parrot, 1988). A compassionate approach is often followed, with the police taking a sympathetic line and not pursuing the matter or leaving it in the hands of social services—with residential care being an informal alternative to custody, and ad hoc arrangements being made between health and welfare agencies and the police (Thomas & Wall, 1993;

Midwinter, 1990). Where mental health is defined, Guardianship under the Mental Health Act 1994 is used to divert older people from the justice system. In relation to cautioning, the Home Office (1990) requires the police to take into account "the offender's age and state of health."

Elders on Probation

Media attention and public attitudes towards elders on probation differ as to the crime. Sex offenders receive a more hostile response both in and out of prison than the adult on public order charges after a demonstration.

Mair and May's (1997) study of offenders on probation consisted of interviews with 1,200 randomly selected offenders serving probation orders or combination orders (see Table 12.2). The age distribution for probationers is similar to that for prisoners, with 40% aged under 25 and only 5% aged over 50. The proportion of offenders aged under 25 is much higher than for the population as a whole; conversely, the proportion of offenders aged over 50 is much lower than for the general population (Mair & May, 1997, pp. 10–11). The age distribution in this study is a fair representation of probationers generally. The study does not distinguish consistently between offenders aged over 50—many of its findings group offenders over 36 or over 40. However, an attempt is made here to identify findings that have relevance to the subject of this book. Offenses to be highlighted here are sexual, fraud/deception, and drink/driving. Older offenders were found to be more likely to have previous convictions than younger offenders (Mair & May, 1997, pp. 26–27).

Content of Supervision

The responses of professionals in the criminal justice system, probation officers and social workers, also receive little attention. In one small study (Phillips, 1996) a welfare rather than a justice approach was seen by offenders as the most important element.

TABLE 12.2   Current Offense and Percentages of Probationers
Over 40 Years of Age

Offense	Percentage over 40	Percentage of all in survey
Violence	18	19
Sexual	11	4
Burglary	4	20
Robbery	1	2
Car theft	0	10
Other theft	16	17
Fraud/deception	13	11
Damage	4	6
Drink/driving	27	12
Other driving	7	12
Drugs related	5	6
N	177	1,208

In Mair and May's (1997) study, older offenders were seen less frequently by their supervisors than younger offenders, although their sessions tended to be longer. The study identified a range of offense-related topics which were generally discussed in supervision sessions. With two exceptions (consumption of alcohol and health problems), all these topics were discussed less with offenders over 40 than with younger offenders. The study also identified a range of specified probation programs. Again, with two exceptions—alcohol management and sex offending—offenders over 40 were less likely to attend than younger offenders (Mair & May, 1997, p. 39). There may be some evidence here that older offenders are being supervised less rigorously than younger offenders.

Effectiveness

In terms of offenders' views on the usefulness of probation, 80% of the survey said it was extremely or fairly useful, whereas 89% of those over 36 said so (Mair & May, 1997, p. 43). This finding has to be considered in light of the fact that 40% of the original intended sample of 3,300 probationers could not be contacted—these respondents were therefore likely to be the "success" stories.

On average, 32% of the probationers in the survey had committed further offenses since the beginning of their current orders, while only 11% of those over 40 had done so (Mair & May, 1997, p. 54). The interviewees were asked the reasons for their offending. The single factor most mentioned by younger offenders was "needed things or money" but for offenders over 40 it was "under influence of alcohol." The other factor mentioned more frequently by older than younger offenders was "depression/mental or emotional problems." Alzheimer's disease also has been used as a defense to major fraud in the Guinness trial, one of Britain's largest fraud trials. Mental and physical health are important factors. Older probationers are much more likely to report long-term illness or disability than in the general population, especially musculoskeletal and mental health problems (Mair & May, 1997).

Elders in Prison

The prison population is much younger than the general population. Data from the 1991 National Prison Survey (Walmsley, Howard, & White, 1992) found that only 1% of the prison population was over 60, compared with 26% of the general population. Only 4% of the prison population was aged 50 to 59, compared with 14 % of the general population. Conversely, 40% of the prison population was aged 17 to 24, compared with 16% of the general population (see Table 12.3).

More recent figures (Home Office, 1997a: Table 1.10, p. 26), however, show that the numbers of men over 50 in prison has increased in the past decade. In 1986, there were 1,090 men aged 50 to 59 in prison (3.1% of the male prison population) compared with 2,047 (5%) in 1996. In 1986, there were 299 men over 60 in prison (0.8%) compared with 699 (1.7%) in 1996. The picture for older women is very different and has changed little. In 1986, there were 56 women aged 50 to 59 in prison (4.6% of the female prison population) compared with 81 (4.7%) in 1996. In 1986, there were

TABLE 12.3 Prison Population by Age, October 1997

Age	Number	Percentage of total
15–17	2451	3.9
18–20	7659	12.1
21–24	11808	18.7
25–29	13753	27.2
30–39	17184	27.2
40–49	6528	10.2
50–59	2880	4.6
60+	963	1.5

Source: Seward (1998).

10 women over 60 in prison (0.8%) compared with 11 (0.6%) in 1996. The biggest age change for women has been the 30 to 49 age group, which has increased at the expense of younger age groups. A similar, but less marked pattern is evident for men in prison.

The Prison Reform Trust says that the oldest prisoner is currently 81 and is in HMP Kingston (Seward, 1998). Home Office figures report that there were 963 prisoners over 60 in October 1997. Since 1990, the proportion of prisoners under 30 has dropped by 6.6%. The number over 50 has increased by 1,750 (Seward, 1998).

Because of ageist attitudes, older inmates are less likely than younger inmates to be able to work in prison, as notions of retirement are transferred from community to institutions. Beyond this, however, we know very little about the transitions of older offenders in and out of prison, the social networks of older offenders, older inmates' connections outside of prison, including family life, or issues concerning the health and social care of older prisoners. Similarly, there is little research on the effects of the aging population and the growing number of older offenders in the prison service. A breakdown of figures on offense by age is not widely available, and a debate on what age defines an older offender has not taken place. Additionally, there are no plans to consider the aging population in prisons (McFadyean, 1998).

Only one prison, HMP Portsmouth, has provision for 30 older offenders over the age of 60. Very little research went into the rationale, design, and strategy for the special prison. Located on the second floor of an existing prison, it does not have easy access for wheelchair users and has been underutilized (McFadyean, 1998). Some criminologists argue that if there are specialized units for older offenders then the courts will fill them, ignoring other alternative programs for offenders and reinforcing the premise that prison is the only solution (McFadyean, 1998).

Disaggregating the routes which lead to an offender being described as old in prison and identifying the nature of their crime is extremely important to understanding the issues and to making a case for treating older offenders as a separate category. Older offenders can consist of those who are first time offenders; war criminals prosecuted years after the crime; those committing a crime in later life; those who are recidivists with a lifetime of crime behind them; and offenders who have grown old in prison. It is this latter group that has interested policy makers, as this population is set to grow with the changes in the system to more mandatory life sentences. The number of life sentences has grown by nearly 60% since 1986 (McFadyean, 1998). Over the same period the average length of a life sentence has risen from 11.1 years to almost 14 years. There are only about 30 people in the United Kingdom imprisoned for their natural lives, the most famous being Myra Hindley, Peter Sutcliffe, and Rose West.

A distinction needs to be made between male and female offenders. In the feminist literature, older female offenders are invisible (Codd, 1998). Similarly, although there has now been considerable study of women in prison in the penal literature, older women are not separated out as a distinct category.

Although the numbers are small, the differences are important to highlight as numbers of both men and women in prison grow and health issues become crucial in such institutional settings. No research currently exists on older women offenders in prison in the United Kingdom, but studies in progress show that poor diet and exercise can have significant consequences for older women inside prison (personal communication with Azrini Wahidin, University of Keele, 1998). Regimes and even the prison wing specifically designed for older offenders over the age of 60 at Portsmouth was based on meeting the health needs of older male prisoners.

We know from limited studies of men in prison that physical threats and taunting from younger inmates can frighten older men (McCarthy & Langworthy, 1988). Women are expected to take on a "mothering role" toward younger prisoners (Carlen, 1983; Peckham, 1985), but recent reports (Howard League, 1997; H M Inspectorate of Prisons, 1997) have identified both the disruption of this role for older women and dangers (bullying, recruitment to prostitution and drugs couriering, etc.) for younger women. Stereotypes of older women offenders also exist—the mad, sad or bad image (Gelsthorpe & Morris, 1990)—resting on the premise that the offender is in need of psychiatric help. The older shoplifter image, or in contrast, the image of the older woman as being manipulative and powerful (Codd, 1998, personal communication) or the good and bad carer are often portrayed by the media.

The media again plays an important part in creating ageist images of those in prison. Headlines such as "Birdman Pop will be doyen of jail's oldie wing" (*Guardian*, October 18, 1994); and "Artful Dodge takes a runner as most wanted oldies lie low" (*Guardian*, February 1, 1995) play on the sensational and unusual, and often present a humorous account (Codd, 1995; Hepworth, 1993).

The voices of older offenders themselves in a prison setting have only been heard through autobiographical and media accounts (*Guardian*, December 30, 1996). In one study the risks associated with prison life created vulnerability, with the threat of violence and the drug culture being alien to many offenders that experienced the penal system for the first time (Phillips, 1996). All 23 offenders interviewed in the study feared for their safety and their health.

Boredom and mental health problems are also cited. One London study (Taylor & Parrot, 1988) found that older offenders had massive social and medical problems. Half had some form of mental disorder, a quarter were alcoholics, a third had "major functional psychosis," and up to three-quarters were "personally isolated." Health care is a major factor of concern and is linked with inadequate architectural design through small, squalid cells leading to overcrowding.

A current study (personal communication with Helen Codd, University of Central Lancashire, 1998) looks at the wider support systems available to offenders and their families. Limited evidence suggests that isolation and loneliness resulting from separation from family exists for older offenders not only within prison but also on release.

Conclusion: Areas for Research

This review of the criminal justice system in England in relation to older offenders leaves many areas unexplored. Further research is needed in relation to the treatment of older people within the system. However, several larger questions need debate, such as: should older people be treated differently from other offenders in the system? Should we create a paternalistic approach in protecting older people or a laissez-faire approach, treating older people as full adults taking control of their own lives?

Finally, to what extent can the problems associated with aging be different for older offenders compared with older people in the community or in residential care? The plethora of research and literature on residential care over the last 50 years is disproportionate to the comparative effort devoted to the older prison population.

References

Bowcott, D. (1995, February 1). Artful dodge takes a runner as most wanted oldies lie low. *Guardian*, p. 20. London: Guardian Newspapers Limited.

Brammer, A. (1994). Registered Homes Act 1984: Safeguarding the Elderly? *Journal of Social Welfare and Family Law, 4*, 423–437.

Brammer, A. (1996). Elder Abuse in the UK: A New Jurisdiction? *Journal of Elder Abuse and Neglect, 8*, 33–48.

Brammer, A., & Biggs, S. (1998). Defining Elder Abuse. *Journal of Social Welfare and Family Law, 20*, 285–304.

Buckinghamshire County Council. (1998). *Independent Longcare Inquiry.* Bedford: Buckinghamshire County Council.

Carlen, P. (1983). *Women's imprisonment: A study in social control.* London: Routledge.

Codd, H. (1995). Older offenders and criminal justice. *Probation Journal, 42*, 152–155.

Corbett, C., & Maguire, M. (1988). The value and limitations of Victim Support Schemes. In M. Maguire & J. Pointing (Eds.), *Victims of crime: A new deal?* Milton Keynes: Open University Press.

Croall, H. (1998). *Crime and society in Britain.* Harlow: Addison Wesley Longman.

Crown Prosecution Service. (1994). *The code for crown prosecutors.* London: Crown Prosecution Service.

Dawson, B., & Faragher, T. (1979). *Battered women project: Interim Report.* Staffordshire: University of Keele.

Decalmer, P., & Glendenning, F. (Eds.). (1993). *The mistreatment of elderly people.* London: Sage.

Dignan, J., & Wynne, A. (1997). A microcosm of the local community? Reflections on the composition of the magistracy in a PSD in the North Midlands. *British Journal of Criminology, 37,* 184–197.

Dyer, C. (1992, June 25). Court film may cheat death. *Guardian,* p. 1.

Formby, W. A. (1992). Should elder abuse be decriminalised? A justice system perspective. *Journal of Elder Abuse and Neglect, 4,* 121–130.

Gelsthorpe, L., & Morris, A. (1990). *Feminist perspectives in criminology.* Buckingham: Open University Press.

Glendenning, F. (1993). What is elder abuse and neglect? In P. Dacalmer & F. Glendenning (Eds.), *The mistreatment of elderly people.* London: Sage.

Griffiths, A., & Roberts, G. (1995). (Eds.). *The law and elderly people* (2nd ed.). London: Routledge.

Griffiths, J. A. G. (1991). *The politics of the judiciary* (4th ed.). London: Fontana Press.

Hepworth, M. (1993). Old age in crime fiction. In J. Johnson & R. Slater, *Ageing and later life* (pp. 32–37). London: Open University Press.

Her Majesty's Inspectorate of Prisons. (1997). *Thematic report on women's prisons.* London: Home Office.

Home Office. (1989). Report of the Advisory Group on Video Evidence. London: Author.

Home Office. (1990). *The Cautioning of Offenders* (re HOC 59/1990). Home Office Circular 59/1990, London, Home Office.

Home Office. (1995). *Digest 3: Information on the Criminal Justice System in England and Wales.* London: Author.

Home Office. (1997a). *Prison Statistics England and Wales 1996* (Cm 3732). London: Her Majesty's Stationery Office.

Home Office. (1997b). *Criminal Statistics England and Wales 1996* (Cm 3764). London: Her Majesty's Stationery Office.

Home Office. (1998). *Speaking up for justice.* Report of the Interdepartmental Working Group on the treatment of Vulnerable or Intimidated Witnesses in the Criminal Justice System. London: Author.

Howard League. (1997). *Lost Inside—The Imprisonment of Teenage Girls.* London: Author.

Kingston, P., & Penhale, B. (Eds.) (1995). *Family violence and the caring professions.* Basingstoke: Macmillan.

Law Commission (1995). *Mental Incapacity* (Law Com No 231). London: Her Majesty's Stationery Office.

Lord Chancellor. (1997). *Who decides? Making decisions on behalf of mentally incapacitated adults* (Cm 3803). London: Her Majesty's Stationery Office.

McCarthy, B., & Langworthy, R. (1988). *Older offenders.* New York: Praeger.

McCreadie, C. (1996). *Elder abuse: Update on research.* London: Age Concern Institute of Gerontology, King's College.

McFadyean, M. (1998, August 1). Lagging behind. *Guardian,* pp. 20–26.

Mair, G., & May, C. (1997). *Offenders on probation* (Home Office Research Study 167). London: Home Office.

Martin, C., & Godfrey, D. (1994). Prisoners' views of Boards of Visitors—A question of credibility. *British Journal of Criminology, 34,* 358–365.

Mawby, R. (1988). Age, vulnerability and the impact of crime. In M. Maguire & J. Pointing (Eds.), *The victims of crime: A new deal?* Milton Keynes: Open University Press.

Midwinter, E. (1990). *The old order: Crime and older people.* London: Centre for Policy on Ageing.

Mirrlees-Black, C., Mayhew, P., & Percy, A. (1996). *The 1996 British Crime Survey. England and Wales, Home Office Statistical Bulletin 19/96,* London: Home Office Research and Statistics Directorate.

Mitchell v. West Sussex County Council. (1991). Registered Homes Tribunal Decision 162, Registered Homes Tribunal Secretariat 1992 (pp. 796–801). London: Department of Health.

Moir, A., & Jessel, D. (1995). *A mind to crime.* London: Michael Joseph.

Offenses Against the Person Act. (1861). Public General Statutes, Ch. 100. London: Queens Printers.

Ogg, J., & Bennett, G. (1992). Elder abuse in Britain. *British Medical Journal, 305,* 998–9.

Pahl, J. (Ed.). (1995). *Private violence and public policy.* London: Routledge and Kegan Paul.

Peckham, A. (1985). *A woman in custody.* London: Fontana.

Phillips, J. (1996). Crime and older offenders. *Practice, 8,* 43–55.

Phillipson, C. (1993). Elder abuse and neglect: Social and policy issues. In *Action on elder abuse,* Working Paper No. 1: A Report of the Ist International Symposium on Elder Abuse. London: Action on Elder Abuse.

Phillipson, C., & Biggs, S. (1995). Elder abuse: A critical overview. In P. Kingston & B. Penhale (Eds.), *Family violence and the caring professions* (pp. 181–203). Hampshire: MacMillan.

Pickering v. Willoughby. (1907). 2 Kings Bench. The law reports of the Incorporated Council of Law Reporting (pp. 297–300). London: C. A. Butterworths.

R v. Stone (1977). 2 All England Reports 341–348. London: C. A. Butterworths.

Sandiford, D. (1998). Boards of visitors: The future. *Prison Service Journal, 117,* 39–41.

Seward, E. (1998, June 2). *Help the aged* (Prison Report No. 43). London: Prison Reform Trust.

Sexual Offenses Act. (1956). Public General Statutes, Ch. 100. London: HMSO.

Taylor, P., & Parrot, J. (1988). Elderly offenders. *British Journal of Psychiatry, 152,* 340–346.

Theft Act. (1968). Public General Acts, Ch. 60. London: HMSO.

Thomas, T., & Wall, G. (1993). Investigating Older People who Commit Crime. *Elders: Journal of Care and Practice, 2,* 53–60.

Wainwright, M. (1994, October 18). Birdman 'Pop' will be doyen of jail's oldie wing. *Guardian,* p. 1. London: Guardian Newspapers Limited.

Walklate, S. (1989). *Victimology.* London: Unwin Hyman.

Walmsley, R., Howard, L., & White, S. (1992). *The National Prison Survey 1991:* Main findings (Home Office Research Study 128). London: Her Majesty's Stationery Office.

Worrall, A. (1994). *Have you got a minute? The changing role of prison Boards of Visitors.* London: Prison Reform Trust.

Chapter 13

Elders and the Criminal Justice System in Germany

Arthur Kreuzer and Ulrike Grasberger

Elder People in German Society

Within the past few decades, significant demographic changes have occurred in Germany. Although the birth rate decreased, life expectancy rose enormously. In relation to the overall population, the number of older people has doubled within the past four decades. It is expected to double again within the next four decades (Kreuzer, 1992b).

Statistically, the average age in Germany is 40 years and thus higher than in almost any other country. By 2020, the average age is expected to be 47. The last census showed that the proportion of persons below age 15 had dropped to 15%; at the same time, the proportion of persons older than 65 had risen to 15%. One-fifth of the population was older than 60. Forty-five out of 1 million inhabitants were older than 100 (Riesenhuber, 1990). In 2030, the proportion of persons older than 60 is predicted to be one-third (Kreuzer, 1997).

As a result of these developments, a continuously decreasing number of people living in Germany will be of employable age, financially supporting an increasing number of retired persons. Today, four working persons have to support one pensioner; in about 50 years, only two working people will have to do the same (Kreuzer, 1997). The term "aging society" was coined and a modification of the "treaty between the generations," on which the current pension scheme is based, was demanded (Gronemeyer, 1991). A new treaty with new responsibilities for elders is called for. Many are demanding the establishment of new areas of work for potential pensioners and the abolition of early retirement options (Schueller, 1995). Some go as far as to predict a new type of "class struggle," that is, a struggle between the generations.

All in all, the demographic changes described above affect the role of elders as offenders and victims in Germany. Statistically, crime rates relatively will decrease. Older people, especially older women, commit comparatively few crimes, and the life expectancy of women in particular will increase (Kreuzer, 1992b). In addition, the number of people over 80—an age with crime rates close to zero—will grow.

On the other hand, the number of crimes committed by older people absolutely will increase (Kreuzer, 1992a) because of the growing population of elders. These statistically increasing crime rates will seem like a new problem at first glance and may be misused as a tool in a predicted conflict between the generations (Kreuzer, 1992b).

Elder People As Victims and Their Fear of Crime

Recently, a study on the victimization of elders was performed. It is the first nationwide quantitive empirical study on violence against elder people and the meaning of criminality in their lives in Germany. Approximately 5,000 persons above age 60 were questioned in 1992. Individuals in need of personal care either at home or in institutions were left out because many of them are restricted in their ability to report about their situation (Wetzels, Greve, Mecklenburg, Bilsky, & Pfeiffer, 1995).

This study found that the victimization risk was low for older people. Notwithstanding their vulnerability, elder people are rarely confronted with violent crime. On the other hand, the material, physical, and psychological problems caused by violent crimes are considerable in every individual case and cannot be neglected. Compared to the violent crime rate as a whole, the victimization rates within the immediate social environment are high. Elders run a higher risk of being confronted with violence in their families than in public (Wetzels et al., 1995).

Another question is whether old people are more afraid of crime than the rest of the population. The study found that the fear of crime among old people is surprisingly low, but that any fear of crime affects their sense of well-being more than is true for young people. Former victimization enhances the fear of being victimized again. According to this study, the "fear-victimization-paradox" (Lindquist & Duke, 1982) has to be revised (Wetzels et al., 1995).

When talking about elders as victims, differentiation between victimization in the public sector, at home, and in institutions is necessary. Within the general social context, older people often fall prey to fraud, robberies, and similar offenses when they are home alone. In cases like fraud, they often don't even realize their victimization (Kreuzer, 1992b). Also, older people often do not report crimes (Birkenstock & Tiedemann, 1982). Therefore, the hidden crime rate is presumedly high in these areas.

The maltreatment of older people by close relatives or the nursing staff of old people's homes or other institutions is more frequent than formerly assumed. Maltreatment comprises physical, psychological, or social harm, from neglect to legal incapacitation, incorrect medication or physical injuries. Within the past few years, several cases of manslaughter in hospitals or nursing homes have been reported, especially some cases of serial offenses. These cases are usually discovered by chance, and many of them presumedly never come to light. The chances of discovering serial offenses are much higher; consequently, cases of killing just one patient are probably never cleared up. A number of conditions can lead to the killing of older people in hospitals or nursing homes. Increasing life expectancy results in increasing burdens on the nursing staff, again producing temptations to rid oneself of difficult patients. Many institutions are understaffed; the staff lack sufficient qualifications to cope with the occurring difficulties; and the jobs are not paid well. In private settings, the lack of supervision and control is a contributing factor; a prospective inheritance can be very tempting. The deplorable physical situation of some older people may induce relatives to put an end to this situation. It is easy to veil these killings; a small change in the medication dose can be lethal, and after a certain age autopsies are rarely performed. Investigations in public or private institutions are obstructed by internal mechanisms to regulate conflicts (Kreuzer, 1992b).

Elders As Criminals

A discussion of elders as criminals requires differentiation between two different offender groups. The first group consists of offenders committing crimes for the first time in their lives at an advanced age. The second group comprises persons whose crimes preceded their transition to old age.

Criminality of elders has been defined as offenses due to physical, psychological, or social processes that accompany aging (Schneider, 1987). This definition entails practical difficulties because it requires careful investigation regarding the causes of the offenses committed. In addition, few offenses can be attributed exclusively to the process of aging, and the process of aging may be present at earlier as well as later periods of life (Kreuzer, 1992b).

Human dignity requires the recognition that every individual, including elders, behaves socially in both positive and negative ways. Advanced age is not an "illness" but rather a period of life requiring specific changes and adaptations which may result in maladaptive criminal actions. Due to changes occurring late in life, elders may commit crimes in different settings than they would have at an earlier age (Kreuzer, 1992b). For example, after retirement, offenses at work are impossible. Often, financial resources are scarce and may result in the illegal acquisition of assets. Two to three million retired persons are assumed to live on incomes below the welfare limit. Every fifth household has less than 1,000 DM available per month (Fronmueller, 1989). On the other hand, many older people adjust to the situation without falling back on illegal means, although a certain correlation of poverty and crime has been proven (Chressantis, 1988).

When elder people commit crimes, they may not be aware of the wrongfulness of their actions at the time (Kreuzer, 1992b). Alcohol easily reduces psychological barriers (Kreuzer, 1983) and may, in combination with cerebral degenerative changes, result in the commission of crimes (Weber, 1987; Fattah, 1991). A strong correlation of cerebral changes and sexual offenses has been found (Greger, 1986).

Certain types of offenses are typical of advanced age. Statistically, shoplifting makes up 80% of all convictions. Women prevail among shoplifters, and males commit more traffic offenses (Kreuzer, 1992b). Fraud, environmental crimes, and minor bodily injuries also bear statistical significance, whereas the rates of serious offenses such as burglary, major bodily harm, sexual offenses, robbery, or drug-related crime are low (Kreuzer, 1992b).

Studies on hidden crime with particular attention to elder offenders are not available. Possibly many offenses by old people are never reported (Feest, 1985; Fattah, 1991). For example, internal mechanisms are applied in old people's homes or other institutions to deal with deviant behavior. Fringe groups, such as communities of homeless people, may also have internal ways of dealing with offenders (Kreuzer, 1992b). On the other hand, offenses like shoplifting are frequently reported. All in all, old people may encounter a higher tolerance level from the community than younger offenders (Kreuzer, 1992b).

The Necessity of Special Regulations for Elder Criminals

German law contains special regulations for juvenile offenders but not for elders (Kreuzer, 1992b). Certain parallels and differences between juvenile and older offenders are evident. During youth, a rapid socialization process takes place. Individuals have to cope with many changes and conflicts during that period. Elders likewise have to adjust to a new situation, especially after retirement. But this is not a socialization process in itself and therefore does not produce a particular risk of criminal actions. Relative to older people, juveniles are also more active, aggressive, and impulsive. Because they don't work, both juveniles and seniors have a lot of free time. However, this also restricts their available financial means. In contrast with juveniles, elders usually adjust to a lower standard of life and accept the situation (Kreuzer, 1992b).

Both young and old people often face a change of their immediate environment. The growing-up process includes leaving home, and growing old often requires moving to an old people's or a nursing home. Juveniles are often members of peer groups, whereas old people may end up in isolation. Members of both groups may lack social competence. But contrary to juveniles, very old persons eventually become socially dependent again, are taken care of, and therefore are automatically "supervised." This factual control possibly reduces the risk of criminal actions (Kreuzer, 1992b).

Juveniles as well as seniors often commit offenses under the influence of alcohol (Kreuzer, 1983), but additional cerebral degenerative processes may also result in deviant behavior among older people (Weber, 1987; Fattah, 1991). Frequently, juveniles and elders commit crimes spontaneously, with little or no consideration for the potential discovery of their criminal acts. Furthermore, investigations against both groups easily lead to a conviction, and juvenile as well as senior offenders rarely lodge appeals (Kreuzer, 1992b).

Notwithstanding the similarities described previously, the crime rates among juveniles are significantly higher. People over age 60 form 25% of the population responsible before the law but only 6% of the registered suspects. The latter number has risen from 4% to 6% since the 1970s due to the demographic development in Germany (Kreuzer, 1992b). The number of juvenile suspects is 7 to 8 times as high. Moreover, judges convict few of the senior suspects at the end of the trial. Supposedly, prosecutors as well as judges are lenient towards older persons (Lindquist, White, & Chambers, 1987).

Special regulations for elders may be needed in order to do justice to their particular situation during their involvement in criminal investigations and trials as witnesses, victims, suspects, or offenders (Schramke, 1996). So far, the protective needs of seniors have been considered as one factor when applying existing regulations. For example, §§153, 153a StPO (Code on Criminal Procedure) legalize the dismissal of minor cases before the actual trial and are extensively applied with senior offenders. Defenders are more often appointed by the courts in trials against elder suspects. Regulations on criminal responsibility are frequently applied (§§20, 21 StGB—German Penal Code). Old age is often considered as one factor in the sentencing process (§46 II StGB) and when deciding on the fitness to undergo detention (Kreuzer, 1992b).

In general, to avoid stigmatization, older persons should not be subjected to special regulations, but age should be noted as one factor for consideration within the existing regulations, for example, on criminal responsibility or sentencing. Age should also be a reason to dismiss cases before the actual trial (Kreuzer, 1992b).

Difficulties After Sentencing

---

§2 StVollzG (Code on Corrections, 1998) defines the purpose of imprisonment as follows: during imprisonment, the inmate is supposed to be enabled to lead a socially responsible life without committing further crimes. This object of imprisonment is of dubious value for senior offenders. The future of elders is of a different dimension than that of younger people. For them, a single day in prison can have a completely different meaning than for other inmates (Schramke, 1996). Their time remaining is usually much shorter, and rehabilitation may be infeasible due to lessened flexibility and adaptability to unknown situations. Many times, the only remaining purpose of imprisonment is thus fighting the loss of socialization caused by detention itself. Specific deterrence is not a valid goal because of the low recidivism rates among elders. The only remaining justification for imprisonment is retribution (Kreuzer, 1992b). Consequently, the German Constitutional Court decided that for offenders sentenced to life in prison, advanced age and illness have to be considered when leave or parole are at stake (BVerfGE 64 1983). Although the court had decided earlier that even those sentenced to life in prison needed to have the chance to be dismissed some time in the future (BVerfGE 45, 1977), old age does not automatically lead to early dismissal from prison, especially not in the most serious cases (BVerfGE 64, p. 281).

The situation of older people in prison differs from that of other inmates. Those imprisoned for the first time are usually not integrated into the prison subculture (Schramke, 1996, p. 199). Many of them are afraid of the younger inmates, although a recent study found that the fear of being victimized is not as strong as often assumed (Schramke, 1996). On the other hand, offenders with long criminal careers often rank highly in the prison subculture (Kreuzer, 1992b).

The biggest problem surrounding older inmates is the integration of this group into the existing work programs (Schramke, 1996). For older inmates, the object of these programs is questionable. Young inmates are supposed to get used to working and be prepared for a job after dismissal, whereas old prisoners often are past the age of retirement or, at least, will have passed that age limit when leaving prison (Kreuzer, 1992b). One positive aspect of this is that elders don't have to worry about their financial situation or about finding a job after dismissal. Their income is secured by the German pension scheme after the age of retirement.

Another problem is older prisoners' need of special health and social care (Schramke, 1996). Their contacts with the outside world are generally limited compared to those of young prisoners (Schramke, 1996). All in all, imprisonment is more burdensome for elder inmates than for the young.

On the other hand, life experience is a positive factor that may help elders cope with the situation in prison. Disciplinary problems with older prisoners are rare (Albrecht & Duenkel, 1981; Fattah, 1991; Schramke, 1996). Often, they enjoy a "bonus" with fellow prisoners as well as with the staff because of their age.

Considering all these facts, we have to raise the question whether special departments for elders should be established within regular prisons or whether special prisons just for old inmates should be established. Both special elder departments and special elder prisons exist in Germany. One prison in Singen, Baden-Wuerttemberg (Schramke, 1996), is for older prisoners only, one prison in Straubing has a geriatric department, and another prison in Bochum has a special department for prisoners in the need of special care. The prison in Singen can accommodate 65 inmates but is usually not filled to its capacity. It was originally established for inmates older than 60, but inmates over 50 are accepted now as well.

There are positive as well as negative aspects to separating older inmates from the rest of a prison population (Kreuzer, 1992b). In separate elder departments or prisons, less security is needed. Such prisons can be adjusted to the special needs of older people. Although a study showed that the risk of being victimized is not as high for older inmates as often assumed (Schramke, 1996, p. 220), potential fears of confrontations with sometimes aggressive younger offenders can be reduced.

On the other hand, prisons are, up to a point, a mirror of society. In special departments or prisons, older inmates are excluded from the rest of that society. They possibly age faster without contact with young people. Moreover, many older people enjoy the company of the young (Schramke, 1996).

Taking all aspects into consideration, we draw the conclusion that elder convicts should not be imprisoned if possible (Schramke, 1996). A change of surroundings can be particularly burdensome for older persons (Schramke, 1996). It is incomparably harder for them to establish new friendships. Thus, home confinement is an adequate alternative to imprisonment (Kreuzer, 1992b, 1992a; Schramke, 1996) as well as probation combined with particular obligations. This way, a change of environment as well as social disintegration of older offenders are prevented.

Of course, imprisonment cannot be avoided in severe cases. For older offenders that must be incarcerated, special departments could be established within regular prisons to meet the special requirements of older inmates. Prisons just for elders are not recommended. The low number of remaining older prisoners would have to be concentrated in few prisons and would result in long distances from home for some of them. This again may lead to further isolation, for example, when visitors are scarce.

Conclusions

The growing number of older people in German society requires studies on elders as perpetrators and victims. Elders rarely commit serious crimes. Shoplifting and traffic offenses are classic examples of crimes committed by older people.

Recently, a study on elders as victims showed that their risk of being victimized was relatively low, but the effects of crime on elders, especially of violent crime, were found to be very serious in every respect. Older people are most likely to be victimized within their immediate social environment. Personnel shortages and inadequate staff training may result in maltreatment of older people in old people's homes or other institutions. Improvements are required in these areas.

Neither the German Penal Code nor the Code of Procedure contains special regulations for elder offenders, but advanced age is given consideration in various decision-making processes within the criminal justice system. Age-specific regulations are not desirable because of their stigmatizing effects.

Imprisoning older people entails additional problems. In Germany, we have one special prison for older inmates as well as special departments for elders within regular prisons. The advantage of such institutions is that they can provide special services to meet the needs of older inmates. On the other hand, they separate older inmates from the young and are thus not representative of society as a whole. Elder people usually enjoy the company of the young. Imprisonment in any type of institution is particularly burdensome on older people and should be avoided as much as possible.

References

Albrecht, H., & Dünkel, F. (1981). Die vergessene Minderheit—alte Menschen als Straftäter (The Forgotten Minority—Elderly People as Offenders). *Zeitschrift fuer Gerontologie (Journal for Gerontology) 14*, 259–273.

Birkenstock, W., & Tiedemann, H. (1982). Die Taeter-/Opfer-Situation alter Menschen als Indikator und Konsequenz gesellschaftlicher Fehlentwicklungen (The offender-victim situation of elderly people as indicator and consequence of a social wrong development). *Die Polizei (The Police), 73,* 137–142.

BverfGE 45 (1977). (Bundesverfassungsgerichtsentscheidung) Decision of the German Federal Constitutional Court.

BverfGE 64 (1983). (Bundesverfassungsgerichtsentscheidung) Decision of the German Federal Constitutional Court.

Chressantis, G. A. (1988). Criminal Homicide and the Elderly Offender: A Theoretical and Empirical Analysis. *Journal of Quantitative Criminology*, *4*, 187–199.

Fattah, E. A. (1991). Alterskriminalität. In R. Sieverts & H. J. Schneider (Eds.), *Handwoerterbuch der Kriminologie* (pp. 239–265). Berlin: de Gruyter.

Feest, J. (1985). Alterskriminalitaet. In G. Kaiser, H.-J. Kerner, F. Sack, & H. Schellhoss (Eds.), *Kleines kriminologisches Woerterbuch*. Heidelberg: C. F. Müller.

Fronmueller, A. (1989). *Eine vergessene Minderheit? Delinquenz und strafrechtliche Sanktionierung "alter" Menschen* (ISS Paper 37/1989). Frankfurt/Main: Institut fuer Sozialarbeit und Sozialpaedagogik.

Greger, J. (1986). Die forensische Bedeutung psychischer Altersveränderungen. *Kriminalistik und forensische Wissenschaften*, *62*, 44–49.

Gronemeyer, R. (1991). *Die Entfernung vom Wolfsrudel: Ueber den drohenden Krieg der Jungen gegen die Alten*. Frankfurt: Fischer Taschenbuch.

Kreuzer, A. (1983). Kinderdelinquenz und Jugendkriminalitaet. *Zeitschrift fuer Paedagogik*, *29*, 49–70.

Kreuzer, A. (1992a, August 28). Mit siebzig auf die schiefe Bahn? *Die Zeit*, p. 69.

Kreuzer, A. (1992b). Alte Menschen in Kriminalität und Kriminalitätskontrolle. In A. Kreuzer & M. Huerlimann (Eds.), *Alte Menschen als Täter und Opfer* (pp. 13–85). Freiburg im Breisgau: Lambertus.

Kreuzer, A. (1997). Gewalt gegen Aeltere zu Hause—Einführung in die Thematik. In *Gewalt gegen Aeltere zu Hause*. Bonn: Bundesministerium für Familie, Senioren, Frauen und Jugend.

Lindquist, J. H., & Duke, J. (1982). The elderly victim at risk: Explaining the fear-victimization paradox. *Criminology*, *20*, 115–126.

Lindquist, J. H., White, O. Z., & Chambers, C. D. (1987). Elderly felons: Dispositions of arrest. In C. D. Chambers (Ed.), *The elderly: Victims and deviants* (pp. 161–176). Athens, OH: Ohio University Press.

Riesenhuber, H. (1990, October 31). DPA-report. *Giessener Allgemeine Zeitung*.

Schneider, H. J. (1987). *Kriminologie*. Berlin: De Gruyter.

Schramke, H. J. (1996). *Alte Menschen im Strafvollzug*. Bonn: Forum Verlag Godesberg.

Schueller, H. (1995). *Die Altersluege: fuer einen neuen Generationenvertrag*. Berlin: Rowohlt.

StGB (Strafgesetzbuch). German Penal Code, code stand: 13 November, 1988.

StPO (Strafprozessordnung). German Code on Criminal Procedure; code stand: 07. April 1987.

StVollzG (Gesetz ueber den Vollzug der Freiheitsstrafe und der freiheitsent-ziehenden Massregein der Besserung und Sicherung—Straf-vollzugsgesetz). Code on Corrections, code stand: 26 August, 1998.

Weber, J. (1987). Spaet- und Altenkriminalitaet in der psychologisch-psychi-atrischen Begutachtung. *Forensia, 8,* 57–72.

Wetzels, P., Greve, W., Mecklenburg, E., Bilsky, W., & Pfeiffer, Ch. (1995). *Kriminalität im Leben alter Menschen.* Stuttgart: Kohlhammer.

Suggested Readings

Amelunxen, C. (1960). *Alterskriminalität.* Hamburg.

Jaeckle, L. (1988). *Aspekte der Altenkriminalitaet in kriminologischer Sicht* (Aspects of delinquency of elderly people seen from a criminology point of view). Dissertation, University of Freiburg, Freiburg, Germany.

Chapter 14

Elders and the Criminal Justice System in Israel

Malca Alek and Sarah Ben-David

> Hearken unto your father who begot you, and despise not your mother when she is old.
>
> —Proverbs 23:22

> You shall stand up before the aged person; you shall show honor to the face of the old and you shall fear God for I am the Lord.
>
> —Leviticus 19:32

These two biblical verses and many similar biblical, Halachic (traditional Jewish law), and other references found in Jewish texts honor older people since they are regarded as the source of knowledge and wisdom. Indeed the first judges in Jewish history were chosen from the town's elders.

However, in modern industrial societies all over the world, including Israel, elders have lost their special role. Their knowledge and experience are too often perceived as useless vis-à-vis rapid societal changes. They no longer hold a prestigious status, since they are considered unproductive and, as such, a burden for society. It still seems strange, however, that in Israel, where tradition and religion play an important role, there is no special consideration for the aged.

The decline in the once-elevated status of elders in Israel is borne out by the experiences of elders who come into contact with the Israeli criminal justice system. As this chapter will demonstrate, elders receive few special privileges or protections under Israeli criminal law or in Israel's correctional system. Moreover, in certain circumstances, including the prosecution and sentencing of older offenders, elders involved in the criminal justice system generally fare no better than younger people and often fare even worse.

Elders in Israeli Law

The state of Israel has been shaped by both its ancient and modern history. In 1998, Israel celebrated its 50th anniversary. It is a young state in the Middle East, surrounded by many hostile Arab states. It is also a state known for its high rate of immigration of Jews from all over the world, including holocaust survivors, refugees from Arab countries, and immigrants from Europe, America, Ethiopia, and the former USSR. These facts have an impact on Israel's legal system in general and on the rate of criminality in the country, in particular.

Israeli law is based on many diverse sources, including the British legal system, the Ottoman law, the religious Jewish and Muslim laws, and Knesset (the Israeli Parliament) legislation (Bensinger, 1997). At the time of the establishment of the state in 1948, the penal code adopted was the ordinance of 1936, as enacted by the British mandate and adopted by the Knesset, along with other laws that were in force at the time.

Since then, the enactment of a number of basic laws has diminished the similarities between the British and the Israeli criminal codes (Kremnitzer, 1997). The last amendments were introduced in 1980. However, in this legislative process, no special consideration for senior citizens is to be found, whether as victims, offenders, or witnesses.

This lack of consideration is demonstrated by the fact that in Israeli law there is no clear definition of old age. Even in the law of compulsory retirement (1957), no criteria for old age exist. A male employee must retire at the age of 65, and a female must retire at 60. Thirty years later (1987), the retirement ages for males and females were equalized, but female employees may nonetheless retire at the age of 60. In addition, members of specific groups, such as university professors, judges, Rabbis, and Kadis retire at the age of 70. The diversity of retirement ages reflect the notion that growing old is a process combining biological, psychological, and social factors (Aring, 1972). It is therefore defined by gender and occupation rather than by chronological age.

It is noteworthy that the Knesset enacted the first law relating explicitly to senior citizens in the form of "licensing and supervision of the institutions for the elderly" only in 1965. Until then, these institutions were in a terrible state, with no supervision or minimal standards.

The "National Health Law" enacted in 1995 makes no reference to elders or to their special needs. By contrast, it does recognize the special needs of the young, as it deals with artificial insemination, childcare, etc. This disregard for special health needs of elders derives, according to Whille (1974), from the notion that senior citizens are a burden to society and from the realization that they lack political power to ensure their rights. Of late, there seem to be some positive developments in that two laws, the "Long-term Care Insurance Law" of 1986 and the "Veteran Citizen Law" of 1989 (Ben-Zvi, 1989, 1994), demonstrate a preference for community care for the aged over institutionalization.

The Older Criminal

As shown previously, the age range that constitutes "old age" is flexible under Israeli law, since "old age" is not defined solely by chronological age. However, among criminals, a convict older than 40 is nicknamed "mandatory" (an old man), implying that his or her criminal career began during the British mandate before 1948.

Criminal behavior in old age may be a continuation of a criminal career from an earlier age, adjusted to the physical and mental conditions of older age (Amir, 1988; Walk, Rustinn, & Scott, 1963). Alternatively, criminal behavior might be brought about by boredom and the urge to be active (Sordu & Fishman, 1981).

The criminal justice system and the criminal code neither give special regard to older criminals nor give differential consideration to the various types of old age criminality. In both, the only differentiation by age is between juveniles (under 18 years of age) and adults.

In 1996, more than 10% of the Jewish population in Israel was over the age of 65. Out of a total population of 4,301,800 Jews, 6.57% were in the age group 65–74, and 4.51% were over 74 years old (Central Statistic Agency, 1997). However, in 1998, only 1.2% of criminal offenders were over age 65 (see Table 14.1).

The most typical offense committed by offenders over 65 is bodily assault. As can be seen from Table 14.1, the incidence of this offense increases from only 21.4% in the age group 19 to 29 to almost half (45.6%) in the age group 66 to 99. By contrast, property offenses decrease from 24.4% among young adults (19 to 29 years old) to

TABLE 14.1   Percentage of Offenses by Age Group for 1998

| Offense category | Age | | | | | | | |
	Under 18	19–29	30–39	40–49	50–59	60–65	66–99	Total N
Security	0.4	0.6	0.5	0.5	0.6	0.3	0.5	306
Public order	14.7	21.5	23.4	26.7	27.4	26.1	25.6	13,292
Against life	0.4	0.4	0.4	0.3	0.5	0.7	0.5	227
Bodily assault	14.98	21.4	31.4	34.6	36.9	40.4	45.6	16,057
Sex offenses	2.7	1.5	2.0	2.2	2.9	4.8	6.7	1,242
Morals	17.9	23.8	14.7	9.0	4.7	2.1	1.9	9,362
Property	46.6	24.4	20.9	18.8	17.9	17.3	13.2	14,070
Fraud	1.3	3.9	4.0	4.7	4.8	3.6	2.8	2,249
Economic	0.0	0.0	0.1	0.1	0.3	0.2	0.4	51
Administrative	0.6	2.0	2.2	2.6	3.4	3.8	1.9	1,257
Licensing	0.4	0.2	0.2	0.3	0.3	0.4	0.5	150
Other	0.1	0.2	0.1	0.2	0.2	0.2	0.3	96
Total (%)	100	100	100	100	100	100	100	
N	6,287	19,722	16,046	10,720	3,838	1,012	735	58,360
Total (%)	10.7	33.7	27.4	18.3	6.5	1.7	1.2	100%

Source: Israeli police.

13.2% among elders (66 to 99 years old). The high incidence of bodily assault committed by elders may be explained by the high rate of involvement in car accidents (Barak, Perry, & Elizur, 1995; Ron & Barak, 1997). In Israel, charges for causing injuries by car are laid in terms of "causing bodily assault" or "offenses against life" (in cases of death).

The second most typical elder offense, undermining public order, accounts for 25.6% of all elder offenses. This offense is not particularly characteristic of elders, however, in that it is almost equally distributed among the other age groups.

It is noteworthy that, although older people in Israel are commonly stereotyped as sex offenders or "dirty old men," older sex offenders are a minority among sex offenders in general. However, the incidence of sex offenses among all offenses committed by the older age group is comparatively high. Sex offenses represent 6.7% of all offenses in the age group of 66 to 99 and 4.8% of offenses in the age group 60 to 65. In contrast, in the younger age categories, sex offenses constitute only about 2% of all offenses.

These findings are somewhat different from those presented by Sordu and Fishman in a 1981 study of 260 male and female elder criminals. This study found that the main offenses committed by older persons are bodily harm (25%), property offenses (16.2%), willful damage to property (1.5%), and acts undermining public order (1.5%). No fiscal offenses and sexual offenses were reported.

It is noteworthy that in these studies the rate of drug-related offenses among older offenders is negligible in comparison with the high rate (around 40%) of this type of offense in the younger population (Barak et al., 1995).

The underrepresentation of elders in the criminal population as a whole is well known. Keller and Vedder (1965) attribute this decrease to retirement from criminal activity due to loss of physical and mental abilities, extra caution when committing crimes, or a tendency to avoid exposure to danger. Another feasible explanation is that the police tend to be lenient towards older criminals.

However, this tendency notwithstanding, a large number of older people in Israel commit crimes for the first time in their life. Sordu and Fishman (1981) found in their sample of older offenders that as many as 53.7% had no prior conviction and that their first offense was committed at the age of 55 and above. The crimes are mostly economic (primarily fraud). A high percentage (17.8%) committed sexually related, nonviolent offenses against minors, and 10.7% were guilty of violent crimes (Barak et al., 1995).

Focusing on first time offenders within the older population, Barak et al. (1995) noted a marked increase in traffic offenses (25%), as compared with those committed by young offenders (10%). These traffic offenses involved hit-and-run accidents and accidents that resulted in severe injuries or death. Similar findings had been reported in a study on traffic accidents in 1991 and 1992 (Ron & Barak, 1997), namely that drivers between the ages 64 and 73 have 7 times more accidents than their proportion in the general population. The severity of these accidents is greater than the severity of those involving young people, and most of these accidents result in severe bodily injury.

In sum, older criminals constitute a small minority of the criminal population. Contrary to existing prejudices, their involvement in sexual crimes is relatively low. Although the incidence of sexual abuse is high among those elders who have begun their criminal career at old age, sex offenses are not typical of older offenders, as they are more likely to be involved in property crimes and bodily assaults resulting from driving accidents. Therefore, the characterization of elder offenders as "dirty old men" is unjustified.

Older Offenders and the Israeli Justice System

There is a dispute in the literature concerning the treatment of older defendants by the justice system. Some argue that the justice system is not generally lenient towards older criminals (Bergman & Amir, 1979; Levi, 1969), whereas others believe that the attitude of the system toward elder offenders is relatively more forgiving (Keller & Vedder, 1968; Moberg, 1953). The attitude of the Israeli justice system may be demonstrated by police decisions not to press charges, requests for psychiatric evaluation of older offenders, and sentencing trends.

In Israel, the main legal justifications to close a file without pressing charges are lack of public interest or criminal responsibility and mental illness. Another category, "closed—no conviction," is usually used in order not to tarnish one's future with a criminal record. More than half of all juvenile cases are closed for this reason, in contrast with less than 1% of elder cases.

In the Israeli justice system, a request for a psychiatric evaluation is usually based on the judge's impression or on the defense's demand. However, in a recent study, Barak, Perry, and Elizur (1995) found that while most elder criminals in their sample suffered from various psychiatric disturbances, only a few were referred for evaluation. Furthermore, in a study of 57 older defendants, Heinik, Kimhi, and Hes (1994) found that only 12% of the study participants had no psychiatric diagnosis. When evaluated before the trial, most of them would have been found incompetent.

As for discretion in sentencing, earlier studies (Amir & Bergman, 1973; Sordu & Fishman, 1981) revealed that 7.5% to 8% of older criminals convicted for the first time were sentenced to prison, while only 6.6% of the comparable general criminal population (including the elders) was sentenced to prison (Criminal Statistics, 1984). No older convict was sentenced to probation. As probation has proven to be very effective for this age group, the decision not to invest in probation and rehabilitation of older offenders seem unjustified (Oberleder, 1966). This decision might reflect ageism and disregard for the elders' needs. For those in power, old age is a stage in life they have not experienced yet, and they might not realize the special needs associated with this age. They also may be more concerned with rehabilitating future generations, viewing elders as people who have already exhausted their social potential.

In conclusion, from the available data on the Israeli criminal justice system, it seems that neither the police nor the courts are especially lenient in dealing with elder offenders. Furthermore, there seems to be unwillingness to invest social resources in older criminals. As a result, it appears that they are rarely referred to psychiatric evaluation or probation.

Special legal provisions are needed for sentencing aged criminals that would require a comprehensive evaluation of the offenders' physical and mental conditions prior to the court's decision. This evaluation should contain a recommendation for proper medical care, and in cases of imprisonment, also periodic follow-ups.

The Older Person As Prisoner

Similar to the police and the court, the Israel Prison Authority does not provide preferential treatment for aged prisoners. Only those incapable of performing their prison duties are transferred to a special ward. Those who are totally disabled are either released (by a special committee headed by a judge) or are hospitalized in a prison hospital or a special care unit (Orit Messer-Harel, personal communication, November 7, 1998).

Prison authorities do not have any official definition for old age. Table 14.2 shows the length of prison terms being served by prisoners in different age categories as reported by the Israeli prison service in 1998. From this Table, it is apparent that prison authorities regard prisoners of over 50 years as old. Currently, there are 241 prisoners in this age group, who comprise 4.2% of the entire prison population.

As Table 14.2 further shows, there is no significant difference between the incidence of prisoners serving shorter and longer terms for this age group. Life sentences are no different; 11.2% of older prisoners are currently serving life sentences and similar percentages are serving shorter terms. Younger prisoners show a wider distribution. For example, between the ages 18 and 21, about one-third (34.4%) of the population are currently serving a sentence of less than one year, as compared with 0.6% who are currently imprisoned for life. These findings are explained by two concurrent facts. First, a life sentence in Israel is usually served for about 18 years (following a presidential definition of the upper limit of the prison term, and a reduction of a third of the remaining period for good behavior in prison). Thus, older prisoners may have been 20 years younger when sentenced for life. Second, the severity of elders' sentences might also account for the data. Analysis of the length of sentences by age at the time of sentencing between 1987 and 1988 revealed that 1,122 (3.6%) criminals sentenced to prison were over 50 years of age. Among them, 1.3% were sentenced for life as compared with a rate of 0.4% for the entire population, and 0.3% for the younger age group of 18 to 21 years. These two factors might explain the high incidence of prisoners over 50 years of age who are imprisoned

TABLE 14.2 Distribution of Prisoners by Age and Length
of Sentence (May 1998)

	Age								
Prison sentence	50+	46–50	41–45	36–40	31–35	26–30	22–25	18–21	Total
Total N	241	273	531	915	1130	1100	855	616	5661
Percentage	4.26	4.82	9.38	16.16	19.96	19.43	15.11	10.88	100
Up to one year	12.45	9.52	7.91	8.32	11.15	14.73	17.90	34.42	827
									14.6
1–2 years	11.20	19.05	15.82	19.23	18.14	17.18	23.27	22.72	1072
									18.9
2–3 years	13.28	13.19	17.89	18.69	18.41	16.18	18.71	17.04	985
									17.6
3–5 years	12.45	20.15	22.03	24.37	23.36	24.10	22.34	14.62	1235
									21.8
5–7 years	8.71	8.79	10.92	10.60	9.92	12.00	8.54	5.03	548
									9.7
7–10 years	9.96	7.69	8.85	6.01	7.17	6.36	4.56	2.27	351
									6.2
10–15 years	9.96	9.16	6.03	4.59	4.78	3.91	1.64	1.63	244
									4.3
15–20 years	3.32	2.20	2.64	1.64	1.50	.54	1.17	1.46	85
									1.5
20 years and more	7.47	4.76	2.64	2.18	1.68	.82	.12	.16	95
									1.6
Life sentence	11.20	5.49	5.27	4.37	3.89	4.18	1.75	.65	219
									3.8
Total %	100	100	100	100	100	100	100	100	100

Source: Israeli prison service.

for life, while sustaining the notion that the Israeli justice system treats older offenders sternly.

One may wonder how older prisoners adjust to prison life. Imprisonment is a critical experience that causes changes in one's lifestyle. It means a break with normal everyday surroundings and a need to function in a new social environment. Is the adjustment of older prisoners to prison life different from that of younger prisoners?

Research in this field has yielded contradictory results. Bergman and Amir (1979) found that the physical and mental conditions of older prisoners deteriorate rapidly in prison. They described the aging prisoners as being at the mercy of younger, more aggressive prisoners who tend to frighten, ridicule, or even harm them. The aged prisoners become depressed and anxious, and consequently dependent on wardens and prison staff for protection. They are deprived of friends, employment, and decent accommodation. This view was supported by Samir, Raiya-leena, and Eyad (1997), who found that old, but not young, Palestinian prisoners perceive imprisonment as suffering and disillusionment.

By contrast, Silfen and Ben-David (1977) found that most older prisoners were well adjusted to prison life. In fact, older prisoners looked healthier and younger than they really were. Amir and Bergman's (1979) findings notwithstanding, these prisoners were not humiliated or intimidated by younger prisoners. On the contrary, the latter respected and helped the aged prisoners with their daily routine. Moreover, when an older prisoner had difficulties in performance, efforts were made by the prison staff to meet him halfway. This was not a product of any policy, but rather part of the dynamics of prison life.

These contradictory findings are probably the result of differences in research tools and subject selection. On the other hand, the differences in the adjustment of older prisoners to prison life might be due to changes in the prison in terms of its population, environment, or regulations.

Older Persons As Crime Victims

Victimization of elders is by itself a demonstration of society's attitude towards older people. The general belief is that the physical and mental weaknesses of older people, along with their deterioration in social status, make them an easy crime target (King, 1995).

Contrary to general belief, the findings of the Israeli 1988 survey show a progressive decline in victimization of elders with the advancement of age. As Shapira (1989) points out, these findings are similar to those obtained in the United States. The findings of the Israeli

1988 survey regarding household victimization are presented in Table 14.3. They show that there is almost equal distribution of victimization (an average of 22%) among households categorized by the age of the household's head. There is one exception, namely, a significant decrease in victimization to 8.2% when the head of the family is over 65.

Thus, the findings in Israel do not support the notion that older people are victimized more often than younger ones. However, one should bear in mind that the impact of victimization is not in the number of cases, but rather in its effect on the victim. Crime severely affects the older victim's health and lifestyle, particularly because older victims are likely to develop severe fear of further victimization (Geva, 1992; Milchinson, 1984).

The relationship between fear of crime among elders and their physical and social environments was studied by Shalhoub-Kevorkion (1987) in the Armenian quarter of the Old City of Jerusalem. She compared Armenians who live within the walls of the patriarchal compound with those who live outside of these walls. The findings showed that both fear of crime and the rate of crime were considerably lower in the protected compound than in the open area. Thus the level of fear of crime was correlated with the actual crime rate. Another factor contributing to the lower level of fear of crime inside the walled quarter was the intensive community activities and social support, that were more available within than outside the walls.

TABLE 14.3   Victimization by Major Types of Offenses According to Age
of Household Head (in Percentage)[1]

| Type of offense | Age of household head | | | | | |
	65+	55–64	45–54	35–44	25–34	18–24
Any offense	8.2	22.5	23.3	20.7	23.8	18.5
Offenses against vehicles	9.6	18.6	22.1	17.0	21.4	27.1
Offenses against apartment	4.5	7.8	7.0	5.5	6.7	6.9
Offenses against individuals	1.7	5.6	4.4	4.8	4.8	4.4

[1]Percentage does not sum up to 100% as some households suffered multiple victimization.

Source: 1988 Survey by Ministry of Police and Israeli Institute for Applied Social Research.

A more comprehensive study on elder's fear of crime in Israel (Milchinson & Rahav, as cited in Shapira, 1989) involved two groups of elders: younger (between 60 and 69 years of age) and older (above the age of 70). Surprisingly, the older group showed a lower level of fear of crime than the younger. In addition, the findings suggest that fear of crime decreases inversely with the level of education and that it is more intensive among Afro-Asian immigrants than among immigrants from Europe.

Katz-Shiban (1989) found in a sample of 200 older victims that only about one-third of the cases were reported to the police. Amir (1988) conducted another study on a sample of 622 aged crime victims from the three largest cities in Israel: Jerusalem, Tel Aviv, and Haifa. He concluded that fear of crime and the nonreporting of crimes to the police are the result of poor communication between the police and elders. However, Shapira (1989) suggests that when the policemen on the scene attend to the older victim's security needs (helping choose locks, bolts, window iron bars, etc.), there is a significant decrease in the level of fear of crime.

Katz-Shiban (1989) further suggests a distinction between three types of older victims in terms of level of acceptance of the victim's role (Ben-David, 1986, 1989):

1. Those who fully accept the role of victims. They develop dependency on social agencies and strengthen the negative labeling of victim by using avoidance behavior. This negative self-labeling is harmful to the well-being of older victims.

2. Those who accept the role of victims only partially or temporarily. While they are legally considered victims, they make no change in their social interactions. By doing nothing other than reporting the crime to the police, they are neutralizing the negative labeling.

3. Those who do not accept role of victims at all. After assessing their loss (injury, property, money, or most often, a car), they continue their usual routine without any significant changes. Usually they report the crime to the police only in order to file an insurance claim.

This typology may contribute to research on crime victims and can be used for crime impact assessment. However, crime victim impact assessment is quite new in Israel (1995) and is currently valid for sexual victimization only.

As mentioned above, in Israel there are few laws that address the status of elders, and none whatsoever relating specifically to older victims. Therefore, it is important to mention the principle set forth by the Chief Justice of the Supreme Court, Meir Shamgar, according to which judges should be stricter in sentencing armed robbery and forceful break-ins where the victims are elders (Avi-Guy, 1983).

As Shapira (1989) showed, victimized elders are often unaware of the assistance and treatment provided by official and voluntary agencies, and once they are victimized, they do not apply for, and, therefore, do not receive, adequate help. Facing this situation, Na'a-mat's (working women organization) 27th convention (1982) adopted a resolution demanding the enactment of a law that would require the municipal authorities to advise older victims of their rights and ensure that they receive adequate assistance and protection.

Elder Abuse

Elder abuse is another type of victimization and a rather cruel one, since the abusers are usually family members and/or caregivers. Elder abuse exposes degrading and humiliating attitudes towards helpless elders. Public responsibility for preventing elder abuse has been recognized only in the last 20 years. This recognition is a result of growing social awareness of victimization in general, and of elder victimization, in particular.

There are several kinds of abuse: physical, psychological, medical, social, and financial (King, 1995). It is difficult to appraise the relative prevalence of the various kinds of abuse, since most of the pertinent information comes from the health institutions, that are concerned mainly with physical abuse. Psychological abuse is treated mostly by social agencies. However, because the abusers in these cases are usually family members, social workers are reluctant to report them; they feel that nothing can be done (King, 1995).

Deception of elders by family members or caregivers has recently received wide publicity. Erelharz (in Shapira, 1989) links this deception to elders' dependency on social agencies and to the difficulties they encounter in securing necessary information. As a result, they are prone to be deceived regarding medical care, insurance, law, investment, and the like.

Frequently, caregivers or even family members exploit inheritance rights, life savings, etc. Elders even fall victim to institutions and organizations such as banks, senior residence centers, health providers, and stores.

The need for personal attention compels some childless, aged persons to bequeath their caregivers excessive rights or gifts. Unfortunately, however, often, after receiving the bequest, the caregivers discontinue their service, thus leaving elders without resources and with no one to tend to their needs. If the case is brought to court, the recipient may be ordered to provide care services, but once the gift has been given, it is impossible to recover. Today it is possible to cancel such agreements on the basis of the General Contracts Law, which states that for the contract to be valid, it is necessary for both sides to fulfill their mutual contractual responsibilities (i.e., the bequest by the elder and the care by the caregiver). Unfortunately, this is only a partial solution, applicable only to some cases; it does not prevent elder abuse from taking place. There is still a need for a more efficient social measure that will prevent such abuse.

Discussion

Although elders do not constitute a homogeneous group (many of them are still productive, while others are dependent on social services), there are a great many myths and stereotypes that relate to them as a group (Hobbman, 1993). Many of these myths and stereotypes convey confusion, misunderstanding, and lack of knowledge about old age. For example, older people are often perceived as helpless victims, even though statistics show a progressive decline in victimization of elders with the advancement of age.

The concept of chronological aging is in itself a manifestation of stereotypical thinking, as physiological and personality indicators have a wider range in old age than in any other age (Butler, 1996). This heterogeneity might be the source of difficulties in the definition of old age. It is also possible that the lack of special consideration for elders in the justice system and in the law is related to the fact that, due to their heterogeneity, elders have disparate needs. It seems that the Israeli social and justice systems tend to judge and treat each person in accordance with his or her personal characteristics, needs, or deeds, rather than according to age.

Despite the heterogeneity of the elder population, however, relative to younger people, elders do have certain unique problems and needs. For example, elders may be more prone than younger people to certain types of victimization, including fraud or deception. Also, once victimized, elders may be more likely to develop severe fear of crime and further victimization than young people.

As a result, official government agencies, including police departments, should develop special procedures for protecting and assisting older people. For example, older people living alone should be connected by distress devices to a social service agency. Upon receiving an alert call, the agency should offer immediate assistance. Police should be trained to assist elders, be aware of elders in their district, and be informed in cases of illness or any other emergency that might endanger the aged person.

Furthermore, various social agencies and community organizations should undertake joint efforts aimed at enabling people to get older safely and with dignity. "Social Watch Groups" should be established with the participation of all existing voluntary agencies, such as neighborhood community centers, youth groups, Civil Guard, and other community-oriented agencies. Such groups should activate elders as self-help groups. Community involvement and close neighborhood relations also should be encouraged for reducing crime and fear of crime.

Finally, special programs for elders must be implemented cautiously in order to avoid stigmatization, envy, and antagonism. They also should be accompanied by further efforts to learn about the aging sector in our society in general and its interactions with the criminal justice system, in particular.

Acknowledgment

The authors thank Israel Nachson for his help in the preparation of the manuscript. Supported by the Schnitzer Foundation for Research on the Israeli Economy and Society.

References

Aiken, I. (1978). *Later life*. Philadelphia: Saunders.

Amir, M., & Bergman, S. H. (1973). Crime and delinquency among aged in Israel. *Israel Annals of Psychiatry and Related Disciplines, 11*, 33–44.

Amir, M. (1988). Police and the Aged Crime Victims. Levin, B. and

Aring, C. D. (1972). On aging senescence and senility. *Annals of International Medicine, 77*, 25–30.

Avi-Guy, Ch. (1983). Don't abuse us at old age. *Naamat, 41*, 14–16 (in Hebrew).

Barak, Y., Perry, T., & Elizur, A. (1995). Elderly criminals: A study of the first criminal offence in old age. *International Journal of Geriatric Psychiatry, 10*, 511–516.

Ben-David, S. (1986). *The social function of the "career victim."* In K. Miyazawa & M. Ohya (Eds.), *Victimology in comparative perspective* (pp. 33–43). Tokyo: Seibundo Publishing Co.

Ben-David, S. (1989). The career victim. *Crime and Social Deviance, 17*, 5–16 (Hebrew).

Ben-Zvi, B. (1989). The contribution of the national security law and long term care insurance law on the well-being of old institutionalized people. *Biteon Sozialy, 34*, 49–60 (in Hebrew).

Ben-Zvi, B. (1994). The long term care insurance law: Achievements and unforeseen implications of its implementation. *Social Security, 3*, 84–100.

Bensinger, G. (1997). Crime and criminal justice. In R. Friedman (Ed.), *Crime and justice in Israel*. Albany, NY: SUNY Press.

Bergman, S. H. (Ed.). *Law and the aging* (pp. 133–141). Jerusalem, Brookdale.

Bergman, S. H., & Amir, M. (1979). Crime and delinquency in Israel. *Israel Annals of Psychiatry and Related Disciplines, 10*, 33–48.

Butler, R. N. (1996). Global ageing: Challenges and opportunities of the next century. *Ageing International, 23*(1), 12–32.

Central statistic agency. (1984). *Criminal Statistics, Pyrsumin Meuchadim, 804,* 28–29 (in Hebrew).

Central statistic agency. (1989). Survey of over 60 year of age head of households. *Pyrsumim meuchdim, 840,* 15 (in Hebrew).

Geva, R. (1992). Feelings of insecurity and fear and cooperation with police: Israeli experience. In S. Ben-David & G. F. Kirchhoff (Eds.), *International faces of victimology* (pp. 281–291). Munchengaldbach: World Society of Victimology.

Heinik, I., Kimhi, R., & Hes, P. J. (1994). Dementia and crime: A forensic psychiatry unit study in Israel. *International Journal of Geriatric Psychiatry, 9,* 491–494.

Hobbman, D. (1993). *Uniting generations: Studies in conflict and co-operation.* London: Ace.

Katz-Shiban, B. (1989). *Effects of victimization experiences in elderly people.* Master's thesis, Hebrew University, Jerusalem.

Keller, C. Y., & Vedder, L. (1968). The crimes that old persons commit. *Gerontologist, 8,* 43–45.

Keller, C. Y., & Vedder, L. (1965). *The elderly offender and theories of crime causation.* Chicago: University of Chicago Press.

King, I. (1995). Violence against the elderly begins at home. *Hagal Hachadash, 60,* 1–3 (in Hebrew).

Kremnitzer, M. (1997). Law and law enforcement. In R. Friedman (Ed.), *Crime and justice in Israel.* Albany, NY: SUNY Press.

Levi, U. (1969). Old age: Legal and criminological issues. *Hapraklit, 25,* 349–364 (in Hebrew).

Milchinson, C. (1984). Fear of crime and behavioral changes among elderly who were victims of criminal offenses. Master's thesis, Tel Aviv University, Tel-Aviv (in Hebrew).

Moberg, C. D. (1953). Old age crime. *Journal of Criminal Law, Criminology and Police Science, 43,* 764–776.

Oberleder, M. (1966). Psychotherapy with the aging or art of the possible? *Psychotherapy Theory Research and Practice, 3,* 139–142.

Ron, H., & Barak, I. (1997). Involvement of old drivers in traffic accidents in Israel. *Refua Mishpatit, 17,* 47–51 (in Hebrew).

Samir, Q., Raiya-leena, P., & Eyad, E. S. (1977). Prison experience and coping styles among Palestinian men. *Journal of Peace Psychology, 3,* 19–36.

Shalhoub-Kevorkian, N. (1987). The effects of the physical and social environment on the fear of crime. Master's thesis. Hebrew University, Jerusalem.

Shapira, N. (1989). *Recommendation for action to reduce the victimization of elders.* Tel-Aviv: Mezila.

Silfen, P., & Ben-David, S. (1977). The adaptation of the older prisoner in Israel. *International Journal of Offender Therapy and Comparative Criminology, 21,* 57–66.
Sordu, I., & Fishman, G. (1981). The elderly criminal in the justice system. *Hevra V'Revaha, 4,* 401–407 (in Hebrew).
State of Israel. (1984). *Criminal statistics, 1981.* Jerusalem.
Walk, R. L., Rustinn, S. L., & Scott, I. (1963). The geriatric delinquent. *Journal of the American Geriatric Society, 11,* 653–659.
Whille, S. (1974). Population of old age in private institutions in Israel. *Bytahon* (in Hebrew).

Suggested Readings

Barrett, H. Y. (Ed.). (1972). *Gerontological psychology.* Springfield, IL: Charles C Thomas.
Lewis, J., with Bernstock, P., Bovell, V., & Wookey, F. (1996). The purchaser/provider split in social care: Is it working? *Social Policy and Administration, 30,* 1–19.
Pinker, R. (1971). *Social theory and social policy.* London: Heinemann.
Pithers, W. D. (1997). Maintaining treatment integrity with sexual abusers. *Criminal Justice and Behavior, 24, 1,* 43–51.

Chapter 15

Elders and Japanese Corrections

Elmer H. Johnson

"Japanese literary expression has long vacillated," Skord (1989, p. 132) deduces, "between attributing to the elderly the vitality of the plum or the frailty of the cherry blossom past its prime." As the first flower of the new year, the blossom sprouting from the gnarled limbs of the plum tree symbolizes renewed vitality where the short-lived cherry blossom, scattered by spring winds, signifies decay and dereliction. The ambivalence of Japanese attitudes about elders has been heightened by the issues associated with the demography of aging.

The combination of lowered birth and death rates has raised the proportion of persons 65 years and older in the total Japanese population. The trend has come later to Japan than other economically developed societies, but the pace has become especially rapid. Ogawa (1989) documents the rapid pace according to the number of years required to move the percentage share from 10% to 20%. Japan will need only 24 years. Among seven European societies, in contrast, Finland will require the shortest time (48 years) and Sweden the most (85 years).

The social and economic impact of this trend on Japanese society will be particularly intensive and extensive because of the contrast between high regard for the elders accorded by traditions inherited from the past and the realities of care for the frail elderly under contemporary circumstances. The confrontation of the past and present will be outlined as background for the central purpose of this chapter: the implications of this demographic crisis for the prisons and community-oriented corrections of Japan.

Japan imprisons remarkably few of its convicted offenders. At the end of 1992, Japanese prisons held only 38.2 prisoners per 100,000 Japanese adults. American prisons confined 332 inmates per 100,000 American adults. The relative position of these two prison systems was reversed for older inmates: 12.7% of Japanese prisoners, but only 2.7% of prisoners in the United States (Maguire & Pastore, 1997; Research and Statistics, 1993). Japan's reluctant use of imprisonment will be explained because, first, this policy affects the qualities of those convicted offenders who do enter prison, and, second, the upsurge in the number of older prisoners is a major exception to the general decline in the imprisonment rate.

This chapter is derived basically from the annual statistics published by the Japanese Ministry of Justice. The age-specific rates of prison admissions, 1970–1995, will document the contrast between the increased imprisonment of older persons and the decline of the admissions of prisoners less than 50 years of age. (This paper limits the study to the population aged 20 years or more because very few admitted prisoners are less than 20 years old.) Older inmates will be compared with younger prisoners in terms of previous exposure to imprisonment, the crimes that brought them to prison, their previous contacts with the criminal justice system, their hospitalization while imprisoned, their involvement with probation and parole, and their heavy representation in halfway houses.

The Traditions: Age-Grading and Familism

"The whole of Japan was torn by factions and plagued by incessant civil war until late in the sixteenth century," Sansom (1963a, p. v) summarizes, "when the process of national unification by forces of arms was begun." The Tokugawa feudal empire (1603–1867) emerged with the Confucian philosophy as its ethical foundation.

"It was the ruler's duty to reward or discipline with the attitude of a father watching over his children," Scalapino (1953, pp. 6–7) comments. "The individual . . . was important only as he completed the unity of his society." A rigid class hierarchy placed the *samurai*, as warriors and administrators, at the peak of the social pyramid, and their obligation was to teach the others higher morality and selflessness. The farmers came in a poor second, but, as producers of rice, they had a crucial role in the economy. Hierarchical control dominated all phases of life: occupation, behavior, and the possession of weapons.

Traditions also identified seniority with authority. The ethics of feudal Japan rested morally on the duty of the son as the head of his family. The theme, Sansom (1963b, p. 88) says, "was carried to extremes by treating filial gratitude not as a natural feeling but as a rule of conduct imposed from outside, thus obligating the child to submit blindly to the parent." The holiday, "Respect for the Elders Day," exists today and has for at least 300 years. Honoring aged persons is in keeping with the Confucian ethic that called for filial piety—children having reverence for their parents (Lock, 1984). The elders were believed to give life and sustenance to the younger persons and, thereby, to merit the deep respect of the younger. Confucian teachings focused on morals within a family system, Sansom (1963b, p. 88) notes, rather than public matters, but the Tokugawa rigid hierarchy of classes "fitted well into a Confucian pattern." Filial piety was extended through a feudal ethic to refer to the submission and obedience of a vassal to his lord.

The *ie* household represented familism as a social pattern giving priority to the interests of the family over those of its members. The *ie* was an agricultural or small-business enterprise—a "corporate residential group" that possessed the property and was controlled by the "family" head in the paternalistic mode. Members, Fukutake (1981, p. 34) declares, "were trained to suppress individual desires and make the goal of their lives the maintenance of the *ie* and enhancement of its name."

"Under the Meiji Civil Code an individual's life was totally ruled and regulated by the family system," Yoshizumi (1995, pp. 187–188) says. Parental permission to marry was necessary until age 25 for women and 30 years for men. Marriage was regarded as a means of perpetuating the family line, and most were arranged to serve the interests of the family, not the will of the couple. Men had priority over women in all areas. Wives entered the husband's family and were expected to serve parents-in-law and give birth to a male successor.

On January 3, 1868, a group of feudal lords took control of the Imperial Court in Kyoto, terminated the Tokugawa Shogunate, and proclaimed the Emperor's direct responsibility for government (Beasley, 1972, pp. 1–2). Aware of the subjugation of the Chinese by foreign powers, the new elite (the Meiji regime) initiated modernization of social, economic, and political institutions with the initial purpose of forestalling Western imperialism.

The Meiji reformers switched the political emphasis gradually from the feudal lord and fief as the focus of loyalties to the nation as a whole. "Since they believed a stable family meant a stable society," Smith (1983, pp. 17, 31) comments, "the oligarchs took a bold step and, as if by a slight of hand, converted filial piety from a private duty into a civil virtue." The Meiji Civil Code made the *ie* the basic unit of Japanese society until 1947, when this aspect of the legal system was abolished (Iwao, 1993). The emperor was portrayed as the patriarch of the common main family, Ishida (1983) explains, and the tradition of ancestor worship and the subordination of branch families to the main family were enrolled in the development of the spirit of nationalism. The *ie* imagery lingers in the conception of the employer as the head of the company existing as a pseudo-family. Nakane (1984, p. 8) explains: "The employer readily takes responsibility for his employee's family for which, in turn, the primary concern is the company rather than relatives who reside elsewhere."

Graying of Japan: An Impending Crisis

"The greatly extended lifespan and the near-zero increase of the birthrate," Iwao (1993, p. 26) asserts, "have greatly accelerated Japan's transformation into an aging society." The number of births per Japanese dropped to 1.53 in 1991, less than the rate for reproduction of the parents. "Japanese in their prime today," she predicts, "cannot expect to be taken care of by their own children." Reduced birth rates ultimately deliver fewer adults to the labor force in the future than birth rates of earlier decades. Because of improved medical care and health, yesteryear's babies are surviving to become today's elders.

Table 15.1 traces the age distribution of Japanese, aged 20 to 25 years. The combination of decreasing birth rates and improved health care has produced contrasting trends for the four age groups. The youngest adults continue to be most numerous in absolute terms, but have lost share, while the oldest ages have scored the greatest percentage gain. The percentage share of young adults (20 to 40 years) declined from 52% in 1970 to 33.5% in 1995—or a

TABLE 15.1 **Comparing Age Groups of Adults in Japan with Prison Admission and Imprisonment Rates, 1970–1995**

Age groups	1970	1975	1980	1985	1990	1995
Percentage distributions of Japanese aged 20 years and more						
20–39	52.02	48.92	45.38	41.65	37.08	33.51
40–49	18.93	20.31	20.23	20.2	21.67	22.13
50–59	13.22	13.63	15.78	17.36	17.42	17.51
60–over	15.83	17.14	18.61	20.79	23.83	26.85
Total percentage	100	100	100	100	100	100
Number[a]	69,833	76,724	81,210	85,994	90,791	95,571
Percentage distribution of adults, aged 20 and more, admitted to prison						
20–39	82.18	75.2	68.06	60.25	52.22	50.56
40–49	12.84	18.18	23.48	26.63	29.56	26.75
50–59	3.81	5.2	6.7	10.86	14.27	16.78
60–over	1.17	1.42	1.76	2.26	3.95	5.91
Total percent	100	100	100	100	100	100
Number	25,553	26,041	28,258	31,550	22,689	21,794
Mean age	32.23	34.5	36.61	38.23	39.44	40.35
Age-specific imprisonment rates per 100,000 Japanese						
20–39	57.8	52.22	52.18	53.07	35.2	34.41
40–49	24.82	30.37	40.39	48.36	34.09	27.56
50–59	10.55	12.94	14.78	22.95	20.48	21.86
60–over	2.71	2.82	3.29	3.99	4.14	5.01
Total rates	36.59	33.94	34.8	36.69	24.99	22.8

[a]Absolute number (in thousands) of Japanese aged 20 years and over.

Source: Research and Statistics Section (1971, 1976, 1981, 1986, 1991, 1996).

decrease rate of 11.8% in absolute numbers. The 40 to 49 year group rose at a rate of 60% and the 50 to 59 year group, at a rate of 81.3%. Those 60 and over gained share at a rate of 132%.

Atoh (1994) identifies two major elements of Japanese population dynamics. First, life expectancy in Japan has increased continuously to become the highest in the world. The world's lowest infant mortality rate as well as a rapid decline in deaths of the middle-aged and older people, mainly due to reduction of cerebrovascular diseases, have been major contributing factors. The Japanese diet emphasizes low-cholesterol meat. Second, the birth rate has dropped precipitously since 1970. Atoh (1994) notes the importance of women in their twenties remaining single. This factor, he explains, is particularly important because few young Japanese cohabit with the opposite sex without marriage or have births outside of wedlock.

The decline of the birth rate is associated with massive changes in Japanese society that also have reduced the capacity (or willingness) of families to be the primary caretakers for elders. Components of the change include: the greater popularity of the nuclear over the extended family; the small size of urban apartments, complicating the inclusion of older parents in the residence of their married children; the rising divorce rate, although short of Western tendencies; delay of marriage for sake of the pleasures of being single; and expanded educational opportunities for women. The Eugenic Protection Law (1948) legalized abortion, Hodge and Ogawa (1991) recall, and the use of contraceptive methods became widespread.

When the Meiji reformers initiated the awesome effort to modernize Japan in rapid order, they faced an insufficiency of resources to meet the urgent need in all sectors of the socioeconomic infrastructure. They relied ultimately on the private sector to assume some of the functions usually handled by the government. The approach persists as is illustrated by the passage of the National Personnel Law (1969), which required each ministry to eliminate one of its bureaus and to cut personnel by 5% within 3 years (Pempel, 1982). The policy preference is to turn social security functions over to the family, community, and private enterprise (Watanuki, 1986).

American elders prefer to maintain their own independent households as long as possible, Akiyama (1984) notes; but, because Japanese values do not place as much emphasis on independence, Japanese appear to feel they deserve support of their children. They are rather proud to be with adult children and even to be supported financially and emotionally by them when they retire.

The lives of the older people of Japan have been improved dramatically since the industrialization of their society, Kiefer (1990, pp. 188–191) notes, but elders have lost the "ability to control the circumstances of their own lives." Familism in the Confucian model had given the aged remarkable power and prestige when compared with Western societies. Power implies differential access of men and groups to its elements: public esteem, capacity to influence others through resources and knowledge, and occupancy of positions of authority in community organizations. Although he summarizes evidence that the socioeconomic lot of elders in Japan compares rather well with those in the United States, Kiefer (1990) finds that current realities (summarized below) fall short of the traditional high prestige and power they enjoyed. In relative terms, the difference between expectations and realities is greater for the aged of Japan.

"Japan's social services to alleviate the problems of the elderly," Asano and Saito (1988, p. 149) report, "are not developed for a number of reasons." Population aging started much later than in the West; the Japanese culture emphasizes family support and care of elders; and the government has emphasized economic growth rather than social services for the aged. The National Health Insurance Scheme provides care for persons over 70 years of age and the bedridden over 65 years, but, Beer (1990, p. 7) reports an out-of-pocket contribution of 30%. Nearly half (48%) of the nursing home residents are bedridden, mostly because of an unusual proportion of stroke victims.

Bedridden elders place particular pressure on the family and the women who continue to be designated as the traditional caretakers. Adult children, by and large, accept the tradition that they should care for their frail parents, but, Freed (1990) discovers, they are experiencing unprecedented ambivalence about accepting this responsibility. The nursing home as an alternative raises special concern among elders because their circumstances in nursing homes are in sharp contrast with the traditions of high regard for elders. "Institutions, by their very nature," Bethel (1992, p. 126) explains, "strip newcomers of their identities, autonomy, social roles, material possessions, and sense of place in a familiar social universe."

Demographic Trend Reaches the Prisons

"From the initial police interrogation to the final judicial hearing on sentence," Haley (1989, p. 495) summarizes, "the criminal justice processing produces a very parsimonious reliance on imprisonment." The vast majority of those accused of criminal offenses confess, display repentance, negotiate for their victims' pardon, and submit to the mercy of the authorities. In return they are treated with extraordinary leniency." (The system of official leniency is explained in greater detail in Johnson, 1996.)

In Japan, public prosecutors are authorized to decide whether or not a suspect should be referred to the courts for formal trial. Article 248, the Code of Criminal Procedure, reads: "If after considering the character, age and situation of the offender, the gravity of the offense, the circumstances under which the offense was committed, and the conditions subsequent to the offense, prosecution is deemed unnecessary, prosecution need not be instituted." In 1995 the public prosecutors disposed of 338,070 general criminal cases: 24.1% went to formal trial, 13.4% went to summary proceedings, 23.3% were not prosecuted, and 39.1% went to family courts (Research and Training Institute, 1996, p. 60).

Article 25, Penal Code, authorizes judges to suspend a sentence to prison under "extenuating circumstances." Of 49,545 adjudications in 1994, 45 were acquittals, 393 were for fines or remission of punishment, 8 for death, 45 for life sentences, and 49,054 usual sentences to prison. Of the 49,054 usual sentences, 29,823 (60.8%) were suspended. Among those whose prison sentences were suspended, 87.6% were released without conditions and 12.4% were placed on probation.

The number of adults, ages 20 years and over, arriving at Japanese prisons totaled 25,553 in 1970 and declined over subsequent years in irregular fashion to reach 21,794 in 1995 (see Table 15.1). A key aspect of the prison admissions has been the consistent rise in average age of newly admitted prisoners, from 32.2 years in 1970 to 40.35 years in 1995. The percentage distribution by age groups shows persons older than 59 years representing just 1.17% of all new inmates in 1970 and gaining percentage share over the years to reach

5.91% in 1995. Meanwhile, the youngest group (20 to 30 years) absorbed the greatest loss of share. Ages 50 to 59 years also recorded a percentage gain throughout those decades. However, our interest will center on the implications of the upsurge in the relative importance of inmates older than 59 years.

Crimes of the Elders and Prison Admissions

Crimes by older persons are increasing, Nakajima (1991) says, probably because they cannot keep up with changes in their environment, worry incessantly about their security, and do not consult other persons about their difficulties. He presents an example and explains that the court imposed a lenient sentence of $4^1/_2$ years because the defendant was older and in an abnormal state of mind. The defendant had worked hard as a laundryman. When retired at age 66, he built a three-story residence. His wife had died when he was 61 years of age; two sons and a daughter were adults and living elsewhere. He occupied the third floor and rented the other floors for income. Soon after retirement, he became acquainted with a 53-year-old divorcee. She pressed him to marry her, but he resisted initially, suspecting that his property, not love, was her target. Although the situation was unprecedented for him, he ultimately agreed. Soon she demanded that the first floor be converted into a bar and the second floor for the bar's hostesses. Believing that she was plotting to obtain a business for herself only, he became determined to protect his own use of the property. He hammered her to death when she was asleep.

The relationships between chronological age and chances for imprisonment are very complicated, but our interest in elder inmates centers on how the increased presence of elders in Japan is related to their level of entry into prison. The increased number of aged Japanese would provide a larger host from which older prisoners could be drawn. However, if one assumes that any criminal tendencies among elders are about the same over the decades and the criteria for decisions remain about the same for public prosecutors and judges, then, the percentage of an age group drawn from the community would remain constant in prison admissions.

The probability of imprisonment pivots on the perceived nature of the given crime. Certain classes of social deviance have been defined as crimes in the Penal Code of Japan because they have been deemed to have serious impact justifying official reactions in defense of the general social order. The reluctant resort to imprisonment mirrors the inclination of Japanese public prosecutors and judges to withhold the sanctions of the criminal law when feasible. The distribution of crimes among offenders admitted to prison reflects some of the reasoning for the decisions that these offenders do not qualify for diversionary policies.

The prison admissions of elders serve as a barometer of the workings of the Japanese criminal justice system when applied to elder offenders. Their inclination to engage in crime is muffled by a decision-making system committed to leniency when feasible. However, that muffling is being reduced, as we shall explain, by the relative greater presence of older persons in certain crimes: homicide among violent crimes, and larceny, fraud, and intrusion among crimes associated with homelessness and poverty.

The Research and Training Institute (1991) investigated the distribution of offenses (1,668) of elders referred to the courts for formal trial in 1990. Of those 1,668 offenses, 52.2% were for larceny, 20.9% for fraud, 4.3% for bodily injury, 3.5% for homicide, 1.8% for bribery, 1.7% for "corruption," and 14% for other offenses.

Admissions of older persons to prisons are portrayed in Table 15.2 in greater detail; but, again, offenses against property continue to be most numerous. Elders held 5.9% share of all prison admissions in 1995. The property offenses of elders represented 10.04% of all property offenses of persons admitted to prison. Larceny was the most common offense of the newly arrived older prisoners, as was true of all inmates. The prominence of larceny is, in part, due to the variety of those offenses: theft from houses, vehicles, shops, and vending machines. Stealing of bicycles and motorbikes also is important.

"Intrusion upon habitation" (Article 130 of the Penal Code) is especially prevalent among the older offenders. The crime is defined as "a person who, without good reason, intrudes upon a human habitation or upon the premises, structure, or vessel guarded by another, or who refuses to leave such a place upon demand." Persons seeking shelter but lacking economic resources would be especially

TABLE 15.2 Crimes of Inmates, Aged 60 Years and Over at Admissions
to Prison, 1970–1995

Crimes	1970	1975	1980	1985	1990	1995	Pct. elder[a]
Violence	8	9.16	8.85	11.22	10.5	12.28	4.2
Bodily injury	2	4.31	1.41	2.38	2.9	2.41	2.67
Extortion	0.33	—	0.6	1.26	1.45	1.17	2.12
Robbery	0.67	1.35	1.21	2.24	1.34	2.41	4.7
Homicide	4.33	2.7	4.43	3.79	3.57	3.81	9.76
Firearms	0.33	—	0.2	0.7	0.33	1.17	4.33
Violence law	0.33	0.27	0.6	0.28	0.78	0.78	4
Property	80.33	78.71	75.05	72.65	67.49	64.8	10.04
Larceny	48.67	55.79	49.3	46.84	47.49	45.07	9.43
Fraud	27	16.17	20.92	20.76	14.86	13.52	12.42
Arson	1	0.81	1.41	1.96	0.78	1.4	7.72
Embezzlement	1	2.96	1.01	1.26	1.56	1.4	8.91
Intrusion	—	1.35	0.6	1.12	1.9	2.8	19.25
Sex	0.67	0.81	1.01	1.12	1.12	0.78	1.91
Illicit trade	7	3.77	2.41	0.7	1	0.7	6.98
Drugs	—	1.35	4.63	8	10.5	12.35	2.54
Traffic	1.33	3.5	6.04	4.35	7.6	6.91	4.65
Other	2.67	2.7	2.01	1.96	1.79	2.18	3.16
Total percentage	100	100	100	100	100	100	—
Total number	300	371	497	713	895	1,287	—
Percentage elder	1.17	1.42	1.76	2.26	3.94	5.9	5.9

[a]The number of elders sent to prison in 1995 for a given crime is divided by the number of adults of all ages sent to prison.

Source: Research and Statistics Section (1971, 1976, 1981, 1986, 1991, 1996).

vulnerable. Arson of uninhabited structures (Article 109) or "setting fire to objects other than structures" (Article 110) has similar implications.

Among violent offenses, homicide stands out, while other violent crimes lag behind the 5.9% rate for all offenses of older inmates. As a very serious offense, homicide holds less prospects for leniency toward aged offenders. "Illicit trades" combine prostitution, gambling and lottery, and pornographic materials. Here the management of illicit enterprises rather than the customers is the target. Traffic offenses are less characteristic of older persons; drugs (primarily stimulant drugs) and sex offenses (indecent assault and rape) were even less numerous. Abuse of stimulant drugs (amphetamines) and traffic offenses reached crisis proportions in the 1970s, resulting in escalating prison admissions.

Changes in the representation of particular crimes also merits attention in examining the prison admissions of older persons over the decades. Perhaps the explanation is that elders have become more active in certain offenses or the criminal justice decision makers have become less tolerant in their decisions for particular offenses of elders. Probably both explanations have merit.

The gain over the decades has been most impressive for drug and traffic offenses. Violence also has become more prevalent among the prison admissions, mostly because of robbery and violations of the Law Against Firearms and Swords, but bodily injury (the most numerous crime) has remained roughly the same. Homicide also has had minor fluctuations. Property offenses—primarily larceny and fraud—have remained dominant over the decades but have lost share because of the escalation of drug and traffic offenses. In spite of the belief in the sexual aberrations of older persons, rape and indecent assault have been of minor importance in the admissions. Illicit trades have lost much of their minor share.

Accumulation of Older Prisoners

Interestingly, the age-specific imprisonment rates in Table 15.1 show that only the oldest prisoners recorded a consistent increase over the 25 years. As indicated, if the selection of prisoners from that age group were unchanged, the rates per 100,000 Japanese aged 60 years and over would be constant. The proportion of prisoners who are elders is increasing at a rate that cannot be explained simply as a consequence of elders' increased presence in the general population of Japanese adults. Conversely, the younger adults (ages 20 to 39 years) have consistently lost age-specific rates in spite of the criminological truism that young adults make the greatest contribution to the crime rates.

Could the explanation be that elders have accumulated exceptionally in Japanese prisons through the coupling of their admissions to prison and the aging of prisoners admitted earlier, especially those serving a long sentence? The question rests on the fact that the aging of the prison population stems from both (a) the increasing age of persons serving long sentences and (b) the greater influx of older persons into prisons among the age groups.

Comparison of age groups is offered by two statistical measurements of the number of prisoners present. Year-end number of prisoners present (their number on December 31 of the given year) gives a summary accounting of the workload of the prison system's staff. It is a barometer of the long-term decline in the number of persons inhabiting Japanese prisons. Table 15.3 shows ages less than 50 years have variously produced the decline over time in the total number of prisoners present. Ages 50 years and over have scored gains in the absolute number of prisoners present at the end of the several years, and ages 60 years and over have had the greatest percentage increases.

The number of persons entering prisons in the course of an entire year is recorded by the prison admissions. The number of admissions reflects directly the immediate fluctuations in the processing by the system of criminal justice of the persons caught in the nets of law enforcement, prosecutors, and judges. Table 15.3 demonstrates that the decreasing number of new prisoners has produced the declining imprisonment rate for ages less than 50 years. One exception has been a slight upturn in 1995 that possibly signals a bottom-outing of the trend. Ages 50 to 59 years joined the downtrend in 1989, while ages 60 years and over were alone in a consistent increase in absolute numbers.

The "percentage carryover" subtracts the number of admissions from the respective year-end population and divides the remainder by the year-end population. For all prisoners in 1983, the 30,725 prison admissions is subtracted from the 44,869 present at the end of 1983. The difference constitutes the "carryover," the number of inmates who were present throughout the year by neither leaving the prisons nor entering them during that year. The carryover is expressed in percentage differences, regardless of the magnitude of absolute numbers, in order to concentrate attention on the relative importance of carryover among age groups.

As the net consequence of absolute gains in both year-end population and admissions, elders have accumulated in Japanese prisons

TABLE 15.3   Accumulation of Prisoners by Age, 1983–1995

Prisoner population by years	Total	Less 30	30–39	40–49	50–59	60–over
1983						
Year-end	44,869	9,673	17,061	12,280	4,749	1,106
Admissions	30,725	7,478	11,676	8,088	2,895	588
Percentage carryover	31.52	22.69	31.56	33.05	39.04	46.83
1985						
Year-end	46,105	10,033	16,294	12,815	5,689	1,274
Admissions	31,656	7,801	11,314	8,401	3,427	713
Percentage carryover	31.34	22.25	30.56	34.44	39.76	44.03
1987						
Year-end	45,958	10,080	14,775	13,233	6,365	1,505
Admissions	29,726	7,574	9,512	8,207	3,702	731
Percentage carryover	35.32	24.86	35.62	37.98	41.84	51.43
1989						
Year-end	42,615	9,347	11,590	13,502	6,348	1,828
Admissions	24,605	6,395	6,774	7,233	3,354	858
Percentage carryover	42.26	31.58	41.55	46.43	47.16	53.06
1991						
Year-end	37,765	8,564	9,205	11,809	6,176	2,011
Admissions	21,083	5,738	5,320	6,272	2,958	795
Percentage carryover	44.17	33	42.2	46.89	52.1	60.47
1993						
Year-end	37,164	8,186	8,926	11,175	6,408	2,469
Admissions	21,242	5,593	5,149	6,149	3,237	1,114
Percentage carryover	42.84	32.07	42.31	44.97	49.48	54.88
1995						
Year-end	38,585	8,554	9,544	10,747	6,839	2,901
Admissions	21,838	5,627	5,437	5,829	3,658	1,287
Percentage carryover	43.4	34.22	43.03	45.76	46.51	55.64

Source: Research and Statistics Section (1987, 1990, 1996).

to a greater extent than any other age group. For every year recorded in Table 15.3, older prisoners (those over 59 years of age) had the greater accumulation (carryover) of their members among the age groups. Their advantage tended to increase over the years, although not with full consistency. Only elders had a persistent absolute increase in year-end population throughout the span of years and, with the exception of 1991, in prison admissions over that span. Ages 50 to 59 years tended to have increases over the years but with considerable inconsistency. Ages less than 50 years have had the greatest impact on the general decline in prison admissions and year-end populations.

Record of Previous Exposure to Imprisonment

Accumulation or not, the underlying issue remains: Why have older persons assumed a greater share of the prison population in spite of the drop in the total imprisonment rate? The association between advanced age and repetitive imprisonment is a major answer. Previous imprisonment is among the criteria used by public prosecutors and sentencing judges when they decide whether or not an offender should benefit from official leniency.

By granting leniency for earlier offenses, the public prosecutors and sentencing judges allowed particular defendants—those who were to come again for later crimes—to age before they were ultimately to become prisoners. Other defendants would not come again—by not committing new crimes or evading detection or prosecution—and would be removed from criminal justice processing. As the second reason for advancing average age of prisoners, official leniency also was frequently denied to those defendants who had been in prison previously. The average age would be raised by the time spent serving several prison sentences.

"We hate crime and not criminals," Nagashima (1990, pp. 4–6) points out, is a Japanese saying with a double meaning. First, offenders should be punished according to both moral and legal responsibility whereas the Western approach concentrates on legal responsibility. Criminals are "our fellow countrymen" who should be accepted into society "when they purify themselves from the tainted past." However, the Japanese assume that the deviants have an innate capacity for eventual self-correction. If the offenders are not repentant and do not undertake self-rehabilitation, they risk denial of the community's fellowship.

For the public prosecutors and judges, blameworthiness is mea-sured in practice by deliberateness in planning, coldheartedness in execution of the criminal plan, infliction of excessive pain on the victim, moral depravity, and repetition of offenses (Suzuki, 1979). As an indicator of the offender's failure to undertake self-rehabilitation, previous imprisonment has special importance as a negative crite-rion.

Table 15.4 documents the special importance of serial imprison-ment for bringing older persons into Japanese prisons. Over the decades, the average number of previous prison admissions for older inmates (age 60 and over) has been consistently greater than that for younger inmates. However, older inmates have not shown a consistent increase over the years in their average number of previous admissions, while the averages for younger inmates have escalated.

The rates of elder admissions per 100 prison admissions further underscore the particular concentration of older persons among serial prisoners. Although in absolute numbers, older prisoners are a minority among prisoners of all ages, there is a significantly higher concentration of elders among serial prisoners than there is among

TABLE 15.4 Previous Exposure to Imprisonment of Older Inmates

Years of admissions	Mean previous admissions		Number of admissions to prison				
	Ages 20–60[a]	Ages 60+	1	2–3	4–5	6–9	10–over
			Number of elders per 100 prison admissions				
1970	2.76	7.57	0.41	0.5	0.96	2.46	13.79
1975	2.96	7.92	0.52	0.48	1.2	2.43	15.57
1980	2.97	7.19	0.74	0.78	1.39	3.72	15.33
1985	3.06	7.3	0.91	1.2	1.39	4.29	18.59
1990	3.27	7.58	1.55	1.62	3.14	6.6	28.33
1995	3.17	7.3	2.65	2.52	4.95	9.21	37.95

[a]For each year the total number of previous prison admissions of inmates 60 years or over is divided by the total number of inmates in that age-group.

Source: Research and Statistics Section (1971, 1976, 1981, 1986, 1991, 1996).

prisoners with only one or a few prior admissions. Moreover, the concentration of elders among serial prisoners has escalated disproportionately; while there has been an increase in the proportion of elders among first-time and serial prisoners alike, this increase has been greatest among prisoners who had entered prison 10 or more times. Thus, the policy of denying leniency to recidivists has had maximum impact upon older offenders.

The growth of elders' first admissions also is noteworthy. The annual reports of the Ministry of Justice do not relate age, number of imprisonments, and crime. To fill that void, Table 15.5 was developed from Ministry tabulations relating the number of imprisonments and crime without specifying age. The estimates in Table 15.5 assume that the patterning of the elder's number of previous imprisonments by crime resembles generally the patterning for total prisoners. Al-

TABLE 15.5 Estimated First Admissions to Prison by Elders by Their Offenses 1970–1995

Offenses of older inmates	Estimated number of first admissions to prison					
	1970	1975	1980	1985	1990	1995
Larceny	45.5	56.5	70	103.1	119	183.5
Fraud	25.4	20.5	35.3	57.9	48.1	61.5
Traffic	3.6	10	19.6	18.8	44.1	52.3
Drugs	—	2	10.3	20	26.8	51.5
Homicide	9.4	7	15.2	18.2	21.7	36.5
Robbery	1.4	3	3.9	10.3	8.4	20.6
Embezzlement	1.8	5.7	3.1	6.2	8.6	13.3
Arson	2	2	4.9	9.9	5	13.2
Bodily injury	2.8	6.6	2.5	6.2	9.8	11.5
Firearms, law against violence	1.6	0.3	1	2.5	2.5	7
Extortion	0.4	—	1	3.2	4.6	6
Rape, indecent assault	1.2	2.1	2.2	4.2	5.8	5.7
Intrusion	—	0.7	0.4	1	2.8	5.4
Forgery	—	1.6	3.9	2.9	4.6	4.1
Illicit trades[a]	4.7	4.3	3.2	1.7	2	3.7

[a]Includes prostitution, gambling and lotteries, and pornography.

Source: Research and Statistics Section (1971, 1976, 1981, 1986, 1991, 1996).

though the estimated figures are only substitutes for precise statistics, they demonstrate that the growth of first admissions of elders may be attributed variously to the crimes that bring them to prisons. The growth is especially marked for certain crimes.

Larceny is the most numerous crime of elders, as Table 15.2 documents. Of those numerous offenses, a significant proportion involve first admissions to prison. Fraud also has been associated with first admissions to an increasing extent over the decades, but the rate of growth has been especially exceptional for traffic and drug offenses as a result of their criminalization in the atmosphere of a perceived public crisis.

Homicide and robbery are relatively infrequent crimes of elders, but they have particular linkage with first admissions. Homicide and bodily injury have long histories of involving older persons, partly because of the crisis situations elders encounter. Commission of these crimes by elders contradicts the general assumption that passivity goes with aging. Other offenses are of minor importance.

The failure of the Ministry's annual statistics to relate age, number of imprisonments, and crime is partly filled by the research of Nozaka, Otsuki, Kashaiwagi, Hashisako, and Ichikawa (1992). They reported a sample of 971 prisoners who had committed their crime while older than 59 years. Frequency of imprisonment was related to type of offense. Of the 971 persons studied, 828 were linked with four major types of crime. Only 12% of the 828 were murderers who were especially likely to be "first termers" and to have favorable social status and relationships. However, some murderers had low intelligence and the personal qualities of a deviant personality. Larceny/theft was the most frequent crime (68%). Prisoners convicted of this offense were heavily represented among recidivists and lacked positive relationships; many were unemployed and had neither a permanent dwelling nor close relationships with others. Fraud (16% of offenses) often involved failure to pay a restaurant bill. Perpetrators of fraud shared some of the characteristics of larceny thieves, but half of those convicted of fraud had less previous imprisonment and more favorable relationships in the community. Older persons who committed arson (4%) were less recidivistic than elders imprisoned for larceny/theft or fraud, but, when compared with murderers, had less favorable living conditions and family ties and were more likely to be senile, alcoholics, or deviants.

Medical Care and Older Inmates

Hospitalization rates demonstrate the heavy demands of aged prisoners for medical services and the growing pressure they place on the budgets for medical care. As for any group of human beings, older prisoners come in variety. Some of them are in special need of medical care either because of the normal vicissitudes of aging or because of experiences while confined. In 1987, the rate of hospital admissions was 24.71 per 100 inmates. For inmates aged 60 to 69 years, the rate was 35.34, and 62.44 for inmates older than 69 years. By 1995, the general rate had grown to 31.69 per 100 adult inmates, but the age-specific rates had reached 41.26 per 100 inmates aged 60 to 69 years and 67.52 per 100 inmates older than 69 years.

Two other rates highlight the especially heavy pressure placed on the medical services by inmates older than 59 years. The percentage share of all inmates present at the end of the year grew from 3.28% in 1987 to 7.52% in 1995. The growth in and of itself suggests a greater demand for services, but elders' share of prison hospital admissions rose from 5.24% to 10.62%.

A visit to the Medical Branch of Osaka Prison dramatized the implications. The limited capacity for the physically ill was being increasingly devoted to older prisoners, especially long-term inmates suffering from cancer. Prisoners who have not yet recovered from an illness upon expiration of their sentences usually require continued hospitalization following their release from prison. Community hospitals located near prison hospitals are reluctant to accept releasees, especially when concentrations of former prisoners are likely to develop over time. Older patients are especially prone to have lost contact with their families. Their offenses and deviant lifestyle frequently lead to the family's rejection. Relatives are very unlikely to be ready and capable to assume responsibility for care of bedridden former felons.

The Correction Bureau has four other medical facilities, with Hachiojo Medical Prison the major institution. Hachiojo and Osaka receive both the physically and mentally ill. Jono Medical Prison in Kitakiushu City and Okazaki Medical Prison receive only mental patients. Kikuchi Medical Branch Prison specializes in leprosy, but, in the absence of such patients, receives a wider variety of the physically ill. The prisons for adults assign older inmates capable of usual prison labor to ordinary cells and workshops. Those incapable of regular labor are assigned to eight-person cells where they perform less arduous labor, usually assembly of paper shopping bags. The frail elderly are housed near the hospital of the particular prison where their medical needs are met.

The Hiroshima Correction Region has developed the small Onomichi Branch Prison, now occupying a new and modern plant and having the primary function of serving older male prisoners who cannot be managed at regular prisons in the region. The plant has separate sections for elders, other medium security males, and those on pretrial detention. The section for the elderly has a workshop, kitchen, and dining room on the first floor. The recreation and living areas are on the second floor. In addition to the custodial staff, a physician and two paramedical nurses are present. The branch has an x-ray machine, an electrocardiograph, and dental equipment.

Elders and Community Corrections

On the rolls of probation offices, adult parolees are more numerous than adult probationers. (In Japan, supervision of both probationers and parolees is conducted by the "probation officers" of the Rehabilitation Bureau, an arm of the nationwide Ministry of Justice.) When suspending prison sentences, the judges choose between unconditional release or probationary supervision. When feasible, they prefer unconditional release because they consider probation more punitive than imprisonment. Paroles are authorized by regional parole boards.

In that context, adult probationers in Japan are likely to have had more previous contacts with the criminal justice agencies than the average American probationers. The Japanese offenders evaluated as sociologically and psychologically worthy would likely be returned to the community unconditionally. Probationers would be considered less worthy but more qualified for leniency than convicted offenders who are sent to prison and then become candidates for parole.

Upon reentering the free community, probationers and parolees rely on their families as the primary buffering institution. For those who lack family assistance, rehabilitation aid hostels have emerged as a substitute. The hostels are operated by volunteer organizations with a governmental subsidy paying a portion of the expenses.

The hostels' clientele represent the failures of families to meet the obligations of a buffering institution. In 1995, 70.5% of the releasees from prisons, including parolees who had been referred to hostels, had no relatives upon which they could depend; 13.0% had been rejected by relatives; 15.2% did not want to go to relatives; and the remainder (1.3%) claimed they sought the resocialization services of the hostels. It is not clear what specifically they meant by "resocialization." We can be certain only that they did not refer to their families. Probationers at the hostels also lacked support of their families but for a different distribution of reasons: no relatives to depend on, 76.8%; relatives refused to help, 12.2%; the probationer rejected relatives, 9.6%; and seeking resocialization services, 14%.

Whether probationers or released prisoners, hostel residents represented 9% of the persons returning to community life (see Table 15.6). Although least numerous among all released prisoners or parolees, older persons were especially likely to be referred to rehabilitation aid hostels. Probationers 50 to 59 years of age matched those aged 60 years and over.

The released prisoners and probationers were similar in rates of hostel use per 100 persons returning to the community, but they differed in the number of days spent at the hostels. That length of time is a barometer of the degree of reentry difficulties for persons who usually lack family assistance.

The rates in Table 15.6 confirm this difference between former prisoners and probationers. Older released prisoners had a greater reentry crisis than the older probationers. Stays of 60 days or more take up the largest share of released prisoners regardless of age, but older prisoners had the greatest concentration in the maximum length of stay. In contrast, the age groups of probationers lacked that concentration.

TABLE 15.6 Probationers and Released Prisoners at Hostels by Age, 1995

Days at hostels	Total persons	Released prisoners or probationers				
		20–39	40–49	50–59	60–over	Rates[a]
Released prisoners		Percentage distributions by rows				
Hostel releasees						
Less 5	327	17.5	15.9	16.3	14.9	13.5
5–20	375	19.6	21.1	15.6	18	14.1
20–60	540	27.1	25.4	29	26.1	14.3
60–over	763	35.8	37.6	39.1	41	15.9
Total percentage	—	100	100	100	100	14.7
Number hostel releasees	2,005	536	622	552	295	—
Percentage hostels	100	26.8	31	27.5	14.7	—
Prison releasees	21,369	9,751	6,125	3,981	1,512	—
Percentage prisoners	100	45.6	28.7	18.6	7.1	—
Rates[b]	9.4	5.5	10.1	13.9	19.5	—
Probationers						
Less 5	115	31.7	20.3	22.2	36.4	10.4
5–20	227	49.1	55.5	56.4	33.3	4.8
20–60	34	6.8	7.8	7.7	12.1	11.8
60–over	63	12.4	16.4	13.7	18.2	9.5
Total percentage	—	100	100	100	100	7.5
Number hostel releasees	439	161	128	117	33	—
Percentage hostels	100	36.7	29.2	26.6	7.5	—
Admissions to probation	4,820	3,354	816	501	149	—
Percentage probation admissions	100	69.6	16.9	10.4	3.1	—
Rates[c]	9.1	4.8	15.7	23.3	22.1	—

[a]Rate: Number of released prisoners aged 60 and over years divided by total released prisoners for each category of days of hostel stay.
[b]Rate: Number of hostel releasees divided by number of released prisoners for respective age group in 1995.
[c]Rate: Number of hostel releasees divided by number of persons admitted to probation for respective age group in 1995.

Source: Research and Statistics Section (1996, 1996a).

Conclusions

The differential demand of former prisoners points up the inadequacy of the policy of relying on the family as the primary buffering institution. The growing presence of elders among prisoners poses a warning of unprecedented difficulties for Japanese corrections as a spin-off of the demography of aging in general. The appearance of more older prisoners suggests that the policy of reluctant use of imprisonment is being affected by the general demographic crisis. The age-specific rates in Table 15.1 show that, in spite of the drop in general prison admissions, older persons are forming a larger share of that population. Japanese elders either are committing more offenses (possibly because they suffer unprecedented pressures in a universe of change) or the previous tolerance of society and the decision making of criminal justice agencies have eroded. Even without any change in previous tolerance, however, the criterion for imposing official leniency, that is, the absence of previous prison stays, has escalated the number of older prisoners.

The linkage between previous exposure to imprisonment and another prison sentence for a new offense, the peculiar linkage of elder crimes with homicide and offenses associated often with homelessness and insufficient economic resources, and a history of previous exposure to criminal justice sanctions—all elements of the increasingly usual older offenders' record—explain their imprisonment. The policy of diversion, ironically, has functioned to increase the number of aged prisoners.

References

Akiyama, H. S. (1984). *Resource Exchanges in the U.S. and Japan: Towards a Theory of Dependence and Independence of the Elderly*, Ph.D. Dissertation, University of Illinois at Urbana-Champaign.

Asano, H., & Saito, C. (1988). Social service delivery and social work practice for Japanese elderly. *Journal of Gerontological Social Work, 12*, 131–151.

Atoh, M. (1994). *Population dynamics: Its social and economic impact and policy responses in Japan*. Kuala Lumpur, Malaysia: Institute for Japanese Studies.

Beasley, W. G. (1972). *The Meiji restoration*. Stanford, CA: Stanford University Press.

Beer, C. (1990). *Japanese health care for the elderly*. Denver: National Conference of State Legislatures.

Bethel, D. (1992). Alienation and reconstruction in a home for the elderly. In J. J. Tobin (Ed.), *Re-made in Japan: Everyday life and consumer taste in a changing society* (pp. 126–142). New Haven: Yale University Press.

Code of Criminal Procedure of Japan. (1907). As amended, Article 248, (English translation).

Freed, A. O. (1990). How Japanese families cope with fragile elderly. *Journal of Gerontological Social Work, 15*, 39–56.

Fukutake, T. (1981). *Japanese society today* (2nd ed.). Tokyo: University of Tokyo Press.

Haley, J. O. (1989). Confessions, repentance, and absolution. In M. Wright & B. Galaway (Eds.), *Mediation and criminal justice* (pp. 195–211). Newbury Park, CA: Sage.

Hodge, R. W., & Ogawa, N. (1991). *Fertility change in contemporary Japan*. Chicago: University of Chicago Press.

Ishida, T. (1983). *Japanese political culture: Changes and continuity*. New Brunswick, NJ: Transaction Books.

Iwao, S. (1993). *The Japanese woman: Traditional image and changing reality*. New York:Free Press.

Johnson, E. H. (1996). *Japanese corrections: Managing convicted offenders in an orderly society*. Carbondale, IL: Southern Illinois University Press.

Kiefer, C. W. (1990). The elderly in modern Japan: Elite, victims, or plural players? In J. Sokolovsky (Ed.), *The cultural context of aging: Worldwide perspectives* (pp. 181–200). New York: Bergin & Garvey.

Lock, M. M. (1984). East Asian medicine and health care for the Japanese elderly. *Pacific Affairs, 57*, 65–73.

Maguire, K., & Pastore, A. L. (Eds.). (1997). *Sourcebook of criminal justice statistics 1996*. Washington, DC: Bureau of Justice Statistics, U.S. Department of Justice.

Nagashima, A. (1992). Criminal justice in Japan. In V. Kusida-Smick (Ed.), *Crime prevention and control in the United States and Japan* (pp. 3–11). Dobbs Ferry, NY: Transnational Juris Publications.

Nakajima, H. (1991). *Current trends of criminal activities and the practices of criminal justice in Japan*. Unpublished paper. Tokyo: United Nations Asia and Far East Institute for Prevention of Crime and Treatment of Offenders.

Nakane, C. (1984). *Japanese society*. Tokyo: Charles E. Tuttle.

Nozaka, Y., Otsuki, T., Kashaiwagi, F., Hashisako, S., & Ichikawa, M. (1992). Actual conditions regarding elderly prisoners. In *Summary of research monographs in the Bulletin of the Criminological Research Department published in 1981–1990* (pp. 49–51). Tokyo: Research and Training Institute, Ministry of Justice.

Ogawa, N. (1989). Population ageing and impact upon health resource requirements at government levels in Japan. *Ageing and Society, 9,* 383–405.

Pempel, T. J. (1982). *Party and politics in Japan: Creative conservatism.* Philadelphia: Temple University Press.

Penal Code of Japan. (1907). As amended, Article 25 (English translation).

Penal Code of Japan. (1907). As amended, Article 130 (English translation).

Penal Code of Japan. (1907). As amended, Article 109 (English translation).

Penal Code of Japan. (1907). As amended, Article 110 (English translation).

Research and Statistics Section. (1971). *Annual report of statistics on corrections for 1992* (Vol. 1). Tokyo: Secretariat, Ministry of Justice.

Research and Statistics Section. (1976). *Annual report of statistics on corrections for 1992* (Vol. 1). Tokyo: Secretariat, Ministry of Justice.

Research and Training Institute (1991). *Summary of the White Paper on Crime.* Tokyo: Ministry of Justice.

Research and Training Institute. (1996). *Summary of the White Paper on Crime.* Tokyo: Ministry of Justice.

Research and Statistics Section. (1981). *Annual report of statistics on corrections for 1992* (Vol. 1). Tokyo: Secretariat, Ministry of Justice.

Research and Statistics Section. (1986). *Annual report of statistics on corrections for 1992* (Vol. 1). Tokyo: Secretariat, Ministry of Justice.

Research and Statistics Section. (1987). *Annual report of statistics on corrections for 1992* (Vol. 1). Tokyo: Secretariat, Ministry of Justice.

Research and Statistics Section. (1988). *Annual report of statistics on corrections for 1992* (Vol. 1). Tokyo: Secretariat, Ministry of Justice.

Research and Statistics Section. (1990). *Annual report of statistics on corrections for 1992* (Vol. 1). Tokyo: Secretariat, Ministry of Justice.

Research and Statistics Section. (1991). *Annual report of statistics on corrections for 1992* (Vol. 1). Tokyo: Secretariat, Ministry of Justice.

Research and Statistics Section. (1993). *Annual report of statistics on corrections for 1992* (Vol. 1). Tokyo: Secretariat, Ministry of Justice.

Research and Statistics Section. (1996). *Annual report of statistics on corrections for 1992* (Vol. 1). Tokyo: Secretariat, Ministry of Justice.

Research and Statistics Section. (1996a). *Annual report of statistics on rehabilitation for 1992.* Tokyo: Secretariat, Ministry of Justice.

Research and Statistics Section. (1996b). *Annual report of statistics on corrections for 1992* (Vol. 1). Tokyo: Secretariat, Ministry of Justice.

Sansom, G. (1963a). *A history of Japan, 1334–1615.* Tokyo: Charles E. Tuttle.

Sansom, G. (1963b). *A history of Japan, 1615–1867.* Tokyo: Charles E. Tuttle.

Scalapino, R. A. (1953). *Democracy and the party movement in prewar Japan.* Berkeley: University of California Press.

Skord, V. (1989). 'Withered blossoms': Aging in Japanese literature. In P. Von Dorotka Bagnell & P. S. Soper (Eds.), *Perceptions of aging in literature: A cross-cultural study* (pp. 131–143). Westport, CT: Greenwood Press.

Smith, R. J. (1983). *Japanese society: Tradition, self, and the social order.* Cambridge: Cambridge University Press.

Suzuki, Y. (1979). Corrections in Japan. In R. J. Wicks & H. H. A. Cooper (Eds.), *International corrections* (pp. 141–161). Lexington, MA: Lexington Books.

Watanuki, J. (1986). Is there a "Japanese-type welfare society"? *International Sociology, 1,* 259–269.

Yoshizumi, K. (1995). Marriage and family: Past and present. In K. Fujimura-Fanselon & A. Kameda (Eds.), *Japanese women: New feminist perspectives in the past, present, and future* (pp. 186–197). New York: Feminist Press of City University of New York.

PART V

Conclusions

Chapter 16

Epilogue: Policy Implications for the 21st Century

Burton D. Dunlop, Max B. Rothman, and Pamela Entzel

In the Foreword, Achenbaum and Schieve observe that "Older people have always had special relationships to the law—ranging from miserable offenders to august magistrates." In this book, we have presented a snapshot of these relationships as they appear at the threshold of the 21st century. We have examined many of the roles that older people play in crime and criminal justice, how older people act in these roles, and how others act towards them.

Because the preceding chapters have provided a lot of information, this chapter first summarizes some of the most important findings, underscoring new data on the characteristics, behaviors, and experiences of older victims, offenders, prisoners, and participants in criminal trials. We then attempt to identify the most salient implications of these findings for the criminal justice system, aging as a field of study, and, to some extent, for society as a whole. Most notably, we explore common perceptions and stereotypes of older people involved in this system because these may serve as important indicators of society's perceptions of older people generally. We examine their validity in light of recent empirical data and current gerontological thought. Finally, we consider policy and ethical issues surrounding age-based distinctions in the criminal justice system, raising the fundamental issue of when, if ever, older people should be singled out for different or specialized treatment. The issues and questions we raise should serve as launching points for further discussion, debate, and research among gerontologists, other social scientists, and criminal justice planners. Indeed, when and how these issues and questions are addressed will shape the future relationships of older people to the law and the justice system.

Roles, Characteristics and Behaviors of Older People in the Context of Crime and the Criminal Justice System

---

Like younger people, older people may be involved in all aspects of crime and the criminal justice system. They may be victims of crime or participants in trials of the criminally accused. They may even be offenders or prisoners themselves. This section summarizes some of the most intriguing characteristics and behaviors of elders in each of these roles.

Elders As Victims

Statistically speaking, and contrary to popular opinion, older people are unlikely victims of crime. In the United States, individuals age 65 and over are less likely to be victimized by crime than any age group over 12 years of age (Wolf, chapter 2). Similarly, older people experience some of the lowest victimization rates of any age group in England, Germany, and Israel, reflecting a common pattern among industrialized countries (Alek & Ben-David, chapter 14; Kreutzer & Grasberger, chapter 13; Phillips, Worral, & Brammer, chapter 12).

Within the elder population, victimization rates are highest among the youngest-old and decline progressively with age (Alek & Ben-David, chapter 14; Wolf, chapter 2). In the United States, elder victimization rates also are linked to gender, race, income, marital status, and place of residence—with men, Blacks, low-income individuals, single people, and urban dwellers experiencing elevated rates of crime (Wolf, chapter 2). However, the strength of the association between victimization and each of these variables also varies by type of crime. For example, although older men are generally more likely to be victims than older women, older women are more likely to experience personal larceny (Wolf, chapter 2).

Again, contrary to popular perception, empirical studies described in previous chapters suggest that older people in the United States are generally less fearful of crime than are younger persons, with the possible exception of the fear of being mugged (see Wolf, chapter 2). To the surprise of many researchers, younger people reported greater fear of victimization than older people in studies conducted in England and Israel, as well as in the United States (Alek & Ben-David, chapter 14; Phillips et al., chapter 12). Moreover, researchers in Israel found that older people in their 60s reported higher levels of fear than individuals age 70 and above (Alek & Ben-David, chapter 14).

Nevertheless, despite both their low risk and their low fear of victimization overall, elders do have a relatively high risk for certain types of crime. Compared to younger age groups, those age 65 and over are less susceptible to violent crime such as homicide or rape, but more susceptible to crime motivated by economic gain, including larceny, fraud, and confidence schemes (Wolf, chapter 2). According to Wolf (chapter 2), older people are thought to be especially vulnerable to fraud and con games because they are more trusting, more readily available, and perhaps more easily confused by fast-talk than younger people. Indeed, elders may be targeted by con artists for their readily available assets.

Furthermore, some older people are financially, physically, and emotionally mistreated by family members and caretakers. According to Wolf (chapter 2), community-based studies carried out at different times in several different countries suggest that elder abuse has a prevalence rate of 4% to 6%; and because most elder mistreatment goes unreported, true prevalence rates are believed to be considerably higher. Although there is no consensus on the causes of elder abuse and neglect, Wolf (chapter 2) identifies four risk factors, namely: (a) declines in victims' mental or physical health that increase their dependence on potential abusers, (b) abusers' dependency (usually financial) on the victims, (c) the psychological state of the abusers, and (d) family social isolation. Older people also may become victims of abuse and neglect in institutional facilities; although, once again, information is lacking on the true nature and extent of this problem.

When they are victimized, older persons appear to sustain more serious physical and economic harm than do younger victims (Phillips et al., chapter 12; Wolf, chapter 2). Recent data reveal that older people are more likely to suffer injuries as a result of criminal attacks, and when they are injured, they are more likely to spend 2 or more days in the hospital (Wolf, chapter 2). Because many elders live on fixed incomes, they also may have more difficulty recovering from economic crimes than younger people (Wolf, chapter 2). Whether they likewise experience more psychological harm remains unclear. Alek and Ben-David (chapter 14) report that older victims in Israel are especially likely to develop severe fear of further victimization, whereas Wolf (chapter 2) cites studies showing no increase in fear among older female victims in the United States.

According to Finkel and Macko (chapter 5), older people also may be less likely than younger people to pursue prosecution of their assailants. Older victims involved in the process report a number of common problems that may lead them to drop their cases. Among these may be mobility and memory problems as well as attorneys' use of technical jargon and high-pressure tactics (Finkel & Macko, chapter 5). With respect to elder abuse and neglect, victims may be hesitant to press charges against an abuser who is a family member or their sole source of care or companionship (Wolf, chapter 2).

In response to real or perceived threats of crime and victimization, increasing numbers of older people are participating in cooperative crime prevention programs. Throughout the United States as well as in England and Canada, elders and social services providers are collaborating with sheriffs and police to try to address crime and public safety needs. (Terry & Entzel, chapter 1; Wolf, chapter 2). In many communities, older volunteers actively participate in neighborhood-watch groups, informal home security surveys, crime victim assistance programs, and various law enforcement initiatives (Terry & Entzel, chapter 1).

Elders As Offenders

Just as they are less likely than younger people to be victims of crime, older people also are less likely to commit crime. They contribute only modestly to crime rates in the United States, England, Germany, Israel, and Japan. For example, according to U.S. arrest data for 1995, those age 65 and over represent 12.8% of the total U.S. population, but only 0.7% of persons arrested (Flynn, chapter 3).

Furthermore, in the United States between 1985 and 1995, persons age 65 and over experienced a 22% decline in their share of all arrests, even though their proportion in the population grew by 8% (Flynn, chapter 3). From 1989 to 1995, arrests of elders declined—and declined at a faster rate than crime among the general population—in the categories of murder, nonnegligent homicide, burglary, larceny/theft, auto theft, arson, stolen property, vandalism, weapons offenses, gambling, vagrancy, drunkenness, and disorderly conduct. Drunken-driving arrests also declined, but at a slower rate than among the general population (Flynn, chapter 3).

During this same period, elder arrests increased in the violent-crime categories of forcible rape, robbery, aggravated assault, and other assault. Overall, their arrests for violent crimes increased by 21%, compared to an increase of 15.2% for the total population. However, because the base numbers of their arrests for forcible rape and robbery are very low, little significance should be attached to rate increases in these categories. Changes in the arrest rates for aggravated assault perhaps present a more worrisome trend. Arrests of older people in this category increased by an impressive 27%, exceeding the 23% growth rate registered for the population as a whole. Again, however, the base number is quite small, representing a rise in the number of arrests from a base of 2,771 in 1989 to 3,510 in 1995. The base number in 1985 for the total U.S. population was 354,735 (Flynn, chapter 3).

Increases in arrests were also recorded in the categories of offenses against family and children, liquor violations, drug offenses, and white-collar crime. With the exception of liquor violations, however, these changes are comparable to increases noted for the total population (Flynn, chapter 3).

As the preceding arrest data illustrate, older Americans commit the full range of offenses committed by younger people. Nevertheless, the preponderance of elder crime in the United States revolves around a small number of offense categories, namely: gambling, sex offenses, DWI (driving while intoxicated), drunkenness, vagrancy, larceny/theft, and family offenses. The bulk of these categories consists of relatively minor offenses; and the more serious categories, including sex offenses, DWI, and family violence, are often linked to substance and alcohol abuse (Flynn, chapter 3). By comparison, in Germany, shoplifting is the most common elder crime reported, accounting for 80% of all criminal convictions of older people (Kreuzer & Grasberger, chapter 13). In Israel, the predominant crime among older offenders is bodily assault. However, this may be an artifact of Israel's broad definition of bodily assault, which encompasses automobile accidents giving rise to injuries (Alek & Ben-David, chapter 14).

Elders As Prisoners

Ironically, despite their relatively low crime rates, older people represent the fastest growing age group in U.S. prisons. The total number of inmates age 50 and over in state and federal prisons increased by more than 240% between 1991 and 1998.[1] In 1998, there were approximately 83,667 individuals age 50 and over in prison (not including local jails), representing about 6% of the total U.S. prison population (Kerbs, chapter 10).

Demographic data underscore that most older prisoners in the United States are non-Hispanic Whites, but the older prisoner population also includes disproportionate numbers of African Americans, Hispanics, and Native Americans. The vast majority of older prisoners (95%) are male, and most enter prison without a high school diploma. Approximately 34% of all older inmates are married, compared to 22% of their younger counterparts. Most important, a substantial proportion of older prisoners have serious health problems, including multiple chronic conditions and a history of alcohol abuse (Kerbs, chapter 10).

---

[1]Although governmental programs often recognize age 65 as the cut-off point beyond which one is considered to be older, criminologists and corrections officials frequently use age 50 or 55 to define older prisoners. The Older Americans Act uses 60.

Although the preponderance of elder criminality revolves around relatively minor, nonviolent offenses (Flynn, chapter 3), older inmates in state prisons often are serving sentences for violent crimes such as homicide (Kerbs, chapter 10). In fact, older state prisoners are more likely to be serving time for violent offenses than are younger inmates (Kerbs, chapter 10). This fact could reflect, in part, the lower likelihood that older persons will be sentenced to prison for less serious offenses (Steffensmeier & Motivans, chapter 9). With respect to their criminal history, the largest proportion (45.6%) of prisoners age 55 and over are career-criminal recidivists who have been convicted repeatedly over the course of their lifetimes. The second largest proportion (41.38%), however, consists of those who were incarcerated for the first time at age 55 or older. The remaining 13% received long sentences before age 55 and grew old in prison. Although the latter category currently represents a minority of all older prisoners, it is expected to grow in number and proportion as a result of three-strikes laws and statutes emphasizing long-term mandatory minimum sentences (Kerbs, chapter 10). Unfortunately, there is little research on how the profiles of these prisoners differ and how patterns of imprisonment might affect potential rehabilitation and release.

Indeed, how incarceration affects older prisoners' physical, psychological, and social well-being is not well understood and likewise merits further research attention. A few studies suggest that older inmates' physical health deteriorates rapidly during incarceration, due in part to the harshness and stress of prison life. Some researchers conclude that these environmental factors exacerbate the aging process, pushing the biological age of a typical older prisoner beyond his or her chronological age. Others argue that prison can potentially slow the aging process below what it would have been had these individuals continued the destructive lifestyles they practiced prior to imprisonment. In any event, the most recent research indicates that prison life has a deleterious effect on the mental health and social relationships of older people. But there is no consensus on whether they have a more difficult time adjusting to incarceration than do younger prisoners, and there is a near total lack of information on the psychological and social needs of older female prisoners (Kerbs, chapter 10).

Elders As Participants in Criminal Trials

In addition to involvement in the criminal justice system as victims and perpetrators of crime, older people sometimes play key roles in the prosecution, defense, and judgment of those criminally accused. They may become involved in the criminal law process intentionally, as judges or attorneys who have chosen criminal law as a career, or inadvertently as eyewitnesses to crime or as randomly selected jurors.

According to Adams (chapter 4), some judicial systems permit judges to work as long as they wish, and it is common for judges to remain on the bench well past age 65. A few of the nation's most distinguished appellate judges have been productive into their 80's. However, the effects of aging on judges' behavior and performance remain largely unexplored. At least one study has concluded that older judges typically adopt the same stance toward older defendants as younger judges, but further research is certainly warranted here (Adams, chapter 4).

Like judges, many prosecutors and defense attorneys continue their careers beyond age 65. They may well benefit from a perception that they represent distinguished symbols of authority. On the other hand, Adams (chapter 4) notes that older attorneys who develop obvious physical problems such as vision or hearing impairments may choose not to practice in the courtroom because of negative perceptions of elders with disabilities.

Declines in physical or mental function associated with old age also may affect the behavior and performance of older witnesses. In a study of the reliability of older eyewitnesses, Yarmey (chapter 6) found that certain effects associated with chronological aging, including gradual declines in sensory efficiency, are detrimental to the completeness and accuracy of eyewitness testimony in selected situations. Compared to younger people, older people tend to be less accurate, on average, in their free recall, cued recall, and descriptions of suspects, victims, and situational factors. In contrast, elders' ability to correctly identify suspects from lineups and photospreads appears to be more comparable to that of younger people. However, studies of recognition memory still tend to show a slight but steady decline in performance with increased age, and older witnesses tend to make significantly more false identifications in suspect-absent lineups than do younger witnesses (Yarmey, chapter 6).

Nevertheless, advanced age does not necessarily diminish the reliability or value of elders' eyewitness testimony. As Yarmey (chapter 6) notes, the testimony of some older witnesses may be more accurate or credible than that of younger people. Moreover, even elders with sensory or cognitive impairments can provide highly reliable and useful information when provided with certain accommodations. For example, police investigators and prosecutors can enhance the recall of many older eyewitnesses by employing facilitative and supportive interview techniques (Yarmey, chapter 6). Similarly, attorneys can facilitate eyewitness recall at trial by carefully preparing the witness for testimony, repeating or rephrasing questions, using documents to refresh the witness' recollection, or seeking leeway from the court (Adams, chapter 4).

Furthermore, according to Bornstein, Witt, Cherry, and Greene (chapter 7), older people with high verbal ability and a relatively high level of education are no more susceptible to misleading suggestions than are younger people. In fact, elders in their study failed to show a misinformation effect, while an effect was detected in younger people. Thus, law-enforcement officials, attorneys, judges, and jurors need not be concerned that older witnesses—at least those who are relatively highly educated—are more suggestible than the population-at-large (Bornstein et al., chapter 7).

Finally, this volume has added to our basic understanding of older people in the role of juror. Most elders appear to value jury service as an important opportunity to participate in the democratic process, and anecdotal evidence suggests that elders report for jury duty in relatively large numbers. However, very little empirical data exist regarding the number, proportion, or demographic characteristics of older people who decline jury service, report for service, or ultimately progress to jury panels. In one recent study (Dunlop & Collett, 1999) of older people who were summoned for jury duty in Florida, elders who reported for jury duty, as well as those who did not report, overwhelmingly agreed that jury service is an important opportunity to participate in the democratic process. Despite their generally positive attitude regarding the value of jury service, however, study participants who had failed to report for jury duty when summoned expressed less interest in actually serving on a jury and more negative attitudes toward the courts than those who reported for service. Those who did not show up were also, on average, less educated, older, and more likely to have self-reported disabilities than those who did appear. The frequency with which elders decline jury service on the basis of age or disability may reflect an assumption that courts cannot provide accommodations to allow them to serve comfortably (Entzel, Dunlop, & Rothman, chapter 8).

How older people behave when they do report for jury duty and ultimately progress to jury panels also is not well understood and merits additional research attention. In particular, further study is needed to determine the importance of age-group affiliation in jury deliberation. Although some attorneys believe that age may be predictive of how an older juror will vote in a particular case, a number of empirical studies have found only a negligible correlation between demographic characteristics such as age and a juror's verdict behavior (Entzel et al., chapter 8).

Further, old age is regarded by the courts as a legitimate justification for striking prospective jurors during the peremptory challenge phase of the jury selection process, whereas striking for reasons of race or gender, even under peremptory challenge, have been ruled unconstitutional. In several appellate cases state prosecutors, accused of eliminating jurors for reasons of race or gender under peremptory challenge, actually have resorted to arguing that the reason was not gender or race but old age (Entzel et al., chapter 8)!

Treatment of Older People in the Criminal Justice System As Compared to Younger People

---

This book contains numerous examples of criminal justice policies and practices that entail age-based differentiation. Criminal justice policymakers, administrators, and service providers regularly note the age of older people and use this to distinguish them from the population-at-large. As a result, older people often are treated differently from younger people at various junctures in the process. The fundamental issue, of course, is whether these age-based distinctions are justified.

The basic organization and structure of the criminal justice system reflects a number of these distinctions. For example, in chapter 1,

Terry and Entzel note the emergence of specialized elder units within law enforcement departments around the country. Cities such as Milwaukee and Miami have devoted small groups of specially trained police officers exclusively to the prevention and investigation of crimes involving older people. Similarly, the Thirteenth Judicial Circuit Court of Florida has created the Elder Justice Center to provide a comfortable environment for older people who must undergo legal process (Adams, chapter 4). Also, in an effort to cut costs and meet the needs of older ailing prisoners, a growing number of states, including Florida, are either building or planning separate penal facilities for older inmates, or at least for those who grow frail (Drummond, 1999).

Furthermore, many states have codified age-based distinctions in criminal statutes. Rather than rely on generally applicable domestic violence or mental health statutes to handle cases of elder abuse and/or neglect, for example, most states have criminalized elder abuse as a separate and distinct misdemeanor or felony with penalties that range from $500 fines to 10 years' imprisonment (Wolf, chapter 2). Other states explicitly designate elder abuse in their criminal codes in order to increase penalties and expedite trials. Additionally, in some states, con artists and perpetrators of other crimes may receive enhanced penalties if their victims are over age 60, 62, or 65 (see Wolf, chapter 2).

A number of states also tie age to eligibility for the roles of juror and judge. In 19 states, advanced age (65, 70, or 72) constitutes grounds for exemption from jury duty and, in two others, older people may be excused from service on age-related grounds alone (Entzel et al., chapter 8). With respect to judges, many state judicial systems mandate retirement at age 70, 72, or 75 (Adams, chapter 4).

Furthermore, it is apparent that age is factored into informal decision-making and exercise of discretion on a daily basis throughout the system. For example, the accused may use age as a criterion for selecting an attorney (Adams, chapter 4); attorneys frequently employ age as a tool for identifying "favorable" and "unfavorable" jurors during jury selection (Entzel et al., chapter 8); and jurors often take age into account when evaluating the reliability of eyewitness testimony (Yarmey, chapter 6). According to Yarmey, studies suggest that jurors enter the courtroom presuming that older witnesses will be less accurate in their eyewitness memory than younger adults.

Thus, jurors may tend to give testimony of older witnesses less weight or consideration than that of their younger counterparts. Lending support to this notion, one recent study found that mock jurors are less likely to find a defendant guilty if an older person has been victimized and no corroborating witness is available. However, when older eyewitnesses contradict negative stereotypes of older people and clearly display competence, jurors may favor their testimony over even that of younger adults (Yarmey, chapter 6).

In chapter 9, Steffensmeier and Motivans provide convincing evidence of an age distinction in criminal sentencing. Relative to younger offenders, older offenders (especially those age 60 and over) are less likely to be sentenced to prison and, when they are imprisoned, they generally receive shorter prison terms. As an exception to this overall pattern, older people convicted of drug offenses (and perhaps sexual offenses as well) receive sentences roughly on par with their younger counterparts (Steffensmeier & Motivans, chapter 9). Nevertheless, in terms of sentencing, older people who face criminal charges are clearly an advantaged group, perhaps because judges take into account the impact of longer sentences on older offenders. Unfortunately, there has been no research and little discussion that analyzes the appropriateness or ethics of such distinctions.

Incidentally, whether older people likewise receive preferential treatment from police officers and prosecutors remains unknown. Early studies indicated that police are less likely to arrest elders than their younger counterparts and that prosecutors are more willing to dismiss charges against them. However, more recent studies have reached contradictory or inconclusive results, again sounding the call for further research (see Adams, chapter 4; see Terry & Entzel, chapter 1).

Finally, Kerbs provides numerous examples of disparate treatment of older prisoners. According to Kerbs (chapter 10), older prisoners are openly denied equal access to rehabilitation, counseling, education, and/or vocational programs that are available to younger inmates. Due in part to these programmatic disparities, a growing number of prisoner advocates, including Kerbs, argue that older prisoners should be singled out for selective decarceration (see Kerbs, chapter 11). A number of states already permit early parole for inmates who have served a minimum amount of their sentences and have reached a designated age (Kerbs, chapter 11).

Perceptions of Older People and Aging in the Realm of Crime and Criminal Justice

As these examples demonstrate, age-based distinctions are integral to the structure and functioning of many aspects of the criminal justice system. Older people are routinely distinguished from younger people in formal laws and policies as well as in daily decision making and exercises of discretion. Advanced age can affect which police unit is sent to a crime scene, the perceived credibility of eyewitness testimony, or the type and length of sentence that an offender receives. Yet, despite the importance of advanced age at many junctures in the criminal justice process, we know very little about its significance. Precisely how are older people perceived by others involved in the criminal justice system, and are these perceptions accurate? Do the preceding age-based distinctions reflect real and meaningful differences between younger and older people or misplaced reliance on inaccurate images and stereotypes of elders and aging?

This chapter examines some of the assumptions and stereotypes about older people and aging that appear to underlie these age-based distinctions revealed in the previous chapters. Anecdotal and empirical data drawn from many of the chapters suggest that elders often are perceived as a relatively homogenous group with certain shared characteristics and attitudes, such as fear of crime, respect for authority, and diminished functional ability. Additionally, information presented in this book alludes to basic assumptions about the effects and meaning of aging. This chapter attempts to place some of these assumptions and stereotypes in the context of empirical knowledge and current gerontological thought.

By exploring attitudes toward older people and aging in the microcosm of the criminal justice system, we may gain a better understanding of the images and norms of growing older that pervade not only that system but other social institutions as well. Additionally, we may gain a better understanding of how social structures like the criminal justice system maintain or reinforce ageist ideas and actions in the larger society.

Elders As a Homogenous Group

At the most basic level, the weight and importance attached to advanced age in the context of crime and criminal justice may reflect a perception that older people are a relatively homogenous group with certain shared characteristics and behaviors. For example, attorneys who base jury selection decisions solely on advanced age rely on the notion that older people are substantially similar in attitudes, beliefs, and behaviors. Similarly, laws that categorically exempt older people from jury service or force older judges to retire appear to be rooted in the assumption that older people share certain traits that make it difficult for them to play meaningful roles in the courtroom. Unfortunately, these laws completely ignore recent research that documents immense variation among elders with respect to competence and functional ability.

Even the professional and academic literature on elders, crime, and criminal justice reflects too often a common tendency to conceptualize older people as a monolithic or undifferentiated mass. As these chapters demonstrate, data sources on elder victimization and criminality seldom draw distinctions among older individuals on the basis of age, gender, race, ethnicity, health status, or other key demographic variables. Instead, older people often are discussed in terms of "people age 50 and over" or "individuals age 65 and over," without reference to within-group variation. As a result, while we know something about how older participants in the criminal justice process differ from their younger counterparts, we have very little solid data on how these older persons differ from each other.

This lack of recognition of subcategories within the elder population is especially troublesome given that, as noted at the outset, older people are increasingly diverse in terms of race, ethnicity, health, and socioeconomic status. For example, the number of Hispanic elders is projected to increase 368% between 1997 and 2030, compared to an increase of 79% for non-Hispanic Whites (AARP, 1998). Older people also vary tremendously in their life experiences and personality traits. Ferraro (1997) emphasizes that people actually become less alike as they grow older because the effects of unique life experiences accumulate over time. Thus, heterogeneity increases with age in a population (Ferraro, 1997). This heterogeneity should be acknowledged and further explored in future studies of elders, crime, and criminal justice.

Common Stereotypes

Given the tendency to conceptualize older people as a homogenous group, what characteristics are members of this group perceived to share? Older people are widely believed to be vulnerable to victimization, fearful of crime, law-abiding, and prone to mental and physical impairments, to name just a few stereotypic traits borne out in the foregoing chapters. According to what we know about the roles, characteristics and behaviors of older participants in the criminal justice process, these and other perceptions of elders tend to have some basis in reality but ultimately reflect only a small part of the truth. As generalizations, they are, at best, imprecise.

Increased Vulnerability to Victimization

We have noted that the belief that older people experience relatively high levels of criminal victimization is among the most common perceptions of older people with respect to crime. Whether they reside in the United States (Wolf, chapter 2), England (Phillips et al., chapter 12), or Israel (Alek & Ben-David, chapter 14), older people often are perceived as being especially vulnerable to criminal attacks. This perception is partly accurate in that older people are particularly susceptible to crimes motivated by economic gain, including robbery, personal theft, larceny, burglary, and motor vehicle theft (Wolf, chapter 2). They also may be more likely than younger people to be victims of homicide-suicide (Flynn, chapter 3). Furthermore, as we have seen, older people appear more likely to sustain more serious injuries than younger people as a result of criminal attacks (Alek & Ben-David, chapter 14; Phillips et al., chapter 12; Wolf, chapter 2) and may be more affected by the loss of even a small amount of money (Wolf, chapter 2). Nevertheless, the overall incidence of crime against elders is largely exaggerated. As mentioned, older people experience fewer criminal attacks than younger people in England, Israel, and the United States. In fact, in the United States, older people are only one-third as likely as younger people to become victims of violent crime (Wolf, chapter 2).

Increased Fear of Crime

Another common misperception underscored in this volume is the belief that older people are especially fearful of crime. Although early theories of fear of crime hypothesized that older people would be more fearful than younger people, recent studies have failed to detect such a disparity (Wolf, chapter 2). According to Wolf, in one study of 10 different types of victimization, younger subjects reported higher levels of fear than older people in every category but one: fear of being approached by a panhandler. These findings suggest that, like their vulnerability to criminal attacks, elders' fear of crime is greatly overestimated.

Respect for the Law and Nonviolence

Other simplified or standardized notions about elders and crime include the generally accepted idea that older people commit few crimes in general, and few violent crimes, in particular (see Flynn, chapter 3). Unlike the mistaken belief that older people are especially vulnerable to or fearful of crime, the perception that most older people are nonviolent, law-abiding citizens finds ample support in empirical crime data. As noted, crime statistics indicate that elders are far less likely to commit offenses than younger people, and the bulk of elder crime consists of relatively minor offenses. Moreover, although older people do commit murder, forcible rape, and robbery, they do not play a significant role in the national crime rate for these offenses. Even within the category of sex offenses, in which older men do play a significant role, arrests for rape—a violent crime—are concentrated among younger men, whereas nonviolent offenses such as offenses against common decency are more prevalent among older men (Flynn, chapter 3).

At the same time, however, in her analysis of national crime data, Flynn made several discoveries that run counter to the stereotype of the nonviolent older offender. She reported that elder arrests for violent crimes increased 21% between 1989 and 1995, exceeding the rate of increase for the population as a whole (15.2%). During this same period, elder arrests for aggravated assault increased by 27% compared to 23% for the general population. Furthermore, Flynn cautions against the assumption that older sex offenders are more likely to play a passive, less harmful role than their younger counterparts, citing a recent study revealing serious predatory behavior, including the use of force, on the part of older sex offenders.

Diminished Functional Ability

We also know that there is a common perception that most older people experience declines in their mental and physical abilities. For example, as mentioned, studies indicate that jurors appear to enter the courtroom presuming that older witnesses will be less accurate in their eyewitness memory than younger adults (Yarmey, chapter 6). The widely held assumption that older people have limited mental or physical capacities also may explain why many states have adopted mandatory retirement laws for judges and age-based exemptions from jury duty.

According to Yarmey (chapter 6), the perception that older people have diminished mental or physical abilities is true inasmuch as the completeness and accuracy of older eyewitnesses' free and cued recall are not as good as that of younger people. Moreover, older eyewitnesses tend to show a slight but steady decline in ability to make accurate identifications and appear to make significantly more false identifications than younger witnesses (Yarmey, chapter 6).

However, the perception that older people are less reliable in their ability to perceive and recall events is false in other respects. Older people have been shown to perform as well as younger people in certain tasks involved in eyewitness testimony, including the retrospective estimation of time duration (Yarmey, chapter 6). Also, according to Bornstein et al. (chapter 7), highly cognitive older witnesses are less susceptible than younger people to misleading suggestions.

Wisdom and Experience

Although advanced age is often perceived as a sign of diminished capacity, at other times it is perceived more favorably. According to

Adams (chapter 4), there is a clear tendency in the criminal justice system to associate advanced age with wisdom and experience. Older attorneys, for example, are generally perceived as being more knowledgeable and experienced than their younger counterparts. Similarly, older judges apparently derive added command and authority from the simplified notion that good judgment is largely a function of age (Adams, chapter 4).

Other Stereotypic Traits

Finally, as discussed in chapter 8, attorneys often rely on a wide, and at times conflicting, variety of stereotypes about older people in making their jury selection decisions. Articles and treatises on jury selection characterize older people as being more prejudiced than younger people, but also more tolerant of human frailty and more sympathetic to the injured. Other stereotypic traits of older jurors reflected in the jury selection literature include stubbornness, indecisiveness, and respect for authority (Entzel et al., chapter 8). Again, empirical data are unavailable to test these assumptions. However, the increasing diversity of the elder population calls into question this or any perception of homogeneity in elders' personality or behavioral traits. Clearly, more research is needed.

It is noteworthy that the perceptions of older people identified previously represent multiple generalizations rather than a single negative or positive stereotype. Older people are perceived as being wise and sympathetic as well as mentally impaired and prejudiced. This finding supports current thinking regarding the complex manner by which older people are perceived or categorized. Although negative stereotypes of older people are thought to be prevalent within American culture, recent research suggests that, in fact, older adults are viewed multidimensionally, with both positive and negative attributes (Hummert, 1990; Hummert, Garstka, & Shaner, 1997; Hummert, Garstka, Shaner, & Strahm, 1994). Several studies have indicated that the general social category, "older adult," functions as a superordinate category encompassing several subcategories or stereotypes of different types of older individuals (Brewer, Dull, & Lui, 1981; Hummert et al., 1994). Given this variability in older adult stereotypes, what factors determine which stereotype is applied to an individual older adult and for what purpose in the context of the criminal justice system? And when is older age an advantage and when is it a liability from the standpoint of the older person interacting with that system?

Current knowledge about elders and the criminal justice system suggests that perceptions of advanced age and older people vary depending on the roles that older people are playing within the system. For example, advanced age, as previously indicated, is perceived as a sign of knowledge and experience in attorneys or judges without obvious disabilities (Adams, chapter 4), whereas older age in an eyewitness, in the absence of countervailing behavior, is viewed as an indicator of diminished memory function (Yarmey, chapter 6). Similarly, advanced age can function as an asset for older convicted offenders, who appear to receive leniency in sentencing (Steffensmeier, chapter 9), but a detriment for older prisoners, who are often denied access to counseling, educational, and/or vocational programs by prison staff (Kerbs, chapter 10).

Additionally, two authors suggest that the process of stereotyping an individual older person is heavily influenced by the individual's outward appearance. Adams (chapter 4) notes, for example, that older lawyers are considered distinguished members of the legal profession up to the point where their physical appearance might belie their mental abilities. At that point, negative perceptions of intellectual capacity associated with declining physical ability in older people may supplant the positive perceptions of advanced age that older attorneys might otherwise enjoy. Similarly, Yarmey (chapter 6) underscores the influence of outward appearance on attitudes toward older eyewitnesses. According to him, although age is an initial barrier to be overcome by older witnesses, what the older witness says and, perhaps even more important, how he or she says it, is ultimately determinative of whether that witness is judged more or less credible than younger witnesses. If the older witness' speech style, for example, a weak or hesitating voice, conforms to negative stereotypes regarding elders' mental or physical abilities, then that witness may be viewed as being less accurate and less trustworthy than younger adults. However, the testimony of older adults whose appearance and demeanor contradict the negative stereotypes is viewed as more credible (Yarmey, chapter 6). These findings suggest that negative attitudes toward older people may be more a reaction to functional declines associated with aging (loss of hearing, loss of vision, decreased mobility, etc.) than a reaction to advanced age itself. These issues warrant much further exploration.

The stereotyping of older people in the criminal justice system, it appears, is further influenced by demographic variables such as gender, race, ethnicity, and socioeconomic status. Yarmey (chapter 6) suggests, for example, that older female witnesses and older witnesses of low socioeconomic status are especially likely to be judged negatively for their speech styles. Further research is needed to determine how demographic variables interplay with outward appearance to activate stereotypes of older individuals in other roles. In particular, more research is needed regarding whether the stereotyping and treatment of older people vary according to the relative age of the older person (young-old, middle-old, old-old).

Finally, the existence of multiple and even conflicting stereotypes of older people in the criminal justice system raises the issue of consistency of stereotypes across different perceiver groups. Studies have indicated that stereotypes of older people vary among age groups, with older adults having more complex representations of aging than younger people (Brewer et al., 1984; Hummert et al., 1994). Thus, older jurors might have different stereotypes of older witnesses than do younger jurors. Similarly, older judges, in fact, may differ from their younger counterparts in their evaluation of older offenders. Moreover, stereotypes adopted by the general public may differ from those held by police officers or judges. Many of the foregoing chapters acknowledge but do not thoroughly address these issues. Further investigation into the degree of consistency of stereotypes across these different groups would greatly enhance our understanding of perceptions of older people in society-at-large.

Age and Causality

The importance of age in the criminal justice system may function as a gauge of basic assumptions about the aging process as well as assumptions about older people. Most notably, the centrality of age at many junctures in the system undoubtedly reflects a tendency to conceptualize aging as not only a marker but a cause of certain characteristics and behaviors. For example, the simplified or standardized notion that older individuals are prone to victimization seems to reflect a common perception that aging increases one's vulnerability. Likewise, the idea that older people make less reliable witnesses or less competent jurors than younger people probably reflects a common assumption that aging itself brings about functional declines.

As gerontologists emphasize, however, aging, though closely correlated, is not necessarily a cause of age-related phenomena (Ferraro, 1997). As mentioned in the Introduction, according to Ferraro, "Age is a very important marker of life events, life transitions, social context, and resources, but age in and of itself is an impotent causal variable" (1997, p. 6). Aging is synonymous with the passage of time, and time in itself does not increase one's vulnerability or diminish one's mental abilities. Instead, biological, psychological, and social changes that occur with the passage of time are the real explanatory variables behind "age-related" changes, and these, of course, occur at different chronological ages.

Thus, as posited in the Introduction, age itself is rarely if ever sufficient to explain patterns in elder victimization, elder crime, or the behaviors of older people in the courtroom. Flynn (chapter 3) suggests, for example, that elder deviance ought to be viewed not as an effect of age, but as the product of the combined effects of bio-psychosocial changes such as illness, bereavement, dementia, stress and strain of aging, and social isolation. Similarly, difficulties some older people may face in reporting for jury duty are more properly understood as the effects of illness, disability, or lack of transportation that may accompany old age rather than a result of age per se. By isolating and identifying the specific causes of age-related phenomena rather than simply writing these phenomena off as products of age, we can greatly improve our ability to identify and meet the needs of not only older people but others interacting with them in the context of the criminal justice or other systems.

Age As a Fixed Chronological Point

Finally, many age-based distinctions embedded in the criminal justice system reflect the idea that aging means growing old beyond some fixed chronological point. Within many laws and policies that attach significance to aging, age is pegged to some arbitrary point in the life course rather than to age-related biological, psychological, or social change. For example, laws that mandate retirement for older judges generally define this population in terms of chronological age rather than terms of functional ability. Similarly, laws that enhance penalties for crimes against older victims or provide jury duty exemptions for older potential jurors often conceptualize aging in chronological terms without consideration for biological, psychological, or social variation.

In reality, however, aging involves more than growing old beyond some fixed chronological point. As Ferraro (1997) points out, aging involves a lifelong series of transitions that occur at different times for different people rather than one great transformation occurring suddenly at age 65 or 70. For example, depending on their career opportunities, attorneys gain experience at varying rates, so that some will reap this age-related benefit earlier than others. Likewise, some attorneys experience declines in their functional abilities later than others (or do not experience them at all), so that not all attorneys will feel the desire or need to retire at the same chronological point (see Adams, chapter 4).

The rate at which the health of older prisoners declines also serves well to illustrate variation in the aging process. According to Kerbs (chapter 10), some studies suggest that the physical health of the typical older prisoner deteriorates more rapidly than the health of other citizens of the same age. In other words, older prisoners are thought to undergo accelerated biological aging, so that the typical older prisoner is considered to have "aged" roughly 10 years beyond the average citizen of the same chronological age. This may result from prison life itself or from the long-term effects of harmful lifestyles practiced during young adulthood or even childhood. Either way, this finding of more advanced "aging" lends support to Ferraro's observation that "while age, as a variable measured in chronological years, increases at equal intervals, aging, as a life process involving transitions, is not necessarily so linearly smooth" (1997, p. 9).

In view of the lifelong nature of the aging process, as Ferraro reminds us, it is important to conceptualize age-related phenomena in terms of transitions that occur early in life as well as changes that occur past the age of 65. For example, Wolf (chapter 2) demonstrates the folly of attempting to explain elder abuse without reference to events that occur before senescence. As Wolf explains, a history of violence and conflict in a family may be more predictive of elder abuse than any transition that occurs later in life. Similarly, transitions occurring throughout the life course are vital to our understanding of older criminals and prisoners. According to Kerbs (chapter 10), a plurality (45.6%) of prisoners age 55 and over are career criminals who have been convicted repeatedly over the course of their lifetimes. Therefore, in an important sense, our understanding of older prisoners is only as good as our understanding of younger offenders.

Policy and Ethical Implications

As demonstrated previously, much of the importance attached to advanced age in the context of crime and the criminal justice system may derive in part from misperceptions of older people and misconceptions of the aging process. In light of this finding, when, if ever, are age-based distinctions appropriate? When should older people involved in this system be singled out for different or specialized treatment?

Age-based distinctions rooted in inaccurate perceptions of older people and aging are bound to produce arbitrary and inequitable results. For example, laws that require older judges to retire, which appear to be rooted in the mistaken belief that older people in general are incapable of performing the duties of a judge, have the arbitrary effect of removing highly competent and capable individuals from their positions. In order to avoid such results, age-based distinctions in the criminal justice system should be abandoned insofar as they rely on perceptions that conflict with objective realities.

In any event, there has been little analysis of whether age-based distinctions intended to aid or assist older people have the unintended effect of further stigmatizing them. Laws that increase penalties for crimes committed against older people, for example, may reflect society's collective judgment that elders should be afforded a positive status and be protected further by stiffer penalties for crimes against them. On the other hand, these laws may perpetuate the inaccurate perception that older people, by and large, are weak, helpless, and vulnerable to victimization. Similarly, the creation of specialized elder police units may convey the impression that older people constitute a separate and dependent class of individuals. This has implications for potential denial of due process if they are viewed as less than competent or complete individuals with all of the rights that pertain to full citizenship. Future studies of elders and the criminal justice system need to analyze carefully the impact that special elder programs and initiatives have on perceptions of elders and whether they are related to legitimate needs and concerns rooted in their daily lives.

Furthermore, to single out older people for differential or specialized treatment based simply on generalized or stereotypic ideas about their characteristics creates a risk of paternalism. The provision of age-based jury duty exemptions serves to illustrate this point. Although many older people no doubt appreciate being relieved from jury duty, others who are both willing and able to serve on juries may find the idea of an age-based exemption demeaning and offensive. Therefore, future initiatives to aid older people through special laws, programs, or practices should include broad assessments of their attitudes, needs, and long-term well-being as well as potential impacts on society as a whole.

However, each of the chapters in this book clearly demonstrates that older people usually do differ from younger people in at least a few important respects. These differences may warrant treating older people as a special class in certain limited circumstances. For example, older people often are targeted for certain types of crime, including fraud and confidence schemes (Wolf, chapter 2). Thus, there appears to be a genuine need for crime prevention policies and programs focusing on economic crime that are aimed specifically at older people. Also, relative to younger people, elders are more likely to have certain health problems and disabilities that call for special accommodations (see e.g., Adams, chapter 4; Kerbs, chapter 10; Yarmey, chapter 6). However, within the context of the courtroom, reasonable efforts should be made to ensure that accommodations are available not only for older persons with impairments, but for individuals of all ages with disabilities who are serving as potential jurors or in other roles. In particular, because older eyewitnesses are, on average, more likely to have recall problems than younger eyewitnesses (Yarmey, chapter 6), police officers and attorneys may have a responsibility to adopt supportive interview techniques in cases involving some older people as well as others with potential memory lapses. Likewise, prison officials and administrators may be obligated to retrofit penal facilities and programs to accommodate older prisoners' unique physical, psychological, and social needs. In so doing, they will be equipped to handle other special populations as well.

Furthermore, age-based categorization and differentiation may serve a number of practical and organizational demands. It may be that elder police units staffed by officers with specialized gerontological training are more successful in meeting elders' safety and security needs than are traditional types of police organization. By the same token, elder courts or court units that provide specialized assistance to elders involved with court proceedings may prove to be highly effective and even efficient innovations. Likewise, as the size of this country's prison population swells (especially given that commission of crime is highly and negatively correlated with age), it soon may become not only efficient but fiscally necessary to target older prisoners for early release (see Kerbs, chapter 11). Practical and organizational concerns such as these should be subjected to further critical analysis so that they can be fairly weighed against countervailing disadvantages of targeting older individuals for specialized treatment, including the potential for perpetuating stigmatization of older age.

To the extent that at least some generalizations about older people do have some basis in reality and may serve important practical and organizational demands, it may be misguided and undesirable to avoid any and all age-based distinctions. Instead, policy and decision makers should strive to avoid false stereotypes of older people and to resist becoming prisoners of popular ideas about the aging process. They should consider how perceptions of older people and aging affect human behavior, including their own. They also should recognize that they routinely, at times perhaps unconsciously, differentiate among individuals on the basis of age, with consequences for the quality and fairness of treatment that older or younger people receive. Furthermore, those who invoke age-based distinctions and generalizations should conform their judgments about older people to objective realities as much as possible. Policies and decisions concerning older people must be grounded in empirical knowledge if they are to succeed.

Finally, actors in the criminal justice field should adopt more flexible notions of age and aging. In particular, they should reject the idea that aging is a causal variable and give much more consideration to the true underlying causes of age-related phenomena. For example, rather than tying continued eligibility for judicial office to age, a vacuous causal variable, lawmakers ought to link eligibility to more direct indicators of the competence of individual judges. Moreover, we should reject the idea that aging means growing old beyond a fixed chronological point, replacing categorical judgments of older people with individual assessments whenever possible. Such efforts will reduce reliance on inaccurate or otherwise inappropriate generalizations about older people, improving the quality and fairness of the treatment that all victims, offenders, and trial participants receive, regardless of age.

Conclusions

Existing empirical data on elders, crime, and the criminal justice system suggest that, on average, older people do differ from younger people in a number of important respects. Among other things, they are less likely to be victims of crime, less likely to commit crime, and more likely to experience functional declines that may require accommodations when they visit a courthouse. However, contrary to some popular perceptions, older people also are similar to younger people in various significant ways: they appear, overall, no more likely than younger people to be fearful of criminal attacks; they commit violent crimes, including, perhaps, increasingly higher rates of aggravated assault; and they can be highly effective participants in the courtroom, depending on their health status and the availability of need-based accommodations. Future studies could greatly improve our understanding of older people and aging by exploring the consistency of these differences and similarities among various elder subpopulations.

What we know about elders, crime, and criminal justice also has implications for our understanding of how older people and aging are perceived throughout society. Perceptions of older people in the context of crime and criminal justice consist of multiple generalizations rather than a single negative stereotype. Reminiscent of the muddled portrayal of old age in ancient Greco-Roman literature (see quote from deLuce [1993] in the Introduction) elders in this context are viewed, sometimes simultaneously it seems, as being vulnerable to and fearful of victimization, law-abiding, prone to mental and physical problems, wise, and experienced. Whether any one of these generalizations is invoked to describe an individual older person appears to depend on a number of variables, including the role in which the person appears, his or her outward appearance and demographic traits, and characteristics of the perceiver. Future studies in this area should further explore images of elders prevailing among different actors in the system for what this might tell us about perceptions of elders generally, as well as what education may be needed to correct misperceptions.

Finally, much of the information gathered here suggests that age still is determinative of the treatment that older people receive at various junctures in the criminal justice system. Within that system, police, judges, jurors, corrections officials and others regularly note the age of older individuals and use this to distinguish them from the population-at-large, with consequences for the opportunities and experiences of older victims, offenders, and other participants in criminal trials. The challenge currently facing criminal justice professionals and academics alike, then, is to determine whether the significance attached to advanced age throughout the process is more a response to real and meaningful differences between younger and older people, or a reflection of misplaced reliance on inaccurate and outdated images and stereotypes of elders and aging. Policies and practices rooted in inaccurate stereotypes and inflexible notions of aging should be identified and revised to conform to current empirical knowledge about older people. The importance of replacing these false assumptions as a basis for age-based differential treatment with more flexible ideas about aging will only increase as the older population expands in size, proportion, and diversity throughout the 21st century.

References

American Association of Retired Persons (AARP). (1998). *A profile of older Americans: 1998*. Washington, DC: Author.

Brewer, M. B, & Lui, L. (1984). Categorization of the elderly by the elderly: Effects of perceiver's category membership. *Personality & Social Psychology Bulletin, 10*, 585–595.

de Luce, J. (1993). Ancient images of aging: Did ageism exist in Greco-Roman antiquity? *Generations, 17*, 41–45.

Dunlop, B. D., & Collett, M. E. (June 4, 1999). *Jury service accessibility for older persons and persons with disabilities in Florida: Full report*. Tallahassee, FL: Florida Supreme Court.

Drummond, T. (1999, June 21). Cellblock seniors. *Time*, p. 60.

Ferraro, K. F. (1997). *Gerontology: Perspectives and issues* (2d ed.). New York: Springer Publishing Co.

Hummert, M. L. (1990). Multiple stereotypes of elderly and young adults: A comparison of structure and evaluations. *Psychology and Aging, 5*, 182–193.

Hummert, M. L., Garstka, T. A., & Shaner, J. L. (1997). Stereotyping of older adults: The role of target facial cues and perceiver characteristics. *Psychology and Aging, 12*, 107–114.

Hummert, M. L., Garstka, T. A., Shaner, J. L., & Strahm, S. (1994). Stereotypes of the elderly held by young, middle-aged, and elderly adults. *Journal of Gerontology: Psychological Sciences, 49*, P240–P249.

INDEX

Index

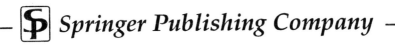 **Springer Publishing Company**

Interventions in Dementia Care
Toward Improving Quality of Life

M. Powell Lawton, MD
Robert L. Rubinstein, PhD, Editors

"The chapters in this volume are an excellent reflection of improvements in dementia care and research that have been achieved in the past decade. Going well beyond the usual recitation of burdens experienced, the chapters emphasize what is known about the daily lives and functioning of persons with dementia. Needed attention is paid to how clinical assessments and treatments can be appropriately standardized, and how interventions can be tailored to improve the quality of life of persons with dementia as well as reduce often overwhelming caregiving burdens."
—From the Afterword by **Marcia Ory,** PhD, MPH
Chief, Social Science Research on Aging

This volume explores the possibilities of favorable change in the domains of functional competence, behavioral symptoms, positive behaviors, and subjective quality of life. According to Lawton and Rubinstein, recognition of these four domains as care targets will result not only in improved programming, but in increased motivation for all caregivers as they begin to recognize some positive result of their efforts. Concise and thoughtfully written, this volume is a valuable resource for the interdisciplinary team of gerontologists, nurses, social workers, and psychologists.

Contents: The Development and Treatment Guidelines for Alzheimers Disease, *Peter V Rabins* • Maximizing the Functional Abilities of Persons with Alzheimer's Disease and Related Dementias, *Carol Bowlby Sifton* • Approaches to the Management of Disruptive Behaviors, *Jiska Cohen-Mansfield* • Psychotherapy with the Cognitivey Impaired, *Deborah Frazer* • Emotion in People with Dementia: A Way of Comprehending Their Preferences and Aversions, *M. Powell Lawton, Kimberly Van Haitsman and Margaret Peret Perkinson* • Interdisciplinary Care Planning for Nursing Home Residents with Dementia

2000   208pp.   0-8261-1325-7   hard   www.springerpub.com

536 Broadway, New York, NY 10012-3955 • (212) 431-4370 • Fax (212) 941-7842

Springer Publishing Company

The Evolution of the Aging Self
The Societal Impact on the Aging Process
K. Warner Schaie, PhD and Jon Hendricks, PhD

The authors examine age-related changes and their impact upon the concept of "self". Self concept is central to well-being, life satisfaction, and quality of life. Topics examined include: the role of the family, aging policy and the health care system, and social values and expectations. Each chapter is followed by two insightful commentaries by nationally recognized experts in the field. For teachers, researchers, and graduate students interested in the sociology and psychology of aging.

Springer Series: Societal Impact on Aging
2000   288pp.   0-8261-1363-X   hard   *www.springerpub.com*

536 Broadway, New York, NY 10012 • (212)431-4370 • Fax: (212)941-7842

Springer Publishing Company

The Many Dimensions of Aging
Robert L. Rubinstein, PhD,
Miriam Moss, PhD and
Morton Kleban, PhD, Editors

Dedicated to M. Powell Lawton and his continuing work in the field of gerontology, this book contains a selection of essays by persons who have worked with him or with his ideas over the last few decades. Each contributor addresses some aspect of Dr. Lawton's contribution to the field and develops it into an essay. Authored by prestigious researchers in the field, the chapters address the latest research findings and their implications in the elderly. Topics include: the environment and aging; health and quality of life issues; emotions and the aged; issues of care-giving; and practice and policy outcomes.

This volume provides a broad overview of advances in the field for graduate students, researchers, and professionals.

Contents:

- Theory and Practice of Place
- The Ecological Theory of Aging
- Adjusting "Person-Environment Systems"
- Time and Function
- Assessing Quality of Care Among Chronic Care Populations
- Family and Nursing Home Staff's Perceptions of Quality of LifeDementia
- Style Versus Substance
- The Assessment and Integration of Preferences into Care Practices
  for Persons with Dementia Residing in Nursing Homes
- Opportunities for Defining Late Life Depression ab initio
- A Stage Theory Model of Adult Cognitive Development Revisited
- Caregiving Research
- Appraisals of Dependence Versus Independence Among Care
  Receiving Elderly Women
- If You Want to Understand Something, Try to Change It
- Community Planning and the Elderly
- Research as a Resource for Planning
- Outcomes for Research in Mental Disorders of Late Life

2000   320pp.   0-8261-1247-1   hardcover   www.springerpub.com

536 Broadway, New York, NY 10012-3955 • (212) 431-4370 • Fax (212) 941-7842